# Evangelical Theological Aesthetics

# Evangelical Theological Aesthetics

*A Theology of Beauty and Perception*

RYAN CURRIE

*Foreword by Samuel G. Parkison*

◆PICKWICK *Publications* • Eugene, Oregon

EVANGELICAL THEOLOGICAL AESTHETICS
A Theology of Beauty and Perception

Copyright © 2025 Ryan Currie. All rights reserved. Except for brief quotations in critical publications or reviews, no part of this book may be reproduced in any manner without prior written permission from the publisher. Write: Permissions, Wipf and Stock Publishers, 199 W. 8th Ave., Suite 3, Eugene, OR 97401.

Pickwick Publications
An Imprint of Wipf and Stock Publishers
199 W. 8th Ave., Suite 3
Eugene, OR 97401

www.wipfandstock.com

PAPERBACK ISBN: 979-8-3852-1945-2
HARDCOVER ISBN: 979-8-3852-1946-9
EBOOK ISBN: 979-8-3852-1947-6

*Cataloguing-in-Publication data:*

Names: Currie, Ryan, author. | Parkison, Samuel G., foreword.

Title: Evangelical theological aesthetics : a theology of beauty and perception / Ryan Currie ; foreword by Samuel G. Parkison.

Description: Eugene, OR : Pickwick Publications, 2025 | Includes bibliographical references.

Identifiers: ISBN 979-8-3852-1945-2 (paperback) | ISBN 979-8-3852-1946-9 (hardcover) | ISBN 979-8-3852-1947-6 (ebook)

Subjects: LCSH: Aesthetics—Religious aspects—Christianity. | Christianity and the arts. | Theology, Doctrinal. | Evangelicalism.

Classification: 2025 (paperback) | call number (ebook)

05/26/25

Unless otherwise indicated, Scripture quotations are from The ESV® Bible (The Holy Bible, English Standard Version®), © 2001 by Crossway, a publishing ministry of Good News Publishers. Used by permission. All rights reserved.

Scripture quotations marked (NIV) are taken from the Holy Bible, New International Version®, NIV®. Copyright © 1973, 1978, 1984, 2011 by Biblica, Inc.® Used by permission of Zondervan. All rights reserved worldwide. www.zondervan.com The "NIV" and "New International Version" are trademarks registered in the United States Patent and Trademark Office by Biblica, Inc.®

"Psalm 8" is from the series "Psalms" by Anneke Kaai of the Netherlands, copyright © 2024 by Anneke Kaai. Used by permission. All rights reserved.

"The Mystery of Babylon" is from the series "Babel" by Grace Carol Bomer, copyright © 2023 by Grace Carol Bomer. Used by permission. All rights reserved.

The figure of Lilias Trotter's painting is copyright © 2020 by Lilias Trotter Legacy and Arab World Ministries. Used by permission of Lilias Trotter Legacy and Arab World Ministries of Pioneers. All rights reserved.

To my mom, Kari Currie, with love.

Restore our fortunes, Lord,
like streams in the Negev.
Those who sow with tears
will reap with songs of joy.

Psalm 126:5

He has made everything beautiful in its time.
He has also set eternity in the human heart;
yet no one can fathom what God has done from beginning to end.

Ecclesiastes 3:11 (NIV)

# Contents

| | | |
|---|---|---|
| *Illustrations* | | ix |
| *Foreword by Samuel G. Parkison* | | xi |
| *Acknowledgments* | | xv |
| *Abbreviations* | | xvii |
| 1 | Introduction | 1 |
| 2 | How Evangelicals Have a Theology of Beauty | 8 |
| 3 | Theological Aesthetic Concepts in Historical Theology | 46 |
| 4 | Balthasar's Theological Aesthetics | 110 |
| 5 | Beauty and Perception in John | 156 |
| 6 | An Evangelical Protestant Theological Aesthetic | 203 |
| 7 | The Aesthetics of the Theo-Drama | 233 |
| 8 | Conclusion | 263 |
| *Bibliography* | | 265 |

# Illustrations

| | |
|---|---|
| *Psalm 8*, from the Psalms series, by Anneke Kaai | 14 |
| *The Mystery of Babylon*, from the Babel series, by Grace Carol Bomer | 29 |
| *Icon of the Nativity of Christ* | 64 |
| *Isenheim Altarpiece* by Mattias Grunewald | 103 |
| *The Descent from the Cross* by Rembrandt van Rijn | 182 |
| *The Incredulity of Saint Thomas* by Caravaggio | 191 |
| "Travel Journal" by Lilias Trotter | 241 |
| *The Storm on the Sea of Galilee* by Rembrandt van Rijn | 253 |

# Foreword

A COMMON EXPERIENCE FOR doctoral students writing their dissertation is the thrill and dread of discovering someone else who has already written cogently on one's topic. Such a discovery is thrilling because it confirms that the student is not alone; others see what he sees, and this is an intellectual comfort. *He's not crazy.* On the other hand, the discovery summons a deep dread. With stomach-turning anxiety, the student wonders, "Does this work render all my research and writing superfluous? Has this person *already* written the dissertation I've been laboring toward?" Had we known each other earlier, Ryan and I may well have given one another this thrilling scare.

As Ryan was putting the finishing touch on his dissertation in preparation for submission and defense, I was putting the finishing touches on the revisions of *my* dissertation in preparation to submit the manuscript for publication.[1] Our respective projects shared the same broad topic: theological aesthetics. Further, both Ryan and I were motivated by the same discontentment with the status quo in this area. Finding some resonance with Hans Urs von Balthasar's criticism that Protestants lack a sufficiently theological account for aesthetics, and feeling like this state of affairs was entirely and tragically *unnecessary*, given the rich reservoir of theological resources available to Protestants (and specifically, evangelicals), we both—in our small ways—aspired to fill the gap by connecting the dots between wholesome Protestant doctrine and theological-aesthetic meditations. In a delightful, unlikely stroke of providence, we now find ourselves ministering at the same seminary in the middle of the Arabian Gulf, safely out of our respective dissertation-writing phases. Though our meeting was thrilling, it was not dreadful.

---

1. Samuel G. Parkison, *Irresistible Beauty: Beholding Triune Glory in the Face of Jesus Christ* (Ross-shire, UK: Mentor, 2022).

Were we to have found each other earlier, however, our fright of each work rendering the other's superfluous would have been short-lived. In terms of construction, argumentation, primary interlocutors, conversation partners, and central biblical passages that orient the project, Ryan's work and my own significantly vary. And this makes the complementary conclusions we have independently drawn all the more remarkable. The upshot is that Ryan's work is a most welcome contribution to a criminally small body of theological-aesthetic work done by Protestants and evangelicals. Currie has eagerly contributed his voice to the growing choir of those harkening the evangelical mind toward the beauty of Christ, and in this work, he makes a lasting impression.

How, specifically, might I commend this book? Narrowing the ways is no small task. Here is a work of deep learning and impressive synthesis. Currie pulls from an intimidatingly wide range of scholarship and presents it to the reader without intimidating him. The net result is a clear, lucid Protestant presentation of theological aesthetics that rhymes with the best reflections on the topic in other traditions. Currie is incredibly irenic while being neither a pushover, nor a synchronist, nor a lowest-common-denominator ecumenicist. He knows what he is about, and where Protestant doctrine parts ways with his primary conversation partners, he is not afraid to say so clearly. And yet, Currie somehow manages to part ways at these junctures without scolding or haughtily lecturing. In this sense, Currie is a "student" in the best sense of the word.

On this note of conversation partners, this work is most impressive for his willingness to tackle the profoundly enigmatic twentieth-century Roman Catholic theologian, Hans Urs von Balthasar. He does so the only way possible: carefully, patiently, humbly, and methodically, bringing much-needed clarity to the (overly?) creative and befuddling theologian. In many ways, having become well-acquainted with Ryan as a friend and colleague, it is clear to me that he was uniquely fitted to write this book. He shows that Protestants have much to learn from the likes of Balthasar, and as the deeply irenic scholar Currie is, he brings such lessons out with clarity and skill. In fact, if there was a point of criticism I would raise with this work, it would be that Currie is *too* friendly toward Balthasar. Throughout the work, I found myself hoping in vain that his criticisms of Balthasar would strike to a deeper root, taking aim at his modernistic revisions of Theology proper and trinitarianism. But, then again, this "criticism"—to the degree it is even rightly so-called—probably says more about me than Currie, for the need of the hour that Currie rose to address was not a takedown of modern theological revisions of figures like Barth or Balthasar, but a fruitful ecumenical dialogue for the sake of theological construction. I confess I simply would not have the patience to pull a thing like this off, and Currie clearly does.

Apart from the strengths of the work itself, I should also like to exercise some personal privilege by speaking to the reader of Currie's character. Sometimes our theological heroes and influences can greatly disappoint us when we have a chance to meet them. Having seen Currie "up close," as it were, I can only say the sensation is exactly the reverse. As a man, a husband, a dad, a churchman, and a fellow colleague in academic ministry, Ryan Currie is exemplary. In this work, the reader will discover a man of great learning, keen wit, and humbling profundity. The reader should be comforted to know that the thinker who wrote this book does not throw his sincerely impressive intellectual weight around. In fact, I suspect he would probably object to so lofty a description of his scholarly chops, but this kind of self-ignorance only proves my point. He is a true friend of Christ Jesus, the Bridegroom of the Church, content to decrease for the sake of magnifying his Lord. This means that the beautiful meditations on the beauty of the Lord found in this book issue forth from—and adorn—the beauty of a life lived in humble service of the absolutely True, Good, and Beautiful.

*Samuel G. Parkison*
Associate Professor of Theology
The Gulf Theological Seminary

# Acknowledgments

THE BEAUTY OF THE mountain ranges of northern New Mexico made an indelible impression on me from my youth and deserve the first acknowledgment. They evoke a love for natural beauty and inspired me to think theologically about beauty. I am always restless when I am away from those mountains. I first learned this love for mountains from my grandma, "Grammy." She taught me to *see* natural beauty. Her insistence to see the *Sangre de Cristo* Mountains in light of the blood of Jesus helped develop crucial ideas in this work.

There have been many other mentors, teachers, and pastors whose influence shaped some aspect of this work. Chris Finnegan taught me to think and organize my worldview. Mark Lincoln and Jesse Taylor taught me the Scriptures. John Piper taught me to desire the beauty of Christ. Rick Shenk developed and sharpened my love for systematic theology and learning. My teachers at Bethlehem College and Seminary trained me and gave me tools and skills I used in this study (and daily in life and ministry). Even though I have never met them, George MacDonald, C.S. Lewis, J.R.R. Tolkien, Charles Williams, and Fyodor Dostoevsky expanded my imagination. Their writings evoke a longing for eternal beauty.

My wife, Emily, is a constant source of encouragement. She is the delight of my life. It goes without saying that she has sacrificed much to enable me to spend so many hours on this project. My mother's support has helped and inspired me in countless ways. I have dedicated this work to her. I am grateful to Parker Landis, Curtis Christensen, Jeremy Elam, and Jeremy Bergevin for their faithful friendship and encouragement.

It is a joy to work with Gulf Theological Seminary in Dubai, UAE. This year at GTS has been a time of healing and recovery from some difficult years in overseas ministry. The team under Eric Zeller's leadership provides an atmosphere that is theologically vibrant and globally focused. I am also grateful for my friend and colleague, Samuel Parkison, for his kind words in the foreword. Samuel has sharpened my thinking in many ways.

I am also thankful to South African Theological Seminary for the support in writing this book in its dissertation form. I was blessed with two excellent supervisors, Robert Falconer and George Coon. Lee Ann Steadman offered much help and encouragement in editing this work. I am also grateful for the editors at Wipf&Stock.

For all these good gifts—and life and breath and everything—I am thankful to the triune God. He is the source of beauty, and as Augustine put it, is himself the beauty so ancient and so new. I love him and long for him and cannot wait to see him face to face.

*Ryan Currie*
November 28, 2024
Thanksgiving in Dubai

# Abbreviations

| | |
|---|---|
| CD | Barth's *Church Dogmatics* |
| DN | Pseudo-Dionysius's *Divine Names* |
| GL | Balthasar's *The Glory of the Lord: A Theological Aesthetics*, 7 volumes |
| KW | *Kierkegaard's Works* |
| LW | *Luther's Works* |
| ST | Aquinas's *Summa Theologica* |
| TD | Balthasar's *Theo-Drama: Theological Dramatic Theory*, 5 volumes |
| TL | Balthasar's *Theo-Logic*, 3 volumes |
| WJE | *Works of Jonathan Edwards* |

# I

# Introduction

### BEAUTY WILL SAVE THE WORLD

MANY BOOKS ABOUT BEAUTY begin with Dostoevsky's words in *The Idiot*, "Beauty will save the world." However, these epigraphs fail to understand Dostoyevsky's statement. In context, the dying Ippolit coughs, "What beauty is going to save the world?"[1] This question resounds through the book. In the haunting conclusion of *The Idiot*, Dostoyevsky shows the hopeless predicament of humanity. *The Idiot* is not a statement that "Beauty will save the world," but a deathly serious question, "What beauty is going to save the world?" Dostoevsky's question invites theological reflection. What is beauty and why is it so enigmatic? Is beauty something that only can be experienced, or are we able to think philosophically and theologically about it? Can beauty be an object of dogmatic investigation in a way that expands and releases its nature and potential? Or does a theological account of beauty by nature degrade and cheapen the mystery of its experience? Is the process of theological construction one of the tools of reductionistic pressures?[2]

The study of aesthetics is shrouded in confusion and ambiguity. Aesthetics deals with the nature of beauty and how we experience it. This existential aspect and the multiplicity of aesthetic tastes generates many

---

1. Dostoevsky, *The Idiot*, 561.
2. See Begbie's critique of the naturalistic reductionism in *Abundantly More*, 1–22.

different perspectives about the nature of beauty.[3] This same confusion carries over into the field of theological aesthetics. The vagueness of "theological aesthetics" has led to a variety of definitions and methodologies. Some consider theological aesthetics to be a method of theology shaped by aesthetic principles.[4] This method emphasizes the beauty of God's revelation and engages in the task of theology in such a way to reflect and reveal this beauty. Typically, though, theological aesthetics is not thought of as a theological method, but a theology of beauty and its perception. In this respect, two main approaches to theological aesthetics have emerged that differ on what is the primary area of focus. One of these approaches treats theological aesthetics as a field of study that examines God's revelation in the beauty of creation and the arts.[5] This type of theological aesthetics shares similarities with studies on the intersection of theology and the arts, but emphasizes discovering God's revelation through a particular work of art. For example, what does Mozart's Symphony No. 40 or Monet's paintings reveal about God? This approach traces its influence to Karl Rahner's transcendental theology.[6]

The other dominant approach was developed by Hans Urs Von Balthasar. For Balthasar, theological aesthetics is the theology of the perception of the splendor of God's revelation in Jesus Christ and all reality in him.[7] This approach offers a theological account of beauty that focuses on the theology of the perception. How do we *perceive* the beauty of God in Christ? For Balthasar, the starting point for a theology of beauty is not in creation and the arts, but in Jesus Christ.

These divergent approaches to theological aesthetics are not simply complementary but reveal a fault line. They represent two competing philosophies of beauty that arise from a perceived tension between spiritual and material beauty. This tension was observed at least as early as philosophers such as Plato and Aristotle.[8] These approaches take different starting points: one with material beauty and the other with spiritual. Those influenced by Rahner begin with material beauty and encounter the infinite through that medium. This approach is better termed "aesthetic theology."

3. Poythress, *Redeeming Philosophy*, 226.
4. See Bychkov and the essays in *Theological Aesthetics After von Balthasar*..
5. Thiessen, *Theological Aesthetics*, 2.
6. Viladesau, *Theological Aesthetics*, 38.
7. McInroy, *Balthasar on the Spiritual Senses*, 134.
8. Sammon, *The God Who is Beauty*, 15.

Balthasar's theological aesthetics has Barthian influences in its focus on revelation from outside the human experience and condition. A theological account of beauty is only revealed in Jesus Christ. Balthasar was comfortable constructing a theological aesthetic that considers created and material beauty, but this is secondary. The primary revelation of the nature of beauty and how humans perceive beauty is found in Christ. He is the source, purest expression, and foundation of beauty.

In this book, I argue that the stream of theological aesthetics that follows Balthasar is more theologically responsible. The approach that emphasizes the arts and material beauty offers valuable insights, but only if it is informed and corrected by a theology of beauty. In Balthasar's language, it is not enough to have an aesthetic theology. We must have a theological aesthetic. Therefore, theological aesthetics, when understood in the Balthasarian sense followed in this book, can be understood in three distinct, but complementary ways: (1) the theology of true perception of the beautiful splendor of God's revelation in Jesus Christ and all reality in him;[9] (2) an approach to theology that is fundamentally shaped by the reality of the true perception of the glory and beauty of God's revelation;[10] (3) a theology of beauty as it is perceived through the senses in creation and the arts as revelatory of divine beauty.[11]

## BALTHASAR AND EVANGELICALS?

Hans Urs von Balthasar (1905–1988) was born in Lucerne, Switzerland. He studied German literature of the eighteenth and nineteenth centuries at the University of Zurich, where he wrote his thesis, *The Apocalypse of the German Soul*. He became a Jesuit priest in 1936 but left the Jesuits in 1950 to establish the Community of Saint John with Adriene von Speyr. The Community of Saint John was a secular institute for lay people to live out a celibate and consecrated life. He was a prolific writer and lecturer. In 1988, he passed away at Basel three days before his investiture as cardinal. Balthasar's famous trilogy is structured around the transcendentals of goodness, truth, and beauty. *The Glory of the Lord: A Theological Aesthetics* (7 volumes) explores the transcendental of beauty, *Theo-Drama* (5 volumes) explores goodness, and *Theo-Logic* (3 volumes) explores truth.

---

9. Dupre, "Balthasar's Theology of Aesthetic Form," 300.
10. Bychkov et al., *Theological Aesthetics After von Balthasar*, 2008.
11. Thiessen, *Theological Aesthetics*, 2.

Balthasar argued that beauty is the neglected transcendental in theology. To counteract the negligence, Balthasar made beauty and theological aesthetics the starting point of his theology of the transcendentals.

Balthasar's emphasis on the necessity of a Christ-centered theology of beauty makes him a better conversation partner for evangelical Protestants than theological aesthetics influenced by Rahner. Evangelical Protestants, in this book, refers to Christians who hold to historic Christian orthodoxy in the Protestant tradition.[12] Michael Bird summarizes that "evangelical" refers to "historic Christian orthodoxy combined with energetic fervor to promote the gospel of Jesus Christ."[13] Apart from obvious and important differences, Balthasar shares many areas of agreement with evangelicals. This agreement is seen in his high regard for the biblical text, Creator-creature distinction, the ontological priority of the immanent Trinity, and appreciation of creation.[14] At the same time, Balthasar strongly critiqued the Protestant approach to beauty: "Contemporary Protestant theology nowhere deals with the beautiful as a theological category... The only question posed by Protestants is that concerning the relationship between revelation and this worldly beauty—certainly a justified question, but not a sufficient one."[15] Balthasar recognized that the Protestant emphasis falls on an examination of the intersection of theology and aesthetics, or "this worldly beauty," rather than an emphasis on the theological nature of beauty.

Evangelical works on beauty and art often quote Balthasar positively. It is a truism that evangelicals produce kitsch art; artistic beauty is not something evangelicals are known for. Balthasar is quoted to help rectify the plight of the arts in evangelicalism. However, Balthasar would not be particularly interested in evangelicals producing better art. The

---

12. Evangelical Protestants believe in the inspiration and sufficiency of sacred Scripture, the triune God, the historical virgin birth, the sinless life, death, burial, resurrection, ascension, and future return of the Lord Jesus Christ, the activity of the Holy Spirit to indwell and sanctify, justification by faith alone in Christ alone, the communion of the saints in the Church, the eternal reality of heaven and hell, and the necessity and urgency of sharing the Gospel of Jesus Christ because he is the only way of salvation. I recognize that within this group of evangelicals there are many subgroups and a multiformity of expressions throughout the world but believe it is still a generally helpful category. For a broad introduction to evangelicals see National Association of Evangelicals, "What is and Evangelical."

13. Bird, *Evangelical Theology*, xxviii. See also: McGrath, *Evangelicalism and the Future of Christianity*, 51. Reeves, *Gospel People: A Call for Evangelical Integrity*, 37.

14. Garrett, "The Dazzling Darkness of God's Triune Love," 423.

15. Balthasar, *GL* 1, 56–57.

shallowness of evangelical art is a symptom of a deeper problem: evangelicals do not have a theology of beauty. Balthasar's specific criticism against Protestants is that they have a truncated theology of beauty. Protestants not only neglect but eliminate beauty from theology as superfluous and spiritually dangerous. This has implications for the method of theology itself as well as the relationship between theology and the arts. Balthasar notes, "Such elimination has meant, broadly, the expulsion of contemplation from the act of faith, the exclusion of 'seeing' from 'hearing', the removal of the *inchoatio visionis* from the *fides*, and the relegation of the Christian to the old age that is passing away."[16] In other words, Balthasar argued that those who emphasize the aesthetic experience of created beauty at the expense of a theology of beauty are trading their birthright for a bowl of soup. The question of the intersection of theology and the arts is a "justified question, but not a sufficient one."[17]

Stephen Garrett encouraged evangelicals "to consider one of the most prominent Catholic theologians of the twentieth century who can help evangelicals sharpen their theological discourse."[18] There is a need for a more developed evangelical interaction with Balthasar's theological aesthetic, particularly the existential aspects of his proposal. Mark McInroy rightly argues that "at the heart of Balthasar's theological aesthetics stands the task of perceiving (*wahr-nehmen*) the form through which God is revealed to human beings."[19] While some evangelicals have begun to study Balthasar and theological aesthetics, there is still relatively little evangelical theology focused on the aspect of perception and the relation of the spiritual and physical senses. This book will seek to explore the theology of the perception of beauty. Balthasar's theological aesthetic and critique of Protestantism can be engaged to help construct an evangelical Protestant theological aesthetic. Thus, the purpose of this work is to build on and nuance Balthasar's theological aesthetic in a way that coheres with the biblical revelation from an evangelical perspective. God has revealed himself not just through the good and the true, but also the beautiful. Faithfulness to God's revelation must consider the beauty of his revelation and respond appropriately. What Balthasar said is true for evangelicals

---

16. Balthasar, *GL* 1, 70.
17. Balthasar, *GL* 1, 56.
18. Garrett, "The Dazzling Darkness of God's Triune Love," 428.
19. McInroy, *Balthasar on the Spiritual Senses*, 134.

today: "the experience of glory must be thought through and formulated for our time anew, directly from the central point of revelation."[20]

This is practically significant for the community of believers and the individual. A biblical theological aesthetic impacts theological method and the proclamation of the church in its preaching ministry. Because theological aesthetics provides a theological basis for the understanding of beauty, it also has implications for how Christians approach beauty, both in creation and in the arts. There is also an existential significance for the individual believer as he encounters God in his beauty through faith in Christ and through the means of created beauty.

## OUTLINE

Balthasar's theological aesthetic and critique of Protestantism as having lost the aesthetic dimension in theology can help develop an evangelical Protestant theological aesthetic. In order to do this, we first need to understand theological aesthetics and its current expression in evangelicalism.[21] In chapter 2, I explore how theological aesthetics concepts are currently finding expression in evangelical Protestantism. Evangelicals have indeed neglected a theology of beauty, but an underdeveloped and tacit theological aesthetic can be seen in the works of many prominent and influential evangelicals. Because theological aesthetics focuses on the perception of God's beauty, I examine how evangelicals speak of the perception of God's beauty.

In chapters 3 and 4, I show how theological aesthetic concepts have developed through the history of theology. Chapter 3 is an analysis of the history of development of the theology of beauty, noting areas of discontinuity and disagreement as well as unity and development of the concepts. Chapter 4 presents Balthasar's theology. Balthasar's works, *The Glory of the Lord: Seeing the Form* and *The Glory of the Lord: The New Covenant*, are examined to better understand his theological aesthetics project and his critique of Protestantism.

Evangelicals recognize the primacy of Scripture for life and doctrine. In order to develop an evangelical Protestant theological aesthetic, chapter 5 presents the teaching of Scripture on the concept of theological

20. Balthasar, *GL* 4, 17.

21. This follows Robert Falconer's "Architectonic Theology" methodology. This systematic theology methodology uses principles and insights from architectural design and building.

aesthetics, especially as it relates to perception. I limit this to John's Gospel and the book of Revelation because these texts provide some of the clearest texts on theological aesthetic themes in the Bible. John the Evangelist is also unique in that he takes up theological aesthetic themes developed in the Old Testament and interprets them in light of the incarnation. Therefore, the study of theological aesthetic concepts in John demonstrates how they progressed and developed in the storyline of Scripture.

In chapter 6, I present foundational principles for an evangelical Protestant theological aesthetic. This chapter builds on the material from the previous chapters to formulate a theological account of beauty and perception. Although I depart from Balthasar's theology at key points, I follow his methodology in explaining the objective and subjective aspects of beauty. This chapter focuses especially on the subjective aspect of perception, which is where evangelical theological aesthetics needs the most development. Chapter 7 gives implications for this evangelical Protestant theological aesthetic. In it I follow Balthasar's lead and show that theological aesthetics rightly understood generates a beautiful life in the theo-drama. I conclude this chapter with noting the implications of theological aesthetics for the artist and the theologian.

# 2

# How Evangelicals Have a Theology of Beauty

## *(Whether They Know It or Not)*

IN *THE DEEP THINGS of God*, Fred Sanders examines popular evangelical theology of the Trinity. Even though evangelicals are often critiqued for their theology, Sanders demonstrated that evangelicals have a tacit awareness of profound trinitarian realities. Sanders's first chapter is subtitled, "How Evangelicals Are Profoundly Trinitarian Whether They Know It or Not."[1] He then moves from surveying popular evangelicalism's tacit awareness of trinitarian theology to constructing an evangelical trinitarian theology that fits within the broader stream of orthodox Christian trinitarianism. In this chapter, I do something similar. Alluding to Sanders, the chapter is entitled, "How Evangelicals Have a Theology of Beauty (Whether They Know It or Not)." The works of evangelical theologians, popular writers, and artists reveal that evangelical theology has a theological aesthetic, although usually undeveloped and tacit. In addition to examining evangelical literature, I also provide examples of evangelical artwork that capture the point of the doctrine discussed. As Karen Swallow Prior has shown, the social imaginary of evangelicalism is at a point

---

1. Sanders, *The Deep Things of God*, 27.

of crisis.[2] The shallow and consumeristic social imaginary of evangelicals generates kitsch art. Even though this is the case, deeper theological aesthetics *are* making their way into evangelicals' artistic expression and popular works on theology.

Theological aesthetics is concerned with the nature of beauty and its subjective perception. The objective revelation of God's beauty is designed to be existentially and aesthetically experienced by people. In aesthetics, perception is related to "taste" within the receiving subject. This aesthetic taste has three aspects: perception, enjoyment, and appraisal.[3] Evangelicals speak of perceiving and enjoying the beauty of God through its revelation in creation, Scripture, and the arts.

## EVANGELICALS ON THE BEAUTY OF GOD

### Ad Intra and Ad Extra Glory and Beauty

In recent years, Jonathan King[4] and Samuel Parkison[5] have been in the forefront of developing theological aesthetics for evangelicals. Johnathan King gives a systematic theology of the beauty of the Lord and theological aesthetics from an evangelical perspective. King argues that, biblically, there is a connection between beauty and glory. His primary focus is the theological nature of beauty and the aesthetic nature of the economy of salvation.[6] For King, the heart of theological aesthetics is the beauty of Christ in his person and work and his ongoing work through the Holy Spirit.[7] The beauty of Christ and the fittingness of the divine plan is demonstrated in the economy through creation, redemption, and consummation. The plan of the triune God in this economy has an inherent aesthetic structure that sets forth the Son and displays God's glory.

King argues the "fittingness" and beauty of the economy of salvation, known as the *ad extra* glory, presupposes and reflects an intrinsic beauty and beatitude of the Trinity *ad intra*.[8] Theologically, it is instructive to define the relationship between glory and beauty and how it relates

---

2. Prior, *The Evangelical Imagination*.
3. Brown, *Good Taste, Bad Taste, & Christian Taste*, xiii.
4. See King, *The Beauty of the Lord*.
5. See especially: *Irresistible Beauty* and *To Gaze Upon God*.
6. King, *The Beauty of the Lord*, 1.
7. King, *The Beauty of the Lord*, 5.
8. King, *The Beauty of the Lord*, 5.

to the ontological *ad intra* and economic *ad extra* trinitarian relations. The immanent glory of God is the abundant perfection of God in all his attributes, informed by the doctrine of divine simplicity.[9] However, this immanent glory of God is not understood in a monadic sense but rather in a distinctively trinitarian way. The triune God is glorious in divine simplicity. This "triadic divine simplicity" is the immanent beauty of God.[10] Creation and redemption were an unveiling of the *ad intra* glory of the Trinity *ad extra* through the fitting revelation of the Son. The structure of the economy of redemption has aesthetic beauty. For King, divine beauty is to be understood as: (1) an attribute of God and an aspect of his divine perfections experienced in the triune life; (2) the plentitude of God's perfections, including his beauty, within the triune God as the ground of his beatitude or perfect delight and satisfaction; (3) the external display of God's glory manifest in the economy of salvation through Jesus Christ so that creatures will respond in faith and delight and thus find their beatitude in him.[11]

Samuel Parkison's contribution to theological aesthetics comes from his retrieval of the beatific vision for evangelicals. In *Irresistible Beauty*, Parkison builds on King's work to explore the relationship of Christ's beauty with regeneration and faith. It is worth quoting his proposal at length as it captures the most developed evangelical theology of beauty to date:

> Beauty is ultimately an attribute of God the Trinity, revealed wherever Triune glory is made manifest, which is permanently so in the person and work of Christ. When the Holy Spirit regenerates a sinner, He imparts the faculties necessary for such a person to behold the beauty of the Trinity, mediated in Christ. The Spirt imparts these faculties by virtue of His own indwelling presence. In regeneration, the Spirit communicates—or, sovereignly brings the regenerate into participation with—the glorious *a se* beatitude of the Trinity, mediated through Christ. This He does by presenting Christ to the eyes of the regenerate's heart and by enabling such hearty vision—which is far more than a mere intellectual act, but also includes the affections— with his renovative presence. The *fiducia* component of saving faith therefore has an accompanying aesthetic aspect; it involves the existential recognition of Christ's infinite beauty.[12]

---

9. King, *The Beauty of the Lord*, 40.
10. King, *The Beauty of the Lord*, 68.
11. King, *The Beauty of the Lord*, 22–25.
12. Parkison, *Irresistible Beauty*, 202.

Parkison emphasizes the need for evangelicals to recover the doctrine of the beatific vision in a way that accords with both Biblical doctrine and classical theology. The works of King and Parkison hold out the promise of a fresh emphasis on the theology of beauty in evangelical circles.

## Transcendent and Immanent Beauty

Related to King's discussion of the *ad intra* and *ad extra* glory of God is the transcendent and immanent relation of God and the concept of the Creator-creature distinction, or God-world relation. This distinction is common in evangelical theological literature. One example of this is Michael Horton in his systematic theology, *The Christian Faith*. Horton gives three paradigms for understanding the God-world relation.[13] Horton's doctrine of the God-world relation offers a developed and representative evangelical understanding of the Creator-creature distinction.

Horton offers a variety of ways philosophers and theologians approach the Creator-creature distinction. He first mentions pantheism and panentheism's "overcoming estrangement."[14] This paradigm blurs the distinction between Creator and creation with an essentially monistic approach to reality.[15] The second paradigm is an atheistic and deistic understanding: "the stranger we never met."[16] God does not exist or at least has nothing to do with humanity. The third paradigm is the biblical paradigm of the covenant: "meeting a stranger."[17] God is personal and triune, and he freely chooses to create and enter into relationships with his creatures. This biblical paradigm is an important backdrop for theological aesthetics and resonates with Balthasar's conception of theological aesthetics. "Covenant," according to Horton, "becomes a central piece in God's revelation and our perception."[18] From Horton's "meeting a stranger" paradigm, we learn of the importance of the Creator-creature distinction as the starting point of theological aesthetics.[19]

---

13. Horton, *The Christian Faith*, 35–43.
14. Horton, *The Christian Faith*, 39.
15. Horton, *The Christian Faith*, 36.
16. Horton, *The Christian Faith*, 39.
17. Horton, *The Christian Faith*, 41.
18. Horton, *The Christian Faith*, 42.
19. Dickens, *Hans Urs von Balthasar's Theological Aesthetics*, 50.

There is a paradox of the Creator-creature distinction and the immanence of God. Unfortunately, many systems of thought collapse this paradox and mingle God with creation. Pantheism treats the revelation of beauty in creation as a manifestation of God. Platonic, Neo-Platonic, Hegelian, and process theology make the mistake of either devaluing the material created order or making creation and history necessary to God for "the realization of his existence, happiness, and perfection."[20] In this line of thinking, the world is a necessary emanation of God's being. In pantheism and later forms of Neoplatonism, the material world and historical process are equated with God. God needs the created order to find full expression.

The doctrine of aseity is central to the Creator-creature distinction. Aseity establishes the distinction between God and his creation and is the basis of his transcendence over his creation. Horton grounds the objective revelation of God in his aseity because God is free from all need and is sufficient in his triune nature. The paradox is that he freely chooses to create as an act of gratuitous grace and then goes further by bringing created beings into fellowship with him. Therefore, God is both transcendent and immanent. The biblical teaching of transcendence and aseity intensifies the staggering nature of immanence.

For Horton, God's creative act did not create his "body" when he created the universe, as in pantheism, but instead created his "house."[21] The created order becomes a "house" where humanity has fellowship with God. Horton explains God's aseity and creation through architectural and literary language. In architectural language, God created the space or place to facilitate the meeting place between God and man. The space itself cannot become the locus of focus, but its beauty and abundance facilitate a place for the meeting of God and man. God created the context and atmosphere for the story and became the "lead character in his own historical drama."[22] God's setting of the story or space is itself a glorious revelation of beauty. God is gratuitous in his revelation of beauty in the beginning stages. The stage is grand enough for the unfolding of his design.

Theological aesthetics begins with God's transcendence, aseity, and generosity rather than a necessity imposed on him. God's aseity is the mystery that God is entirely self-sufficient and "self-existing, perfect,

20. Horton, *The Christian Faith*, 233.
21. Horton, *The Christian Faith*, 233.
22. Horton, *The Christian Faith*, 233.

and independent" and yet freely chooses to create and reveal himself with astounding beauty.[23] The "extravagant variety" in creation is itself a beautiful revelation and, at the same time, provides materials for the creatures themselves to become artists. The reason God created this place and drama is so that he could reveal himself to his creatures. Therefore, while God is transcendent, he is also immanent with his creation in a covenantal relationship. The covenantal relationship with God is possible through Jesus Christ, the Word, and God is "radically present" and yet "utterly distinct" from his creation as Father, Son, and Spirit.[24] Jesus Christ is the center of this covenant relationship with God, and we have the eschatological promise that we will be brought into the consummation of this covenant and participate in the beatific vision of the glorified Jesus Christ.[25]

An artwork from an evangelical artist that reveals God's transcendence and immanence is Anneke Kaai's *Psalm 8*.[26] Kaai is a Christian artist who collaborated with Eugene Peterson to artistically represent the Psalms with artwork inspired by *The Message*. This work is an artistic expression of Psalm 8, in which the psalmist senses the transcendence of God in his handiwork in the heavens, yet also affirms the immanence of God's care and concern for human beings. Kaai expressed the transcendence of God in the light and the hands in her work. In God's hands is written out the tetragrammaton, God's holy name. However, she also expresses the immanence of God's work in the world by writing the tetragrammaton on the face of the earth. Kaai's art communicates a theology of transcendence and immanence. The Creator-creature distinction and the relation of transcendence and immanence are beginning presuppositions of evangelicals' approach to theological aesthetic themes.[27]

---

23. Horton, *The Christian Faith*, 230.
24. Horton, *Covenant and Salvation*, 229.
25. Horton, *Covenant and Salvation*, 283.
26. Kaai, *The Psalms*.
27. Anneke Kaai (the Netherlands) describes this work from her series *The Psalms*: "In the fingers is the Hebrew name of God (JAHWEH). At the top of the work of art we see God's creative hands. When the poet sees the greatness of the creation of the universe and the earth, he realizes that it is a miracle that God still goes to a person looks after." Online: www.annekekaai.nl.

*Psalm 8* (1999) by Anneke Kaai. Used with permission.

## A Particular Transcendence that Points to the Triune God

The related themes of transcendence and immanence and Creator-creature distinction and their implications for general aesthetics have been a concern of Jeremy Begbie. Begbie notes that the theme of transcendence is common in discussions of art and theology.[28] Even those who do not believe in the biblical witness are now fascinated with the notion of the transcendent and the sublime. Begbie notes a new "turn to the transcendent" in many contemporary works.[29] Both Christians and non-Christians alike see within this turn an existential desire and longing for the "Other" or "beyond" within this fractured and broken life.[30]

Begbie's survey of the literature on the relationship between art and the transcendent leads him to give four common and unquestioned tenets:[31]

1. Divine transcendence perceived in the arts emphasizes our own limitations and tends toward apophatic experiences. Rothko's Chapel and Malevich's Black Square are examples of avoiding depiction and emphasizing our limitations in perceiving the transcendent.

2. Transcendence in the arts avoids the specifics of revealed truth, such as the work of God in Jesus of Nazareth. Transcendence emphasizes the general nature of the world's relationship with God.

3. There is a presupposition that humans can perceive the transcendent God in his otherness and respond appropriately.

4. Related to the second tenet, transcendence does not relate to God's triunity. In other words, transcendence presents a generic, unknown, or unitarian god.

Begbie grapples with the question of how the arts attest to divine transcendence. He concludes that the experience of transcendence in the arts does not point to the bare "otherness" of the unknown transcendent.[32] Instead, the experience of transcendence points to the triune God revealed in the Scripture. Begbie agrees with Horton that the immanence of Jesus Christ presupposes the Creator-creature distinction

---

28. Begbie, *Redeeming Transcendence in the Arts*, 1.
29. Begbie, *Redeeming Transcendence in the Arts*, 8.
30. Begbie, *Redeeming Transcendence in the Arts*, 36.
31. Begbie, *Redeeming Transcendence in the Arts*, 34–35.
32. Begbie, *Redeeming Transcendence in the Arts*, 2.

and transcendence.[33] Scripture disturbs the secular conceptions of the transcendent and sublime and teaches us to reform the concept of divine transcendence considering the immanence of God in Jesus Christ.[34] God's freedom from the world allows freedom for the world and allows God to be the agent of renewal and restoration and free from the depravity of the world.[35] This relates to theological aesthetics because there are streams of theological aesthetics, such as we will see with Karl Rahner, that conflate the revelation of God with its manifestation in the world. Horton, King, and Begbie show that God is distinct from the world and transcendent. However, the perception of God's transcendence does not evoke an experience of the sublime devoid of content. Instead, God uses his creation to reveal his beauty, including his transcendent beauty. God's transcendence first establishes the distinction between Creator-creature and then affirms God's revelation of himself to the creature. Both truths are crucial for theological aesthetics to avoid an overemphasis on God's transcendence and unknowability or an overemphasis on his immanence and blurring the distinction between God and creation.

Considering the Scripture's teaching, Begbie reorients the notion of divine transcendence around the particularity of Jesus Christ. The four tenets of transcendence and the arts noted above are challenged and transformed:[36]

1. Instead of emphasizing our finitude and limitations to the point of absolutizing the apophatic, the incarnation of Jesus Christ gives meaning and value to our language, thought, concrete particularity, creation, expression, and life. Considering the incarnation and the immanence of God within the world, God's transcendence and our limitations are affirmed. The transcendence of God and our limitations are only truly understood when we consider that God works from within our world and limitations so that we may enter into a relationship with him.

2. The concept of transcendence is not enhanced by stopping at the general revelation, perception, or experience of a nondescript "Other." Rather, the biblical texts lead one to affirm that divine transcendence is revealed at its zenith in the particular and concrete

---

33. Begbie, *Redeeming Transcendence in the Arts*, 120.
34. Begbie, *Redeeming Transcendence in the Arts*, 78.
35. Begbie, *Redeeming Transcendence in the Arts*, 121.
36. Begbie, *Redeeming Transcendence in the Arts*, 122–126.

facts of the life, death, and resurrection of Jesus Christ of Nazareth. All notions of true transcendence will not negate or undermine this.

3. Instead of assuming that all people have an innate ability to perceive and respond appropriately to transcendence, the assumption is that sin drastically affects our perception and ability to respond appropriately to God's transcendence. While humanity may perceive inklings of the transcendent, what is needed is a recreation brought about by a turning or divine-initiated repentance in the human heart to respond correctly.

4. Transcendence in the arts points toward the triune God. The trinitarian relations of Father, Son, and Spirit and the action of the triune God within the world become the conceptual basis for an understanding of transcendence in the arts. A concept of transcendence in unitarian terms is insufficient.

Therefore, God designed the experience of transcendence within creation to reveal the particular transcendence of the true God and point toward Jesus Christ. Begbie challenges the artistic community not to be content with worshiping an unknown God but to press on toward delight in the transcendent one, the triune God revealed in the Bible.

## Jesus Christ and His Work as the Pinnacle of Beauty

King, Parkison, Horton, and Begbie present a robust doctrine of the Trinity but also focus on the person and work of Christ. The transcendent *ad intra* glory of the Trinity is revealed in the economy by the beauty of the person and work of Jesus Christ, who is the "Stranger" we meet in the covenant.[37] In Jesus Christ, God is revealed both as the transcendent Trinity and the immanent redeemer.[38] Evangelicals are known for their Christocentrism, an approach to theology in which the person and work of Jesus Christ is central and decisive. Evangelicals emphasize that everything in the Christian life hinges on how one views and responds to Jesus.[39] Another

---

37. Horton, *The Christian Faith*, 41.
38. Begbie, *Redeeming Transcendence in the Arts*, 126.
39. Ortlund, "Christocentrism," 309–312. This is not necessarily a Christomonism, which is a reductionistic approach that neglects other crucial aspects of theology. Ortlund surveys the historical literature and reveals that responsible Christocentrism has an honorable pedigree in historical theology, including theologians such as Augustine, Luther, Calvin, Edwards, Kierkegaard, Schleiermacher, Bonhoeffer, Barth, and

aspect of being Christ-centered is the focus on Jesus's work on the cross.[40] Some evangelicals combine their theology's Christ-centered and cross-centered aspects and speak of being "Gospel-centered." In its healthiest forms, being "Christ-centered," "cross-centered," or "Gospel-centered" is not reductionistic at the expense of other crucial doctrines or aspects of the Gospel. Although this type of language is broad and begins to lose its meaning, it is popular in evangelical works.

The evangelical focus on Christ, the cross, and the gospel reveals a crucial aspect of evangelicals' theological aesthetics. Many evangelicals do not articulate the connection between Jesus Christ and his cross-work and beauty. However, evangelicals often connect Christ and the cross with the glory of God. This is because many evangelicals, based especially on the exegesis of John's Gospel, believe that the Father and the Spirit hold out Jesus Christ in a way that displays the glory of the Trinity and brings believers into fellowship with the Father and the Spirit.[41] Evangelicals often conflate God's beauty with his glory and use the words as synonyms.[42] Therefore, when they speak of the glory of God revealed in Jesus Christ and the cross, evangelicals are referring to both the glory and beauty of Jesus Christ and his work on the cross as a revelatory event.

This emphasis includes an implicit affirmation of the beauty of Jesus and the cross as those who perceive this beauty are drawn in. The beauty of Christ is displayed through the Gospel being spoken and shared in local churches between members and evokes wonder and thrill.[43] John Piper gives an example of an evangelical articulation of the glory and beauty of Jesus and his cross-work. Like Balthasar, Piper emphasizes Christ's glory using the exegetical ground of 2 Corinthians 3:18 and 4:4–6.[44] Piper sees his ministry as seeing, savoring, and "showing the supreme worth and the beauty of God."[45] In describing the reasons he wrote his classic book, *Desiring God*, he said it is because "breathtaking beauty

---

Balthasar. Ortlund demonstrates Christocentrism in a number of evangelical authors: Belcher, Clowney, Chapell, Goldsworthy, Greidenus, Johnson, Eswine, and Poythress. Many authors could be added to the bibliography provided by Ortlund who brings Christocentrism to different areas of study.

40. As seen in D.A. Carson's *The Cross and Christian Ministry*, R.C. Sproul's *The Truth of the Cross*, and John Stott's *The Cross of Christ*.

41. Sanders, *The Deep Things of God*, 173.

42. Crain, "Towards an Evangelical Theological Aesthetics," 29.

43. Ortlund, *The Gospel*, 19.

44. Piper, *God's Passion for His Glory*, 82. Piper, *Expository Exultation*, 82.

45. Piper, *Expository Exultation*, 17.

has visited us."[46] He not only magnifies the beauty of Jesus Christ, but he says that his beauty is an active, moral beauty that culminates in the cross. He explains, "The seeming weakness of the cross, endured by the most majestic and innocent person, is the peculiar glory that draws us into a well grounded faith."[47] Piper speaks of the aesthetic aspects when he mentions the "majestic person" and "peculiar glory" and then being allured or "drawn" by the majesty. Both aspects of aesthetics are present: the objective beauty or majesty and glory and the existential response of the perceiving subject, namely faith.

Brian Zahnd is another popular theologian who has influenced evangelicals in their approach to beauty. He develops the connection between beauty and cross-centered theology. Zahnd articulates the beauty of the cross, "The cross is the beauty of Christianity because it is at the cross that we encounter co-suffering love and costly forgiveness in its most beautiful form…the cruciform is the aesthetic of our gospel."[48] The beauty of Christ's love and forgiveness on the cross displays a "transcendent beauty" that saves us from self-centeredness that manifests itself in pride and greed.[49] Zahnd argues that the systems of the world are dominated by an axis of power that perpetuates envy, bitterness, pride, greed, and all forms of wickedness. Jesus' cross-work offers the world a new axis of love that is the beauty that will save the world.[50] This new axis that Jesus offered has a profound aesthetic allure that draws us into a reorientation of life around this beauty. Zahnd's appeal to the staggering beauty of Jesus Christ and his work on the cross as the axis to arrange the world around is an aesthetic way of articulating orientation to the beauty of Jesus Christ that resonates with many evangelicals.

Although the cross as a central focus is a basic tenet of evangelicals, not all evangelicals formulate their conceptions of God's beauty from a cross-centered perspective. For example, Vern Poythress gives a sketch of a Christ-centered Christian philosophy of beauty from a redemptive-historical and philosophical standpoint without specific reference to the cross. He argues from the temple's beauty and artistry. Just as the tabernacle and temple were designed with beauty and artistry, Jesus himself is the fulfillment of that beauty. He concludes, "Thus the climactic beauty

46. Piper, *Desiring God*, 293.
47. Piper, *A Peculiar Glory*, 239.
48. Zahnd, *Beauty Will Save the World*, 7.
49. Zahnd, *Beauty Will Save the World*, 7.
50. Zahnd, *Beauty Will Save the World*, 83.

and artistry of God appears in Christ. On this basis we may infer that God is indeed beautiful as one can see also in Revelation 4:3. His beauty is the original, archetypal beauty. Beautiful things in the world possess beauty only because they find their source in God. Their beauty has been specified by Christ, who is the Word of God."[51]

The evangelical focus on the glory or beauty of Jesus Christ and the cross is not merely a theological idiosyncrasy but a fitting articulation of profound theological truths that coincide with the Christological aspects of beauty.[52] In the incarnation, Jesus did not hide his beauty but displayed it. The beauty of God cannot be spoken of without reference to the beauty of Christ crucified, even as horrific as that event was. King argues:

> Our theological aesthetic sees the fittingness of God's *wisdom* and *power* manifest in Christ crucified as being perfectly correlated with the fittingness that characterizes the *beauty* of Christ crucified. For through the form of Christ crucified is the radiance of his glory, radiating a beauty reflective of and dramatized in the self-giving love of God.[53]

In other words, although some popular evangelicals, such as Grudem,[54] speak of the God's beauty as simply an attribute of God, King argues that this does not go far enough. God's beauty is Christological and reveals God's own self-giving-love.[55]

Evangelicals' Christ-centered focus has implications for how they approach theological aesthetic concepts. It also reveals that many evangelicals have a tacit theological aesthetic awareness that aligns well with Balthasar's theological aesthetic. Evangelicals emphasize that the person and work of Jesus Christ is the objective display of God's glory and, therefore, also the display of God's beauty. The beauty of God is seen most clearly in Jesus's work on the cross as the self-giving love of God.

## Sehnsucht and Lewis's Influence

Up to this point, I have primarily focused on the objective aspects of God's glory and beauty. This section will primarily focus on evangelicals'

---

51. Poythress, *Redeeming Philosophy*, 228.
52. King, *The Beauty of the Lord*, 48.
53. King, *The Beauty of the Lord*, 169.
54. Grudem, *Systematic Theology*, 219.
55. King, *The Beauty of the Lord*, 169. Also, Piper, *A Peculiar Glory*, 144.

teaching on the subject's perception of God's glory and beauty. This will be a bridge to begin exploring the ways God reveals his beauty through creation and the arts in the next sections. The issue of perception and sense of God's beauty is the most undeveloped aspect of current evangelical thought on concepts related to theological aesthetics. The evangelical theology of the subject's existential perception of God's objective beauty is heavily influenced by the works of C.S. Lewis. Lewis's works have a profound impact on evangelicalism, especially American evangelicalism.[56] Lewis's theological aesthetics emphasize longing, yearning, or homesickness for beauty. Lewis used the German word *Sehnsucht* to describe this experience. He gave an autobiographical account of his own longing for joy in *Surprised by Joy*.[57] However, the autobiographical experience of *Sehnsucht* is not merely something that Lewis felt personally, but something he believed all people feel or are at least capable of feeling because we were made for heaven and the infinite.[58] *Sehnsucht* is described in both Lewis's fiction and his non-fiction. Indeed, it has been argued that the concept of *Sehnsucht* is implicitly or explicitly present in all of Lewis's works.[59] One of the classic expressions of *Sehnsucht* is in his allegory, *Till We Have Faces,* when Psych, the main character says, "The sweetest thing in all my life has been the longing—to reach the Mountain and, to find the place where all the beauty came from. . .do you think it all meant nothing, all the longing? The longing for home? All my life the god of the Mountain has been wooing me."[60]

Often, *Sehnsucht* is a wandering desire that never meets the object of its true longing, God himself.[61] This is because people substitute God for the stuff of creation, such as books, flowers, music, natural beauty, sex, drink, ambition, and so on.[62] However, *Sehnsucht* was never designed to end in these things. The things of creation are only supposed to stimulate

---

56. Noll, *The Scandal of the Evangelical Mind*, 218. Carter "C.S. Lewis and the Church," 200. McGrath *C.S. Lewis*, A Life, 371–376.

57. Lewis, *Surprised by Joy*, 14–18.

58. Lewis, *The Weight of Glory.*

59. Crawford, "C.S. Lewis's Concept of Sehnsucht," 46. Lewis, *Surprised by Joy*, 17. Lewis, *The Four Loves*, 17. Lewis, *The Pilgrim's Regress*, 7, 202–204. Lewis, *Mere Christianity*, 150–151.

60. Lewis, *Till We Have Faces*, 75.

61. Lewis, *The Weight of Glory.*

62. Lewis, *The Weight of Glory.*

*Sehnsucht* and be signs that evoke longing for true and eternal beauty.[63] *Sehnsucht* is the existential longing or desire for the transcendent God, and that longing can only be met through him.

*Sehnsucht*, this longing for God, is only satisfied by the encounter with the triune God in Jesus Christ. *Sehnsucht*, for Lewis, is a surprising joy. It is like "arrows of Joy" that are shot through created reality and our experiences to give us inklings of the source of true joy.[64] These arrows of joy that beauty evokes creates a longing for the source of that beauty. Even when *Sehnsucht* directs people toward God, the source of beauty, there is still a longing for complete fulfillment. This longing is still an unsatisfied desire for the Christian. The fact that earthly pleasures never completely satiate the longing of *Sehnsucht* reveals that people were made for another country.[65] Lewis connects this longing and homesickness for beauty with the "weight of glory" of meeting Jesus Christ. Only when the Christian hears the words "well done, good and faithful servant" can he say, "Here at last is the thing I was made for."[66]

Lewis wanted his readers to experience this *Sehnsucht* or longing. Lewis argued that a person is more likely to experience *Sehnsucht* if he adopts an aesthetic stance toward life and experience that he describes as "looking along" rather than a mere "looking at."[67] Lewis describes the difference with the metaphor of standing in a dark toolshed with a beam of light coming through a crack at the top of the door. One can "look at" the beam of light and explain the beam of light and the dust particles floating in the light, or you can step back and "look at" and explain the seeing subject and explain the optical nerves and the process in which the person sees the beam of light. In other words, for Lewis, "looking at" something is observing and explaining facts from a disinterested scientific point of view. Lewis maintains that this type of knowledge is a part of knowledge but not the whole picture. To have true knowledge, one must look "along" the beam of light. Looking along the beam is to step into the beam of light so that it hits the perceiver's eyes, and that person begins to see through the light into the world outside. When someone looks "along" something, he steps into the existential nature of reality. This allows one to experience the subjective or existential aspects of reality. Lewis says, "One must

---

63. Lewis, *The Weight of Glory*.
64. Crawford, "C.S. Lewis's Concept of Sehnsucht," 59. Lewis, *Surprised by Joy*, 230.
65. Lewis, *Mere Christianity*, 138.
66. Lewis, *The Problem of Pain*, 151.
67. Lewis, *God in the Dock*, 230.

look *along* and at everything."⁶⁸ This is an encouragement to approach life through the vantage point of aesthetic wonder and coincides with theological aesthetics. *Looking along* something is about true perception and evokes *Sehnsucht* and the aesthetic experience of beauty.

Lewis's concept of *Sehnsucht* has shaped evangelical articulation of theological aesthetics. *Sehnsucht* has both an objective and subjective dimension that presupposes transcendence and finds its *telos* in Jesus Christ.⁶⁹ Created beauty reveals God. We never encounter an undiluted vision of the infinite God in this life. We perceive him now as we *look along* his revelation. The aesthetic wonder and longing the believer experiences now is like a signpost that leads him home, where he will meet God face to face. There, the longing will be satisfied.

## EVANGELICALS ON ENCOUNTERING GOD IN CREATION

### Tensions within Evangelicalism: Spiritual or Created Beauty?

Although evangelicals are influenced by Lewis's concept of spiritual beauty being communicated through created beauty, there is confusion on the relationship between spiritual and material beauty.⁷⁰ In this tension, created beauty and the arts compete with spiritual beauty and ethical goodness. Michael Wittmer argues that the pressure is seen especially in popular American evangelical arguments by David Platt and John Piper. Platt and Piper espouse a lifestyle of living radically on mission and not wasting your life.⁷¹ Wittmer believes that this emphasis is pushed to the point of neglecting the good gifts of creation. He argues this view that is influenced by a Platonic and spiritualistic reaction to naturalism.⁷²

Joseph Rigney also recognizes these tensions within evangelicalism and within the Scriptures themselves. Rigney asks the question, "What do we do with the things of the earth?"⁷³ He notices a false dichotomy evangelicals have between the beauty of Christ and the beauty of creation. Often, evangelicals resolve this tension by landing on one side of

---

68. Lewis, *God in the Dock*, 234.
69. Crawford, "C.S. Lewis's Concept of Sehnsucht," 77.
70. Tripp, *Awe*, 11. Dyrness, *Visual Faith*, 149.
71. Wittmer, *Becoming Worldly Saints*, 101.
72. Wittmer, *Becoming Worldly Saints*, 15.
73. Rigney, *Things of the Earth*, 20.

the tension.⁷⁴ Both Rigney and Wittmer attempt to answer the question of these tensions within Christianity and contemporary evangelicalism considering the doctrines of creation, redemption, and new creation. For some evangelicals, the concept of encountering God in creation and in culture and the arts is a neglected topic. However, as Rigney and Wittmer point out, God has given us the gifts of creation and culture as a means of experiencing him. The gifts are enjoyed in themselves but simultaneously point to God. This section and the next will present evangelical theologies of encountering God through creation, Scripture, and culture.

## God as Artist

The doctrine of God as the Great Artist is immensely popular in evangelicals' theology of the arts. This teaching also has precedence in the history of art. Nicholas Wolterstorff demonstrates that this idea was present in artists of the modern and contemporary period, like Gauguin, who said "Creating like unto our Divine Maker is the only way of rising to God" or Klee, who said, "Art is a simile of the Creation."⁷⁵ The first suggestion that God could be viewed as an artist was in the late 15th century.⁷⁶ Before that time, it was considered impious to make that assertion. The refusal to call God an artist because of impropriety at best and blasphemy at worst is a stark difference from the self-assertive and self-expressive rising to heaven that Gauguin envisioned for the artist. Today, evangelical authors do not fear being impious by saying that God is the artist, but they distance themselves from Gauguin's prideful assertions. Many evangelicals see their creative action as an imitative action of God as creator in faith and submission. Evangelical books on arts and creativity claim that God's nature as an artist is the foundation of creative impulses and the art making process.⁷⁷

Dorothy Sayers was influential for evangelical writers in connecting God's creative work with the artistic processes. She argues that the trinitarian imprint is on the artist's process of creating.⁷⁸ More importantly,

---

74. Rigney, *Things of the Earth*, 22–24.
75. Wolterstorff *Art Rethought*, 52.
76. Wolterstorff *Art in Action*, 51.
77. Sayers, *The Mind of the Maker*. Anderson, *The Faithful Artist*, 242. Terry and Lister, *Images and Idols*, 21. Fujimura, *The Splendor of the Medium*, 28. Barrs, *Echoes of Eden*, 20.
78. Sayers, *The Mind of the Maker*, 55.

she articulates an understanding of the transcendence of the author from his work while also maintaining immanence in such a way that something is revealed about the artist through his work. One cannot identify the work of art with the artist, such as pantheism would do with God and his creation. For example, we would not take up Shakespeare's plays and say that those plays were Shakespeare himself. In our response to God's art in creation and the drama of redemption, "we are brought into the mind of the author and caught up into the stream of his Power, which proceeds from his Energy, revealing his Idea to us and to himself."[79]

In evangelical theology, God is the creator who reveals himself through his creation. He is *the* Artist. Terry and Lister note that God's artistic creativity includes his activity as an architect, artist or painter, and author.[80] God is the great song writer, symphony conductor, and musician. He is the one who conducts the saints or plays the instruments of their lives. God is also the Great Architect. The universe's cosmological structure and the sky's architecture reveal God's glory, character, and authority.[81] This is similar to Horton's notion of God creating his "house," which was the space for him to dwell with his people.[82] God's architecture includes both the present world and the world to come. God is the "designer and builder" (Heb 11:10) of the new heavens and earth. God is also the artist, designer, or painter who fills his architecture with unsurpassed beauty. Through his design of Eden as a staggeringly beautiful home or temple, God demonstrates his artistry, and Eden is like an "aesthetics lecture taught in garden form."[83] The beauty of Eden finds its source in God and reveals his glory. Eden is his art gallery, and he is the great etcher who etches his beauty into every detail of life.[84]

God is also the author.[85] Related to God's authorship, God is a playwright. Kevin Vanhoozer expounds on the playwright as a prominent metaphor for the Christian life. In redemption history, God is the playwright, actor, and director of the drama.[86] The triune God conceived the play from eternity, with all of creation as the theater for the drama,

---

79. Sayers, *The Mind of the Maker*, 55.
80. Terry and Lister, *Images and Idols*, 25–39.
81. Terry and Lister, *Images and Idols*, 29.
82. Horton, *The Christian Faith*, 233.
83. Terry and Lister, *Images and Idols*, 32.
84. Terry and Lister, *Images and Idols*, 34.
85. Terry and Lister, *Images and Idols*, 34.
86. Vanhoozer, *Faith Speaking Understanding*, 28.

with actors and agents. The plot concerns how the playwright enters into communion with the actors by becoming an actor himself in Jesus Christ.[87] The theologian stands as a dramaturge, the assistant of the director and actors.[88] God is the playwright of the most outstanding drama ever told and is himself the audience when no one else is watching.

God is the great artist whose artistry reveals but does not contain him. He is the great architect, composer, musician, designer, painter, author, and playwright. In emphasizing these things, evangelicals consistently maintain that all types of artistry in some ways reflect God's artistry. All the artistic endeavors have an analogical relationship in some limited way with the Creator and his creativity. These analogies may not be pressed too far in any way that undermines the prior commitment to biblical faithfulness, but they reveal the truth of God as the infinite artist. For evangelicals, a crucial difference between the artistry of a human person and God's artistry is that God is the Artist-Creator, and he creates *ex nihilo*. His design, form, and materials provide the ability for creatures to be artists.[89]

## The Perceiving Subject Awake in the World in Wonder

For evangelicals, God is the great artist. He also delights in the beauty of his artistry. When God is pleased with his art, he also invites his creatures to be pleased with created beauty.[90] God created Eden beautifully. He also created the human sense perception with the capacity for pleasure and aesthetic delight. The senses are not sinful. God is full of aesthetic delight and not an ascetic.[91] The senses are a gift from God, given to reveal himself. Appealing to Lewis's categories of "looking at" and "looking along," John Piper argues that all our physical senses work alongside the eyes of our heart to reveal the glory of God in creation.[92] "Looking along" could be placed alongside "heard along," "smelled along," "tasted along," or "felt along." The senses are designed to allow individuals to perceive and delight in God's glory through creation.

87. Vanhoozer, *Faith Speaking Understanding*, 74–75.
88. Vanhoozer, *The Drama of Doctrine*, 244.
89. Kilby *The Arts and the Christian Imagination*, 52.
90. Rigney, *Things of the Earth*, 78.
91. Kilby *The Arts and the Christian Imagination*, 29.
92. Piper, *When I Don't Desire God*, 185.

Evangelicals are comfortable with saying that God reveals himself in creation in such a way that God gives himself through creation.[93] N.D. Wilson says the world is a reflection of God, the artist himself, and what seems to us to be the vast expanse of the cosmos with all its manifold particularity is merely a small confining frame for God to express himself in.[94] Because creation is God's art and means of expressing himself, God invites us to look at this finite picture of the infinite. Wilson says that the human perceiver is invited to:

> Assess it like prose, like poetry, like architecture, sculpture, painting, dance, delta blues, opera, tragedy, comedy, romance, epic. Assess it like you would a Fabergé egg, like a gunfight, like a musical, like a snowflake, like a death, a birth, a triumph, a love story, a tornado, a smile, a heartbreak, a sweater, a hunger pain, a desire, a fulfillment, a desert, a dessert, an ocean, a leap, a quest, a fall, a climb, a tree, a waterfall, a song, a race, a frog, a play, a song, a marriage, a consummation, a thirst quenched.[95]

Reality is enchanted with beauty because of God's revelation. The perceiving subject is thrown into wonder at this revelation. The Creator-creature distinction is maintained, but creation is simultaneously a display of divine life, light, and glory, so we can look at everything and say, "This also is Thou: neither is this Thou."[96] Thus, the disenchanting influences of secularism, atheism, and naturalism are put in check, and a healthy use of both imagination and reason is established.[97]

## The Fall and the Ugly

One of the complicating factors of God's revelation in creation is the reality of the fall and its effects. Although evangelicals have developed theologies of the fall, they do not typically use aesthetic categories to speak of the impact of sin and the fall as "The Ugly," though the concept is present. The doctrine of sin is the marring of God's good creation and the image

---

93. Rigney, *Things of the Earth*, 85.
94. Wilson, *Notes from the Tilt-A-Whirl*, chapter 6.
95. Wilson, *Notes from the Tilt-A-Whirl*, chapter 6.
96. Rigney, *Things of the Earth*, 67.
97. McGrath, *Born to Wonder*, 146.

of God.[98] In other words, evangelicals typically focus on metaphysical realities and effects of the fall rather than its aesthetic effects.

In popular evangelical theology textbooks, Erickson gets the closest to addressing some of the aesthetic implications of the fall.[99] He notes that sin may be construed both as the "bad" and the "wrong." In Erickson's terminology, he blends the good and the beautiful nature of God's original creation. The good, he says, is the beautiful. He then uses aesthetic words such as "harmonious" and "attractive" to describe it. The evil is "ugly" and "repulses."[100] Evil has a turbulent and inharmonious property that pierces through the state of all creation. The bad is the ugly effect of the fall on all creation and the state of things, while the "wrong" is the conscious transgressing of the Law of God.[101] Although evangelicals do not have a strong theology of "the ugly," the doctrine of the fall profoundly effects how they approach creaturely beauty, culture, and the arts. This is especially the case in circles influenced by the doctrine of total depravity without a counterbalance of a strong doctrine of common grace. The effects of the fall often create a deep suspicion for the things of this earth among evangelicals.

An evangelical artistic expression of the pervasive ugliness of sin created by the fall is seen in Grace Carol Bomer's, *The Mystery of Babylon*. This work is a part of her series that explores the themes of Babel, sin, and chaos. In *The Mystery of Babylon*, there are references to the Great Prostitute of Revelation 17 and 18. New York City is inverted and, in a reference to Pieter Bruegel the Younger's 1563 and 1566 paintings, the form of the ancient tower of Babel is portrayed in outline form. The picture demonstrates the darkness, chaos, and ugliness of society apart from God.

---

98. Grudem, *Systematic Theology*, 449.
99. Erickson, *Systematic Theology*, 553.
100. Erickson, *Systematic Theology*, 553.
101. Erickson, *Systematic Theology*, 553.

*The Mystery of Babylon* (2015) by Grace Carol Bomer. Used with permission.

## ENCOUNTERING GOD IN SCRIPTURE

### Kevin Vanhoozer's Doctrine of Scripture and the Author and Reader

Humanity also experiences the glory and beauty of the Lord through the Scriptures. Kevin Vanhoozer's hermeneutics are full of aesthetic insights. The whole canon of Scripture is a communicative act of the divine Author.[102] Vanhoozer criticizes postmodern deconstructionism and the dethroning of authorial intention. The key difference between Christian theories of language and deconstructionist theories is the difference between Christian "joy" and deconstructive "play."[103] The Christian respects the Author's moral rights and receives the communication, opening the possibility for joy. Deconstructionists "play" with the text to make it mean whatever they would like. True interpretation is faithful to what the author is doing with the text. The author is an "aesthetic agent"

102. Vanhoozer, *Is There a Meaning in This Text?*, 265.
103. Vanhoozer, *Is There a Meaning in This Text?*, 202.

who designs the text in such a way that it has a profound effect on the reader.[104] In God's design the Bible reveals Jesus Christ. Christ presents himself in the text. He explains, "The Bible is part of the pattern of divine communication and communion over which the risen Lord presides in and presents himself."[105] This is a unique dynamic unparalleled in any other type of reading. The primary author of the covenant canon is God. This does not undermine the human authors of the Bible, but it does nuance our hermeneutical approaches. Vanhoozer says, "Unlike the human authors of Scripture who are dead and buried, then, the risen Christ is alive — communicatively present and active."[106] This does not mean that the words of the human authors are distorted, but that they are reinforced and authoritatively applied to each generation by the God who inspired their words.[107]

Therefore, the Bible is the primary place we perceive the risen Lord's form and splendor. The Spirit awakens the heart to behold the grace of Jesus Christ and see the light of God's glory in his face as the believer reads. Vanhoozer summarizes, "To read in the economy of grace is to read with faces exposed to the face of God shining on us through the text."[108] The end goal is not only beholding God's glory, but also being transformed by it into Christ's likeness. In Scripture, God himself is placed before the believer and he or she is brought up into fellowship with the Trinity as they are transformed into the likeness of Jesus Christ. In the act of reading, the Spirit is forming and shaping that person's reason, imagination, emotion, and volition.[109] In other words, reading Scripture becomes a shaping action as the one who apprehends becomes transformed in their tastes and judgments. The Bible is not an object of judgment as other aesthetic objects but trains aesthetic taste.

To highlight the Bible's effect on the readers, Vanhoozer uses another aesthetic metaphor. The Bible not only creates an Author-reader relationship between God and a believer, but also a Conductor-performer relationship. Scripture is like a musical score. God is both the conductor and the composer of the symphony. As the composer, he puts notes, accents, dynamics, tempos and so on to show how the symphony should be

---

104. Vanhoozer, *Is There a Meaning in This Text?*, 234.
105. Vanhoozer, *Mere Christian Hermeneutics*, 8.
106. Vanhoozer, *Mere Christian Hermeneutics*, 8.
107. Vanhoozer, *Mere Christian Hermeneutics*, 10.
108. Vanhoozer, *Biblical Authority After Babel*, 60.
109. Vanhoozer, *Biblical Authority After Babel*, 86.

played out in life. God is the orchestra conductor who leads the music of Scripture to be "performed."[110]

In another aesthetic metaphor, Scripture is a gallery that shapes the Christian imagination and allows them to live in the world in a truly Christian way.[111] Vanhoozer's goal in employing these aesthetic metaphors is to engage the imagination and influence the use of the Scriptures so that the church becomes a living Bible.[112] Believers read the Bible and let it influence and direct their lives. God, as the playwright, gives each believer a particular part to play in his drama. The Bible has the power to produce a sanctified and transformed imagination in actors who act on the stage of life. Vanhoozer's project presents a nuanced hermeneutic that is intrinsically connected to theological aesthetic categories and concepts.

## ENCOUNTERING GOD IN CULTURE AND ART

### Evangelicals' Variegated Approach to Culture and Art

Evangelicals have a variety of approaches to culture. This is partly because culture and cultures are multifaceted.[113] From a biblical perspective, cultures have elements of both staggering beauty and obscene depravity. The beauty of culture is based on the fact that mankind is made in the image of God and was given the culture mandate. The depravity within the culture and its artifacts are present due to the profound effects of the Fall, rebellion against God, and the activity of Satan in the world. Wolterstorff offers a scathing critique of the fine arts institution within society.[114] The fine arts institution consistently distorts our vision, is hostile to religion and God himself, creates and leads to oppression and self-aggrandizement, destroys lives, and deflects responsibility. A theology of art that does not recognize this will fall into a simplistic acceptance of all culture as good and revelatory.[115] The paradox of beauty and depravity within culture is what makes some evangelicals completely reject all culture

---

110. Vanhoozer, *Pictures at a Theological Exhibition*, 87.
111. Vanhoozer, *Pictures at a Theological Exhibition*, 77.
112. Vanhoozer, *Faith Speaking Understanding*, 2.
113. Frame, *The Doctrine of the Knowledge of God*, 888.
114. Wolterstorff, *Art in Action*, 192–193.
115. Treier et al., *The Beauty of God*, 10.

while others move toward practical wholesale acceptance of it. The evangelical approach to culture and art is rightly complex and variegated.[116]

God delights in his human creatures and the truly beautiful things that they create or reflect.[117] Aesthetic delight in art is a type of aesthetic joy. This joy comes from God and can be experienced even in this broken world.[118] God designed culture and art to be a forum where we can experience glimpses of his beauty. Art reveals two things.[119] First, art reveals beauty and the inherent sacredness of the world that God has charged with that beauty. Second, art is the revealer of the values and questions of a particular cultural moment.[120] This explains the ambivalence of art. It may reveal the beauty that finds its source in God or unveils attitudes and values stemming from sinful nature. It is possible to find both these elements within the same work of art. Therefore, how a Christian is to approach art and cultural artifacts is a particularly important topic.

An influential treatment of the Christian's approach to culture was presented by Richard Niebuhr in *Christ and Culture*. Although Niebuhr was not an evangelical, his work has become the point of departure for evangelicals' discussion of how to relate to culture.[121] He argued that the Christian's approach to culture has five possibilities: (1) Christ above culture, (2) Christ against culture, (3) Christ of culture, (4) Christ and culture in paradox, and (5) Christ transforming culture. Niebuhr also argued that there is a cycle that typically occurs in the life of a church.[122] The church begins with a "Christ against culture" stance, where the church is set against culture. There then comes a stage where there is a time of peace with culture, and there is almost no difference between those in the church and the broader culture. This is followed by the third stage of revival, where the church again sets itself against culture.

Niebuhr's insights provided a basis for discussion for evangelicals. Anderson argues that the "Christ against culture" position best represents

---

116. Wolterstorff, *Art in Action*, 193.

117. Mouw, *He Shines in All That's Fair*, 36. Dyrness, *Visual Faith*, 140–141.

118. Wolterstorff 1980, 169.

119. Dyrness, *Visual Faith*, 142.

120. Dyrness, *Visual Faith*, 142.

121. Crouch, *Culture Making*, 179. Carson, *Christ and Culture Revisited*. Frame, *The Doctrine of the Christian Life*, 863–887. Anderson, *The Faithful Artist*, 27. Chatraw and Prior, *Cultural Engagement*, 36.

122. Niebuhr, "Toward the Independence of the Church." See discussion in Keller, *Center Church*, 237.

the fundamentalist position in the late 19th and early 20th century, which deeply influenced streams within evangelicalism.[123] The posture of Christ against culture, however, failed to realize that as humans, we exist by necessity within a culture. By nature, culture shapes the individuals of a culture.[124] Thus, the Christ against culture model as a sole posture is untenable. In the 1970s, some evangelicals were encouraged to take a different approach to culture and the arts through the works of Schaeffer, Rookmaaker, Wolterstorff, and Seerveld.[125] These authors influenced some streams of evangelicalism, especially within the Reformed sections of evangelicalism.

Two evangelicals who have been influenced by a more positive approach to engaging and creating culture are Andy Crouch and Timothy Keller. Keller demonstrates that each of Niebuhr's cultural approaches has strengths and weaknesses.[126] He argues that there are basically four different models in Niebuhr's five positions: (1) Transformationist, (2) Relevance, (3) Two-Kingdoms, and (4) Counterculturalist. He goes on to say that these models operate under an assumption about how much common grace is within culture and how active engagement should be with culture. Since no single model can encompass what it means to have a biblical approach to culture, Keller argues that we should learn from the blended insights of these approaches. Keller's discussion is helpful as a basis for understanding differences among evangelicals in their approach to culture and the arts. There is no monolithic approach to culture within evangelicalism.

Crouch likewise urges caution because "the culture" is a highly complex concept.[127] Culture has different spheres and scales, and it is influenced profoundly by the meeting of many cultures through the ethnic diversity in our age.[128] We are born into culture, and our task is to cultivate what has been handed down to us. To cultivate the good and beautiful within the received culture is the discipline of "culture keeping" to be distinguished from culture making.[129] Crouch also adjusts Niebuhr's five approaches to culture and speaks of the responses of "critiquing culture,"

123. Anderson *The Faithful Artist*, 235.
124. Anderson *The Faithful Artist*, 236.
125. Anderson *The Faithful Artist*, 231–233. Crouch, *Culture Making*, 86.
126. Keller, *Center Church*, 192–232.
127. Crouch, *Culture Making*, 60.
128. Crouch, *Culture Making*, 43–49.
129. Crouch, *Culture Making*, 77.

"condemning culture," "consuming culture," and "copying culture."[130] Instead of saying that one of these approaches should characterize the Christian approach to culture, he says that each of these responses or "gestures" is needed for different cultural goods and artifacts.[131] He says it is a problem when one of these responses becomes an overall posture adopted toward culture. Similar to Keller, Crouch argues that a problem occurs when the Christian refuses to learn from other approaches to culture. He says that each response or approach is good and acceptable if rightly applied to a particular aspect or artifact of culture. However, Crouch's main concern is not with Christian's approach culture. He wants evangelicals to cultivate and create beautiful culture within the various spheres of life to live out who God has created us to be as "artists and gardeners."[132]

Therefore, while Keller gives us a platform for understanding variegated evangelical engagement with culture, Crouch ushers in a call to make or generate culture and cultural artifacts. Crouch argues that understanding and approaching the broader culture is not enough. He critiques a worldview analysis approach as merely cognitive. However, he also admits that this starting point of "keeping culture" is how we move toward generating culture and beautiful cultural artifacts from a Christian perspective.[133] Thus, in the following sections I will examine the work of Nancy Pearcey, a worldview analyst in the tradition of Francis Shaeffer. Crouch offers a gentle critique of Shaeffer and Pearcey, saying their approach creates critics of art rather than artists.[134] Therefore, I will present Pearcey's work and then move on to examine some culture makers within evangelicalism.

## Art as Worldview Revealer

Some evangelical scholars approach art, both in its high and low forms, as something that reveals an aspect of the worldview and system of thought of the artist behind that artwork. Pearcey sees a secular assault in the west on morals, meaning, and thought and argues that it is the Christian's

130. Crouch, *Culture Making*, 90–93.
131. Crouch, *Culture Making*, 90.
132. Crouch, *Culture Making*, 97.
133. Crouch, *Culture Making*, 77.
134. Crouch, *Culture Making*, 62.

responsibility to develop a biblical and Christian worldview as an alternative.[135] Pearcey argues that art functions as stories and images that express worldviews and ideologies.[136] She builds on Francis Schaeffer's two-story metaphor that truth has been divided into "upper-story truths" of theology, morality, and aesthetics and "lower-story truths" of the scientific, empirically proven facts.[137] She calls this the fact/value dichotomy.

If a person's worldview falls solely on either side of this dichotomy, it will eventually lead to secularism.[138] On the fact side, empiricism, rationalism, evolution, logical positivism, and linguistic analysis all move toward secularism.[139] However, emphasizing only the value side of truth leads to secularism through various forms romanticism, Idealism, Marxism, phenomenology, existentialism, postmodernism, and deconstructionism.[140] Pearcey maintains that while these ideologies have elements of truth, the problem comes when an element of truth becomes absolutized and pushed to its extreme without the nuance of other truths providing balance. This is a reductionistic approach to reality where the worldview emphasizes part of reality and forces everything to fit within that box.[141] The absolutized element (e.g., sense experience in empiricism, the natural in naturalism, the spiritual One in pantheism), becomes a mental idol and denies the Creator's transcendence and creativity.[142]

The relation of Pearcey's works to theological aesthetics is especially apparent in her development of the theme of transcendence in relation to these systems of thought and the art that expresses them. Taking in a work of art is to encounter the artist's worldview, which is true even for the postmodern deconstructionists.[143] This is congruent with Horton's suggestion that philosophy follows the models of "overcoming estrangement" and "the stranger we never met."[144] To overemphasize or even absolutize the values side of truth seeks to "overcome estrangement" and

---

135. See *Total Truth, Saving Leonardo, Finding Truth*, and *Love Thy Body*.
136. Pearcey, *Saving Leonardo*, 4.
137. Pearcey, *Total Truth*, 21. Pearcey, *Saving Leonardo*, 26.
138. Pearcey, *Saving Leonardo*, 3.
139. Pearcey, *Saving Leonardo*, 172.
140. Pearcey, *Saving Leonardo*, 245.
141. Pearcey, *Saving Leonardo*, 244.
142. Pearcey, *Saving Leonardo*, 244.
143. Pearcey, *Saving Leonardo*, 236.
144. Horton, *The Christian Faith*, 35–43.

inevitably blends into monism. To overemphasize or absolutize the fact side of truth rejects God, treating him as the stranger we never met.

When art absolutizes the fact side of truth, it becomes ineffective at pointing beyond itself. This can be seen in such works as Francisco Goya's *The Third of May* (1814), Edgar Degas' *Ballerina and Lady with a Fan* (1885), Pablo Picasso's *Demoiselles d'Avignon* (1907), Marcel Duchamp's *Fountain* (1917), and Frank Stella's *Single Concentric Squares* (1974).[145] Pearcey traces the progressive descent into chaos expressed in the artwork of those who deny the ability of art to convey transcendence.

On the other hand, when the value side of truth is absolutized, transcendence is yearned for, but ultimately undermined. Transcendence is undermined in different ways by the various streams of thought within this grouping. For example, romanticism undermined transcendence through pantheistic tendencies and emphasis on the light within the artist.[146] Imagination and creativity became savior and substituted art for religion. The romantics were not tasked with seeing beauty but creating it.[147] However, while the romantic heritage yearned for transcendence, the refusal to find it outside themselves led to despair and nihilism.[148] The progression from romantic pantheism to nihilistic postmodernism is seen in works such as Sanford Robinson Gifford's *October in the Catskills* (1880), Carlos Schwabe's *Death of a Gravedigger* (1885), Giorgio de Chirico's *Love Song* (1914), John Pollock's *Number 33* (1948), Rothko's *Chapel* (1971), and David Salle's *Angels in the Rain* (1998).[149] These works of art and others like them may indeed be beautiful but they undermine the transcendent Creator either through substituting him with self or buckling under despair.

Pearcey not only emphasizes being able to read worldviews from art. She is also interested in Christians creating good art. Pearcey encourages Christians to develop good taste so that we can perceive and create what is good and true and beautiful in painting, literature, architecture, music, or any of the arts.[150] From the biblical perspective, the Creator is transcendent and the source of all things. Christian discernment and creativity must start with this basic presupposition and eschew the sacred/

---

145. Pearcey, *Saving Leonardo*, 109–169.
146. Pearcey, *Saving Leonardo*, 191.
147. Pearcey, *Saving Leonardo*, 184.
148. Pearcey, *Saving Leonardo*, 215.
149. Pearcey, *Saving Leonardo*, 89–239.
150. Pearcey, *Saving Leonardo*, 271.

secular and the fact/value dichotomy. In other words, the romantic or empirical reductionism that characterizes much of art must be undone. Art forms can enshrine reductionistic thinking, but they also have the powerful ability to burst apart the bonds of reductionism. Christian art must include creation, fall, and redemption in a way that allures people to the biblical worldview.[151] Pearcey sees this responsible and beautiful Christian art in works such as Jasper Francis Crospey's *Autumn on the Hudson River* (1860), Henry O. Tanner's *The Banjo Lesson* (1983), Casper David Friedrich, Georges Rouault's *Christ Mocked by Soldiers* (1932), Grace Carol Boomer's *Weep for the Wiping of Grace* (1998), and Makoto Fujimura's *Zero Summer* (2005).[152]

Where Pearcey's emphasis is reading worldview in art for the purpose of discernment and apologetics, theological aesthetics' concern is with encountering God in his beauty. Art tends to become a kind of sacred ritual that is a substitute for God.[153] People, craving for beauty and transcendence that can only be satisfied by God, end up creating an idol of art or some good gift. Pearcey refers to the beauty of God when she speaks about the alluring quality of the beauty of the biblical worldview.[154] The biblical worldview is alluring because the God behind that worldview is beautiful. This alluring is part of theological aesthetics. Allured by the beauty of truth, people are drawn in to meet the God of truth. Pearcey's insights on the fact/value dichotomy and the broad streams of art and philosophy are instructive for the streams of theological aesthetics that engage with art.

## The Integrated and Scriptural Imagination

As noted above, Crouch points out the insufficiency of analysis and critique when it comes to culture and its artifacts. Pearcey's work offers a penetrating analysis of general themes and styles of art and shows the longing and hunger for God, the Transcendent One. It is not enough from an evangelical point of view to merely be consumers; rather, believers must be culture makers and use God-given talents, abilities, and worldview to create beauty that reveals what is good, true, and beautiful

---

151. Pearcey, *Saving Leonardo*, 272.
152. Pearcey, *Saving Leonardo*, 110–209.
153. Pearcey, *Finding Truth*, 38.
154. Pearcey, *Saving Leonardo*, 272.

about God. This involves two steps that will be addressed in the following two sections. The first has to do with an imagination that is formed by the true perceiving of God's revelation. Thus, I begin by examining Peterson's concept of the integrated imagination and Begbie's concept of the scriptural imagination. The second step will discuss making art that reveals truths about God and what it means to be generative.

To make art that reveals the beauty or truth of God requires imagination. Fujimura explains that imagination is powerful enough to create the good and beautiful while the lack of imagination can only destroy and lead to a culture of cynicism.[155] Embedded in the art process is an imagination that dares to hope even when the broader culture context is infected with apathy, cynicism, and terrorism. Leland Ryken argues that since the 19th Century, imagination has replaced imitation as the way to understand art's relationship to life.[156] Imagination is "image-making and image-perceiving capacity, the creative faculty, the contemplative act, the ability to synthesize disparate details into a single whole, and the human capacity for artistic form and beauty."[157] Thus, in the arts, there is a need to develop a distinctively Christian imagination.

Author and musician Andrew Peterson addresses the problem of "imaginational segregation."[158] This segregation of the mind is the divorcing of Christianity and its truths from the enjoyment of art and its creation. This parallels Pearcey's Fact/Value dichotomy but is somewhat different. The segregation Peterson discusses is where the truths of the Christian faith do not touch the enjoyment and creation of art. He speaks of his youthful love for novels, comic books, films and music, and he understood that this love was a desire to enter into beauty.[159] The desire is often to enter the "other side" of the world of creativity, where everything is better than the things of this earth. However, Peterson says that what we need is the imagination that allows art forms to be used not merely as an escape from this world but as a revelation of what is already within the real world. Lewis and Tolkien are examples who produce the kind of art that enlivens everyday life. He explains, "Tolkien and Lewis, both in their own way, lifted me out of this world to show me a thundering beauty, and when I read the last sentence and came tumbling back to earth, I could

---

155. Fujimura, *Refractions*, 112.
156. Ryken, *The Christian Imagination*, 61.
157. Ryken, *The Christian Imagination*, 61.
158. Peterson, *Adorning the Dark*, 67.
159. Peterson, *Adorning the Dark*, 67.

still hear the peal. I hear it to this day."[160] In the language of theological aesthetics, these works of art do not only have form, but the splendor of beauty shines out from them. Karen Swallow Prior similarly shows that Lewis and Tolkien appeal to evangelicals because they are "a symbol-starved people." She explains, "We need enchanted worlds to help us to help us see the enchantment in our own."[161]

This type of enchanted art integrates imagination with the real world to illuminate reality rather than shroud or critique it. Peterson says, "God allowed the stories to lift the veil on the imaginary world to show me the real world behind it — which ended up being, in the end, the one I was already in."[162] Good art is an imitation of the art of the Great Artist. Good art reveals the splendor of beauty and trains the mind to know the good, true, and beautiful. Art is a tool of the imagination that allows us to see through the mundane aspects of life to the beauty within it. However, the aesthetic experience of good art is revelatory for the individual because it allows the splendor perceived in the art form to illumine this present world as it beckons us to enter everyday life with that newly formed imagination that opens our eyes to beauty and brokenness around us.[163] Or, as Wolterstorff argues, art is not escape from the world, but action within the world.[164]

In this art, the beauty of real life is amplified and deepened rather than detracted from. The art form is like a "bridge" used to "smuggle back some of its light into this present darkness."[165] Peterson does not know if the bridge exists in the perceiving person or in the art itself. For the perceiving subject, the goal is to receive the beauty and bring it back to illuminate the perception of the real world. To smuggle beauty back into real life is the goal of the perceiving person. The incredible thing is that the beauty perceived is not apophatic or world-shunning that assumes God's sheer transcendence, but it is the transcendent revealed in the beauty of the world.[166]

After perception is the creative act. Creating art that radiates beauty so that the perceiver experiences this bridge is the task of the artist. This

---

160. Peterson, *Adorning the Dark*, 71.
161. Prior, *The Evangelical Imagination*, 249.
162. Peterson, *Adorning the Dark*, 71.
163. Fujimura, *Refractions*, 17.
164. Wolterstorff, *Art in Action*, 5.
165. Peterson, *Adorning the Dark*, 73.
166. Begbie, *Redeeming Transcendence in the Arts*, 131.

is accomplished through the uniting of truth and beauty within the art form.[167] The form of beauty that is captured in excellent art, such as the art by Rembrandt or novels by Tolkien, arrests and may create *Sehnsucht* in the perceiver.[168] The creative process is "profoundly spiritual, and therefore profoundly mysterious."[169] Peterson speaks of the difficulty of the creative process. Inspiration comes in an exhilarating flash, but the "potential is shimmering beyond the veil somewhere," while the finished product is accompanied by the haunting sense of not reaching that potential.[170] The author or artist senses transcendent beauty and attempts to convey that beauty through their work, but it will always fall short of the flash of the transcendent inspiration. Peterson describes this with a metaphor. A mountain is seen through the clouds. The artist, a songwriter in his case, tries to find a way to communicate in a way that gets as close as possible to the summit. He goes on, "Most often, I am nowhere close. I end up in the desert somewhere ... But sometimes I end up in the foothills and go to bed happy. I haven't summited, but I can at least see the peak and imagine what it would be like to stand there."[171]

Peterson's integrated imagination and transposing the transcendent into the art form is related to Begbie's concept of transcendence in art. Transcendence is experienced in art when the artist is guided by and dependent on the Holy Spirit. This artist assists this world in becoming fully itself as God has designed it.[172] In this creative act, creatures are responding to the majesty of God's revelation as the Great Artist and stepping into their role as worshippers. Begbie writes, "In humans, the nonhuman world finds a conscious answering voice, a mortal from the dust of the earth who can know and respond to God's love as a creature and love God in return, and, as part of this response, 'voice creation's praise.'"[173]

In art, the imagination is to be shaped by the transcendence of God and the particularity of how he has revealed himself through Jesus Christ. The artist uses "integrated imagination" and perceives the goodness and beauty of the creation and is informed by the "scriptural imagination."[174]

167. Peterson, *Adorning the Dark*, 85.
168. Peterson, *Adorning the Dark*, 86, 100.
169. Peterson, *Adorning the Dark*, 90.
170. Peterson, *Adorning the Dark*, 92.
171. Peterson, *Adorning the Dark*, 93.
172. Begbie, *Redeeming Transcendence in the Arts*, 131.
173. Begbie, *Redeeming Transcendence in the Arts*, 149.
174. Begbie, *Redeeming Transcendence in the Arts*, 185. Begbie, *A Peculiar Orthodoxy*, vi.

This perception and imagination then inspires art that helps others live in the fullness of this created world.[175] This does not preclude nonrepresentational art, but rather encourages a type of nonrepresentational art informed by the concepts of scriptural and integrated imagination. For an evangelical example, Makoto Fujimura's art does not pull us away from the sensory material of this world, but communicates a transcendence, splendor, shalom, and eschatological hope.[176]

Good art gives a glimpse of deeper perception into the wonder of this world and its future eschatological destination. Scriptural and integrated imagination of the artist are the ways the artist sees what is there and then guides the process for making art. Voicing creation's praise results when an artist embarks on the creative processes for the good of others and in praise of God. The calling of the artist is to use their gifts to help people really see the enchanted reality of God's creation and inspire praise. Scriptural and integrated imagination are the tools to help artists see created reality so that they can generate God-honoring art that voices creation's praise.

## Culture Care and Being Generative

Worldview and imagination are part of formation and the perception of God and the world. For those who have been deeply formed by a biblical worldview and integrated, scriptural imagination, the next step is to be a culture maker as Crouch argues. For evangelicals, being a culture maker is part of God's calling to live responsibly before God, our neighbor, ourselves, and nature.[177] This means engaging in the action of making art and having goals for that art in a manner consistent with the Christian commitment.[178]

Mukato Fujimura calls Christian artists to be generative. To be generative is to use creativity to bring about something life giving and fruitful.[179] It is a way to be a good steward with what God has given and engage with culture in such a way that future generations may thrive. A generative approach to culture catalyzes and enables future growth and

---

175. Begbie, *A Peculiar Orthodoxy*, 158.
176. Fujimura, *The Splendor of the Medium*, 3–4.
177. Wolterstorff, *Art in Action*, 72–78.
178. Wolterstorff, *Art in Action*, 195.
179. Fujimura, *Culture Care*, 23.

production of beauty within a culture. Fujimura challenges the approach to culture that is always at battle with it.[180] He argues that culture, rather than a battle ground to wage a war on, is a garden to be cultivated. Fear and anxiety do not create art, but rather, it is faith and love for neighbors that causes us to be generative.[181] The goal of culture care and being generative within culture is to swim upstream above the over-commodification and utilitarian within culture and become a culture estuary that produces clean water for others to thrive off.[182] The truly generative artist will be able then to display the truths of God and the biblical worldview. In this way, the generative artist becomes an instrument of God in giving tastes of God's transcendence and immanence and evoking *Sehnsucht*.

## Kitsch Art and Evangelicalism

Creating art with a biblical worldview and imagination involves considering creation, fall, and redemption in a way that draws people into the beauty of Christianity.[183] Unfortunately, evangelical Christians are known for kitsch and sentimental art. Kitsch evangelical art undermines the reality of the fall by ignoring it. It is a reductionistic approach that refuses to deal with evil through the cross and redemption but ignores it altogether. Kitsch art is a substitute for culture care and being generative. Unfortunately, kitsch art as a substitute for deeply biblical art is a constant temptation of evangelicals.

Roger Scruton reveals the danger of kitsch art.[184] As we have seen, art has the incredible ability to reveal the transcendent in a way that corresponds to humanity's innate spiritual longings. In Lewis's language, art inspires *Sehnsucht*. Because art has the incredible potential of being "sacred" in its revelation of transcendence, kitsch art is a degradation and desecration much like pornography or gratuitous violence in art.[185] However, it is difficult to determine when art really becomes kitsch as there are no clear-cut boundaries between kitsch and non-kitsch.[186] Even the

---

180. Fujimura, *Culture Care*, 40.
181. Fujimura, *Culture Care*, 129.
182. Fujimura, *Culture Care*, 134.
183. Pearcey, *Saving Leonardo*, 272.
184. Scruton, *Beauty*, 188.
185. Scruton, *Beauty*, 188.
186. Scruton, *Beauty*, 188.

reaction against being kitsch can create an overly gritty and edgy art that is itself kitsch in a different way.[187] Another overreaction to kitsch art is an elitist mentality that pervades fine art institutions.

It is not just evangelicals that have a tendency toward producing kitsch art. It is a problem for all branches of Christianity and can be seen in other religions as well.[188] The reason for this is that kitsch art reveals a disease in the faith, ideology, and doctrine of a community and continues to spread to the whole of the culture or sub-culture. Further, kitsch art is particularly detrimental to the theological aesthetic project because it attempts to evoke religious sentiments without truly encountering or knowing God. The classic expressions of kitsch evangelical art, at least in America, are Precious Moments collectable figures and Thomas Kinkade paintings.[189] This type of kitsch evangelical art is pervasive in Christian bookstores, the homes of many evangelicals, and even in evangelical churches. Reductionistic art conveys an ideology that only emphasizes a perfect and wonderful world.[190]

Kinkade's art has much to offer in terms of skill, appeal, and inspiration. Many of his individual pieces deserve praise. However, the body of his work reveals a reductionism and deficient understanding of the fall and redemption. Kinkade is the self-proclaimed "Painter of Light" and explains, "Light is what we're attracted to. This world is dark, but in heaven there is no darkness . . . I like to portray a world without the Fall."[191] Against his critics who point out the kitsch and sentimental nature of his art, Kinkade responded, "High culture is paranoid about sentiment, but human beings are intensely sentimental. And if art does not speak the language of the people, it relegates itself to obscurity."[192] Kinkade self-professedly desires to paint Eden, and his work has been described as "quintessentially evangelical."[193]

Great art must echo Eden in its original glory as well as the Eden that was lost to us and promises to be restored.[194] However, while Kinkade's

---

187. Brown, *Good Taste, Bad Taste, & Christian Taste*, 123.

188. Scruton, *Beauty*, 190–191.

189. Brown, *Good Taste, Bad Taste, & Christian Taste*, 140–141. See pictures of Thomas Kinkade's art online at: https://thomaskinkade.com/the-art/.

190. Brown, *Good Taste, Bad Taste, & Christian Taste*, 141.

191. Balmer, "The Kinkade Crusade," 50–51.

192. Balmer, "The Kinkade Crusade," 55.

193. Balmer, "The Kinkade Crusade," 55.

194. Pearcey, *Saving Leonardo*, 272. Barrs, *Echoes of Eden*, 26.

art popularity among evangelicals belies a defect in faith and doctrine, the body of his work shows a marked difference from art that comes from an integrated imagination and biblical worldview such as the works by artists such as Christopher Powers, Anneke Kaai, Grace Carol Bomer, and Makato Fujimura. These and other examples of robust biblical art demonstrate that the Precious Moments and Kinkade's type of art is not the only expression of evangelical art. This does not mean that popular art is by nature kitsch and that we need to engage only in the fine arts. Rather, it means that theologically robust evangelical art, whether it is popular art or high art, acknowledges the fall and its effects and creates bodies of work that present the truths of the Scripture.[195]

## SUMMARY

Evangelicals do indeed have a theological aesthetic, even if they don't know it. In this chapter, I presented how representative evangelicals speak of the beauty of God in theology proper, creation, Scripture, and culture and art. God's beauty in creation and redemption presupposes and reflects an intrinsic beauty and beatitude of the Trinity. Evangelicals affirm the Creator-creature distinction. God is the great, infinite artist who created all things *ex nihilo,* whom artists imitate in a finite way. Even though the fall has profound effects on the beauty of creation, creation is meant to be enjoyed in wonder because it has intrinsic value and reveals God in some way. The beauty revealed in creation evokes a deep longing and desire for God himself.

For evangelicals, God's beauty and glory are especially related to Christology. Jesus Christ's person and work objectively display God's glory and, therefore, also the beauty of God. The beauty of God is seen most clearly in Jesus's work on the cross as the self-giving love of God. Christ is revealed most clearly in Scripture. God reveals himself and places himself before the believer who receives him in faith and is brought into fellowship with the Trinity and transformed into the likeness of Jesus Christ. Evangelicals have a variegated response to God's revelation in culture and the arts. There is common agreement that Christians are called to submit their thoughts, tastes, imagination, and creativity to the Bible. While evangelicals are known for kitsch and sentimental art, many evangelicals

---

195. Frame, *The Doctrine of the Christian Life,* 892.

recognize the need to create art that is informed by the concepts of theological aesthetics explored in this chapter.

Evangelicals' approach to theological aesthetics may not be systematic or uniform, but evangelicals do interact with theological aesthetic concepts regularly. This summary of the current context of theological aesthetics in evangelicalism gives a picture of what concepts need further development and clarification. It also reveals the type of theological aesthetics that resonate with evangelicals. In the next two chapters I explore the historical development of the concepts of theological aesthetics.

# 3

# Theological Aesthetic Concepts in Historical Theology

CONCEPTS SUCH AS PERCEPTION and revelation, subjectivity and objectivity, hiddenness and revelation, the form of Christ, and the climax of revelation on the cross developed through the course of history. These concepts are crucial in helping understand Balthasar's theological aesthetics and a distinctively evangelical Protestant theological aesthetics. In this chapter, I delve into the development of theological aesthetics in the history of theology. While this chapter could include numerous other theologians, those chosen here represent pivotal moments and contributions.

As noted in chapter 1, theological aesthetics diverges into two broad streams. The first emphasizes the revelation of beauty in the concrete in creation and art forms, while the second applies aesthetic insights to theology proper and how we experience God and his revelation. This divergence comes from a felt tension concerning the nature of beauty as a spiritual and a material reality. This tension between beauty's spiritual and material nature has been noted at least since Plato and Aristotle. Brendan Sammon notes, "The difficulty of beauty that reveals itself with Plato's and Aristotle's attempts to subject it to rational inquiry concerns primarily the perennial tension between the identity of transcendental, spiritual beauty and the differences that arise with its concrete, material manifestations."[1] Philosophers such as Plato and Aristotle could not resolve the tension between beauty as a spiritual reality and its expressions

---

1. Sammon, *The God Who Is Beauty*, 55.

in the physical world.[2] Theologians also grapple with this tension. However, Christian theology has consistently maintained that the resolution to this tension is Jesus Christ. The transcendent God, the source of beauty, was made flesh and became concrete and material for us and our salvation. His person and work are beautiful.

Athanasius's theology of the incarnation is a good place to start. According to Athanasius, Jesus renewed and restored the good, true, and beautiful within creation through his incarnation. I then discuss the tensions within Augustine's approach to beauty that have reverberated through the centuries. Next, I examine Pseudo-Dionysius's theology of the procession and return of all things from and back to God, who is the source of the beautiful and good. After Pseudo-Dionysius's mystical approach to theological aesthetics, I explore John of Damascus's more tangible and practical defense of the materiality of creation and the acceptability of using icons and the arts for worship and discipleship. Then, I present Aquinas's view of transcendental beauty as a definitive development in theological aesthetics and an outworking of Pseudo-Dionysius's theology.

The subsequent section delves into Reformation and Modern contributions. These contributors share common ground with Balthasar, but also present areas of tension with his theological aesthetic. Luther's theology of the cross and his critique of a theology of glory marked a pivotal moment in the evolution of theological aesthetics. While Balthasar offers a critique of Luther, his theology of the cross was a necessary revolution in theological aesthetics that significantly influenced Balthasar's project. The theological aesthetics of Jonathan Edwards then provides a starting point for a synthesis between early theologians and Protestant emphases. The section further examines how Kant's philosophy and theory of transcendental apperception influenced theological aesthetics. Kierkegaard's contribution is also explored. Kierkegaard, alongside Luther and Barth, is one of Balthasar's most frequent Protestant dialogue partners. The third section then delves into contemporaries of Balthasar, Barth and Rahner.

---

2. Sammon, *The God Who Is Beauty*, 15.

## PRE-REFORMATION CONTRIBUTIONS TO THEOLOGICAL AESTHETICS

### Athanasius on the Incarnation

Athanasius (296–373), bishop of Alexandria, was the great defender of Nicene orthodoxy in the face of the Arian crisis. His life was a triumphant defense of the *homoousios* divinity of the second person of the Trinity. This was not only true when he was a young man at the Council of Nicaea, when orthodoxy was in favor, but also when it faced fierce opposition. His tenacious stand for truth amid tensions with emperors and numerous exiles is captured by the catchphrase that described his ministry: *Athanasius Contra Mundum*. Athanasius is famous for his crucial contribution to trinitarian and Christological doctrines. His theology systematically emphasizes "the distinction and simultaneous relation, between God and the world."[3] Unlike the apophatic Hellenistic tradition, Athanasius held together the paradox of the transcendence of God with his immanence. This paradox is seen most clearly in the incarnation, which defines God's relation to the world.[4] Athanasius's theme of the incarnation and God's relation to the world is important for theological aesthetics. Athanasius's focus on the incarnate Word as the meeting place of the divine and the material set the stage for future theologians to articulate decisively Christ-centered theological aesthetics. This robust theology of creation and the incarnation influenced theologians for centuries as they thought about the relationship of the divine and the material creation.

In *On the Incarnation*, Athanasius displayed the creation and redemption of all things through the Word who became incarnate. The doctrine of creation *ex nihilo* was the significant backdrop for the Arian controversy. This doctrine defines the dividing line between God and creation. For Arius, the Logos was on the creation side of that dividing line; for Athanasius, the Logos was none other than God himself.[5] The Logos or Word shared the same nature with the Father and should not be counted as a created being. Athanasius chastised Arius for making God too aloof from creation.[6] Arius maintained that God created the Son so that the Son might make all things. For Athanasius, Arius had made God

---

3. Anatolios, *Athanasius*, 3.
4. Anatolios, *Athanasius*, 5.
5. Anatolios, *Athanasius*, 95.
6. Leithart, *Athanasius*, 90.

wholly other to the point that there is no sense of immanence or care for his creation.[7] Arius made God too transcendent to have any real relation to the world or creation. Therefore, Athanasius counteracts Arius's hyper-transcendence of God and focuses on the pre-Incarnate divine Word's activity in creation. Athanasius held the paradox of transcendence and immanence, while at the same time maintaining the Creator-creature distinction.

Creation, for Athanasius, was the miraculous act of God, who was the "Maker and Artificer" of all things.[8] Athanasius argued that God, through the Word, is the great Artist who reveals himself through his art. The Artificer made himself known in creation. Mankind only had to look up to heaven to clearly see God's revelation of himself.[9] In Athanasius's understanding, the revelation of God in creation or through general revelation is to be understood Christologically.[10] The Word is the Image of the Father, but he is also the pattern or archetype of creation because the Logos is impressed on all of creation. This is especially true of mankind themselves, who are made in the image of God. Not only that, but they could see God's "Image Absolute," the reflection of God's Word within themselves. This Image that mankind bore allowed them to perceive God and have a relationship with him.[11] Thus, the Word became the meeting place of God and man even in the event of creation. God the Father created through the Word and loved creation because the image of the Word, who was the Image of God, was impressed and revealed through creation. At the same time, man could look at creation and perceive true things about the Word of God in creation and themselves.[12]

The fall, however, was a turn away from God and his revelation to the corruptible and non-being.[13] Athanasius said that in the fall, three things happened. The three things he notes are thematically connected with the transcendentals. The fall was the corruption of what was beautiful, true, and good. First, mankind threw away the beauty that they had been invited into in paradise. "But if they went astray and became vile,

---

7. Leithart, *Athanasius*, 90.

8. Athanasius, *On the Incarnation* §2, 27.

9. Athanasius, *On the Incarnation* §11, 39.

10. Leithart, *Athanasius*, 92. This theology was developed by Irenaeus, *Against Heresies* 4.6.6.

11. Athanasius, *On the Incarnation* §11, 38.

12. Leithart, *Athanasius*, 99.

13. Athanasius, *On the Incarnation* §3, 30.

throwing away their birthright of beauty, then they would come under the natural law of death and live no longer in paradise, but dying outside of it, continue in death and corruption."[14] Paradise was a place of exquisite beauty, but mankind threw away beauty and descended into chaos.

Secondly, fallen humanity descended into non-truth and non-existence. In losing the knowledge of the truth about God, "they lost existence" because God himself alone is the One who exists and the source of all existence.[15] Athanasius argued there was a striking disjunction between who humanity was designed to be and who they became.[16] The distance between God's intention for humanity to image God and where they ended up in depravity and loss of existence is tragic. Paul Kolbet explains, "Human beings used the power derived from the Logos to turn away from the source of life."[17] Without being focused on God as the source of life, humanity moved away from him and, in turn, moved away from the order that was in the Logos. This is related to Athanasius's theology of sin as the soul's forgetfulness of God. Because the Logos is the source of life and existence, the human choice of sin is a choice towards a lack of ontological grounding and only brings death.[18]

In addition to turning away from the beautiful and the true, the good was also undermined as the sinning was limitless. In a reflection of Romans 1:18–32, Athanasius describes how the good was undermined progressively without limit to the point that even sins against nature such as homosexuality were committed.[19] John Behr notes, "Athanasius thus uses idolatry, especially that of the body, as a kind of barometer, measuring the perversity into which humans have fallen, the degree to which their knowledge has been lost, and the extent to which the image of God in them has been obscured."[20] The fall and the resulting idolatry "demands the drastic solution presented in *On the Incarnation*."[21] Athanasius's theology of the fall sets guardrails for theological aesthetics. Anyone who would construct a theological aesthetic concerning the beauty of God in any of its manifestations must first realize the fallen nature of

---

14. Athanasius, *On the Incarnation* §3, 29.
15. Athanasius, *On the Incarnation* §4, 30.
16. Kolbet, "Athanasius, the Psalms, and the Reformation of Self," 91.
17. Kolbet, "Athanasius, the Psalms, and the Reformation of Self," 92.
18. Kolbet, "Athanasius, the Psalms, and the Reformation of Self," 92.
19. Athanasius, *On the Incarnation* §5, §31.
20. Behr, *The Nicene Faith*, 227.
21. Behr, *The Nicene Faith*, 227.

humankind and the need for grace as the starting point. This point will be taken up especially by Augustine and Luther.

Throughout his discussion of creation, Athanasius uses art and the artist as metaphors. The fall is understood as a corruption of artistic beauty: "You know what happens when a portrait that has been painted on a panel becomes obliterated through external stains. The artist does not throw away the panel, but the subject of the portrait has to come and sit for it again, and then the likeness is re-drawn on the same material. Even so was it with the All-holy Son of God."[22] It would be unfitting for God to discard his original creation.[23] God is the great Artist who created the world by the Son, his Word. Creation was not something to be discarded but redeemed and restored when mankind filled the world with evil. Athanasius says that it was fitting and necessary that the Word of God who ordered creation should be the One who also renewed that creation. The Word of God renewed his art through the Incarnation.

Athanasius heralds the wonder of the incarnation of the Word of God. The incarnation itself was an artistic display of God. The God who created the senses took on a body so he could present himself to their senses.[24] Furthermore, by being in the body, he deepened the wonder of physical creation. In taking on a body, he cleansed and sanctified the body.[25] He accomplished this both through the work of the cross, the center of the faith, and the resurrection.[26] In Athanasius's theology the paradox of the transcendent and the immanent meet in the paradox of the enfleshed Word displayed as crucified. The crucifixion was the infinite display of an event of beauty. The transcendent God, the form of beauty, publicly and paradoxically became the formless one for our salvation.[27] Thus, the Word of God became flesh so that we could see him and be saved by entering the chaos of human existence brought about by sin. Athanasius argued that the incarnation was both necessary and sufficient to restore humanity and reveal God.[28] In the Word's revelation of God to the senses through the incarnation, the inward turn of sin is overcome. Man's sin violated God's intention and design for humanity

---

22. Athanasius, *On the Incarnation* §14, 41–42.
23. Meijering, "Athanasius on God as Creator and Recreator," 183.
24. Athanasius, *On the Incarnation* §15, 43.
25. Athanasius, *On the Incarnation* §18, 46.
26. Athanasius, *On the Incarnation* §19, 48.
27. Little, "The Paradoxical Beauty of the Cross," 72.
28. Roselen, "The Incarnational Christology of Athanasius," 87.

and mankind moved away from life. In a staggering act of grace, "the Logos, having drawn near in Jesus Christ, once again makes possible the task of realizing the divine intention: that is of conforming oneself to the vivifying Logos; the soul renewing its agency and power, becoming truly itself for the first time and moving toward complete stability in God."[29]

Athanasius's theology is profoundly cataphatic. God was presented to the senses. However, there is also an element of apophatic theology. Apophatic theology does not define the content of revelation but is reflected in mankind's limited ability to articulate the infinite depth of what has happened in Christ.[30] God's revelation in Christ is clear. The senses have perceived the revelation and the eyewitnesses have testified. However, for Athanasius, the apophatic aspect reminds the finite cannot fully grasp the infinite, even in the face of clear revelation. In response to the objective revelation of God in the incarnation of the Logos, Athanasius called for a subjective or existential response of wonder that is an attitude of "apophatic reverence" that maintains the "otherness between God and the World."[31] However, Athanasius's apophaticism is not simply negation but necessitates positive theological statements.[32] It is an apophaticism that does not leave empty but chastens and demands humility and reverence in the reception of revelation and our speech about it.

Athanasius made many contributions to the themes of theological aesthetics. The very center of Athanasius's thought, the relation of God to the world through the incarnation of the Word, is directly related to theological aesthetics. This Creator-creature distinction is the starting point of theological aesthetics. Athanasius's clear articulation of this distinction set the parameters for orthodox theological aesthetics. Athanasius demonstrates God's creative power as Artist in both creation and redemption. Creation is a painting that reveals God. However, as Peter Leithart notes, "Athanasius insists that the creation reveals not some generic 'deity' but specifically the Son. As Logos, the Son is the framer and arranger of creation."[33] The Son is revealed in creation.

Athanasius theology of the fall has implications for theological aesthetics. For Athanasius, when the painting of creation was marred and ruined through evil, the redemption of that painting itself through the

---

29. Kolbet, "Athanasius, the Psalms, and the Reformation of Self," 93.
30. Anatolios, *Athanasius*, 97.
31. Anatolios, *Athanasius*, 98.
32. Anatolios, *Athanasius*, 99.
33. Leithart, *Athanasius*, 99.

incarnation was an artistic move of the creator that revealed him even more clearly. Athanasius emphasized both the majesty and goodness of creation as well as the creation of the senses of mankind and their ability to perceive God's revelation. Yet, at the same time, he has a profound understanding of the need for grace because of the perversion of sin. Humanity needed to be redeemed and restored. God restored humanity and creation through the incarnation of the second person of the Trinity and the paradoxical work of the cross. The incarnation was an event taken in by the senses as God took on flesh and was manifested physically. Through the incarnation, God's original art was restored.

## Augustine on Beauty

### *The Relation of Created Beauty and Divine Beauty*

Augustine (354–430), the bishop of Hippo in North Africa, is widely recognized as one of the most influential theologians in the history of church. Balthasar said of Augustine's theological aesthetics, "No one has praised God so assiduously as the supreme beauty or attempted so consistently to capture the true and the good with the categories of aesthetics as Augustine in the period during and after his conversion."[34] While he often showed his Neo-Platonic influences, he was "fundamentally more Hebraic than Hellenic."[35] Augustine's approach to beauty's relationship with God is seen most clearly in Book X of *Confessions*. This section presents Augustine's reflections on beauty and the love of beauty.

In *Confessions*, Augustine argues that the beautiful is that which allures or attracts and creates desire. Before his conversion, Augustine recalls that he was in love with the beauty of created things, which pulled him away from higher beauty. He was so enamored with beauty and proportion at that stage that he wrote two or three volumes called *Beauty and Proportion*, which he somehow lost.[36] David Jeffrey argues that while Augustine's approach to beauty and proportion would have been different in the lost volumes, Augustine's concern for beauty and proportion continued. He explains, "The questions which he had attempted to pursue in the lost books, first among them the nature of the beautiful and its

---

34. Balthasar, *GL* 2, 95.
35. Jeffrey, "Augustine on Beauty," 57.
36. Augustine, *Confessions* IV.13, 83.

compelling 'allure' (*allicit*, from *allicere*, to entice) are here in the *Confessions* and throughout the whole body of his works reframed in a larger intellectual context in which, far from being dismissed as spiritually or philosophically unworthy, they are re-valorized and made central to the meaning of his new life."[37] The question of true beauty and its compelling nature is the center of Augustine's work.[38]

After his conversion, Augustine obtained a new perspective on the created world of beauty and the senses. Even in his early theology, Augustine adopted a distinctively Christian view of creation. The transcendence of God, creation from nothing, and the goodness of creation are consistent throughout his writings. Indeed, Carol Harrison argues that the doctrine of creation from nothing helped him overcome the Manichee philosophy and provided a structure and framework for his faith.[39] Here, Augustine's theology of creation is like Athanasius's. There is an emphasis on the Creator-creature distinction or a "radical ontological divide" that exists between Creator and creation as well as the beauty and goodness of creation.[40]

Augustine has an unmistakable metaphysical and spiritual focus, but this does not undermine his emphasis on the legitimacy of physical senses to experience and enjoy creation. Indeed, the spiritual beauty is perceived and known through a person's sense perception and experience.[41] Augustine's doctrine of creation and the senses is paradoxical. The beauty of creation and the sense perception are gifts from God. They have a teleological purpose. However, ultimately creation was transient and the senses "sluggish."[42] Augustine prays that creation will evoke an aesthetic response of wonder and praise within him, but that the pleasure would not terminate on the sensual experience. An escape from creation to the interior of the soul was not the answer. Retreat from creation into contemplation also gives a measure of pleasure but is not inherently good. This is because the soul and the practice of contemplation is fallen and subject to sin, just like the body is. Augustine was clear that moving toward spiritual contemplation in and of itself is not the answer for the needs of man. Creation and contemplation need to lead us to rest in God.

37. Jeffrey, "Augustine on Beauty," 57.
38. Jeffrey, "Augustine on Beauty," 57.
39. Harrison *Rethinking Augustine's Early Theology*, 76.
40. Harrison *Rethinking Augustine's Early Theology*, 89, 103.
41. Jeffrey, "Augustine on Beauty," 57.
42. Augustine, *Confessions* IV.10, 80.

In Book X of *Confessions*, Augustine attempts to explain his faith and give the reason why he wrote his confessions. He reflects on his sense experiences and the temptations associated with them and how the senses relate to the soul. In this section of *Confessions*, Augustine describes the objective aspects of creative beauty and how it relates to the perceiving subject through the senses. He wrestles with both the legitimate and illegitimate pleasure of the senses in the reception of the beauty and how the beautiful things of creation relate to God, the source of all beauty.

Augustine is clear that God is the creator of not only the material world, but the senses as well. The soul of the person is united to the material senses. For Augustine, the soul animates man's body and receives the input through the bodily senses.[43] Thus, the soul, even though it is "the better part," is inextricably linked to the physical body and the senses that God has given the body.[44] Augustine's quest in *Confessions* Book X is to demonstrate how both the senses and the soul point toward God himself as he is beyond both body and soul. The things of the earth are "admitted by the door of the senses," and they preach a continual sermon.[45] Augustine says the things of the earth proclaim that God is the creator and that we are to love him. In a poetic passage, Augustine personifies wind, sea, animals, sky, and the stars and asks them questions about God. The personified creation then tells Augustine about God. He explains, "I asked these questions simply by gazing at these things and their beauty was all the answer they gave."[46] For Augustine, God is the source of beauty wherever it is found in creation.[47]

Augustine celebrates the God given source of creation's beauty, but he carefully differentiates God from creation. The Creator-creature distinction is firmly established. However, the delight evoked by creation's beauty teaches humanity what it means to delight in God.[48] The sense perception of creation's beauty becomes an analogy for perceiving God's beauty. Humanity is invited into aesthetic delight in God, to taste and see that he is good. Creation and the senses teach us what it means to have aesthetic delight and are a means to know God himself. This is reflective of Plato's teaching about beauty in *The Symposium* 210d–211b.

43. Augustine, *Confessions* X.6, 213.
44. Augustine, *Confessions* X.6, 213.
45. Augustine, *Confessions* X.6, 212.
46. Augustine, *Confessions* X.6, 212.
47. Augustine, *Soliloquies* I.1.3. Quoted in Jeffrey, "Augustine on Beauty," 62.
48. Augustine, *Confessions* X.6, 212.

Although he does not quote it, Augustine seems to have been influenced by Plato's teaching that the beauty in the physical realm lifts the perceiver to encounter divine beauty.[49] Jeffrey explains, "It is clear thus that contemplation of beauty in the natural order is . . . an upward leading way or ascent of the soul towards a fuller vision of intelligible beauty."[50] Augustine's emphasis on rightly ordered love in response to beauty reflects Plato's teaching. Although there are similarities, Augustine approaches beauty and love in a particularly Christian and biblical way. Augustine, like Plato, viewed love as the proper response to beauty, but, unlike Plato, saw a deep need for the grace of God to allow the person to love and respond properly to beauty, both material and spiritual.

Augustine reflected that God alone is the "beauty at once so ancient and so new" whom he longed for and loved.[51] Once God called Augustine and "shone upon" him, God's fragrance, touch, and taste left Augustine "inflamed with love of your peace."[52] The salvation of man from sin and evil has an aesthetic component. Harrison explains Augustine's Christian aesthetic, "God has chosen to motivate man's fallen will to the true and good through the delight occasioned by his beautiful revelation of Himself."[53] The beautiful things of creation and physical senses are a blessing if they lead to God, but an idol if they lead away from God. James K.A. Smith explains that this affectional delight in God is the rightly ordered love (*ordo amoris*), which provides the foundation for the subjective aspects of Augustine's theological aesthetic.[54] Everything in creation is to be used (*uti*) for the enjoyment (*frui*) of God. The heart of idolatry for Augustine, Smith says, is to delight in creation in a way that is reserved for God himself. Rightly ordered love uses and receives the good gifts of creation to bring us true enjoyment of God and love for him.[55]

The fundamental goodness of creation is taught by Augustine, not just in *Confessions* Book X but throughout his writings.[56] However, Harrison does not do justice to Augustine's theology of the fall and the

---

49. Sammon, *The God Who Is Beauty*, 28.
50. Jeffrey, "Augustine on Beauty," 59.
51. Augustine, *Confessions* X.27, 231.
52. Augustine, *Confessions* 232.
53. Harrison, *Augustine: Christian Truth and Fractured Humanity*, 76.
54. Smith, "Staging the Incarnation," 127.
55. Smith, "Staging the Incarnation," 82.
56. Harrison, *Rethinking Augustine's Early Theology*, 76.

effects of the fall on creation and the will of man.[57] Even the goodness of creation can be twisted by a fallen will so that creation may "veil more than unveil the radiance of divine beauty."[58] This is the reason for Augustine's caution with the arts and created beauty. Robert O'Connell asks the question, "How could so great a literary artist, in his passion for truth, become the very same man whose theory of art amounts at times to the banishment of art?"[59] He says the answer is in Augustine's Neo-Platonic influences. Augustine's aversion to the arts came from these influences as well as a profound understanding of the radical extent of the fall on the human and the propensity toward idolatry.[60] Harrison is right to critique O'Connell for extending the Neo-Platonic influences to every aspect of Augustine's theology of beauty.[61] However, O'Connell is correct in his emphasis that the Neo-Platonic influenced Augustine's view of the arts.[62]

Smith argues that Augustine's critique of theater and the arts was twofold.[63] The first was an ontological critique. Augustine, following Platonic metaphysics, argued that the arts are a movement away from being toward nothingness.[64] Jeffrey also addresses this when he says that, for Augustine, Aristotelian mimesis is not an option because ontologically, the representation is only able to refract in its representation.[65] The second critique of the arts was ethical. The arts arouse passions and desires for some sensible object itself rather than for God. This desire by nature leads away from God.[66] Augustine's aesthetic motifs of the goodness of creation, the incarnation, and the resurrection "undermine his Neoplatonism" and overturn his dismissal of the arts.[67] For this reason, Harrison is right to critique O'Connell for overemphasizing the Neo-Platonic in Augustine.[68] The biblical view triumphs over the Neo-Platonic in

---

57. Djuth, "Veiled and Unveiled Beauty," 91.
58. Djuth, "Veiled and Unveiled Beauty," 91.
59. O'Connell, *Art and the Christian Intelligence in St. Augustine*, 2.
60. Harrison, *Rethinking Augustine's Early Theology*, 32–35.
61. Harrison, *Rethinking Augustine's Early Theology*, 32–35.
62. Smith, "Staging the Incarnation," 126.
63. Smith, "Staging the Incarnation," 128.
64. Smith, "Staging the Incarnation," 125, 128.
65. Jeffrey, "Augustine on Beauty," 64.
66. Smith, "Staging the Incarnation," 128.
67. Smith, "Staging the Incarnation," 128.
68. Harrison, *Beauty and Revelation in the Thought of Saint Augustine*, 32.

Augustine's theology of creation, though he capitulated to Neo-Platonism in his theology of the arts, as O'Connell maintains.

## The Beauty of Christ

As mentioned above, rightly ordered love is a deep concern for Augustine.[69] Because of the temptation of both body and soul, Augustine knew he needed a guide to walk through life. He does not simply avoid the material creation in favor of the spiritual soul because the soul has the subtle and more severe temptation of pride.[70] Rather, he relies on God to lead him, both body and soul, in truth and trusts God to forgive him when he sins. Ultimately, though, the resolution for the temptations and sins of body and soul is the mediator, Jesus Christ.

It is significant that Augustine closes *Confessions* Book X with a reflection on Jesus Christ as both Victor/Victim and Priest/Sacrifice. By doing this, Augustine shows that Jesus Christ is the mediator and bridge between God and man. Creation can point to God but cannot lead to him. The contemplations of the soul also cannot lead to God. Where creation and the soul can only point, Jesus Christ is the actual mediator between God and man. As a result of his struggle with the material creation and sensual pleasure, Augustine says he was tempted to an ascetic life in the desert. He says that God forbade him this lifestyle and pointed him to the death of Christ. Because of this, Augustine recognizes his only hope is Jesus Christ and the price he paid with his own blood. The answer to Augustine's sensory temptations was not an ascetic life but rather a focused faith in Jesus Christ and his work. Augustine believed that Jesus was not only the mediator between God and man, but also that he was the clearest expression of God's beauty. Harrison notes that for Augustine, Jesus had a beauty "which is at once immanent within the temporal mutable realm, but which yet belongs to and originates in transcendent Divine Beauty."[71] Transcendent beauty entered the temporal and mutable so that beauty could be displayed in the flesh to draw fallen humanity to himself.

Augustine's theology of beauty and aesthetics cannot be understood without referencing the *theologia crucis*.[72] The theology of the cross is

---

69. Smith, "Staging the Incarnation," 127. Jeffrey, "Augustine on Beauty," 62.
70. Augustine, *Confessions* X.36–39.
71. Harrison, *Beauty and Revelation in the Thought of Saint Augustine*, 39.
72. O'Collins, *The Beauty of Jesus Christ*, ix. Jeffrey, "Augustine on Beauty," 62.

the ultimate expression of beauty even though it was an image of suffering because it moves us to "find our delight and meaning in God."[73] Augustine explains, "The deformity of Christ forms you. For if He had not wished to be deformed you would not have received back the form you lost. Therefore, He hung deformed on the cross, but His deformity was our beauty."[74]

In summary, beauty for Augustine finds its redemption and fullest expression in Jesus Christ. Augustine appreciated created beauty but was keenly aware of the sensual temptations and idolatry often associated with it. Created beauty leads us to God and gives an analogy for experiencing God's beauty. For Augustine, the primary aesthetic response to the revelation of God's beauty in creation and, ultimately, Jesus Christ is a rightly ordered love. However, because of the sin nature and a perversion of the will, we do not naturally have a rightly ordered love and illegitimately love and use creation and art as a substitute for God, rather than a pointer to him. Augustine prays, "Your beauty drew me to you, but soon I was dragged away from you by my own weight and in dismay I plunged again into the things of the world."[75] This rightly ordered love for the objective beauty of God and his creation provides later theologians with a basic category for understanding the subjective and objective aspects of theological aesthetics. Thus, Augustine paved the way for theological aesthetics to understand the profound effect of sin on the will and aesthetic delight, the paradox of the goodness of creation as well as its temptations, the objective and subjective aspects of beauty, and the centrality of Jesus Christ in the revelation of God's beauty.

## Pseudo-Dionysius and the Procession and Return

Pseudo-Dionysius's contribution to theological aesthetics is immense.[76] His identity remains a mystery. For many centuries, Pseudo-Dionysius was considered to be the Areopagite mentioned in Acts 17:34. He most likely was a Greek or Syrian in the fifth or sixth century. His theology had a profound impact on the development of theology. Pseudo-Dionysius's metaphysics, epistemology, and teaching on the perception of God were

---

73. Smith, "Staging the Incarnation," 129.
74. Jeffrey, "Augustine on Beauty," 62.
75. Augustine, *Confessions* VII.16–17, 150–151.
76. Balthasar, *GL* 2, 147.

profoundly influential for Aquinas's metaphysics and later for Balthasar's theological aesthetic project.[77]

Pseudo-Dionysius's metaphysics was influenced by Neo-Platonic thought. However, like Augustine, while Pseudo-Dionysius employed Neo-Platonic terminology and categories, he operated from a biblical or Christian theology. While his Neo-Platonism influence is indeed significant, it is irresponsible to read him simply as a Neo-Platonist.[78] In his metaphysics, he views the triune God as the source or cause of all things. God is transcendent above all things, but at the same time present to all things.[79] God does not dwell at the top of a Neo-Platonic ladder of Being, but rather is the preexistent one, who is the cause, source, and goal of all things.[80] God is thus decisively differentiated from creation and being, but is related to it in that all things flow from him. Everything relates to him because he is the source and goal of all things. Pseudo-Dionysius's metaphysics was theocentric, and he describes all things circling and moving toward this transcendent God.[81] Christopher Iacovetti argues that the differentiation between God and creation is seen through Pseudo-Dionysius's emphasis on God's "transcendent hiddenness."[82] This is who God is in himself and his *ad intra* activity, which becomes the basis for apophatic theology. However, God freely chooses to "overflow" his abundance and communicate himself to created being *ad extra*.[83] This language will profoundly influence the history of theology, especially Thomas Aquinas and Jonathan Edwards.[84]

God is the Cause and Source of all things and is described as the Good and the Beautiful. God, in himself, is eternally good and beautiful and he is "the superabundant source . . . of every beautiful thing."[85] Pseudo-Dionysius emphasized that God established these two transcendentals. He explains the procession and return of all things, "To put the matter briefly, all being derives from, exists in, and is returned toward

---

77. Sammon, *The God Who Is Beauty*, 7. Iacovetti, "God in His Processions," 298. Balthasar, *GL* 2, 147.

78. Sevier, *Aquinas on Beauty*, 148.

79. Pseudo-Dionysius, *Divine Names* 825B, 102.

80. Pseudo-Dionysius, *Divine Names* 824A, 101.

81. Pseudo-Dionysius, *Divine Names* 704D, 78.

82. Iacovetti, "God in His Processions," 299.

83. Iacovetti, "God in His Processions," 299.

84. Iacovetti, "God in His Processions," 301.

85. Pseudo-Dionysius, *Divine Names* 701C, 76.

the Beautiful and the Good. Whatever there is, whatever comes to be, is there and has being on account of the Beautiful and the Good . . . Here is the source of all which transcends every source, here is an ending which transcends completion."[86] God is the transcendent Source, the Good and Beautiful himself, from whom the good and beautiful proceed to all of reality and then return to him.

For Pseudo-Dionysius, this procession from and return to God was the structure of existence and being. God dwells in simplicity and unity. In the procession, God creates a multiplicity and then reveals himself to the diversity of creation, which then returns through the creature's response to that revelation. The controlling metaphor for this procession and return is light.[87] Morgan notes the metaphor of light has both an objective and subjective aspect. Although the divine light gives itself ceaselessly and liberally, it must be received willingly for its soteriological benefits to be appropriated.[88] As light proceeds from the sun and illuminates, so also God's splendor is like a light that proceeds from him and then illumines all creation, and especially the mind and heart of mankind. The illumination of the mind enables the perceiver to see the splendor of illuminated creation and redirects the person back to the source. As the illuminated mind is directed to the source it begins a return of this illuminating light back to its source until the creature is eschatologically united to God.[89] Andrew Louth describes Pseudo-Dionysius's articulation of the relationship between God and created things as "theophanic beauty."[90] Created beings are related to their source and reveal him. He explains, "The theophanic beauty reminds those beings who are struck by this beauty of their own derivation from the source and cause of all."[91] This does not blur the Creator-creature distinction but is a revelation of the source of theophanic beauty and a beckoning to return to the source of beauty, God himself.[92] For this reason, Balthasar emphasizes Pseudo-Dionysius's "aesthetic delight" in all of creation and the invitation to embrace and love creation.[93] For Balthasar, Pseudo-Dionysius is creation-affirming by

86. Pseudo-Dionysius, *Divine Names* 705D, 79.
87. Louth, *Denys the Areopagite*, 39.
88. Morgan, "A Radiant Theology," 134.
89. Pseudo-Dionysius, *Divine Names* 592C, 679D, 713D.
90. Louth, "Apophatic Theology," 75.
91. Louth, "Apophatic Theology," 76.
92. Morgan, "A Radiant Theology," 129.
93. Balthasar *GL* 2, 179.

the theophanic nature of creation. Colors, shapes, and the particular are "immediate theophanies" that share an "unlike likeness" with God.[94]

Pseudo-Dionysius is known for his apophatic theology, a theological method that emphasizes the transcendence of God and his ultimately unknowable nature. Apophatic theology focuses on knowing God not through positive statements about him but negative statements about what he is not. Cataphatic theology is the opposite, which makes positive theological statements about God. Even though Psuedo-Dionysius is known for his negative theology, it must be noted that he does not disregard cataphatic theology.[95] He articulates a positive theology based on Scripture and the incarnation.[96] Louth convincingly argues that Pseudo-Dionysius's "apophatic theology complements cataphatic theology."[97] Apophatic theology can only have meaning in relation to cataphatic theology. This is true even for Dionysius, who tended to push apophatic theology to the extreme.[98] The "apophatic reverence" or "chaste silence" is the aesthetic response of reverential awe and wonder at the incomprehensibility of God even in response to his positive revelation.[99]

Through Scripture and the incarnation of Christ, the means for the return to God was established.[100] One can see both the apophatic and the cataphatic in his treatment of the incarnation, though the emphasis falls on the cataphatic nature of the incarnation. The incarnation is "beyond words," but can positively be explained, "the simplicity of Jesus became something complex, the timeless took on the duration of the temporal, and, with neither change nor confusion of what constitutes him, he came into our human nature, he who totally transcends the natural order of creation."[101] In Jesus, the Transcendent One was revealed in the "realm of the senses."[102] God presented himself positively in Jesus so that we could see the invisible God. Pseudo-Dionysius goes on to say that in contemplating him we become like him and will be made like him. Pseudo-Dionysius

---

94. Balthasar *GL* 2, 179.

95. Rorem, "Negative Theologies and the Cross," 319.

96. Balthasar *GL* 2, 179.83. Pseudo-Dionysius, *Divine Names* 872A, 109.

97. Louth, "Apophatic Theology," 73. Rorem has shown that this is a feature of apophatic theology in general. Rorem, "Negative Theologies and the Cross," 314.

98. Rorem, "Negative Theologies and the Cross," 318.

99. Anatolios, *Athanasius*, 98.

100. Pseudo-Dionysius, *Divine Names* 588C, 50.

101. Pseudo-Dionysius, *Divine Names* 591A, 52.

102. Pseudo-Dionysius, *Divine Names* 591A, 52.

speaks of apophatic reverence in his emphasis that the incarnation is "beyond words."[103]

The apophatic allows for the Creator-creature distinction in Pseudo-Dionysius's theology and is the basis of his liturgical theology. In the apophatic nature of his theology, "space" from God is created.[104] Pseudo-Dionysius protects against a transcendentalism that mingles the Divine source, God himself, with creation by emphasizing this space for created beings. This is the primary argument against pantheism in Pseudo-Dionysius's theology. The space between God and creation is filled by the hierarchy of being that is not a hierarchy of subordination but the arena or structure of reality where the life of creation takes place. In both the *Celestial Hierarchy* and the *Ecclesiastical Hierarchy*, the drama of procession from God's love and return to God is on display. Louth explains, "Far from being a structure of ordered and repressive authority, hierarchy for Pseudo-Dionysius is an expression of the love of God for everything that derives from him—that is, everything—a love that seeks to draw everything back into union with the source of all being."[105] It is within this hierarchy that the divine light is bestowed.[106] The space of being opens the possibility of a truly creaturely existence where the drama of the return to God takes place. This is the reason liturgy is so important in the life of the Church. "Liturgy takes place in space" and the liturgy becomes a reenactment of deeper spiritual truths that calls people to participate in that liturgy in their lives.[107] Liturgy is an "orientation towards the transcendent . . . a form of art" that is "something that we begin to grasp by participating in it, that in terms of which we interpret the rhythms of our lives, and our hopes and fear."[108]

In addition to his theology of the liturgy, Pseudo-Dionysius had a profound influence on iconography.[109] Katerina Bauer demonstrates that Pseudo-Dionysius's theology of the procession and return, apophatic and

---

103. Pseudo-Dionysius, *Divine Names* 591A, 52. Maximus the Confessor later develops Dionysius apophatic theology in relation to the incarnation. Rorem claims that Pseudo-Dionysius does not apply apophatic theology to the incarnation. Rorem, "Negative Theologies and the Cross," 324.

104. Louth, "Apophatic Theology," 77.

105. Louth, "Apophatic Theology," 78.

106. Morgan, "A Radiant Theology," 139.

107. Louth, "Apophatic Theology," 80.

108. Louth, "Apophatic Theology," 81.

109. Bauer, "Iconic Light as Incarnate Grace," 84.

cataphatic theology, and metaphor of light became an essential aspect of icons. This is shown through an examination of the Icon of the Nativity. Bauer points to the use of light in this icon and shows the contrast of Christ with the darkness of the cave. She also points out the sacred triangle that "bathes everything in light."[110] The art of the icon presents both the apophatic transcendence and mystery of God as well as the positive content of revelation in Christ. Bauer maintains that this type of use of light in the icon was due to the influence of Pseudo-Dionysius.[111]

*Icon of the Nativity of Christ.* Public Domain / Wikimedia Commons

110. Bauer, "Iconic Light as Incarnate Grace," 88.
111. Bauer, "Iconic Light as Incarnate Grace," 88.

Pseudo-Dionysius's apophatic and cataphatic theology have a distinctively aesthetic emphasis. The response to God's revelation is contemplation, which is desire, yearning, or love for the beautiful and good. God himself, from eternity, had a desire, yearning, and love of the beautiful and good. It was this love that "stirred him to use the superabundance of his powers in the production of the world."[112] God's desire and yearning for the beautiful and good has a corresponding expression within those who bear his image. This is a theological aesthetic desire or yearning for the beautiful and good that ultimately is a yearning for God himself that Scripture calls us to. God himself creates and causes this yearning within people and uses it to prompt the person who perceives and knows of God's beauty to return to him. Balthasar later develops his theological aesthetics in light of Pseudo-Dionysius's reference to the procession of God's splendor and the return of the creature to that splendor through contemplation.[113]

## John of Damascus's Defense of Icons

John of Damascus (655–750) is well-known for his defense of the use of icons against the iconoclasts during the Iconoclastic Controversy (717–787). His defense of icons and the treatises he wrote became the intellectual framework for the Seventh Ecumenical Council at Nicaea.[114] In response to a ban against icons in 726, John immediately responded with his first treatise on this subject. Two subsequent treatises were written to further develop his arguments. In these three treatises, as he is responding to a ban on icons, John carefully situated himself squarely within orthodoxy and begins his treatise with a confession of the triune God, who is the source of all things, and is invisible and without form. He makes clear the distinction between the Creator and his creation, though he believes that many of the iconoclast's arguments are tantamount to Manicheism. John puts forward three main reasons for why icons, and by extension all artistic representations, are acceptable. These reasons are Christological, exegetical, and what Payton describes as "an innovative theory of human cognition which placed a high value on created materiality."[115]

---

112. Pseudo-Dionysius, *Divine Names* 708A, 80.
113. Balthasar, *GL* 2, 164.
114. Payton, "John of Damascus on Human Cognition," 173.
115. Payton, "John of Damascus on Human Cognition," 173.

John of Damascus developed Athanasius's argument on the implications of the incarnation and applied it, particularly to the use of icons and artistic representation. This Christological argument is John's main defense of the legitimacy of artistic representations. The incarnation of the Word establishes the possibility of drawing images of the human Christ, God clothed in flesh.[116] For John, the representations of Christ are not the representation of God in his invisible nature but representations of the flesh.

John of Damascus did not shy away from venerating or honoring matter because God used the flesh of Jesus Christ to accomplish salvation.[117] Although John makes it clear that the incarnation legitimizes artistic depiction, Louth claims that John goes further than this by emphasizing the soteriological implications of the incarnation. The saving work of Christ "is about God's restoring the meaning and relatedness of the created order and human life within it by entering into the 'order of signs'. . . to heal brokenness and restore meaning and relatedness."[118] The fall fractured the signs of creation from the things they signified, but Jesus's work restored this. Christ's restoration of the sign and the thing signified had profound theological and practical implications for John. In his third treatise, John argued that those who tear down images of Christ and the saints are doing violence not only to the sign, but the person signified by those signs. God created matter to lead us to the spiritual. Therefore, matter should be treated as holy when it points to God. Signs signify and lead to the spiritual. This is true in creation and in Scripture. The thing signified is vitally connected to the sign itself. John argued, "Everything has a double signification, a corporeal and a spiritual."[119]

This is true on the objective side, but God has also designed human beings in such a way that they are able to perceive the thing signified within the sign. Payton demonstrates that an often-overlooked aspect of John's argument is his anthropological argument for icons and by extension the legitimacy of the arts.[120] John's primary point of argumentation is Christological, namely, material should be used because of the fact of the incarnation of the Word of God. However, the anthropological argument of how God structured perceiving human beings also supports the use

---

116. John of Damascus, *On Holy Images* 1.
117. John of Damascus, *On Holy Images* 1.
118. Louth, "Beauty Will Save the World," 75.
119. John of Damascus, *On Holy Images* 1.
120. Payton, "John of Damascus on Human Cognition," 178.

THEOLOGICAL AESTHETIC CONCEPTS IN HISTORICAL THEOLOGY 67

of icons and artistic representation.[121] God created humans with both a body and soul, and the material realm is necessary for knowing God.[122] Adrahtas likewise notes, "Thus body-ness is a *sine qua non* feature of the whole human existence: the body is not something man has, but the basis of his/her essence."[123] Human existence is inherently material. God created people as embodied souls. Therefore, the sensible realm and creation must be used in the processes of learning and worship. John said, "Just as we listen with our bodily ears to physical words and understand spiritual things, so, through corporeal vision, we come to the spiritual."[124] Because man is endued with both body and soul, God uses matter or body to teach concerning the spiritual. This is true of Jesus Christ himself, baptism, communion, and prayer. John cites Pseudo-Dionysius as his patristic authority for the use of the material world as a means to teach about the immaterial.[125] John developed a theory of how God designed sense perception to work alongside human cognition. Payton argues that "no Christian thinker preceding him had explored the significance of human materiality for the process of human cognition."[126]

In addition to the Christological and anthropological argument, John of Damascus made an exegetical argument in his defense of icons.[127] In response to the iconoclast argument citing the Old Testament commands not to make an idol or image, John insists that these commands were given to prohibit idolatry rather than an absolute prohibition of images.[128] In each of the treatises, he points out that the Cherubim in the tabernacle were images of angels. John returns frequently to the descriptions of the tabernacle and temple and the materials used for their construction to make the point that God cared both about what types of materials were used as well as commanded a certain type of image making. The signs or images are to be adored or venerated (προσκυνησις) in a way that is distinct from the worship of God. These signs and symbols are to be venerated, but only God is to be given the worship of λατρεία. Thus, John presents two types of veneration. One is adoration, veneration, or

121. Payton, "John of Damascus on Human Cognition," 183.
122. Payton, "John of Damascus on Human Cognition," 179.
123. Adrahtas, "The Notion of Symbol," 16.
124. John of Damascus, *On Holy Images* 2.
125. Payton, "John of Damascus on Human Cognition," 180.
126. Payton, "John of Damascus on Human Cognition," 183.
127. Payton, "John of Damascus on Human Cognition," 173.
128. John of Damascus, *On Holy Images* 2.

respect (using the Greek word προσκυνησις) and the other is the worship (λατρεία) that only belongs to God.[129] In this understanding, an icon or a saint may be venerated in such a way that it is not worship and therefore avoids idolatry.[130]

John of Damascus's contribution to the concepts of theological aesthetics is his defense of artistic expression against iconoclastic tendencies. He demonstrates nuanced exegesis that guards against idolatry but simultaneously legitimizes the use of the materials of creation to help worship. He does this by showing the precedence in the Old Testament of the use of symbols and images such as the tabernacle and the temple as well as the indisputable fact that God took on flesh in the second person of the Trinity. John of Damascus followed elements of Pseudo-Dionysius's apophatic theology because he elevated the use of artistic expression over theological formulation.[131] John goes further than Augustine in uniting sign and thing signified. However, in the distinctions of worship (λατρεία) and veneration (προσκυνησις), John also wanted to guard against idolatry.

One does not need to follow all of John of Damascus's conclusions or arguments to appreciate the value of the main points from his defense. Michael Rhodes has recently shown the impossibility, from a biblical perspective, of making hard distinctions between the two types of worship, λατρεία and προσκυνησις, that is crucial to John's theology of icons.[132] Others argue that the insights in John's theology find both responsible expression, such as at the Seventh Ecumenical Council of Nicaea, and irresponsible expression, such as Theodore the Studite's (759–826) argument that the icon shared the same *hypostasis* as its subject.[133] John's defense of icons, at least, established a theological and exegetical case for the connection between sign and things signified and the use of the arts in worship, which was crucial in the development of theological aesthetics.

---

129. Narinskaya, "On the Divine Images," 141.
130. Narinskaya, "On the Divine Images," 142.
131. Louth, "Beauty Will Save the World," 76.
132. Rhodes, "Handmade," 14–26.
133. Foster, "The Veneration of Icons," 292.

## Aquinas's Transcendentalism

Thomas Aquinas (1225–1274), the Italian Dominican known as the *Doctor Angelicus*, has been called "the great liberator of the human intellect."[134] It is difficult to exaggerate the significance of Aquinas in the development of theology. His contribution to the field of theological aesthetics is no exception. Aquinas's theology of beauty, perception, and aesthetics is complex. Aquinas's development of theological aesthetics was profound due to his theological argument for the transcendental nature of beauty, a theology of created beauty and its characteristics, and his argument that material and spiritual beauty evokes love in the perceiver.

In his work of synthesizing and developing the contributions of the past, Aquinas leaned heavily on Aristotle, Augustine, and Pseudo-Dionysius. Although Aquinas's relation to Aristotle has been well established, recent scholarship recognizes that Pseudo-Dionysius was perhaps even more of an influence if the criteria is frequency of citation.[135] It could be argued that Pseudo-Dionysius also influenced Aquinas in the structure of the *Summa Theologica* as it reflects Pseudo-Dionysius's emphasis on the procession from and return to God (*exitus—reditus*).[136] Aquinas's dependence on Pseudo-Dionysius is most clearly seen in his claim that God is the beauty and the good who causes all things.[137] Aquinas followed Pseudo-Dionysius in maintaining a hard line of distinction between God the creator and creation, but at the same time, treated created being as having a "theophanic" nature in that it reveals God.[138]

Aquinas says that beauty has three conditions, "For beauty includes three conditions, 'integrity' or 'perfection,' since those things which are impaired are by the very fact ugly; due 'proportion' or harmony'; and lastly, 'brightness' or 'clarity,' whence things are called beautiful which have a bright color."[139] These three conditions, integrity or perfection (*integritas sive perfectio*), proportion or harmony (*proportio sive consonantia*) and clarity (*claritas*) are conditions of both spiritual and material beauty.[140]

---

134. Chesterton, *Thomas Aquinas*, 13.

135. Sammon, *The God Who Is Beauty*, 7. Sevier, *Aquinas on Beauty*, 147. Iacovetti, "God in His Processions," 298.

136. Nichols, *Redeeming Beauty*, 17.

137. Sevier, *Aquinas on Beauty*, 16.

138. Louth, "Apophatic Theology," 75.

139. Aquinas, *ST* 1.39.8.

140. Aquinas, *ST* 1.39.8.

This famous passage is often used when discussing Aquinas's aesthetics. However, it is important to note the context of these conditions in the *Summa* is not a discussion of Aquinas's aesthetics, but rather a discussion of the essential attributes of the Father, Son, and Spirit. In this section, Aquinas argued that beauty itself is a property of the Son.[141]

In *ST* 1.39.8, Aquinas explained how the Son, the second person of the Trinity, has all the conditions of beauty within himself. Aquinas builds upon Augustine's Christology and quotes from *On the Trinity* to explain how the Son has the conditions of beauty. First, the Son has integrity and perfection because he shares the nature of the Father. The Son possesses the whole nature of divinity and is the supreme and primal life.[142] Secondly, the Son has proportion or harmony because he is the image of the Father. The proportion and harmony between the Father and his image, the Son, is exact and perfect. Aquinas says that an artwork that perfectly represents even an ugly thing can be said to be beautiful in a way. However, the Son perfectly represents the Father. Thirdly, the Son has the beauty of clarity because he is the Word. This Word is "the light and the splendor of the intellect."[143] He is the one who shines out with clarity and enlightens the mind that sees him who is the "art of the omnipotent God" through faith. The Son holds all things together and is the "splendor of the intellect" and "art of the omnipotent God," and the clarity of his beauty shines forth objectively. He is, therefore, the key to understanding and comprehending all of life. The Son is the clarity and light that allows the beauty of all reality to be seen.[144] The beauty of the Son is especially seen in the aesthetic fittingness of the incarnation.[145] The beauty of the Son in his person, as well as his work, is the link between beauty and virtue. It is possible to perceive this link between beauty and virtue by reason.[146]

Considering Aquinas's theology of the Son's beauty, Christopher Sevier has developed some implications for the conditions of beauty for aesthetics.[147] He notes that Aquinas's explanation of beauty in this section has two stages. First, Aquinas notes the three conditions of integrity or

---

141. Sevier, *Aquinas on Beauty*, 104.
142. Augustine, *On the Trinity* 6.10.
143. Aquinas, *ST* 1.39.8.
144. Sevier, *Aquinas on Beauty*, 112.
145. Aquinas, *ST* III.1.1.
146. Sevier, *Aquinas on Beauty*, 113.
147. Sevier, *Aquinas on Beauty*, 104.

perfection, proportion or harmony, and brightness and clarity. In the second stage it is shown how these relate to the Son. Eco attempts to speak of a subjective and objective aspect of these conditions, but it seems more likely, as Sevier suggests, that these conditions are the objective formal properties of beauty that the subject perceives.[148] In his discussion on the condition of proportion, he demonstrates the difficulty in separating Aquinas's passage on beauty from the context of speaking about the beauty of the Son to make it apply to aesthetic principles of beauty.[149] The same can be said about applying these conditions to the transcendental nature of beauty. To apply these conditions to the beauty of a particular object for aesthetic judgment runs into the problem of subjectivism and taste. Aquinas's conditions give some measure of insight into the nature of beauty in the created order. For Aquinas, the objective nature of beauty is specifically related to the Son. The Son is the clarity of beauty that reveals the objective beauty of God himself. The Son also reveals the beauty and intelligibility of God in created reality.[150] In other words, for Aquinas, the Son is the illuminating *claritas* of beauty that shines forth and illumines the perceiving mind to not only the beautiful, but also the good and the true.

There was also a development in the subjective aspect of theological aesthetics in Aquinas's theology. For Aquinas, perception is an act of the senses, the will, and the cognition or intellection. One can tell that something is beautiful when it pleases upon being seen.[151] Eco argues that this is where Aquinas's theology of *claritas* as a condition of beauty is so important.[152] The *claritas* is the manifestation of the beauty of the form to a perceiving subject. Eco says that this *claritas* allows the form to have a rationality to the perceiver so that a "light . . . manifests itself to aesthetic seeing."[153] Thus, when a sound mind perceives something objectively beautiful through the senses, it is able through the intellect to reflect on the manifestation of the *claritas* of this beautiful particular object in such a way as to understand the universality of the beautiful.[154]

---

148. Eco, *The Aesthetics of Thomas Aquinas*, 94.
149. Sevier, *Aquinas on Beauty*, 109.
150. Sevier, *Aquinas on Beauty*, 116.
151. Aquinas, *ST* I.5.4 *ad* 1.
152. Eco, *The Aesthetics of Thomas Aquinas*, 119.
153. Eco, *The Aesthetics of Thomas Aquinas*, 119.
154. Bychkov, "Metaphysics as Aesthetics," 148.

This ability to move from particulars to universals is what sets the human being apart from the animals.

Aquinas argues that when the perceiver sees a beautiful object, this experience is mediated through the senses and gives pleasure. However, the experience of the beautiful must be reflected upon if it is to move beyond the particular to the universal. This reflection enables the perceiver to move toward a more universal understanding of spiritual beauty with God as the source.[155] For Aquinas, beauty relates to the cognitive faculty.[156] Bychkov argues that Aquinas's movement from the particular and the senses to the universal and spiritual is unexplainable, but for Aquinas this tension between the particular and the universal or transcendental beauty is solved by the cognition of the perceiver even if he is not specific as to how this happens.[157] Eco is right to maintain that Aquinas is very specific in his assertion that there are two stages of perception of the beautiful: first, the sense perception and, subsequently, intellectual abstraction.[158] Aquinas differentiates the sensitive appetite from the rational appetite, and both are in operation in perception. The first relates to the immediate perception of the particular, and the second to the universal or spiritual. To understand Aquinas's teaching on perception, one must keep these two stages and appetites differentiated.

Aquinas follows Augustine and Pseudo-Dionysius to show that the good and the beautiful evoke love.[159] Here again objective beauty and the subjective perception of that beauty meet. In this discussion on the passions, Aquinas says that love is chief of these passions. Passions begin when an agent or object reveals its form to an apprehending subject, and the affections are evoked, and it begins a movement of the perceiver toward the object. This first passion or movement is love, followed by desire, and finally joy.[160] Passions, then, are passive and respond to the beauty and good nature of the object. The cause of love is not from the person but from the object that evokes love and brings about a movement toward it.[161] For Aquinas, love is most fundamentally passive in nature as one stands in relation to God, who is actively revealing himself and

---

155. Bychkov, "Metaphysics as Aesthetics," 148.
156. Aquinas, *ST* I.5.4 *ad* 1.
157. Bychkov, "Metaphysics as Aesthetics," 152.
158. Eco, *The Aesthetics of Thomas Aquinas*, 63.
159. Augustine, *On the Trinity* 8.3.
160. Aquinas, *ST* I.26.2.
161. Aquinas, *ST* II.I.27.1.

helping the perceiver.[162] This passive love becomes the precondition of a more active, rational love of God.

Aquinas's theology of perception is related to his distinction between the sensitive appetite and the rational appetite.[163] In the sensitive appetite, the person is drawn toward the perceived object. In the rational appetite, the perceiver takes the object within himself. This movement of the sensitive and rational together make a union of subject and object. When the object apprehended or loved is a person, this allows for a union and mutual indwelling between lover and beloved. This is the result of the love of a person for another, whether this be within the persons of the Trinity, or between human relationships, or between man and God.[164] Love, then, for Aquinas is important for understanding the perception of the good and beautiful. The love of the beautiful, which begins as a passive passion, is what inspires the cognition and intellectual reasoning about that object.[165] Thus, this movement toward the beautiful object has to do with both the passions, which is initially passive reception, and the active intellect. This loving movement toward the object is the union of object and subject. This love draws the perceiver to God and his beauty.

Aquinas argues that God himself is man's last end and it is only through God that we arrive at the happiness we were created for.[166] People perceive God's revelation and respond in love, desire, and joy. As this happens, the creature experiences the blessings of union and communion with God. This is described as a mutual indwelling is a unity-in-distinction as the Creator-creature distinction remains, but true union occurs. Furthermore, Aquinas provides a way to understand how the perception of physical objects relates to the revelation and beauty of God himself. Through the senses and the recalling of sensory experience, humans, as image bearers, can move to the depths of things through cognition. While this begins with sense experience, it is only after reflection and intellectual engagement that the perceiver is able to know something of God's beauty. Due to Aquinas's emphasis on pleasure, passions, and cognition, Kevin O'Reilly attempts to show his "dynamic interplay between reason, emotion and the body of our response to an appreciation

---

162. Miner, *Thomas Aquinas on the Passions*, 121.
163. Miner, *Thomas Aquinas on the Passions*, 19.
164. Aquinas, *ST* II.I.29.
165. Aquinas *ST* I.5.4 *ad* 1; Miner, *Thomas Aquinas on the Passions*, 121.
166. Aquinas, *ST* II.1.1.8; *ST* II.1.2.8.

of objects of beauty."[167] This argument gives equal weight to the will and intellect in the Thomistic perspective.[168] However, this synthesis of the will and intellect goes against Aquinas's emphasis on cognition, reason, and abstraction *after* the encounter with beauty. It does not give the proper distinction between the sensitive and the rational in Aquinas.[169] Eco is correct to note that Aquinas had "defined, secured, and ordered the stages," so it does not work to synthesize sense perception and intellectual abstraction.[170]

Those who read Aquinas through the lens of Balthasar must be aware that, for Aquinas, metaphysical principles are to be reasoned from sense perception. The human being, as made in God's image, has an incredible ability of abstraction from the particular to the universal. He also has an imagination which connects the universal form to the particular. This does not mean that the perceiver can immediately grasp the universal form or the depths of being immediately through the senses without reason. For Aquinas, the intellect and reason are necessary to perceive universal beauty from beautiful things. This is different than Bychkov, for example, who argues from the viewpoint of Balthasar scholarship's interpretation of Aquinas, "Aquinas's metaphysics is 'aesthetics', or to be more precise, 'revelatory aesthetics', in the sense that in his metaphysics, ontological—metaphysical principles can be seen immediately, as in aesthetic experience, and not reasoned to."[171] As Eco argues, this intuitive and spontaneous approach to aesthetics is congruent with Maritain and Balthasar, but not consistent with Aquinas.[172] This I believe is due to a partial misunderstanding of his complex argumentation. It can indeed be said that Aquinas's metaphysics is a "revelatory aesthetics" and begins with sensory or "aesthetic experience," but this experience brings the subject to reason about that experience in order to understand it and its relation to universal beauty and its source. Aquinas opened the way for a clearer treatment of theological aesthetics, especially in his concept of perception.

---

167. O'Reilly, *Aesthetic Perception*, 17.
168. O'Reilly, *Aesthetic Perception*, 63.
169. Miner, *Thomas Aquinas on the Passions*, 19.
170. Eco, *The Aesthetics of Thomas Aquinas*, 63.
171. Bychkov, "Metaphysics as Aesthetics," 167.
172. Eco, *The Aesthetics of Thomas Aquinas*, 63.

# REFORMATION AND POST-REFORMATION CONTRIBUTIONS

## Martin Luther on the Cross and Beauty

Martin Luther (1483–1546) was the seminal leader of the Reformation in Germany. One of his most important and enduring contributions is his theology of the cross. This theology has profound implications for theological aesthetics. Rosalene Bradbury situates Luther's theology within a tradition of crucicentric theologians such as the Apostle Paul, Athanasius, Bernard of Clairvaux, Johannes Tauler, and Nicolas of Cusa.[173] Luther's theology was complex and both critiqued and appropriated aspects of the traditional school of thought (*via antiqua*) and the nominalism (*via moderna*).[174]

The Heidelberg Disputation of 1518 presents many of Luther's most staggering theological insights. This Disputation has profound implications for the concept of beauty.[175] While the Nominalist scholastics of the day were rejecting the *via antiqua*, Luther self-consciously placed himself in line with Augustine. Luther opens the Heidelberg Disputation, "We humbly present these theological paradoxes...so that it may become clear whether they have been deduced well or poorly from St. Paul...and also from St. Augustine, his most trustworthy interpreter."[176] Following Paul and Augustine, Luther denounced the theologians of glory and the late scholastics who slavishly followed Aristotle. Luther reoriented the discussion of ethics and metaphysics toward Christ and his cross.

The Heidelberg Disputation, in its first eighteen theses, addresses anthropological concerns as well as good works and free will. Luther's theology of the cross is only understood in light of a theology of sin. For Luther, sin and the bondage of the will leave people morally bankrupt and unable to achieve anything before God. Indeed, as Thesis 4 states, even the works of God seem evil to fallen humanity. Forde notes a parallel construction in Theses 3 and 4 that sets up a fundamental contrast between the works of humans and the works of God.[177] The works of humans may appear splendid and good, while God's works often look

---

173. Bradbury, *Cross Theology*, ix.
174. Bradbury, *Cross Theology*, ix. Vainio, "Martin Luther on Perception," 88–89.
175. Mattes, "Luther's Theology of Beauty," 49.
176. Luther, *Annotated Luther* 1, 81.
177. Forde, *On Being a Theologian of the Cross*, 31.

deformed and ugly. Nevertheless, the works of humans are "in all probability mortal sins," while God's works are "immortal merits."[178]

The first eighteen theses prepare the way to explain the theology of the cross. Theses 1–12 demonstrate the inability to keep the law, while Theses 13–18 show the bondage of our will.[179] Humanity's bondage to sin makes a "theology of glory" based on creation, natural reason, and logic an effort in futility. The scholastics were following this theology of glory by neglecting the cross. Luther's main complaint against the scholastics was that they did not recognize the crucified and hidden God, but rather they deduce things about the invisible nature of God from the "glorious manifestation" in creation. This theologian of glory follows Aristotle in the love of the good in all of creation, but as a result avoids the cross with its suffering, punishment, and death.[180]

Luther noted that the theologian of glory refuses to see all of life and reality through the revelation of God on the cross. He critiqued the theology of glory as a cross-less Christianity based on general revelation and reason. He explains, "Because people do not know the cross and hate it, they necessarily love the opposite, namely, wisdom, glory, power, and so on."[181] Humans, in their fallen nature, cannot love the cross, the pinnacle of God's revelation, because they hate the works of God by nature. Humans attempt to avoid the cross and peer into the invisible things of God rather than seeing all of reality "through suffering and the cross."[182] Luther's theology of the cross gives a completely new outlook on all of life.[183] All of reality is tested by the cross, and the Christian sees all of reality in light of it.

In the Heidelberg Disputation, Luther critiqued abuses of the law and wisdom derived from natural theology. However, in Thesis 24 he adds nuance to his critique of these abuses. He says, "That wisdom is not of itself evil, nor is the law to be evaded; but without the theology of the cross a person misuses the best things in the worst way."[184] This nuance is important for theological aesthetics because it establishes that creation and the wisdom derived from creation are intrinsically very good. Still,

---

178. Forde, *On Being a Theologian of the Cross*, 31.
179. Rosebrock, "The Heidelberg Disputation and Aesthetics," 348.
180. Rosebrock, "The Heidelberg Disputation and Aesthetics," 348.
181. Luther, *Annotated Luther* 1, 100.
182. Luther, *Annotated Luther* 1, 99.
183. Preus, "The Theology of the Cross," 87.
184. Luther, *Annotated Luther* 1, 101.

they can be misused and twisted in the worst way. This explains why Luther had such a high view of created beauty and aesthetic enjoyment. The cross redeems creation. Luther explains that every gift of creation is good but cannot be enjoyed apart from the cross. For Luther, the cross and faith in Christ become the prerequisite for enjoying God's good gifts in creation.[185]

Matthew Rosebrock develops the connection between Luther's *theologia crucis* and theological aesthetics.[186] Theological aesthetics often assumes beauty's power to reveal but forgets that sinful humanity by nature misuses the gift of beauty.[187] Rosebrock states that the Heidelberg Disputation condemnation of the theologian of glory in Thesis 24 parallels Balthasar's condemnation of aesthetic theology as opposed to theological aesthetics.[188] The theologian of glory takes created beauty apart from the cross. It can even take the cross itself and abstract it from suffering and affliction and make it "beautiful" in a way God never intended. For Luther, the cross is only beautiful as God intended it to be to those who have been crucified with Christ through faith and share in his affliction. It is this person who can now see and enjoy created beauty. This is a new perception of reality through the cross. It is a new type of sight, "so that we might begin to see the way things are."[189] Rosebrock explains, "The theologian of the cross is the only one who can properly delight in the aesthetic because he or she has died and continues to die daily to the sinful allure that beauty can be captured by his or her efforts."[190]

Luther's theology of the cross is the basis of his theological aesthetics. The theology of the cross is the wisdom of God that becomes the prerequisite for understanding and perceiving true beauty. Therefore, Luther reoriented the discussion of the nature of beauty. Beauty is not determined by conditions of integrity or perfection (*integritas sive perfecto*), proportion or harmony (*proportio sive cosonantia*), and clarity (*claritas*). Beauty is determined by what God declares is beautiful, even if human wisdom declares that same thing ugly.[191] Luther's theology of the cross inspired art that focused on the cross and Jesus's humility, suffering, and

---

185. Forde, *On Being a Theologian of the Cross*, 98.
186. Rosebrock, "The Heidelberg Disputation and Aesthetics," 350.
187. Rosebrock, "The Heidelberg Disputation and Aesthetics," 352.
188. This distinction will be explored in the next chapter.
189. Forde, *On Being a Theologian of the Cross*, 36.
190. Rosebrock, "The Heidelberg Disputation and Aesthetics," 354.
191. Mattes, "Luther's Theology of Beauty," 47.

sacrifice. Luther was favorable to the use of art to instruct and embody the truths of Scripture.[192] This theology also influenced a Lutheran theology of the arts.[193] His Christological theology of beauty is from below, in the sense that it focuses on the beauty of Jesus in his work on the cross. This emphasis is seen especially in the paintings of Matthias Grünewald (1470–1528), Lucas Cranach the Elder (1472–1555), and Albrecht Dürer (1471–1528). An examination of the crucifixion artwork of these artists shows that they uniquely highlight the sufferings of Christ.[194] They also portray the beholders of the crucifixion arrested in attention on the sufferings of Jesus, pointing the viewer to the crucified Savior.

Luther emphasized God's perspective in his theology of beauty as opposed to the perspective of man or the flesh.[195] God is the primary Perceiver, and we are invited to see things as he sees them. This has soteriological implications as God creates what is beautiful even out of that which is ugly. In Thesis 28, Luther states, "God's love does not find, but creates, that which is pleasing to it."[196] God is unlike humans in that he is not merely pleased with the beautiful, but rather he creates what is beautiful and thus pleasing to him.[197] He did this through the cross. In the cross, Jesus became ugly so that we could be created new and beautiful in the sight of God.[198] This is an aesthetic approach to Luther's theology of justification. Mattes explains, "For Jesus' sake, God regards what is ugly as something beautiful, loves the unlovely, and sees sinners as righteous."[199] The justified person affirms God's aesthetic perspective concerning what is beautiful and what is ugly, rather than the human perspective. This person is the true theologian of the cross. He has been considered beautiful in Christ, and his focus is on the cross. Because he sees all reality through the lens of the cross, he is now able to enjoy the good gifts of creation in the way God intended. In this way, the cross becomes the window through which we view all of life, whether that is the experience of suffering or the aesthetic delight in creation. Once

---

192. Mattes, "Luther's Theology of Beauty," 45.

193. See Rosebrock, "The Heidelberg Disputation and Aesthetics," 2012 and Heal, *A Magnificent Faith*.

194. See Noble, *Lucas Cranach the Elder*.

195. Mattes, "Luther's Theology of Beauty," 49.

196. Luther, *Annotated Luther* 1, 104.

197. Mattes, *Luther's Theology of Beauty*, 77.

198. Mattes, *Luther's Theology of Beauty*, 85.

199. Mattes, "Luther and Beauty," 17.

the theology of the cross is firmly established, humanity can receive the good gifts of creation, such as music or art.[200] Thus, in his sermons on the Gospel of John, Luther said, "Now if I believe in God's Son and bear in mind that He became man, all creatures will appear a hundred times more beautiful to me than before. Then I will properly appreciate the sun, the moon, the stars, trees, apples, pears, as I reflect that He is Lord over all and the center of all things."[201]

Luther's theology of the cross in distinction from a theology of glory is a crucial development in theological aesthetics and became a major influence on Balthasar. However, as we will see in the next chapter, Balthasar did not sufficiently emphasize the pervasive nature of the bondage of the will to sin. Therefore, Balthasar's project lacks a sufficient understanding of the ugliness of sin and how it pervades human thinking and perception. Luther's understanding of the radical nature of the fall made him despair of the contribution of the philosophers and human reason. Yet, he nuanced this by recognizing the legitimacy of reason and philosophy if it was tested and refined by a theology of the cross (*crux probat omnia*). Luther's theology of beauty offered an understanding of the ugliness of sin and the need for the cross. The cross makes beautiful and allows humanity to enjoy the beauty of creation and art in the way God intended.

## Jonathan Edwards's Synthesis

Jonathan Edwards (1703–1758) is considered America's greatest philosopher before the twentieth century.[202] He was a pastor, theologian, and president of the College of New Jersey, later named Princeton. McDermott argued, "Edwards made beauty more central to theology than anyone else in the history of Christian thought including Augustine and the twentieth-century Swiss Catholic Hans Urs von Balthasar."[203] Edwards's theology is, in effect, the fulfillment of Balthasar's challenge concerning theological aesthetics to Protestants.[204] His contribution to theological aesthetics was his synthesis of the Protestant theology of the cross with

---

200. Heal, *A Magnificent Faith*, 17.
201. Quoted in Arand, "God's World of Daily Wonders," 53.
202. McDermott, "How to Understand the American Theologian," 4.
203. McDermott, "How to Understand the American Theologian," 4.
204. Gibson, "The Beauty of the Redemption of the World," 46.

the tradition of the beauty and glory of God as developed by Pseudo-Dionysius and Aquinas. However, his theology of the beauty and excellence of God is not simply a synthesis but a developed theological aesthetics in its own right.[205] Balthasar appears to have been unaware of Edwards. If he had been, he would not have claimed that Protestants banished beauty from theology.[206] Edwards's theological aesthetic has a developed understanding of beauty, excellence, and fittingness based on the triune God. He provides a detailed explanation of how the objective glory of God is displayed in Christ and the aesthetic aspect of how creatures perceive and partake of the divine beauty. To be a Christian, for Edwards, is to perceive and partake in God's beauty.[207] In this section, I briefly overview Edwards's theology of beauty based on the trinitarian relation of love, displayed most clearly in Jesus Christ, and the subjective perception of God's beauty.

In *A Dissertation Concerning the End for Which God Created the World*, Edwards demonstrates the reason for all creation and reality. He says God's end or purpose for creating the world needs to be known: "That which God had primarily in view in creating, and the original ordination of the world, must be constantly kept in view, and have a governing influence in all God's works, or with respect to everything he does in creation."[208] Edwards's conclusion about God's end for creating the world is that God made "*himself* his own *last end* in the creation of the world."[209] God makes himself and his glory his own last end in creation and redemption because of the *ad intra* splendor and majesty of the Trinity. Edwards's trinitarian theology is robust and seen as the ground for God's aseity and self-sufficiency. The love of the triune God is his holiness, and this holy love is his infinite beauty.[210] This love within the triune God is the basis of primary beauty. Thus, love, for Edwards, is the highest beauty.[211]

Edwards was clear that, from all eternity, the inter-trinitarian relation of love was infinitely excellent and glorious and was decisively independent from creation. By making himself and his glory his ultimate

---

205. Louie, *The Beauty of the Triune God*.
206. Sherry, *Spirit and Beauty*, 15.
207. Louie, *The Beauty of the Triune God*, 19.
208. *WJE* 8:413.
209. *WJE* 8:467.
210. *WJE* 6:363; *WJE* 13:57.
211. Lee, "Edwards and Beauty," 114.

end in creation, God wanted to display and share his *ad intra* love and glory with *ad extra* creatures.[212] God has a disposition to communicate his beauty. Within the Trinity, God "is eternally the infinite fullness of the highest beauty and the communication of that beauty."[213] Because of the fullness and sufficiency of the triune life of God, Lane Belden misrepresents Edwards when he says, "The God he sought most to realize, in both his preaching and writing, was a God filled with a restless longing for relationship."[214] God possesses the fullness of relationship within himself and has no need outside of himself. God freely chose to create to manifest his glory, or in Lee's explanation of Edward's theology, to "communicate beauty."[215] In explaining this himself, Edwards echoes Pseudo-Dionysius's language of procession or emanation of God's glory and fullness and return.[216] Edwards explains, "a respect to himself, or an infinite propensity to, and delight in his own glory, is that which causes him to incline to its being abundantly diffused, and to delight in the emanation of it."[217] God's display of holiness, glory, and beauty is an act of love. This love begins within God himself and flows outward to communicate this love with creatures so that they partake of "excellence and beauty."[218]

Ultimately, the way God accomplishes his ultimate end of glorifying himself is through Jesus Christ. Jesus Christ, the second person of the Trinity, displays the beauty of God. He is the display of "infinite beauty."[219] This is seen especially in his sermon, *The Excellency of Jesus Christ*.[220] In this sermon, Edwards says that Jesus, in his humanity, "is the most excellent of all creatures" and explores the different ways Jesus has "excellence."[221] Edwards often equates "beauty" and "excellence" or uses them as synonyms.[222] The excellence of Jesus is seen most clearly in the hypostatic union. Jesus brings to his humanity all the excellence and beauty of his infinite divinity, while at the same time, clothes himself in

212. Belden, "Jonathan Edwards on Beauty, Desire, and the Sensory World," 49.
213. Lee, "Edwards and Beauty," 115.
214. Belden, "Jonathan Edwards on Beauty, Desire, and the Sensory World," 47.
215. Lee, "Edwards and Beauty," 115.
216. Gibson, "The Beauty of the Redemption of the World," 60.
217. *WJE* 8:439.
218. *WJE* 6:364.
219. *WJE* 16:415.
220. Mitchell, "The Theological Aesthetics of Jonathan Edwards," 41.
221. *WJE* 18:203.
222. Delattre, *Beauty and Sensibility in the Thought of Jonathan Edwards*, 66.

humility so that we can see him.²²³ As Louie explains Edwards's theology, "Since Christ is the infinite glory of God dressed in the perfection of a human person, we have every possible reason to adore and love him."²²⁴ Jesus Christ reveals the beauty and excellence of God and in him God accomplishes his end for creating the world.

The beauty of Christ as the infinite display of God's glory in Edwards's theology is not a neglect of the other two members of the Trinity. The second person of the Trinity is the exact image of the Father. The Spirit also is beautiful. Patrick Sherry notes that the Spirit is the personified Love between Father and Son, which makes the Spirit intrinsically tied to beauty in Edwards's theology.²²⁵ Holiness, the infinite love of God, is specifically related to the Holy Spirit. When the Holy Spirit is communicated or given to the creature, God is giving the creature his own holiness and love. In Edwards's theology, the Holy Spirit is the person of the Trinity who makes all things beautiful, and conforms the creature to the beauty of holiness.

Thus, for Edwards, beauty is intrinsically tied to goodness and has ethical implications. Beauty is the display of holiness, and this holiness is essentially love, first in God himself, and then in the life of the believer.²²⁶ In Augustine's language, Edwards was deeply concerned with rightly ordered love. God's love for himself is infinite beauty and this is the basis of his holiness. Likewise, for the believer, love for God is the basis of holiness. Holiness of life and the affections is a moral display of beauty in the life of an individual. The person who loves God and lives in holiness lives according to God's design. However, like Augustine and Luther, Edwards maintains that the natural man cannot love, or even apprehend, the beauty or excellence of God or live a life of holiness or moral beauty.²²⁷

In his sermon "*The Divine and Supernatural Light*," based on Matthew 16:17, Edwards demonstrates that "mortal man" can understand the arts and sciences, but is unable to truly know God. He argues for the need of a supernatural light of the Spirit imparted to the soul in order that the person may be able to perceive "a true sense of the divine excellency of

---

223. *WJE* 19:590.
224. Louie, *The Beauty of the Triune God*, 135.
225. Sherry, *Spirit and Beauty*, 85.
226. Lee, "Edwards and Beauty," 113–116.
227. *WJE* 14:93.

the things revealed."²²⁸ The person with this divine light is now able to apprehend beauty and glory in what God revealed. In other words, the divine and supernatural light opens the eyes of the heart so that it may aesthetically appreciate the beauty and excellency of God. For Edwards, the subjective side of theological aesthetics begins with this supernatural light, and it transforms the tastes and affections of the perceiving subject. This spiritual sense can now perceive the "beauty, amiableness, or sweetness" of God's revelation, "so that the heart is sensible of pleasure and delight."²²⁹ Through the spiritual sense, Edwards describes how fallen humanity can come to know and aesthetically appreciate the beauty of Jesus Christ and the Scriptures. God imparts the divine and supernatural light to the soul and the individual is given the ability to perceive God. The spiritual sense is nothing less than God's own disposition and delight in himself shared with the person.²³⁰

Miller demonstrated the central place that this theology of the spiritual sense or the "sense of the heart" had in Edwards's theology.²³¹ The scholarship following Miller's article described the use of the spiritual sense in three possible ways. The first claimed that the spiritual sense operated almost like a sixth sense with no direct link to the physical senses.²³² The second claimed that the spiritual sense was a supernatural enlivening of the other five senses. Thus, the spiritual sense is woven into everyday experience and perception.²³³ The third approach is the synthesis of the two approaches that says the spiritual sense is both a new sense and interwoven with the physical senses. In this view, the spiritual sense is new in that it allows the perceiving subject to sense the spiritual beauty of God within the created order.²³⁴ The spiritual sense interprets the sensory input of the physical senses in such a way that allows the believer to perceive God's glory within the physical. In a way, then, the spiritual sense operates somewhat like Kant's transcendental unity of apperception. The sense experience is placed into *a priori* affective and rational

---

228. *WJE* 17:413.

229. *WJE* 17:413.

230. Lee, "Edwards and Beauty," 121.

231. Miller, "Jonathan Edwards on the Sense of the Heart," 123–145.

232. Helm, "John Lock and Jonathan Edwards," 51–61. McClymond, "Spiritual Perception in Jonathan Edwards," 196.

233. Davidson "From Locke to Edwards," 355–372. Balthasar's theology of the spiritual sense is like this second interpretation of Edwards, with the spiritual sense experienced through the perception of the physical senses.

234. McClymond, "Spiritual Perception in Jonathan Edwards," 209.

categories. The spiritual sense thus includes rational and affective aspects that allows the believer to perceive, know, and delight in God's beauty.[235]

The spiritual sense is intrinsically related to the physical senses in that the spiritual sense allows the perception of God's primary beauty through the vehicle of the secondary beauty of creation. God is "infinitely the most beautiful and excellent" and he has "diffused" his beauty throughout creation.[236] Thus, Edwards speaks of the typology of creation as pointing to the beauty of God in Jesus Christ.[237] Again, echoing Pseudo-Dionysius, Edward speaks of the "emanations of the sweet benevolence of Jesus Christ" in the flowery meadows and gentle breeze. He continues, "When we behold the fragrant rose and lily, we see his love and purity. . . When we behold the light and brightness of the sun, the golden edges of an evening cloud, or the beauteous bow, we behold the adumbrations of his glory and goodness."[238]

For Edwards, the world is charged with a majestic beauty that points people to the beauty of Jesus Christ. This passage explains what Edwards means by primary beauty and secondary beauty. Primary beauty is the spiritual beauty that is signified through the secondary or physical beauty.[239] Because of the way God created it, the world is charged with spiritual beauty and is revealed through natural beauty and the arts, especially music. However, this secondary beauty is only derivative of the primary beauty.[240] Edwards defines this natural or secondary beauty in a way similar to Aquinas's definition, "a mutual consent and agreement of different things in form, manner, quantity, and visible end or design; called by various names of regularity, order, uniformity, symmetry, proportion, harmony, etc."[241] Secondary beauty is designed to point us to the spiritual beauty most clearly revealed in Jesus Christ.[242] Natural man can only appreciate secondary beauty and does not perceive the glory of God in it. However, those who have the spiritual sense and have been awakened to the glory of God are able to perceive primary spiritual beauty in the secondary beauty. Lee explains, "To perceive beauty in the world in

---

235. McClymond, "Spiritual Perception in Jonathan Edwards," 213.
236. WJE 8:550.
237. WJE 13:279.
238. WJE 13:279.
239. WJE 8:565.
240. Lee, "Edwards and Beauty," 113.
241. WJE 8:561.
242. Lee, "Edwards and Beauty," 120.

the true way is to perceive that beauty first and then also to perceive its harmony or 'fitness' with the beauty of God as embodied in the life of Jesus Christ."[243]

Edwards also emphasizes the beauty of the virtuous life.[244] The nature of true virtue is love for God and neighbor and this is the same thing as spiritual beauty.[245] Joseph Woodell explains, "True virtue or true, spiritual beauty consists in a propensity of heart (i.e. good will or benevolence and ultimate love and obedience) toward God and his ultimate good, glory, and will, for God's own sake."[246] In relation to this, Edwards also sees beauty in justice.[247] Justice demonstrates a harmony with society and a sense of proportion of a life lived in virtue. This is seen on the larger scale of society, where evil is punished and the good rewarded, as well as the individual who lives in harmony and proportion with that society. The individual is called to live a morally beautiful life. For the individual, "just affections and acts have a beauty in them."[248]

It is unfortunate that Balthasar did not interact with Edwards's theological aesthetics. Edwards provides a Protestant theological aesthetics that synthesizes Protestant convictions with the tradition of theological aesthetics reaching back to Pseudo-Dionysius and Aquinas. His contribution to theological aesthetics is seen most clearly in his emphasis on the objective and subjective aspects of divine beauty. Like Pseudo-Dionysius, his use of the Neo-Platonic language of procession and return in a thoroughly Biblical way provides the framework for his theological aesthetic. Edwards was systematic in his thinking and one can perceive a movement in his theology of beauty. It moves from its primary source in the triune God and is revealed most clearly in Jesus Christ, to whom all of creation and the history of redemption points. The objective nature of beauty has its source in the triune God's love and holiness and his free choice to create and emanate that beauty in all of his creation. The culmination of beauty is Jesus Christ and the economy of redemption. People who have their eyes opened by the divine and supernatural light to the beauty of Christ are now able to perceive all of reality in light of him. They are given tastes and affections that respond appropriately to

---

243. Lee, "Edwards and Beauty," 115.
244. Lee, "Edwards and Beauty," 123.
245. Woodell, "Jonathan Edwards, Beauty, and Apologetics 86.
246. Woodell, "Jonathan Edwards, Beauty, and Apologetics," 87.
247. *WJE* 8:561.
248. *WJE* 8:561.

the beauty of Christ in revelation and in all of creation. Those who have their eyes opened are enabled to love God as they were designed to and live a life that is in keeping with the end for which God created the world. This is a life of true virtue and love to God and neighbor and is a morally beautiful life. Edwards's emphasis on the objective and subjective aspects of beauty was eclipsed in later developments in philosophy and theology through modernity's radical turn to the subject, especially seen in Kant's philosophy.

## Immanuel Kant and the Turn to the Subject

Immanuel Kant (1724–1804), the German philosopher, inspired a seismic shift in philosophy. He is a crucial figure in the history of the development of theological aesthetics because his work transformed theology as well as philosophy. Kant's philosophy of perception set a path for theologians to follow and develop theological aesthetics. Balthasar made the claim that "Rahner chose Kant" in his transcendental approach to theology, while he himself chose the more organic and literary method of Goethe.[249] Rodney Howsare notes, "It would probably not be overstating the case to suggest that Balthasar understands his theological project as an alternative to what can only be called the Kantian captivity of modern thought."[250] However, Balthasar was indebted to Kant in many ways, so much so that Balthasar's theological aesthetics could be called a "Kantian critique of Kant."[251] This section will be a brief overview of how Kant's philosophy, especially the *Critique of Pure Reason*, influenced the development of Balthasar's theological aesthetics. Unlike the theologians in this chapter, Kant's impact on theological aesthetics is indirect rather than direct. Kant's philosophy will be presented to show its impact on theological aesthetics.

Kant's project is a decisive "turn to the subject" that attempted to synthesize elements of Descartes's rationalism with the skeptical empiricism of Hume.[252] He shifted the point of departure in philosophy to the human person and the conditions that make experience and thought possible. In this way, he redefined objectivity and emphasized the

---

249. Levering, *The Achievement of Hans Urs von Balthasar*, 26.
250. Howsare, "On True and False Humility," 445.
251. Levering, *The Achievement of Hans Urs von Balthasar*, 26.
252. Grube, "God or the Subject?," 313.

THEOLOGICAL AESTHETIC CONCEPTS IN HISTORICAL THEOLOGY 87

perspective, perception, and conceptions of the subject. Kant claimed, "Our knowledge springs from two main sources in the mind, first of which is the faculty or power of receiving representations (receptivity for impressions); the second is the power of cognizing by means of these representations (spontaneity in the production of conceptions)."[253] In experience, the person receives the impressions through the impression made to the senses. As this happens, the understanding spontaneously categorizes these impressions into conceptions. He explained that the subject had an "*a priori* relation to objects."[254] Because of this, the subject is able to "cogitate objects entirely *a priori.*"[255] This is known as the transcendental unity of apperception.

The transcendental unity of apperception is the process by which the self-conscious subject experiences a unified point of view based on the transcendental conditions of the subject that make this unified experience possible.[256] The transcendental unity of apperception is the simultaneous experience of the transcendental aesthetic and transcendental analytic. The first of these, the transcendental aesthetic, describes the reception of sensory impression the process by which the perceiving subject imposes "pure *a priori* intuitions" of space and time onto the perception, making it intelligible.[257] Secondly, the transcendental analytic describes how the understanding spontaneously categorizes the impressions made by the senses into conceptual categories. This simultaneous experience of the transcendental aesthetic and analytic is the transcendental unity of apperception.

Even though Kant tried to situate his philosophy within Christian religion, this radical reorientation to the conditions that make knowledge and experience possible ultimately rejects the necessity of God's action and revelation. He affirms, "It is not essential and therefore not necessary for everyone to know what God does, or has done, for his salvation."[258] Not only this, but Kant was agnostic when it came to the knowability of the *noumena* and the nature of things in themselves (*Ding an Sich*). Thus, his use of the term "transcendental" was focused not on the objective and classic transcendentals, but on the prerequisites of cognition and thought

253. Kant, *Critique of Pure Reason*, 115.
254. Kant, *Critique of Pure Reason*, 121.
255. Kant, *Critique of Pure Reason*, 121–122.
256. Scruton, *Kant*, 44.
257. Kant, *Critique of Pure Reason*, 114.
258. Kant, *Religion Within the Bounds of Bare Reason*, 59.

in the subject. For Kant, the "transcendentals have to do with thought about things, not with the things in themselves."[259]

Though Kant's philosophy was a radical turn to the subject, he did not do away with objectivity, even when it comes to aesthetics.[260] Aesthetic judgment is a "subjective universality," which attempts to consider taste as well as objective beauty. Aesthetic taste is the "free play" between imagination and understanding and is not determined by concepts.[261] Thus, when someone says something is beautiful, the subjective taste is implied in such a way to assert universality. However, Kant's main contribution to the field of theological aesthetics, at least in the Balthasarian understanding, is in his epistemology and transcendental unity of apperception.

Balthasar intentionally situates his theological aesthetics in relation to Kant when he says that theological aesthetics develops in two phases. These phases are the *theory of vision* and the *theory of rapture*, which will be explained in the next chapter. The *theory of vision*, he says, is understood "in the Kantian sense as a theory about the perception of the form of God's self-revelation."[262] While he is influenced by Kant's theory of perception in the *Critique of Pure Reason*, he also rejects Kant's basic theology and soft agnosticism concerning God. Prior to the subject's perception and theory of vision (the first phase of theological aesthetics), Balthasar re-establishes the objectivity of God's revelation and action. To do this, he emphasizes against Kant that it is not only the perspective of the human subject that matters, but God's perspective and revelation. Balthasar maintains a transcendental realism and argues that we can truly know, in a limited way, the essence of things rather than simply the phenomena or appearances shaped by our perceptions and categories.[263] At the same time, however, he agrees with Kant that theology is not a discussion of bare facts, but the subject's perception and aesthetic response to God's objective act and revelation. God's revelation is "a genuine self-representation on his part, a genuine unfolding of himself in the worldly stuff of nature, man, and history."[264]

---

259. Levering, *The Achievement of Hans Urs von Balthasar*, 34.
260. O'Connor, "Theological Aesthetics and Revelatory Tension," 206.
261. O'Connor, "Theological Aesthetics and Revelatory Tension," 206.
262. Balthasar, *GL* 1, 124.
263. Levering, *The Achievement of Hans Urs von Balthasar*, 45.
264. Balthasar, *GL* 1, 119.

Balthasar synthesizes Kant's emphasis on the perception of the subject with the historical orthodox emphasis on God's primacy and revelation. He explains this synthesis, "The object with which we are concerned is man's participation in God, which, from God's perspective, is actualized as revelation (culminating in Christ's Godmanhood) and which, from man's perspective, is actualized as 'faith' (culminating in participation in Christ's Godmanhood)."[265] God's perspective and consciousness has been revealed most clearly in Jesus Christ and God has determined that all of reality relates to this center. This then becomes the transcendental ground for the perceiving subject. Jesus Christ is the form (*Gestalt*) of contemplation for the perceiver, and the believer has the categories of perception and cognition that relate and unite all of reality and all "forms" to this center.

Balthasar said that "what Kant called 'transcendental apperception'... alone does full justice to the full concept of *Gestalt*."[266] However, for Balthasar, a pure Kantian transcendental apperception must be rejected because aesthetic judgments are ultimately grounded in the perceiving subject.[267] Matthew Levering summarizes, "Kant's quest for the ground of the unity of all forms (transcendental apperception), a quest that for Kant has its terminus in one's own consciousness, is here transformed: the ground for the unity of all forms, and the truly beautiful form (not least because of its supreme moral goodness), is the divine consciousness, the self-surrendering love of the Father and the Son, incarnate in Christ on the cross."[268] Balthasar would recover a theocentric view of theology and revelation in a way that utilized Kant's theory of perception.

## Søren Kierkegaard's Stages and the Aesthetic

Søren Kierkegaard (1813–1855) was a prolific author of Copenhagen, who is often associated with the beginnings of existentialism. Kierkegaard's authorship is particularly difficult to understand, and he defies systemization due to his use of pseudonyms who approach life from a variety of different perspectives. However, despite his idiosyncratic method, when one examines the corpus of his writings it becomes evident

---

265. Balthasar, *GL* 1, 125.
266. Balthasar, *Epilogue*, 62.
267. O'Connor, "Theological Aesthetics and Revelatory Tension," 403.
268. Levering, *The Achievement of Hans Urs von Balthasar*, 81.

that he had a project he was systematically working on. He explains his project in *The Point of View for My Work as an Author* (1848). Kierkegaard claims he was primarily a religious author who used pseudonyms to help those in Christendom become truly Christians who existentially relate to God. This is seen especially in his exploration of the aesthetic, ethic, and religious spheres or stages of life. Kierkegaard's critique of the aesthetic mode of existence earned him a sharp rebuke from Balthasar. Balthasar accused Kierkegaard of being the heir of Luther and "eradicating from theology all traces of the aesthetic."[269] However, Balthasar misunderstood Kierkegaard's critique of the aesthetic. Kierkegaard's critique of the aesthetic sphere of life is not a critique of beauty and aesthetic appreciation. Instead, he critiqued an existential aestheticism caught up in the immediacy of life and characterized by a "narcissistic obsession with arbitrary particularity."[270] Kierkegaard's contribution to theological aesthetics cannot be avoided because he emphasizes the importance of interiority and decision as opposed to mere existential aestheticism. The emphasis on interiority inherited from Kierkegaard became a key feature of Balthasar's theological aesthetic project. This section will explain Kierkegaard's spheres of existence and the importance of interiority as a needed development on the subjective side of theological aesthetics.

Kierkegaard's understanding of the aesthetic emphasizes the psychological or subjective side of the aesthetic rather than the objective or metaphysical.[271] Kierkegaard is concerned with the existential nature of the individual. Thus, even though he acknowledges the transcendentals, he emphasizes their existential nature. In *Concluding Unscientific Postscript*, Kierkegaard's pseudonym, Johannes Climacus, says, "The true is not superior to the good and the beautiful, but the true and the good and the beautiful belong essentially to every human existence and are united for an existing person not in thinking them but in existing."[272] True existence is incorporating the good, the true, and the beautiful into the life of the individual.

There are three different interpretations of the stages in scholarship. The first interpretation is to see a definitive progress to the stages. In this interpretation, the individual may move through the aesthetic and the

---

269. Balthasar, *GL* 1, 50.

270. Stan, "From Singularity to Universality and Back," 619.

271. Dadosky "Recovering Beauty in the Subject: Balthasar and Lonergan Confront Kierkegaard," 78.

272. *KW* 12.1:348.

ethical to the religious stage. This interpretation, which Balthasar followed, explains why he believed Kierkegaard dismissed the aesthetic altogether.[273] The second interpretation notes that the three stages are always present within the individual. It is not as if one leaves behind the previous stage in the progression of the stages. Christopher Barnett, for example, explains that the stages "are not mere steps on a ladder, arranged in such a way that to reach the ethical is to abandon the aesthetic and so on. Rather, these stages are permanent domains within the self, which . . . overlap at certain key junctures."[274] In this view, the three spheres are existential possibilities that are always in tension within the life of the individual.[275] The third interpretation notes that there is a progression in these stages or spheres, but each stage is transformed within the next stage.[276] Thus, the aesthetic is taken up and transformed in the ethical, and both are taken up and transformed within the religious.[277] Price explains this interpretation, "the aesthetic as an attitude towards life must inevitably disappear, but the ethical, which replaces it, does not annihilate its content, it simply transforms it, gathers it up and redirects it."[278] This, however, does not undermine the dialectic of Kierkegaard's *Either/Or*. The ethical is contrasted to the simple aesthetic, and the religious stands in contrast to them both. To say otherwise is to make the embarrassing mistake that one of Kierkegaard's readers made when they told him they had read portions of "*Either and Or*" rather than *Either/Or*.[279] However, when a person existentially comes to the religious stage, he finds within himself what the second interpretation noted: the spheres of aesthetic and ethical remain in their transformed nature within the religious as a "permanent domain within the self."[280]

All humanity is born into the aesthetic stage.[281] Kierkegaard explains this stage in the first volume of *Either/Or*. Some people stay in this stage

273. Balthasar, *GL* 1, 50.
274. Barnett, *The Dynamics of Faith*, 77.
275. Feijoo and Protasio, "The Aesthetic Character of Existence in Kierkegaard Philosophy," 1475.
276. Price, *The Narrow Pass*, 159–160. Also, Dadosky "Recovering Beauty in the Subject," 85–87)
277. Evans, *Kierkegaard*, 69.
278. Price, *The Narrow Pass*, 159–160.
279. Garff, *Søren Kierkegaard*, 481.
280. Barnett, *The Dynamics of Faith*, 77.
281. Evans, *Kierkegaard*, 68.

and are simply an isolated individual. Judge William, the pseudonym who embodies the ethical stage, describes the aesthetic stage in his attempt to show a young man the beauty of the ethical stage. The aesthetic stage is merely accidental and fleeting.[282] It approaches the beautiful in life, but this beauty is merely superficially beautiful. He explains the aesthetic view of life as a love of the "accidental" and a fleeting appreciation of the "imaginary erotic."[283] The evasion of "pain, boredom, or difficulty" is the preoccupation of the one in the aesthetic stage.[284] Judge William explains, "To me your view of life's beauty seems very similar to the gaiety that prevailed in the age of drinking songs."[285] In the ethical stage's critique of the aesthetic, the moral nature of beauty comes to the forefront. However, this does not undermine physical beauty but rather connects spiritual beauty with physical beauty. The aesthetic way of life ultimately rejects spiritual or infinite beauty, while the ethical unites them and thus sees through the superficial or accidental into the essential nature of beauty. This approach opens the world up to both a physical and spiritual aesthetic appreciation of beauty.

The young man stuck in the aesthetic stage struggles with the monotony and boredom of life. He must psychologically and existentially create moments of aesthetic delight, as seen in the *The Seducer's Diary*.[286] On the other hand, those in the ethical stage are awakened to the beauty of all life. They see through the accidental into the real. This is described as the "faith in the victory of the beautiful."[287] Judge William explains, "With this faith, I see the beauty of life. . . The beauty I see is joyous and triumphant and stronger than the whole world. And this beauty I see is everywhere, also there where your eyes see nothing."[288] This type of apprehension of beauty in all of life sees individual people as the pinnacle of beauty. Judge William speaks of looking out his window and seeing all people "according to their beauty."[289] As opposed to the aesthetic young man, Judge William does not struggle with boredom because he sees all reality charged with beauty.

282. Evans, *Kierkegaard*, 70.
283. *KW* IV:7, 10.
284. Hanson, *Kierkegaard and the Life of Faith*, 10.
285. *KW* IV:277.
286. *KW* V.
287. *KW* IV:276.
288. *KW* IV:276.
289. *KW* IV:275.

The ethical approach to life does not appreciate the beauty of poetry and the arts and the beauty of creation. However, Judge William's critique of poetry is ironic because his prose and description of moral beauty throughout the second volume of *Either/Or* is poetic and beautiful. The critique of poetry is only a critique of poetic language that merely celebrates the superficial and accidental. This was Kierkegaard's view, which is seen in *Works of Love*, where he tells the story of an aesthetic artist who travels the world but finds no face worth painting. Someone unable to find a face beautiful enough to paint is no real artist. The true artist is awake to the beauty of life, especially the beauty of every individual, no matter how outwardly unimpressive.[290]

For Kierkegaard, content is more crucial than form because the content is essential in helping the person push through to existential interiority. However, Kierkegaard also recognized the importance of form as the vehicle for delivering the content. *Concluding Unscientific Postscript* reads, "As long as there is a human being who wants to claim a human existence, he must preserve poetry, and all his thinking must not disturb for him the enchantment of poetry but rather enhance it."[291] Poetic language and art is useful as far as it reveals hidden beauty. Kierkegaard wrestled with the tension of how the aesthetic and art can be used properly for upbuilding and edification.[292] Poetry and art are tools that could be used, but they easily become distractions and encourage a merely aesthetic existence. He even described the need for a poet of the religious sphere in order that people might encounter the existential need of the religious.[293] He saw himself as this needed poet.[294] Even in the comment concerning the "sadness and the gloominess that are inseparable from the beauty of all nature and art,"[295] he does not say that the beauty is worthless, but rather that physical beauty contains an element of sadness due to its fleeting and superficial nature.

Luther's theology of the cross influenced Kierkegaard's theology of the incarnation. Kierkegaard's approach to the incarnation is crucial in understanding the religious sphere. In *Philosophical Fragments*, Johannes Climacus tells the parable of a king who falls in love with a maiden and

290. *KW* XVI:158.
291. *KW* XII.1:348.
292. Ziolkowski, *Kierkegaard, Literature, and the Arts*, 39.
293. Barnett, *The Dynamics of Faith*, 68.
294. Ziolkowski, *Kierkegaard, Literature, and the Arts*, 4.
295. *KW* IV:276.

takes on the servant form to win her love. This form of the servant, who hides glory and majesty, is Jesus Christ. Likewise, the Lutheran influence is seen in Anti-Climacus's *Practice in Christianity* and the explanation of the divine incognito. Jesus's lowliness is the only way humanity comes to know Christ. Only those who move past admiration and actually join in Jesus's sufferings have genuinely grasped the servant form of Jesus Christ.[296] This distinction between the admirer and the imitator is a key distinction that influences Kierkegaard's approach to art. In *Practice in Christianity*, Anti-Climacus writes a scathing rebuke of Christian art, especially those that depict the sufferings of Christ.[297] Christian art cheapens the religious and makes it an aesthetic experience. It focuses on the appearance of the picture itself rather than Christ himself and thus "abstracted the aesthetic from the religious."[298] A painting of Christ, Anti-Climacus argued, is not looked at with religious love for Christ but rather as an art expert. The religious calls for the individual to imitate Christ, while the aesthetic simply allows for artistic admiration. Art, in all forms, is only useful if inspires imitation and discipleship.

Ragni Linnet calls for caution in interpreting Kierkegaard's approach to art.[299] He says, "Kierkegaard would not be Kierkegaard if the different statements in his writings about the capacities of a picture were formulated in a straightforward manner."[300] His approach to art is under the guise of pseudonyms and full of irony and intentionally reflects different points of view. It is possible that Kierkegaard used irony and satire to make his pseudonyms adopt extreme approaches to the arts that are not representative of his own approach.[301] Although Kierkegaard's approach to the arts is ambivalent, Barnett has provided an interpretive key through Kierkegaard's use of the word *Billede* (image).[302] Kierkegaard's concept of *image* (*Billede*) demonstrates that he is most concerned with the life lived rather than mere admiration.[303] Art may be approached lust-

296. *KW* XX:172.
297. *KW* XX:254–256.
298. Barnett, *The Dynamics of Faith*, 182.
299. Linnet, "Kierkegaard's Approach to Pictorial Art," 193. Pattison has documented Kierkegaard's extensive positive reception of both elite and "low" or popular art. Pattison, "Kierkegaard's Literary Kaleidoscope," 44.
300. Linnet, "Kierkegaard's Approach to Pictorial Art," 193.
301. Tseng, "Bringing Mozart's *Don Giovanni* to Terms with Kierkegaard," 411.
302. Barnett, *The Dynamics of Faith*, 2018.
303. Barnett, *The Dynamics of Faith*, 71.

fully, like the aesthete in *The Seducer's Diary*. The seducer gazes at the image of his desire through a mirror tilted toward the woman he lusts over. He says, "Unhappy mirror, which assuredly can grasp her image but not her."[304] The seducer grasps only her image. Kierkegaard is using irony here because the seducer is never able to truly have this woman, but only her image.[305] Those in the aesthetic sphere, cannot go beyond the superficial image. It is this aesthetic view of the image (*Billede*) that Kierkegaard rejects and implies through his authors that the artist is often guilty of. For Kierkegaard, the image can either be dangerous or useful depending on how it is approached by the individual.[306] Even Anti-Climacus, with his criticism of artwork depicting Christ, encourages the beholding of Christ's image (*Billede*) if it prompts a life entirely devoted to him.[307] Kierkegaard's understood both the danger and power of images to form lives. He also knew the human proclivity to merely get caught up in appearances and live an aesthetic existence. However, Kierkegaard approved if the image inspired the beholder to imitation and a life well-lived, in truth before God. Kierkegaard himself used word images in order to produce this effect in his readers.[308]

Kierkegaard desires to help his reader "become concrete" and truly Christian in a relation to God. In *Sickness Unto Death*, Kierkegaard again uses his pseudonym Anti-Climacus to describes this: "To become oneself is to become concrete. But to become concrete is neither to become finite nor to become infinite, for that which is to become concrete is indeed a synthesis."[309] The concrete in life is experienced in the religious sphere when the individual is in relation to God and God alone. In this sphere, which Kierkegaard aimed to live in and inspire in his readers, the individual is before God alone and both the aesthetic and ethical sphere have met their limits. In *The Concept of Anxiety*, pseudonym Haufniensis examines the contribution of *Fear and Trembling* and says that both the aesthetic and ethical spheres are shipwrecked in sin and repentance. Specifically, the aesthetic sphere is shipwrecked by ethical ideals. The reality of sin renders the ethical ideal impossible when it meets the human and

---

304. *KW* V:315.
305. Linnet, "Kierkegaard's Approach to Pictorial Art, 207.
306. Barnett, *The Dynamics of Faith*, 72.
307. *KW* XX:194–195.
308. Barnett, *The Dynamics of Faith*, 73.
309. *KW* XIX:30.

concrete.³¹⁰ The collision of the aesthetic with the ethical and the ethical with concrete life begins the religious in a person's life. Jeffrey Hanson argues that even though the aesthetic and ethical are destroyed in one sense, the religious incorporates the "aesthetically desirable" and the "ethically required."³¹¹ The shipwreck of the ethical sphere on the religious creates a new type of ethical sphere of existence that does not tend toward the despair caused by sin and anxiety. Hanson explains, "The religious ideal is as lovely as the aesthetic ideal and not as impossible to realize as the ethical ideal; it is the marriage of the beautiful and the just."³¹² In an existential sense, the religious person is not an aesthete of the immediate or someone striving for the universal ethical ideal, but the individual who is repentant before God in the concrete life situation. The truly religious person has authentic interiority and is the synthesis of the finite and the infinite. As John Frame summarizes, "The religious stage combines the immediacy of the aesthetic with the personal commitment of the ethical, but it transforms both into a higher life."³¹³

Contrary to Balthasar's critique that Kierkegaard banished the aesthetic from religion, Kierkegaard transforms the aesthetic by bringing it into the religious sphere of existence.³¹⁴ Kierkegaard's project pushes for the truly religious person, who is the concrete synthesis of the infinite and the finite, enabling the enjoyment of creation and beauty. Kierkegaard asks what the truly religious person would choose, the amusement park or the monastery? He says the temptation of the religious person is to go into the monastery and reflect on his relationship with God, but this would undermine what it means to be truly concrete as it is an attempt to be more than human. Instead, the concrete individual who has authentic interiority and exists in the religious sphere goes to the amusement park and "does not dare to choose the way to the monastery." He explains, "Because the humblest expression for the relationship with God is to acknowledge one's humanness, and it is human to enjoy oneself... Enjoying oneself... is the humblest expression for the relationship with God."³¹⁵

Balthasar, therefore, was mistaken about Kierkegaard's project. Balthasar says that based on *Either/Or*, Kierkegaard can "no longer

---

310. *KW* VIII:17–18. Hanson, *Kierkegaard and the Life of Faith*, 6.
311. Hanson, *Kierkegaard and the Life of Faith*, 15.
312. Hanson, *Kierkegaard and the Life of Faith*, 15.
313. Frame, *A History of Western Philosophy and Theology*, 317.
314. Balthasar, *GL* 1, 50.
315. *KW* XII.1:493.

achieve a meeting of the religious and the aesthetic." Balthasar continues, Kierkegaard "is impelled to use the concept of 'the aesthetic' to stake out and define a basic attitude which, for the Christian, is unacceptable."[316] This is true in a sense, but it shows that Balthasar's critique is mainly based on his understanding of the aesthetic sphere as presented in *Either/Or* and does not properly consider Kierkegaard's later writings. For Kierkegaard, the religious and the aesthetic meet in the concrete individual who is a synthesis of finite or aesthetic immediacy and the infinite or truly religious.

Because of the synthesis in the concrete existence of the individual's life, the religious person also has a certain incognito or hiddenness. This is because the individual lives a transformed aesthetic existence. Because the individual's relation to God is interiority and hidden, this person becomes aware of the contradiction and synthesis of the finite and infinite within himself. This contradiction is explained, "he, with all this inwardness hidden within him, with this pregnancy of suffering and benediction in his inner being, looks just like all the others—and inwardness is indeed hidden simply by his looking exactly like others."[317] This person lives in the concrete and the moment, enjoys beauty and the amusement park just like the aesthete, but is existentially different in his relationship with God.[318]

In one sense, the incognito and concreteness of existence are critiques of immediacy and focus on the moment of the existential aesthete. However, the individual before God establishes the possibility of aesthetic appreciation of beauty within the religious sphere. Thus, although Kierkegaard attracted the ire of Balthasar, a closer reading is necessary. Kierkegaard critiques a mere aesthetic existence, but at the same time his project sets the groundwork for living a truly theological aesthetic existence before God. Kierkegaard and Balthasar were united in pushing for interiority and existential truth for the individual subject. While Kierkegaard critiques aesthetic enjoyment where the "religious is completely dislocated,"[319] Balthasar critiques the religious where beauty "is no longer loved."[320] The overlap in their theology is that both were guarding against those who

316. Balthasar, *GL* 1, 50.
317. *KW* XII.1: 499.
318. Evans, *Kierkegaard*, 69.
319. *KW* 20:254–256.
320. Balthasar, *GL* 1, 18.

made beauty "a mere appearance."³²¹ Kierkegaard critiques those who were making beauty a mere appearance of the immediate moment in the aesthetic sphere, while Balthasar responded to those who completely disregarded beauty in the religious. Balthasar's project was complementary and not diametrically opposed to Kierkegaard's insights.³²² Kierkegaard's aesthetic stage addresses the same thing as Balthasar's critique of the "aestheticization of the beautiful."³²³ In concluding this section, it should be noted that despite the criticisms against Kierkegaard, Balthasar paid him great respect when he said, "Pascal and Kierkegaard were able to speak both existentially and impartially because they both stood under Christ's fiery glance . . . they are both undoubtable great artists of the word who, in this regard, placed all their art in the service of Christ's truth."³²⁴ In the next section, we will examine contemporaries of Balthasar, beginning with Karl Barth. Though Protestant, Barth was a fellow Swiss theologian who influenced Balthasar profoundly.

## CONTEMPORARIES OF BALTHASAR

### Barth on Beauty

Karl Barth (1886–1968) was one of the most influential theologians of the 20th Century. In 1921, his commentary on Romans, *The Epistle to the Romans*, was a sharp critique of the prevailing liberal theology. His influence was further established through the Barmen Declaration and *Church Dogmatics*. When it comes to theological aesthetics, Barth reframes Kant's discussion on the beautiful and sublime.³²⁵ Barth does this by focusing on the "givenness *for us* in the form of the Son."³²⁶ Barth reestablishes the priority of the freedom of God. God's free choice of giving himself in the Son as the basis of the creature's enjoyment of beauty.

This reorientation to God gives context to Barth's response to Brunner regarding natural theology. In 1934, Brunner wrote *Nature and Grace*, where he claimed that God revealed himself and self-communicated

---

321. Balthasar, *GL* 1, 18.
322. Dickens, *Hans Urs von Balthasar's Theological Aesthetics*, 38.
323. Dickens, *Hans Urs von Balthasar's Theological Aesthetics*, 39.
324. Balthasar, *GL* 1, 515.
325. Kirkland, "Glory Over Sublimity," 1010.
326. Kirkland, "Glory Over Sublimity," 1010.

through creation.³²⁷ Barth's firm rejection of Brunner's argument comes from his rejection of Descartes and Kant and all subsequent "subject-theologies" that replace God as the Subject with the human subject.³²⁸ Barth's rejection of natural theology also has implications for his approach to art and culture. At least in his early writings, Barth made a sharp distinction between God's revelation and human culture.³²⁹ Barth's approach to beauty definitively makes God the Subject who reveals his glory and, subsequently, his beauty to the creatures. Barth is clear that he wants to discuss beauty theologically, not from man's perspective.

Barth's most extensive discussion of the beauty of God is in *Church Dogmatics* II.1. The theology of beauty is addressed at the end of his exploration of the "Perfections of the Divine Freedom."³³⁰ Barth summarizes this section: "The divinity of the freedom of God consists and confirms itself in the fact that in himself and in all His works God is One constant and eternal, and therewith also omnipresent, omnipotent, and glorious."³³¹ The freedom of God is his majesty, sovereignty, and sufficiency, but primarily relates to his love.³³² God's perfections are shown in his freedom to love. This is important because in the precious section (§ 30), Barth expounded on the "Perfections of the Divine Loving." The simplicity of God emphasizes the unity of the perfections of God. Each perfection is related and a simple unity with the other perfections. Barth wants his discussion of the perfections to be mutually interpreting. For example, in the discussion of the perfections of divine freedom, he relates unity with omnipresence, constancy with omnipotence, and eternity with glory.³³³

Barth's discussion of the beauty of God is a subsection of his treatment of glory. For Barth, the eternity of God and the glory of God have a special relationship. After an extended exposition of God's eternity, Barth says, "God is glorious in the fact that He is eternal" and that God's eternity means that "God endures in glory."³³⁴ God's glory is pre-temporal, supra-temporal, and post-temporal. God does not stand aloof or separate in his

---

327. Dyer, "Lewis, Barth, and the Natural Law," 8.
328. Grube, "God or the Subject?," 321.
329. van der Kooi, "Herman Bavinck and Karl Barth," 74.
330. Barth, *CD* II.1 §31, 440–677.
331. Barth, *CD* II.1 §31, 440.
332. Barth, *CD* II.1 §31, 441.
333. Barth, *CD* II.1 §31, 441.
334. Barth, *CD* II.1 §31, 640.

eternality but is moved in love to manifest his glory in time.[335] His glory is the "self-revealing sum of all His divine perfections. It is the fullness of God's deity, the emerging, self-expressing, and self-manifesting reality of all that God is. It is God's being in so far as this is in itself a being which declares itself."[336] Barth puts glory at the end of his discussion of the perfections because it is the manifested sum of these perfections. He relates glory to eternity to convey the eternality of the life of God as a glorious reality that He manifests and declares. This eternality then is manifested in his glory. Glory is the climactic display of the unity of the multiple perfections of God.[337] Barth concludes that since all these perfections are manifested in the climax of God's glory, the whole of *CD* II.1 "can be read as a deliberately and carefully crafted theological aesthetic." Barth defines the glory of God as the "fullness, the totality, the sufficiency, the sum of the perfection of God."[338] This sum of perfection is then manifested and declared to perceiving subjects. The glory of God does not "go out to an empty place" but reveals God himself to his creatures.[339] The creature then echoes and reflects the glory that it receives. Jesus Christ overcame man's rejection of God's glory so that man himself is pulled into the eternal joy and glory of God himself.[340]

Barth then asks a series of questions about the glory of God and indicates that something is missing in his discussion. These questions press into whether more can be said about the form of revelation that is the manifestation of glory.[341] Here in particular, Barth's theological aesthetics are most clearly articulated. Barth says that "beauty" is what is missing in the discussion of glory because in beauty, form and content are objectively revealed in a way that draws, convinces, and persuades the perceiving subject. Barth explains that the beauty of God is a subset of God's glory. It is the form of his revelation that draws and aesthetically attracts humanity.[342] Barth's addition of beauty shields us from thinking of God's glory as a brute fact and cold omnipotence without form.[343] In-

---

335. Barth, *CD* II.1 §31, 641.
336. Barth, *CD* II.1 §31, 643.
337. Kirkland, "Glory Over Sublimity," 1013.
338. Barth, *CD* II.1 §31, 645.
339. Barth, *CD* II.1 §31, 646.
340. Barth, *CD* II.1 §31, 648–649.
341. Barth, *CD* II.1 §31, 649.
342. Barth, *CD* II.1 §31, 650.
343. Kirkland, "Glory Over Sublimity," 1014.

stead, Barth speaks of the warmth and attraction of God's beauty in his shape and form (*Form und Gestalt*), which goes to the heart of theological aesthetics. Barth goes on to explain that the beauty of God is what makes him the object of "desire, joy, pleasure, yearning, and enjoyment."[344] God's beauty is the aspect of his glory that inspires aesthetic responses within those who glimpse his beauty.

Barth self-consciously builds on Pseudo-Dionysius and Augustine's concepts of the beauty of God. He retrieves some of Pseudo-Dionysius's arguments outlined in this chapter, which show that God is the source of the beautiful and the good. As the source, God provides harmony to all things and is creation's teleological goal. Barth makes it clear that this is not Neo-Platonism, but a true conception of reality.[345] Barth was disappointed that Reformation and Protestant theologians neglected this doctrine. He appears unaware of Edwards's development of this theology from a Protestant standpoint. However, Barth also critiques Pseudo-Dionysius and Augustine for making beauty an essential perfection of God rather than a subset of the perfection of glory. This is dangerous, he argues, because beauty is a derivative perfection *ad extra*.[346] In Barth's opinion, the beauty of God goes hand in hand with discussions of God's revelation rather than part of a discussion of his *ad intra* perfections.

Because beauty goes hand in hand with revelation, Barth has strong warnings for those who make "aestheticism" the final word or key to unlocking all of theology. He says that speaking of the beauty of the Lord is not only legitimate, but necessary or essential to theology. However, to make aestheticism and beauty the sole focus is to embark on a road toward idolatry.[347] In order to give adequate articulation to the relation of beauty to God and revelation, Barth says he would have to go back through all of his doctrine of God with this question in mind.[348] Barth is aware of the profound place the beauty of God has in theology, especially the theology of revelation. Instead of rewriting his theology with this question of beauty in mind, he offers some preliminary examples of the importance of beauty. Although theology must be beautifully articulated, it is more important to experience the beauty of God.[349]

344. Barth, *CD* II.1 §31, 654.
345. Barth, *CD* II.1 §31, 651.
346. Barth, *CD* II.1 §31, 651.
347. Barth, *CD* II.1 §31, 653.
348. Barth, *CD* II.1 §31, 656.
349. Barth, *CD* II.1 §31. 657. Kirkland, "Glory Over Sublimity," 1017.

Like Kierkegaard, Barth's focus on the beauty of Jesus Christ leads him to call artists to stop depicting Christ. This is partly because he believes no artist can capture the dialectic between humiliation and glory and the divine and humanity. He is adamant, "If at this point we have one urgent request to all Christian artists, however well intentioned, gifted or even possessed of genius, it is that they should give up this unholy undertaking, for the sake of God's beauty."[350] This call to Christian artists is interesting because of his appreciation for Grünewald's crucifixion scene of *Isenheim Altarpiece*, displayed in front of his writing desk.[351]

This is a tension in Barth's theology, but he may have viewed the *Isenheim Altarpiece* as a notable exception to his rule that Jesus Christ should be depicted. Another solution is that he was prohibiting artists from painting Christ's face. Barth's emphasis is on event and he may allow depictions of the crucifixion or Christ's action.[352] Whatever the case, Barth, like Edwards, preferred non-representational art.[353] In contrast to his statement that there is "no theological visual art,"[354] he said of Mozart, "if I ever get to heaven, I would first of all seek out Mozart and only then inquire after Augustine, St. Thomas, Luther, Calvin, and Schleiermacher."[355]

Barth's contributions to theological aesthetics are many. Indeed, one can interpret Balthasar's entire theological aesthetics as "an extension of Barth's reflections on the beauty of God in *Church Dogmatics* II/1."[356] Balthasar himself affirms that what Barth presented in *Church Dogmatics* II.1 was "an overview" of what he presented more extensively.[357] It appears Balthasar took up Barth's comment that he could rewrite his dogmatics from the perspective of beauty.[358] For Barth, the revelation of beauty God's comes from his freedom to love. Barth also clarifies an important distinction and relationship between the glory of God and the beauty of God. A crucial development Barth introduces is the relationship between

---

350. Barth, *CD* II.1 §31, 666.

351. Barth, *CD* I.2, 125. Wheeler, ""Three Theologians and Their Favourite Paintings," 6.

352. Barth, *The Humanity of God*, 55.

353. Gouwens, "Mozart Among the Theologians," 464.

354. Barth, *The Humanity of God*, 55.

355. Barth, *Wolfgang Amadeus Mozart*, 16.

356. Kerr, "Assessing this 'Giddy Synthesis," 9.

357. Balthasar, *GL* 7, 23.

358. Barth, *CD* II.1 §31, 657.

the form and content of God's beauty. The form is the content of God's revelation. God reveals himself in his beautiful form as he truly is. The beauty of God is ultimately Christological for Barth. Like Edwards, Barth argued that Jesus Christ, in his hypostatic union, is the form of divine beauty and the source of all beauty.[359] However, the beauty of Christ also has specific reference to his action. It is the crucified and risen Christ who is the beautiful. Barth explains, "The crucified is revealed and known as the risen Christ . . . If the beauty of Christ is sought in a glorious Christ who is not the crucified, the search will always be in vain."[360] Another key emphasis of Barth is that the form of God's beauty evokes pleasure, joy, desire, and attraction in the perceiver. God's beauty attracts and compels us so that we are drawn into the content of the form, God himself. Balthasar has developed these key themes extensively. Barth's warning against making aestheticism an idol that unlocks all of theology is a needed guardrail for theological aesthetics. Paying attention to this guardrail differentiates Balthasar from another one of his contemporaries, Karl Rahner.

*Isenheim Altarpiece* (1512–1516) by Mattias Grünewald. Public Domain / Wikimedia Commons.

359. Barth, *CD* II.1 §31, 664.
360. Barth, *CD* II.1 §31, 665.

## Rahner's Transcendental Theological Aesthetics

Karl Rahner (1904–1984) was a contemporary of Balthasar who is considered one of the most influential Catholic theologians of the 20th Century. He was a progressive theologian who adapted Aquinas's theology to Kant and Heidegger's philosophical systems and profoundly influenced the Second Vatican Council with his transcendental and existential approach. His approach to theology radically differed from Balthasar, which led to tensions between the two influential Catholic theologians.[361] These differences set the trajectory for two different approaches to the field of theological aesthetics. This section will briefly explain Rahner's theological aesthetics and how they differ from Balthasar's. While Rahner's development of theological aesthetic concepts was somewhat sparse, his anthropology and concept of the supernatural existential inspired an approach to theological aesthetics different from Balthasar's.

The center of Rahner's theology is God's "self-sharing" in the human person: "We arrive at a Christian understanding of existence when we say: the human person is an event of a free, unmerited and forgiving, and absolute self-communication of God."[362] For Rahner, Christology matters because of what it says about anthropology and the nature of man.[363] In Christ, the ultimate symbol of God is expressed to humanity. Therefore, in Rahner's theology, Christology is a feature of anthropology.[364] Christology is built within the structure of human existence and is, therefore, not a revelation from God outside of humanity that needs to be responded to. God's grace is given within the structure of human consciousness, which Rahner called the "supernatural-existential." The reality of grace permeates all things, and life is the experience of the supernatural.[365] Grace and nature are mixed and intertwined in all reality and should not be separated.

Karen Kilby argues that Rahner's theology should not be read in light of his philosophy.[366] In Kilby's desire to make Rahner more palatable to orthodoxy, she argues that one must detach the philosophy from the

---

361. Endean, "Von Balthasar, Rahner, and the Commissar," 33.

362. Quoted by O'Meara, "Paul Tillich and Karl Rahner: Similarities and Contrasts," 448.

363. Little, "Anthropology and Art in the Theology of Karl Rahner," 943.

364. O'Meara, "Paul Tillich and Karl Rahner: Similarities and Contrasts," 448.

365. Little, "Anthropology and Art in the Theology of Karl Rahner," 940.

366. Kilby, *Karl Rahner Theology and Philosophy*, 2.

ideas presented in *Spirit and the World*. She claims that although Rahner insists on the validity of the anthropological turn and borrowed concepts from Kant and Heidegger, this does not mean his theology is liberal.[367] However, Kilby's reading of Rahner is questionable.[368] Though it may be true that there was nuance to Rahner's work and that elements of orthodoxy permeate his work, one cannot read his theology separate from his philosophy as Kilby suggests. Peter Fritz has demonstrated the key place of *Spirit in the World*, not only in Rahner's philosophy, but also in his theology.[369] Fritz, like Kilby, has attempted to read Rahner not as a subjectivist, though at the same time admits that Rahner is modern in appropriating Kant and using the subject as the starting point for theological reflection.[370] Although elements of orthodoxy are mixed in Rahner's theology, even his most strident defenders recognize that modernism and liberalism influenced him profoundly. This is what earned him the criticism of Balthasar.[371]

Rahner's theological anthropology and the consciousness of the human subject are radically different from Balthasar's.[372] While Balthasar utilized Kant's theory of perception, Rahner adapted Kant's theory to make conclusions about the transcendental nature of consciousness. Balthasar wrote about the possibility and action of perception, but Rahner emphasized the essential transcendental nature of the person.[373] Rahner's emphasis was on the transcendental nature of the subject in life and spoke of man's experience of an "ever greater transcendence" and mystery.[374] This led him to devalue the *event* of perception in vision and rapture that Balthasar's theological aesthetics were based on. This led to many tensions between the two. Balthasar emphasized that *seeing* the Form of Christ was crucial, but Rahner argued that the human's essential constitution made Balthasar's seeing the unique form of Christ unnecessary. Rahner argued that the importance Balthasar placed on seeing the world with a coherent worldview was only possible for God.[375] This led

367. Kilby, "Balthasar and Karl Rahner," 260.
368. Marmion "Review of *Karl Rahner*, 121.
369. Fritz, *Karl Rahner's Theological Aesthetics*.
370. Fritz, *Karl Rahner's Theological Aesthetics*, 137.
371. Kilby, "Balthasar and Karl Rahner," 260.
372. Schindler, *Hans Urs von Balthasar and the Dramatic Structure of Truth*, 153.
373. Endean, "Von Balthasar, Rahner, and the Commissar," 34.
374. Endean, "Von Balthasar, Rahner, and the Commissar," 34.
375. Endean, "Von Balthasar, Rahner, and the Commissar," 35.

to disagreements on the possibility of "anonymous Christians." Rahner believed that an "anonymous Christian" could experience God's grace, even if they were not conscious of living in the experience of grace.[376] Balthasar critiqued Rahner and his theology in a polemical fictional dialogue published after Vatican II.[377] This fictional dialogue was between a Christian who embodied Rahner's theology and a commissar representing secularism and atheism. By the end of the dialogue, the commissar pronounces that there is no difference between himself and the Rahnerian Christian.[378] Balthasar's point in this dialogue is to demonstrate that Rahner's theology is essentially the same as secularism. Balthasar's fictional dialogue reveals that he believed Rahner was guilty of the same thing he accused Hegel, namely, a (a fluid identification of the natural and the supernatural which at the same time humanized Christianity and ignored its true message).[379]

Because Balthasar stresses the need for revelation and the objective priority of God, the theological aesthetics of Rahner and Balthasar are very different.[380] In his emphasis on the supernatural existential and the subject's openness to the mystery of God in the concrete, Rahner prioritized experiencing the arts.[381] However, for Rahner, that human experience is also shrouded in mystery. Just as God is an incomprehensible mystery, so also is man. Therefore, the Christian is the "most radical skeptic" who throws himself in "capitulating love to the incomprehensible God."[382] This throwing oneself into the mystery includes the mystery of aesthetics and enjoyment of art. Rahner's theological aesthetics are existential and focus on the mystery of the incomprehensible human encountering the incomprehensible God in the enjoyment of art.

While Balthasar's theological aesthetics focus on the perception of the Form of God in Christ and his beauty, theological aesthetics in the tradition of Rahner focuses on the encounter with the mystery of God in the concrete expression of the work of art. In Rahner's theological

---

376. Little, "Anthropology and Art in the Theology of Karl Rahner," 941.

377. Kilby, "Balthasar and Karl Rahner," 257.

378. Endean, "Von Balthasar, Rahner, and the Commissar," 33.

379. "Fliessenden Identifikation des Natürlichen und Übernatürlichen, die gleichzeitig das Christentum humanisierte und es in seiner wahren Botschaft überhörte." Balthasar, *Herrlichkeit* 1, 85.

380. Viladesau, *Theological Aesthetics*, 125.

381. Rahner "Theology and the Arts," 29.

382. Rahner, "Thomas Aquinas on the Incomprehensibility of God," 125.

aesthetics, God is mediated through the concrete, including art.[383] Rahner gives an example:

> It is precisely this which constitutes the essence of a work of art. I can understand Dürer's "The Hare" as a *concretissimum*, as an utterly concrete and definite given in an innocuous human experience. But if I really look at it with the eyes of an artist, there looks out at me, if I can put it this way, the very infinity and incomprehensibility of God.[384]

Each work of art is an expression of the transcendental incomprehensibility of the nature of the artist and an encounter with the mystery of God in that art. For Rahner, theological aesthetics focus on this world and expressions of created beauty. Therefore, many who are interested in the intersection of art and theology follow Rahner rather than Balthasar in their development of theological aesthetics.[385] Those who follow Rahner emphasize foundational theology and concepts like the "supernatural-existential" at the expense of dogmatic or systematic theology.[386]

## CONCLUSION

This chapter shows how theological aesthetics developed in the history of theology. The concepts of theological aesthetics have developed through the centuries and provide a context for the current discussion. One can see a movement from the objective approach of Athanasius toward a more nuanced approach that includes both objective and subjective aspects of theological aesthetics. It is also clear that the theologians wrestled with the classic tensions between spiritual or transcendental beauty and its concrete manifestation or revelation in creation. These theologians, following Pseudo-Dionysius, noted that God himself is beautiful and the source of all beauty. He created in such a way that his goodness, beauty, and truth shine through creation and artistic beauty. However, because of the fall, the good gifts of God can be turned into temptations. The theologians presented in this chapter followed Athanasius and emphasized

383. Little, "Anthropology and Art in the Theology of Karl Rahner," 944.
384. Rahner "Theology and the Arts," 29.
385. Little, "Anthropology and Art in the Theology of Karl Rahner," 948.
386. Viladesau, *Theological Aesthetics*, 38. Quash, *Found Theology*, 4–5. Fritz, *Karl Rahner's Theological Aesthetics*, 182.

that the incarnation was the revelation of God to the human senses and the restoration of fallen creation. These theologians understood Jesus as the revelation of God's beauty, though each had a distinctive way in how they articulated this. Some, like Augustine, Pseudo-Dionysius, Aquinas, focused more on the spiritual beauty of Christ. Others, like Luther, Kierkegaard, and Barth, focused on the beauty hidden and revealed in his redemptive action.

Luther provided a watershed moment in his theology of the cross over against a theology of glory. After Luther, discussions on God's hidden and manifest beauty in the ugly event of the crucifixion became emphasized and appreciated. Ironically, this event solves the tensions between the spiritual and physical beauty. Perfect moral beauty was on display in the person of the Son. Creation was redeemed, and the door was opened for proper enjoyment of created beauty. Even though Balthasar critiqued Luther, Balthasar was influenced by his theology of the cross and the event of the cross became the decisive and climactic element in his theological aesthetics as we will see in the next chapter. Theological aesthetics after Luther emphasized the spiritual beauty of the second person of the Trinity with a newfound appreciation for the beauty of his redemptive work. For Luther, all of reality is seen in light of the cross. It is because of the cross that the beauty of creation and arts can be legitimately enjoyed. Through the cross and resurrection, creation and the arts are enabled to fulfill their God established purpose to reveal the beauty and glory of God. The objective beauty of creation and the arts point to and reveal the glory of God and spiritual beauty, as Augustine, John of Damascus, and Edwards argued.

The subjective response to beauty in creation and revelation is a recurring emphasis in this chapter. Augustine's response of rightly ordered love sets the stage for Pseudo-Dionysius's, Aquinas's, and Barth's emphasis on pleasure, desire, and joy as a response to God's beauty. This is consistent with Edwards's spiritual sense and theology of the transformed affections. Kant's subjective turn provided a more developed theory of perception, In the next chapter, I will show how this is critiqued and transformed by Balthasar. Kierkegaard's existential interiority underscores the need for a proper subjective response in the concrete nature of life. Kierkegaard follows Augustine in teaching that we were not made for a mere immediate aesthetic existence, but an aesthetic existence transformed by the ethical and religious. Kant's theory of perception and Kierkegaard's emphasis on interiority and becoming concrete are part of the crucial context that informs Balthasar's theological aesthetics. Rahner's theological aesthetics provide an example of a contemporary of Balthasar who had a very different approach and eventually inspired an approach to theological aesthetics that blurred the Creator-creature distinction or focused on the intersection of art and theology.

In the next chapter, we will conclude the survey of the context of theological aesthetics by examining the distinctive emphases of Balthasar's theological aesthetics. We will particularly focus on his understanding of the theory of vision and the theory of being enraptured, which are key elements of his unique contributions.

# 4

# Balthasar's Theological Aesthetics

IN THE PREVIOUS TWO chapters, I explored the context of theological aesthetic concepts in evangelicalism and representatives from the history of theology. In this chapter I complete the exploration of context by presenting the theological aesthetics of Hans Urs von Balthasar. After a discussion on his method and metaphysics, I present Balthasar's definition of beauty and theology of perception (or theory of vision). I do this by examining Balthasar's first volume, *The Glory of the Lord: Seeing the Form*, which is programmatic for his theological aesthetics.[1] This is followed by an examination of the second part of Balthasar's concept of perception, called the theory of rapture, explained in *The Glory of the Lord: New Covenant*. Balthasar's theory of vision and rapture in these two volumes is the heart of his theological aesthetics.

## BALTHASAR'S METHOD AND METAPHYSICS

### Balthasar's "Polyphonic" and Synthesizing Method

The style and rhythm of Balthasar's work is idiosyncratic and difficult to follow. This presents a difficulty in any attempt to understand his method or systematize his thought. Balthasar wanted to move away from a theology that felt like a science lab in order to present a theology that was a dramatic work of art. He followed a method that incorporated and

---

1. Davies, "Von Balthasar and the Problem of Being," 131. Levering, *The Achievement of Hans Urs von Balthasar*, 30.

systematized many systems of thought. Aidan Nichols says, "His own mature theology would attempt to identify the elements for truth in both Existentialism, represented here by Kierkegaard, and Neo-Platonism summed up in Plotinus, while at the same time identifying over against these the specifying features of a distinctively Christian metaphysics."[2] Vetö vigorously critiques Balthasar for "surfing" from one system of thought to another even when these systems are inherently contradictory.[3] She views Kant, Schelling, and Heidegger as the most influential sources for his work. Others identify the primary influence as contemporaries of Balthasar, such as Erich Pryzwara, Henri de Lubac, Karl Barth, and Adrienne von Speyr.[4] Schindler argues that Erich Przywara, Gustav Siewerth, and Ferdinand Ulrich were the most significant philosophical influences.[5]

Each of these authors identifies influences on Balthasar's work. However, that each of these note different influences as the most important indicates that Balthasar is difficult to categorize and situate. Balthasar both synthesized and critiqued different systems of thought in light of the revelation of Jesus Christ. It is impossible to restrict his influences to a select few. He viewed reality, history, and the great philosophers and theologians as all part of a great symphony. Balthasar explains, "By performing the divine symphony, all the instruments of creation discover why they have been assembled together. Initially they stand or sit next to one another as strangers, in mutual contradiction. Suddenly, as the music begins, they realize how they are integrated. Not in unison, but what is far more beautiful—in symphony."[6]

Vetö argues that we should dismiss Balthasar because he too neatly smooths out different philosophical systems.[7] However, a much better approach is offered by Levering.[8] Levering notes Balthasar's engagement with Kant, Hegel, and Nietzsche was simultaneously constructive and critical. Balthasar is constructively and critically engaging various systems of thought in a way that shows how they fit within the structure of truth and symphony of beauty. In order to do this, he engages with philosophical

2. Nichols, *The Word Has Been Abroad*, x.
3. Vetö, "Kilby Verses Balthasar," 431.
4. Howsare, *Balthasar: A Guide for the Perplexed*, 5–25. and Garrett (2010, 417–419
5. Schindler, *Hans Urs von Balthasar and the Dramatic Structure of Truth*, 7.
6. Balthasar, *Truth is Symphonic*, 9.
7. Vetö, "Kilby Verses Balthasar," 431.
8. Levering, *The Achievement of Hans Urs von Balthasar*, 5.

systems by taking on their various perspectives. Balthasar approached these systems of thought "*from the inside* and seeks to expose their fruitfulness when stripped of their erroneous aspects."[9] This appropriation "from the inside" is often surprising because Balthasar utilized modern philosophers who were diametrically opposed to Christian metaphysics. Balthasar entered their systems of thought, enjoyed them, and employed them, even as he derailed them from their "hubristic ends."[10]

## Synthesis of Foundational and Dogmatic Theology

Even though Balthasar is polyphonic in his approach to theological aesthetics, the primary way to understand Balthasar's theology is that it is a synthesis of foundational and dogmatic theology.[11] Howsare notes that theology continues a debate that was important in medieval universities between what he calls radical Aristotelians and radical Augustinians.[12] The Aristotelians maintained that reason gives the human access to God through universals and the reasoning process. The Augustinians regarded this as hubris and argued that God's revelation in Scripture was the proper place to encounter God. This debate was noted in chapter 3 in the section on Luther. Luther argued from the Augustinian perspective and regarded the Aristotelian approach to reason as the classic expression of a theologian of glory.

Howsare argues that the radical Augustinian emphasis was found in Luther's and Barth's assertion that the analogy of being was the creation of the antichrist.[13] However, in the modern era, the Aristotelian approach to reason found expression in what is known as correlational or foundational theology.[14] Foundational theology argued that generally accepted truths can be used to reason to the specific truths of Christianity. Dogmatic theology, on the other hand, emphasizes revelation's priority and absolute necessity. This is not simply a debate between Catholicism and Protestantism, as representatives within Catholicism and Protestantism adhere to both sides of the discussion. Balthasar sought to synthesize

---

9. Levering, *The Achievement of Hans Urs von Balthasar*, 6.
10. Quash, "Drama and the Ends of Modernity," 141.
11. Howsare, *Hans Urs Von Balthasar and Protestantism*, 5.
12. Howsare, *Hans Urs Von Balthasar and Protestantism*, 1.
13. Howsare, *Hans Urs Von Balthasar and Protestantism*, 1.
14. Howsare, *Hans Urs Von Balthasar and Protestantism*, 3.

foundationalism and dogmatic theology so that they are mutually informative rather than at odds with one another. This synthesis is seen most clearly in Balthasar's attempt to show the congruence of Barth's theology with Przywara's analogy of being despite Barth's suspicion and categorical rejection of the analogy of being.[15] Howsare summarizes, "Balthasar is neither the way of foundationalism—the truths of revelation built upon the foundation of being/nature—nor the way of *sola fide*—the truths of revelation crashing into the idols of human culture—but represents a 'third way' of love alone."[16] For Balthasar, God's loving gift of self and being is congruent with dogmatic and foundational theology. Thus, Balthasar's approach synthesizes the debate between radical Aristotelians and radical Augustinians.

Nichols notes Balthasar's synthesis of foundational theology and apologetics and calls it the synthesis of apologetics and doctrine.[17] Balthasar's approach allows him to understand the usefulness of reason chastened by faith and nature in reference to grace. Synthesizing these two approaches to theology, however, is no simple task. There is a reason the debate between foundational and dogmatic theology has raged for centuries. Balthasar simultaneously distinguishes created and spiritual beauty and argues they are interrelated.[18] Balthasar's project of synthesizing this debate is a key aim in his theological aesthetics. The way he synthesizes this debate is through his metaphysics and subordinating the analogy of being to the analogy of faith.[19] This synthesis and all of Balthasar's theological aesthetics has its foundation in his metaphysics.

The weakness of this synthesis is that it too neatly irons out the differences between the claims of foundational and dogmatic theology, or the Aristotelian and Augustinian, schools of thought. There are areas where real tensions and competing truth claims cannot be resolved. While a synthesis is possible, the question is, did Balthasar do justice to the real tensions or smooth out the differences to force this synthesis? I believe that Balthasar made steps toward a legitimate synthesis. However, to make this synthesis, Balthasar underemphasized the Augustinian emphasis on the extent and nature of sin. This doctrine of sin is present but deemphasized and underrepresented in Balthasar's trilogy. Balthasar

15. Balthasar, *The Theology of Karl Barth*, 255–257.
16. Howsare, "On True and False Humility," 3.
17. Nichols, *The Word Has Been Abroad*, 413.
18. Kilby, *Balthasar*, 18.
19. Barrett "Von Balthasar and Protestant Aesthetics," 97.

does not fully appreciate the effects of the fall and sin both metaphysically on the cosmos nor the pervasive effects of sin on the human individual. Balthasar's doctrine of sin is present. He describes sin as idolatry, non-being, and defiantly rejecting God.[20] However, Balthasar's emphasis on reconciliation in Christ undermines the *effects* of sin on the created order and the human person. Therefore, Protestant interaction with Balthasar must consider how a robust theology of sin challenges his synthesis. Although he does not have a strong doctrine of sin and its effects, Balthasar follows Augustinian and dogmatic theology, underlining the infinite qualitative difference between God and man and the Creator-creature distinction.

## The Fourfold Distinction

In his metaphysics, Balthasar synthesizes aspects of the systems of realism, phenomenalism, and existentialism.[21] He also synthesizes Aquinas's and Kant's disparate transcendentalism, though he himself is closer to Aquinas in his metaphysical and realist approach to the transcendentals.[22] I explain Balthasar's approach to the transcendentals in the next section. As noted above, Balthasar puts beauty first because it is experienced first existentially by the person.[23] In beginning with theological aesthetics and beauty, Balthasar wants to highlight the "given-ness" of Being. Being, for Balthasar, is "not dead matter but a translucent event: it is a gift."[24] Balthasar's metaphysics then is based on the unity of the gift of Being and the reception of that gift. The reception of the gift of Being is a dramatic movement toward the giver.[25] For Balthasar, Being includes both material form as well as the event and history of action of gift and reception. Balthasar, therefore, starts his theological project with theological aesthetics because he saw the crucial nature of the aesthetic response of wonder to the gift of Being.

20. Balthasar, *GL* 5, 217.
21. Schindler, *Hans Urs von Balthasar and the Dramatic Structure of Truth*, 31.
22. Davies, "Von Balthasar and the Problem of Being," 11.
23. Howsare, *Balthasar: A Guide for the Perplexed*, 68.
24. Schindler, *Hans Urs von Balthasar and the Dramatic Structure of Truth*, 29.
25. I follow Balthasar's translators and capitalize "Being." Although this is capitalized, this "Being" does not refer to God but to Balthasar's conception of "Being" as all created reality taken as a whole, which will be described in this section.

Metaphysical aesthetic wonder is the proper response to God's gift of Being.[26] Balthasar builds his metaphysics and the description of the aesthetic response on Aquinas's conditions of beauty because these conditions are intrinsic within Being and beings. Davies explains, "Proportionality sustains a universe in which one thing is ordered harmoniously to another, and the whole is ordered harmoniously to a single principle."[27] Metaphysical aesthetic wonder is not merely wonder at the beauty of this proportionality and harmony, but a wonder at the *claritas* or splendor of Being which transcends the horizon of the particular. Like Kierkegaard, Balthasar points out that metaphysical aesthetic wonder is never mere admiration at physical beauty, though it includes this. Rather, this type of wonder has an element of *surprise* at the experience of Being as a gift and revelation.[28] Balthasar began his trilogy with theological aesthetics because this experience of aesthetic wonder at the gift of the beauty of Being must be present in the subject as he perceives and receives the gift of Being in all of life and any subsequent theological articulation.

Balthasar thus desires to explain his ontology in a way that makes this metaphysical aesthetic wonder a core aspect of Being itself. Thus, he explains his ontology by explaining four crucial differences called the *Die vierfache Differenz*, the "Fourfold Difference."[29] The "Fourfold Difference" is a philosophy that is at once ontological and existential and is key to understanding Balthasar's theological aesthetic. These four basic differences or distinctions are:[30]

1. The difference the child experiences from his mother.
2. The difference of Being from being.
3. The difference of beings from Being.
4. The difference between God and Being/beings.

Because of Balthasar's concern to maintain the existential nature of the perceiving subject's reception of the gift of Being in aesthetic wonder and surprise, Balthasar's first distinction is a personal and relational distinction that is at the same time a metaphor for the subject's relationship to Being. The first distinction is the difference the child experiences from his

26. Balthasar, *GL* 5, 615.
27. Davies, "Von Balthasar and the Problem of Being," 11.
28. Schindler, *Hans Urs von Balthasar and the Dramatic Structure of Truth*, 32.
29. Schindler, *Hans Urs von Balthasar and the Dramatic Structure of Truth*, 36.
30. Howsare, *Balthasar: A Guide For the Perplexed*, 57.

mother as he or she becomes self-consciously aware. Balthasar explains, that "[the child's] 'I' awakens in the experience of a 'Thou' in its mother's smile through which it learns that it is contained, affirmed and loved in a relationship which is incomprehensively encompassing, already actual, sheltering, and nourishing."[31] The event of the child awakening to his mother's love is "glorious" and the "first experience of miracle and play" that is carried throughout life. This experience is an analogy of the subject's experience with Being. The tenderness and love that accompanies the experience is set in stark contrast with the transcendental ego of German Idealism.[32] This child recognizes in joy and aesthetic wonder that life is fundamentally a gift. The difference between the child and mother is maintained and never abolished, but it is a difference that is encompassed by the unity of love.[33] This unity of love in distinction leads Balthasar to say that the subject opens up to Being, but at the same time remains distinct from Being.[34] Much like the child and the mother, there is a relationship but also a distinction. The distinction between the subject and Being reinforces the fact that the subject is receiving the gift of Being and is in no way necessary to Being. Life and existence is gratuitous grace rather than necessity that accentuates "our wonder at its existence."

For Balthasar to begin with this distinction demonstrates both an existential and personalist emphasis. Indeed, the personal and existential nature of human experience is the reason Balthasar began his theology with theological aesthetics and his fourfold-difference with the distinction and experience of a child with his mother. This differs from approaches to theology that emphasize the metaphysical or epistemological as the theological starting points. I argue that Balthasar begins with this distinction in a careful and nuanced way that assumes the value and truth of other approaches to theology and philosophy. For example, Balthasar moves on to discuss ontology and metaphysics but does not begin there. His approach is a polemic against merely approaching theology metaphysically or epistemologically at the expense of the existential and personal nature of reality and the perceiving subject's actual experience. His aim was that theology reflects the experience of the subject.

The second distinction is the difference between Being and beings and therefore moves on to more metaphysical considerations. After

---

31. Balthasar, *GL* 5, 616.
32. Schindler, *Hans Urs von Balthasar and the Dramatic Structure of Truth*, 37.
33. Howsare, *Balthasar: A Guide for the Perplexed*, 58.
34. Balthasar, *GL* 5, 618.

establishing the existential and personal aspect of the distinction in the first distinction, he moves to a more metaphysical distinction. The nature of "Being" in Balthasar's understanding is the most difficult of these distinctions. For Balthasar, Being is *completum et simplex sed non subsistens* (complete and simple but nonsubsistent).[35] Being then becomes actual or unfolds in particular subsistent beings or entities (*Wesen*) that are at the same time distinct from Being. Thus, Being transcends beings but at the same time is expressed through them.

Being, for Balthasar, is the gift of God, God's communicative action whereby he reveals himself.[36] It is perhaps easy to become uneasy at this point and begin to think that Being is something between God and creation. This would be a dangerous misunderstanding. To avoid this misunderstanding, Balthasar says that Being not only finds expression in real things but is at the same time a non-subsistent mystery that transcends the particular because it is God's dynamic communicative action.[37] Davies demonstrated that this is where Balthasar's reliance on Aquinas's metaphysics shows up most clearly.[38] Aquinas held also that that Being is true act, *actus essendi*, and there is a distinction between this and *essentia* or *Wesen*. Balthasar argues that the reason he so imperfectly addresses the concept of Being is because it is by nature a mystery tied inherently to God's action.[39] Being's mystery is that it is simultaneously action as well as revelation. Being is a light or splendor that illuminates the meaning of all *Wesenheiten*, finite beings. In a later section I discuss Balthasar's theology of perception or "seeing the form" and how the Form (*Gestalt*) reveals to the depths or splendor of Being. This distinction reminds us that the particular form, is not Being itself, but reveals the light of God's gift of Being. Being, thus, is the reason for the enchantment of reality. This gives rise to aesthetic "wonderment" because, "man is astonished that Being has been opened up to him, to the very one who knows himself as a fragment (in the midst of countless fragmentary beings in the world)."[40]

---

35. Schindler, *Hans Urs von Balthasar and the Dramatic Structure of Truth*, 42.

36. Schindler, *Hans Urs von Balthasar and the Dramatic Structure of Truth*, 53.

37. Balthasar, *TL* 1, 107. Balthasar, *Epilogue*, 51. Schindler, *Hans Urs von Balthasar and the Dramatic Structure of Truth*, 53.

38. Davies, "Von Balthasar and the Problem of Being," 12.

39. Balthasar, *Epilogue*, 109.

40. Balthasar, *Epilogue*, 48.

The third distinction is related to the second. The multiplicity of beings is distinct from Being. This is important because it creates a space between beings and Being, which allows for freedom. Being itself "gives" every particular entity or being its own "being in itself" (*in-sich-Sein*) but at the same time its capacity to "be with" (*Mit-Sein*) and its ability "to be for another" (*Für-ein-ander-Sein*).[41] This opens space for the particular being from the whole of Being and other finite beings so that the entity can be perceived or in the case of humans, both perceive and be perceived and ultimately love and be loved. The distinction between beings and Being is Balthasar's attempt to maintain the particular and the multiplicity of things while at the same time preserving the unity of Being.

The final distinction is the "highest distinction" between God and Being/beings.[42] I have referred to this distinction in the previous chapters as the Creator-creature distinction, affirmed both in the history of the development of theological aesthetics as well as the evangelical context of the doctrine. God is distinct from both Being in general and particular beings. God is transcendent above all Being yet at the same time chooses to reveal himself in Being and in the expressions of Being in beings. God in his triunity, moves to self-showing (beauty), self-giving (goodness), and self-expressing (truth) which establishes all Being and creates beings.[43] For Balthasar, this is the reason the whole of Being and all beings are related to the transcendentals, which is what I address in the next section.

It is important to note that God's self-communication through the transcendentals of beauty, truth, and goodness has Christological contours. Jesus Christ, as the Word of God maintains the unity of relation that undergirds the Fourfold Distinction. Balthasar explains that the Christological word of God is "written into the word of Being," and likewise the "word of Being" is written into the "words of creatures."[44] The Logos therefore is the unifying form of Being. Balthasar's theological aesthetic is thus Christocentric. I will show in a following section that in Balthasar's aesthetic, Jesus Christ is the *Übergestalt* (Super-Form) that gives meaning to all other forms. This is because Jesus Christ as the Logos

---

41. Balthasar, *Epilogue*, 51.
42. Balthasar, *GL* 5, 631.
43. Balthasar, *Epilogue*, 109.
44. Balthasar, *GL* 5, 631.

of God is the self-showing, self-giving, and self-expression of the triune God who holds together all Being and illuminates beings.[45]

The question that arises is, is this category of Being essential for theology? For Balthasar, Being is the self-giving, self-showing, and self-expressing of God himself that has decidedly Christological contours. However, Balthasar is imprecise about what exactly what the nature of "Being" is. He conceives of Being as both non-substantial but at the same time inhering within the particular. Being, then, becomes a category that unifies the multiplicity into a whole and becomes a tool through which Balthasar can build a metaphysical connection to Being and the transcendentals and his Christocentrism.

The only way it is possible to understand Balthasar's category of Being is through a modified construction of transcendental idealism. God is the creator of this transcendental category of Being and he holds it together by his omnipotent understanding and will. I argue that Balthasar does not want to create Being as a type of mediator between God and the world or person so it must be understood in an idealist way. God therefore establishes this concept of Being through his self-giving act of creation. He also allows creatures to experience the concept of Being through a type of transcendental apperception by which the experience of reality allows the perceiver to conceive of the whole mystery of Being in the act of perception. For most people, this is merely a tacit understanding following the experience of reality. In other words, for Balthasar, Being, with all its mystery, is experienced whether the perceiver knows it or not. If this is the case, part of the task of the theologian is to help bring this experience of Being, and the encounter with God through Being, to a more intentionally understood conception of Being that corresponds to the transcendental nature of reality as God has established it. The goal of theology is to unearth a tacit understanding of Being and God that we have based on experience to a more consciously held understanding. When what is tacit becomes consciously understood, the person may then respond appropriately. However, here again it is my contention that Balthasar does not give enough credence to the debilitating nature of sin and the noetic effects of the fall. Conversion is not simply the unearthing and making explicit tacit knowledge that we already have. This is because the fall makes us willfully blind and fundamentally alienated from God.

---

45. Balthasar, *Epilogue*, 89.

In any case, Balthasar's "Fourfold Difference" provides an outline of his metaphysics. It begins with the awakening of the subject to the experience of being loved by his mother. This establishes the relational and existential nature of Balthasar's metaphysics. It is also the basis of wonder and joy in his theological aesthetic as all reality is a gift that is to be perceived. The distinctions create space for the relationship between the worldly beings and entities as well as between God and creation. Balthasar's distinctions guard against blurring the line between God and creation. As Howsare notes, in these distinctions he also provides a synthesis of the cosmological perspective with the anthropological or subjective. In other words, his metaphysics affirms both objectivity and the place of subjectivity.[46] The relation in distinction also establishes the nature of the transcendentals and their Christological nature.

In the next section, I complete the explanation of Balthasar's metaphysics with a discussion of the transcendentals. In order to understand Balthasar's theological aesthetics, it is crucial to understand his use of the transcendentals.[47] These transcendentals are directly related to the Fourfold Difference. The transcendentals and the form of Christ are the unity that hold together these differences. Balthasar's understanding of the transcendentals and their coinherence also provides a framework for understanding the nature of beauty.

## The Transcendentals as God's Gift of Being

Balthasar's theological aesthetics is informed by his philosophy of the transcendentals.[48] These transcendentals are directly related to the Fourfold Difference. The transcendentals and the form of Christ provides the unifying aspect in the midst of these differences. There is discussion about whether Balthasar followed Scholasticism or German philosophy in his use of the transcendentals.[49] This is because Balthasar, like Kant, emphasized the transcendentals of the good, the true, and the beautiful rather than the one, the true, and the good like Scholasticism.[50] Schindler disagrees with Peter Henrici who claims that Balthasar follows German

---

46. Howsare, *Hans Urs Von Balthasar and Protestantism*, 57.

47. Nichols, "An Introduction to Balthasar," 8.

48. Nichols, "An Introduction to Balthasar," 8.

49. Henrici, "La Structure de la Trilogie," 15–17. Schindler, *Hans Urs von Balthasar and the Dramatic Structure of Truth*, 362.

50. Balthasar, *Epilogue*, 87.

philosophy and Kant rather than Scholasticism and Aquinas. However, due to Balthasar's synthesizing methodology, and his use of both Aquinas and Kant, it can be argued that he was responding to Kant's use of the transcendentals in his critique by utilizing Aquinas's metaphysics within a Barthian understanding of the priority of revelation in Christ. For Kant, the use of "transcendental" shifted from a metaphysical statement about Being to epistemological conditions for the *a priori* possibility of knowledge. Balthasar was rejecting transcendentalism in the Kantian sense and recovering the metaphysical sense.[51] Davies explains, "The transcendentals as Balthasar appropriated them, served as a platform for his realignment of Kantianism, modernism, and liberalism."[52]

Even though Balthasar says that the nature of the transcendentals is undefinable and mysterious, he describes them as the "properties of being . . . which transcend every species and belong to every existent as such."[53] For Balthasar, then, the transcendentals are intrinsically related to both Being and beings. The transcendentals of goodness, truth, and beauty for Balthasar are qualities that both transcend and at the same time in here in every particular being to various levels. These transcendentals establish the legitimacy of the analogy of being and teach us about God who is the Source of Being.[54] Thus, for Balthasar, against Kant, they are metaphysical realities. However, Balthasar did not simply reproduce the scholastic arguments, but spoke of the transcendentals in light of Kant's critique.[55] The transcendentals are a metaphysical reality based on God's communicative action, and are experienced by the individual. For Balthasar, they are not only metaphysical, but the key to epistemology and existentialism. The experience of the transcendentals evokes aesthetic wonder in the individual. The transcendentals are true outside of and apart from the subject in a realist sense but must be received and existentially lived out. These transcendentals "require the reception by a self-conscious subject."[56]

Balthasar wanted to establish that Being and beings are a gift of God. This gift of Being has two sides: the Giver, God, and the receiver, the receptive human being. Thus, Balthasar speaks of the transcendentals

---

51. Schindler, *Hans Urs von Balthasar and the Dramatic Structure of Truth*, 352.
52. Davies, "Von Balthasar and the Problem of Being," 133.
53. Balthasar, *GL* 4, 371, 441.
54. Nichols, "An Introduction to Balthasar," 8–9.
55. Davies, "Von Balthasar and the Problem of Being," 133.
56. Schindler, *Hans Urs von Balthasar and the Dramatic Structure of Truth*, 367.

from two different angles. On one side the Being and the transcendentals can be spoken of as a gift given, or on the other side they can be spoken of as a gift received. I mentioned above in the discussion on Being that Being itself is the result of the triune God's self-showing (*Sich-Zeigen*) beauty, self-giving (*Sich-Geben*) goodness, and self-expressing (*Sich-Sagen*) truth.[57] God gifts Being, which means that he actively communicates himself and expresses himself to the self-conscious subject through the medium of Being. This action creates the possibility for the self-conscious subject to know God's revelation and respond in the freedom of the life that God has given that perceiving subject. Balthasar thus also speaks of the existential aspects of the transcendentals. The human subject responds in aesthetic wonder, self-giving goodness, and relational self-communicating truth.[58]

Schindler provides an excellent explanation of the way that Balthasar understood the transcendentals.[59] Ontologically, the transcendentals are not to be isolated from one another. Unity is indeed a transcendental, as the Scholastics argued, but the transcendental of unity is the circumincession of the transcendentals of beauty, goodness, and truth and cannot be treated by itself.[60] Beauty, as mentioned above, is the first transcendental that should be emphasized in Balthasar's perspective. This is because Being has an epiphanic and theophanic nature and is the first transcendental to be experienced by the human subject. The transcendental of beauty, though, is not to be isolated from the other transcendentals, is the first transcendental to be experienced in the aesthetic wonder of encountering Being/beings. Being by nature is beautiful because it has an epiphanic nature and "is the movement of inner ground to outward appearance."[61] This epiphany of Being is manifestly beautiful. For Balthasar, the manifestation of a particular entity's form (*Gestalt*) carries within it a reference to the whole unity of Being. In perceiving the part in one particular form, the splendor of all of Being shines through and the perceiver is brought into the depths of being as he himself is a part of Being as a whole. I further explore Balthasar's understanding of beauty as it relates to form in a following section.

57. Balthasar, *Epilogue*, 109. Schindler, *Hans Urs von Balthasar and the Dramatic Structure of Truth*, 365.
58. Balthasar, *Epilogue*, 59–86.
59. Schindler, *Hans Urs von Balthasar and the Dramatic Structure of Truth*, 364–374.
60. Schindler, *Hans Urs von Balthasar and the Dramatic Structure of Truth*, 402.
61. Schindler, *Hans Urs von Balthasar and the Dramatic Structure of Truth*, 365.

For Balthasar, the transcendental of goodness refers to the action of self-giving. Being is the gift of God as he gives himself to others. Therefore, Being is transcendentally good because it is the gift of God as he gives himself in relationship. Goodness relates to beauty, the epiphany of Being, and this epiphany or manifestation is an action of goodness from the self-giving God. In response to the gift of Being, all things desire this good.[62] The transcendental of goodness evokes an aesthetic response of desire in the perceiving subject, which leads to the free reception of this gift. In turn the receiver offers the gift of self-giving love back to God. Goodness, as an existential reality in the life of the human subject, begins with the perception of God's gift of Being. Then, in response, the perceiver has an aesthetic desire for the good, receives the good, and gives the "good" back in a life of love.

Truth, for Balthasar, has a particular reference to thinking, judging, and speaking. Truth is a mode of communication as a person speaks and communicates self. From the perspective of God's gift, truth as a transcendental means that God communicates truly through his revelation in Being. God, Balthasar maintains, created Being in truth, which means that he communicated in the perfect freedom of self-expression and surrender as he gives himself and speaks through creation and the incarnate Word.[63] Truth is God revealing and disclosing what is real in the gift of Being.[64] Therefore, truth is most fundamentally God's revelation of himself. From the perspective of the transcendentals as God's gift of Being, truth is united with goodness and beauty. From the perspective of the reception of the gift by the perceiver, truth completes an organic order of the transcendentals. The perceiver receives the beauty, lives in goodness, and then is enabled to speak as a person who expresses himself in truth and the freedom of speech as one who has received God's gift of Being.

The transcendentals speak of a personal and relational self-showing, self-giving, and self-expression.[65] The transcendentals are seen first in God's gift of Being and, secondly, existentially in the receptive human subject as he or she receives this gift and responds in aesthetic wonder, dramatic goodness, and speaks the truth. The transcendentals yet again demonstrate an area where a lack of the theology of sin impacts Balthasar's

62. Schindler, *Hans Urs von Balthasar and the Dramatic Structure of Truth*, 366.
63. Balthasar, *Epilogue*, 85.
64. Balthasar, *TL* 1, 37.
65. Balthasar, *Epilogue*, 59–86. Schindler, *Hans Urs von Balthasar and the Dramatic Structure of Truth*, 367.

project. Balthasar envisions natural man as morally neutral, or even positively because of the reception of the gift of the transcendentals. All people must do is receive these transcendentals and gifts and respond appropriately. However, Balthasar omitted a biblical emphasis on the effects of the fall on all of reality. In spite of this omission, Balthasar's concepts of the Fourfold Distinction and the transcendentals establish his project's metaphysical framework, which undergird his theological aesthetic.

## BALTHASAR'S THEORY OF VISION

Balthasar begins his trilogy with an aesthetic approach to the glory and beauty of the Lord. Balthasar begins his first volume by explaining, "We here attempt to develop a Christian theology in light of the third transcendental."[66] His attempt was "*die Sicht des Verum und des Bonum zu ergänzen durch die des Pulchrum*" (to supplement the vision of the good and true with that of the beautiful). Balthasar's project in the seven volumes of *The Glory of the Lord: A Theological Aesthetic* is to present a theological aesthetic that is an exposition of God's beauty in its objective form and its subjective perception.

Howsare gives three reasons why Balthasar begins with beauty.[67] First, Being and all of reality simply appears to the subjective perceiver and its appearance is inherently beautiful. To begin with theological aesthetics emphasizes an existential perspective, where the subject awakes to the gift of Being. Balthasar begins here because the experience of beauty is prior to the experience of truth or goodness. Secondly, Howsare notes, "modernity-in both its progressive and conservative guise-is more forgetful of beauty than it is the other two transcendentals." For too long, Balthasar laments, the true and the good have been taught at the neglect of the beautiful.[68] These transcendentals must be held together, and if one is neglected, the other two will become skewed. Balthasar puts beauty first because it is experienced first by the individual person and secondly because it has been the most neglected of the transcendentals. Thirdly, Howsare says that Balthasar begins with beauty because beauty

---

66. Balthasar, *GL* 1, 9. "Versucht wird hier, die christliche Theologie unter dem Lichte des dritten Transzendentale zu entfalten: die Sicht des Verum und des Bonum zu ergänzen durch die des Pulchrum" (Balthasar, *Herrlichkeit* 1, 9).

67. Howsare, *Balthasar: A Guide for the Perplexed*, 68.

68. Balthasar, *GL* 1, 18.

is displayed in the encounter between two loving persons.[69] According to Balthasar, the beauty of the loving, concrete encounter between God and the person needs more emphasis. Theology often has the unfortunate feel of being conducted in a science lab.[70] In Balthasar's theological aesthetic, he desired to restore an atmosphere of personal love and wonder to theology. In restoring beauty to theology, Balthasar argued, the truth and goodness of theology will again be able to convince and attract by its radiance.[71]

The first volume in *The Glory of the Lord, Seeing the Form,* is programmatic for Balthasar's theological aesthetics.[72] In the rest of this section, I explore the concepts of *The Glory of the Lord, Seeing the Form* that are at the heart of his theological aesthetics. As mentioned above, Balthasar is often difficult to follow as his method is idiosyncratic.[73] He takes freedom and liberties as an artist to produce an artistic rather than a precise theology. This tendency is seen throughout the seven volumes of *The Glory of the Lord.* The contribution of the various parts to the whole is assumed by Balthasar to be self-evident, though it is often not as self-evident as he assumed. Before examining the concepts presented in this programmatic volume it is helpful to see its overview and structure.

Volume 1 of *The Glory of the Lord* is broken up into three parts: (1) Introduction,[74] (2) The Subjective Evidence,[75] and (3) The Objective Evidence.[76] The Introduction criticizes both Catholics and Protestants for eradicating aesthetics or the beautiful from theology. He then presents the difference between "theological aesthetics" and "aesthetical theology" and introduces the task and structure of theological aesthetics. The second part, "The Subjective Evidence," focuses on the element of faith as the subjective perception of beauty. This section is divided between "The Light of Faith" and "The Experience of Faith" and then moves on to give examples of "archetypes" who experienced this type of faith. The second section closes with a description of the spiritual senses that enable the perception of the form and the corresponding subjective experience.

69. Howsare, *Balthasar: A Guide for the Perplexed*, 68.
70. Balthasar, *GL* 1, 31.
71. Viladesau, *Theological Aesthetics*, 12.
72. Levering, *The Achievement of Hans Urs von Balthasar*, 30.
73. Davies, "Von Balthasar and the Problem of Being," 131.
74. Davies, "Von Balthasar and the Problem of Being," 17–127.
75. Balthasar, *GL* 1, 131–425.
76. Balthasar, *GL* 1, 427–683.

The third part, "The Objective Evidence," begins with an apologetic for the objective form of revelation and demonstrates why this is needed for the subjective apprehension of beauty. Revelation and its form become central in this section. Jesus Christ is presented as the center and clearest form of revelation. The Scripture and the Church display this beautiful revelation. The final and concluding section is the "Eschatological Reduction" which maintains that all people will objectively perceive Jesus Christ as glorious and as Lord of the cosmos on the day of judgment.

## The Beautiful: Form, Splendor, and Perception

For Balthasar, the beautiful and its relation to theology is determined by three elements. The first element is the transcendental nature of beauty. The second is the objective form and splendor of beauty. The third is the perception and the spiritual sense that allows the seeing of beauty. In the previous chapter, I noted that Balthasar's project can be called a "Kantian critique of Kant."[77] Balthasar critiques Kant's decisive turn to subject and retrieves a theocentric view of reality. This reinforces God's action and revelation. God's revelation in Christ is the ground of Christianity, rather than the religious impulse within humanity. Balthasar maintained a transcendental realism and argued that we can truly know, in a limited way, the essence of things rather than simply appearances shaped by our perceptions or categories.[78] People find themselves within God's world responding to God's creation and revelation. Balthasar retrieved a theocentric theology of revelation and synthesizes it with a modified Kantian transcendental apperception. Thus, both the objectivity of the transcendentals of Being and subjectivity of perception find emphasis in Balthasar's theological aesthetics. God is the one who is the Source of all things, and all of reality is a theophanic manifestation, or a self-showing revelation of God, intended to be perceived by his creatures.

God's self-showing is his beauty and the subject's perception of that beauty happens through the perception of what Balthasar calls form and splendor. The beautiful is both the form (*Gestalt*) or figure (*Gebilde*) as well as radiance or splendor (*Glanz*) that shines out from that form.[79] For Balthasar, both material form and interior or spiritual splendor flow

---

77. Levering, *The Achievement of Hans Urs von Balthasar*, 43.
78. Levering, *The Achievement of Hans Urs von Balthasar*, 45.
79. Balthasar, *GL* 1, 19–20.

out simultaneously from an object.[80] In relation to the discussion of Being and beings, the beings or entities possess a form through which the splendor of Being shines through. A particular form, then, is the meeting place of the finite and the infinite because the splendor of Being, God's self-showing and the unity of all beings, shines through the particular form.[81] William Dickens notes that for Balthasar this establishes the mystery of Being manifest in the form of the particular. In all things there is a "manifest non-manifest" that is the mystery of Being.[82] The splendor of Being is revealed in the form, but at the same time it is concealed and mysterious.[83] The mystery that is maintained finds its roots in the Fourfold Difference discussed above. The "manifest" that Balthasar speaks of is the revelation of beauty, truth, and goodness of God in the particular. However, it is simultaneously "non-manifest" because that revelation is not immediately apparent, and it transcends the particular. Balthasar wanted to maintain distinction and mystery but at the same time affirm the surprising and manifest reality of revelation in the particular. This doctrine of the "manifest non-manifest" has implications for his Christology and the cross where God was simultaneously revealed and hidden.

The most profound influence on Balthasar's theory of form was Goethe.[84] Schindler notes that Balthasar chose Goethe's notion of *Gestalt* (form), because of his desire to maintain the existential nature of aesthetic perception while at the same time establishing the revelatory nature of objective Being. For Goethe, the mechanistic view of the universe was to be rejected in favor of a more organic vision and the individual parts are not to be divided up but seen as a unified whole permeated by a soul.[85] Goethe argued that different forms operate within a unified hierarchy. There are some forms, such as inanimate forms, that possess no life principle within itself. A stone's shape, for example, is formed from without rather than from within and thus low on the hierarchy of forms. Inanimate objects, plants, animals, and humans each move up the hierarchy of forms in a similar way to Dionysius' hierarchy of being.[86] However, Balthasar, appeals to the Psalmist (Psalm 19:2–4) and Goethe to argue

80. Balthasar, *GL* 1, 19.
81. Schindler, *Hans Urs von Balthasar and the Dramatic Structure of Truth*, 188.
82. Dickens, *Hans Urs von Balthasar's Theological Aesthetics*, 53.
83. Dickens, *Hans Urs von Balthasar's Theological Aesthetics*, 53. Balthasar, *GL* 1, 442.
84. Schindler, *Hans Urs von Balthasar and the Dramatic Structure of Truth*, 12.
85. McInroy, *Balthasar on the Spiritual Senses*, 144.
86. McInroy, *Balthasar on the Spiritual Senses*, 145.

that all forms, even inanimate forms, express themselves by presenting a form and "a kind of voiceless, yet not inarticulate, speech" that reveals Being and the mystery of God.[87]

Thus, for Balthasar, following Goethe, each individual form is brought together and unified by the transcendental nature of reality so that all of creation participates in Being as a unified whole. This emphasis was seen in the previous chapter in both Pseudo-Dionysius and Aquinas as well, who were major influences on Balthasar. The unified whole of Being is an important emphasis in Balthasar's theology. Each form as a part of the whole reveals the depths of transcendental Being. A particular form simultaneously reveals the whole of Being in its relation to the whole and points beyond itself to transcendental Being.[88] Balthasar notes that intellectual history falls into emphasizing one of these two things: either the external form or the depths of Being beyond and within the form. These two aspects, external form and the depths of Being, must be united in the act of perception. While Being and beings maintain their essential distinction or difference, in the act of perception these two things are united. This is what Balthasar means by his appropriation of the Kantian theory of perception.[89] His version of Kantian transcendental unity of apperception is that Being and beings, form and splendor are united in the act of perception. In the perception of forms, the perceiver does not leave that particular form behind to plunge into the splendor of the depths of Being, rather he or she experiences form (*Gestalt*) and splendor (*Glanz*) of the depths of being simultaneously in the concrete.[90]

When a person views something beautiful, for example a tree, three things are revealed simultaneously.[91] First, the form of the tree reveals its own particular beauty. Secondly, it reveals the splendor of Being and the place of the tree within the whole of Being. Thirdly, the tree, as it reveals its own particular beauty and form, it reveals the mystery of the Creator who has given the gift of this appearance of Being.[92] This happens simultaneously and in a natural way as the perceiver experiences the beauty of the form of a particular entity like a tree. The perceiver does not leave behind the concreteness of the tree, but rather the particular

87. Balthasar, *Epilogue*, 59.
88. Balthasar, *GL* 1, 118.
89. Balthasar, *GL* 1, 112.
90. Balthasar, *GL* 1, 119.
91. Schindler, "Beauty in the Tradition."
92. Nichols, *The Word Has Been Abroad*, 24.

form of the tree itself reveals the depths of Being and the mystery of the Creator. This is due to both the objective nature of form and splendor as well as the nature of perception. The brilliance of Balthasar's theology is it simultaneously allows for the mystery and enchantment of the particular and even mundane, without dissolving the particular into the whole or created reality into God. There is a revelation of God and Being in the form of the particular, but also a fundamental distinction.

An area that reveals a potential weakness or confusion for Balthasar's construction of form and splendor is his argument that the splendor of Being is simultaneously beheld in the act of perceiving the form. This means that by nature everyone who has consciousness perceives the splendor of Being in the perception of form. However, for most, this remains an implicit or tacit perception. While seeing the splendor of Being in perception, they do not know that they perceive it. Again, this seems to imply an inherent goodness of the perceiver and does not account for the effect of sin on perceiving the glory of God. Balthasar did argue clearly for the need to move on from the implicit perception of Being to a more conscious contemplation of the form of Jesus Christ, where the splendor of Being is most clearly perceived and understood. However, it was inconsistent for Balthasar to critique Rahner for his concept of an anonymous Christian, while at the same time arguing for an implicit transcendental perception of the splendor of Being. While Balthasar is more careful than Rahner, his truncated theology of sin and its effects at least put him on the road toward the same conclusions Rahner made of the possibility of anonymous Christians who had no need of special revelation.

The three elements examined in this section, namely, the transcendental nature of beauty, the concept of the form and splendor, and the centrality perception are all needed to understand Balthasar's project. With this preliminary understanding, we can now see how Balthasar uses these concepts to construct his theological aesthetic.

## Theological Aesthetics or Aesthetic Theology?

Balthasar wanted to distance himself from what he calls "aesthetic theology," which stands in distinction from his "theological aesthetics." It should be noted that "aesthetic theology" provides an example of a lack of unified terminology that plagues the field of theological aesthetics. For example, Richard Viladesau argues that theological aesthetics includes an "aesthetic theology," which is the "language, method, and contents of the aesthetic realm."[93] It seems that Viladesau is consciously critiquing Balthasar as his positive treatment of aesthetic theology comes at the end of a section explaining Balthasar's theological aesthetic. Viladesau is much more sympathetic to Rahner's approach to theological aesthetics. However, Balthasar's rejection of aesthetic theology is not a rejection of the "language, method, and contents of the aesthetic realm," but rather a rejection of approaching aesthetics and created beauty in a way that blurs the Creator-creature distinction.[94] By "aesthetic theology," Balthasar means the tendency toward pantheism and equating God with creation, that marked theologians such as Herder and characterized romantic theology and German Idealism.[95] This theology was excessively aesthetic and blurred the Creator-creature distinction and fell into "aesthetic and religious monism."[96] Theological aesthetics, as Balthasar understands it, does not confuse the natural with the supernatural, nor does it use a this-world understanding of aesthetics. Rather, theological aesthetics "develops a theory of beauty from the data of revelation itself with genuinely theological methods."[97]

Balthasar, then, sees the need for a synthesis of the experience of perception of a particular form of creation and the splendor of the depths of being radiating from that form. The synthesis between creation and Creator is an experience at the level of perception rather than a synthesis at the level of ontology. A synthesis at the level of ontology leads to a Spinoza-like pantheism or what Balthasar calls "aesthetic theology." There is a need to affirm both the revelation of God through the material of creation and at the same time underscore the "ever-greater difference" ontologically between Creator-creature.[98] However, it is not only the romantic tendencies or the pantheists who are guilty of aesthetic theology. Unfortunately, it can be argued that those who follow Rahner in their construction of theological aesthetics will inevitably end up with the type of aesthetic theology that Balthasar critiques. Rahner's approach, which I presented in the previous chapter, blurs the lines between

---

93. Viladesau, *Theological Aesthetics*, 38.
94. Levering, *The Achievement of Hans Urs von Balthasar*, 200.
95. Balthasar, *GL* 1, 90. Nichols, *The Word Has Been Abroad*, 14.
96. Balthasar, *Herrlichkeit* 1, 85.
97. Balthasar, *Herrlichkeit* 1, 110.
98. Balthasar, *GL* 1, 431.

Creator and creature. This is because for Rahner, art is an expression of the transcendental incomprehensibility of the nature of the artist and an encounter with the mystery of God in that art. Rahner's contention that God is mediated through art does not have Balthasar's clear articulation of the fourfold distinction in order to guard it from an aesthetic theology. Theological aesthetics today is more influenced by Rahner than Balthasar, driven by the desire to show how God is mediated through art.[99] Balthasar, however, provides a better model.

Again, here it is the theocentric structure of his theology and the Fourfold Distinction that provides the protection from a blurring of the Creator and creature. Aesthetics in the general sense can only provide an analogy for theological aesthetics. However, if an aesthetic of this worldly beauty constitutes theological aesthetics too much it will lead to the pantheistic conflation of Creator and creature of the "aesthetic theology." Even though aesthetics provides a helpful analogy, the problem is this worldly aesthetics are inherently man-centered. Balthasar explains, "Man's habit of calling beautiful only what strikes *him* as such appears insurmountable, at least on earth."[100] This leads Balthasar to appreciate even some of the iconoclastic arguments of Constantine V and some of the Reformers.[101] The iconoclastic arguments are a "permanent warning," similar to the Old Testament's ban on images, not to allow the beauty of God's decisive revelation in the person of Christ Jesus to be merely equated or supplanted by an inner-worldly beauty. This warning is one that the current field of theological aesthetics must hear. If the field of theological aesthetics does not heed this warning, it will continue to move toward a blurring of the Creator and creature into an aesthetic theology. While many who follow Rahner look to works of art for the revelation of God, Balthasar allows aesthetics to have its proper place, but keeps his focus on Jesus Christ as the clearest revelation of God's beauty. Aesthetics in general provides an analogy for theological aesthetics but, in the Balthasarian sense, the object of theological aesthetics is especially the aesthetic perception of the revelation of God in Jesus Christ.

---

99. Rahner "Theology and the Arts," 29.

100. Balthasar, *GL* 1, 38. "Des Menschen Gewohnheit, als schön nun einmal nur das zu bezeichnen, was ihm als solches einleuchtet, ist auf Erden zumindest, unuberwinder." Balthasar, *Herrlichkeit* 1, 35.

101. Balthasar, *GL* 1, 41.

## The Subjective and Objective Aspects

The emphasis in Balthasar's theological aesthetics falls on the subjective side of human perception. "Existential Christianity" is the goal of the whole study of theological aesthetics.[102] Beginning with perception and experience with an existential goal is immediately suspect of having liberal theology as the underlying presupposition. Indeed, the danger in liberalism is that the existing subject undermines the truth of objective realities. Objective truth is replaced with mysticism, feeling, and experience. Although this is a danger with the structure Balthasar follows, he strongly holds on to the objective reality of revelation outside of the perceiver. Balthasar critiques liberal Protestant theology for the "*Verflechtung der objektiven Evidenz in die innere Erfahrung hinein*" (conflation of the objective evidence with the inner experience).[103] Balthasar said this is the tragedy of Protestantism and claims that Catholic theology protected itself from the slide into mere subjectivity. Unfortunately, Balthasar seems unaware of conservative branches within Protestantism and is also seemingly naïve about the liberalism within Catholicism. His treatment of Protestantism traces the movement from Luther down the path of theological liberalism. While it is true that liberalism was the direction of one branch of Protestantism, he does not interact with Pentecostal, Evangelical, or Fundamental movements. Nor does he mention conservative theologians such as Herman Bavinck, Benjamin Warfield, Cornelius Van Til, Carl F.H. Henry, or their theological pedigrees. Unfortunately, Balthasar's treatment and critique of Protestantism is focused only on liberal and neo-Orthodox theology.

However, Balthasar is clear, "the act of faith is dependent on God's antecedent revelation" and "the subjective is totally dependent on the objective evidence."[104] The section on "The Light of Faith" concludes with acknowledging the need for a "radical objectivity" that is the foundation for the existential interiority.[105] The emphasis on subjective perception and interiority can only be thus rightly understood in the broader structure of his metaphysics and theocentrism.[106] Being and each of the forms that participate in the whole of that Being become an objective form of

---

102. Balthasar, *GL* 1, 298.
103. Balthasar, *Herrlichkeit* 1, 283.
104. Balthasar, *Herrlichkeit* 1, 131, 156.
105. Balthasar, *GL* 1, 216.
106. Levering, *The Achievement of Hans Urs von Balthasar*, 45.

revelation through creation and redemption. Creation as a whole is a form of revelation that reveals and radiates the glory of God and allows us to "grasp" him in a way.[107] This is ultimately because of the structure of creation as God designed it, but also because Jesus Christ's incarnation purified creation and brought it into participation with God.[108] The paradox of the Creator-creation distinction is maintained even while the objective theophanic radiance of glory is seen in creation.

Balthasar desired to give a unique exposition of the nature of subjectivity and objectivity. This is seen most clearly in the subject-object relationship between the perceiver and Jesus Christ. The discussion of form in Balthasar leads to the climactic form of Jesus Christ. Jesus Christ is objective truth and Lord overall. The various forms of revelation in creation becomes the context of the revelation of the form of Jesus Christ. The person of Christ is the central theme of Balthasar's theological aesthetics and the whole of his trilogy. Jesus Christ gives Being and the transcendentals their meaning and ontological basis. Indeed, the trilogy can be seen as the intentional and rigorous defense of the Jesuit devotion to "Jesus's Sacred Heart" against the arguments that this Christ-centered devotion was mere sentimentality.

Balthasar noted that it is a common misunderstanding to understand him as a "theological aesthete" who theologically approached beauty. His primary goal was to explore beauty as it related to Jesus Christ and his work. He explained, "What is involved is primarily not 'beauty' in the modern sense or even in the philosophical (transcendental) sense but the surpassing of beauty in the 'glory' in the sense of the splendor of the divinity of God himself manifested in the life, death, and Resurrection of Jesus and reflected, according to Paul, in Christians who look upon their Lord."[109] Theological aesthetics is a Christ-centered theology of revelation.[110] Jesus Christ is the super-form (*Übergestalt*) who is the *telos* and unifying form of all Being. Balthasar explains, "the word of God must be written into the word of Being, and the word of Being into the words of creatures."[111] Jesus Christ is the *Gestalt Gottes*, the form of God himself, who holds together Being and gives meaning to all beings.[112] While Be-

---

107. Balthasar, *GL* 1, 431.
108. Balthasar, *My Work in Retrospect*, 118.
109. Balthasar, *My Work in Retrospect*, 96.
110. Viladesau, *Theological Aesthetics*, 32.
111. Balthasar, *GL* 5, 631.
112. Balthasar, *My Work in Retrospect*, 118.

ing and its splendor reveals God, Being itself is distinct from God. Jesus Christ, on the other hand, is the form of God himself. It is also important that Jesus Christ is truly man so that he can be a form that is presented to the senses. Furthermore, in Jesus Christ's hypostatic union of God and man, he is not merely a form to be observed, but a living form who draws perceivers into himself by his splendor. Balthasar notes, "If this form really is the crowing recapitulation of everything in heaven and on earth, then it also is the form of all forms and the measure of all measures, just for this reason it is the glory of all glories of creation as well."[113] Jesus Christ then is the central form of revelation and the one through whom splendor radiates. It is through Jesus that "God's incarnation perfects the whole ontology and aesthetics of created Being."[114] Balthasar returns to the form of Christ in the seventh volume of *The Glory of the Lord* to describe the dynamic movement of the form of Christ in history. The dynamic or dramatic form of Christ in his redemptive work then becomes the bridge between theological aesthetics and theo-dramatics.

Jesus Christ is the objective form of God's revelation. However, Balthasar wants to emphasize that God's objective revelation and form does not go out to empty space. This objective revelation is designed to be perceived by people. Individual persons themselves are a form, a unity of soul and body, placed in the world to behold and become the image of God, which is in the world.[115] Balthasar recognizes that there are ages where the beauty of forms and splendor is clearly seen and acknowledged but there are also ages of humiliation and the denial of form and beauty. The Incarnation is the clarion call to men and women stuck in lethargy and the "uncertainty and melancholy" that plagues most human forms in the world.[116] Jesus Christ and his work in the Incarnation is the objective revelation or super-form and point of departure for waking the perceiving subject from this "uncertainty and melancholy" to the reality of the beauty of theological aesthetics and gives them a part to play in the theo-drama.

David Schindler notes that, for Balthasar, form is fundamentally connected to the notion of drama.[117] Even though form is always physical and open to the senses, it cannot be understood without reference to

113. Balthasar, *GL* 1, 432.
114. Balthasar, *GL* 1, 432.
115. Balthasar, *GL* 1, 432.
116. Balthasar, *GL* 1, 28.
117. Schindler, *Hans Urs von Balthasar and the Dramatic Structure of Truth*, 17.

drama.[118] Form and forms are created as the space for dramatic movement and the dramatic movement itself becomes a form of revelation.[119] This is especially true in the case of the human form. Unlike other forms, such as rocks, plants, or animals, the dramatic aspect to the form of a human is evident. The human is a form that is to orient himself or herself to the divine form of revelation. If the human does this, the form of Christ constitutes the form of that person. This for Balthasar becomes the meeting place of the subject and object. The subject meets with the object of revelation in Jesus Christ and finds true form and true interiority in the perception and transformation that occurs and the "subject comes to itself through the object."[120] For this reason, the Christian form enters the "miracle of the forgiveness of sins, of justification, of holiness, which is the miracle that transfigures and ennobles the whole sphere of being and which in itself guarantees that a spiritual form will thrive as the greatest of beauties."[121] Balthasar explains, "*Die gelingende Gestalt des Christen ist das Schönste, was es im menschlichen Bereich geben kann*" (the successful Christian form is the most beautiful thing in the human realm).[122] The Christian form is the dramatic dynamic of the human responding to perception of the form and splendor of God's revelation and allowing this revelation to constitute their own form. This makes it possible for the Christian to image Christ and take on his form.

The supreme object or super-form of God's revelation in Christ can only be seen and fittingly apprehended by mankind through the spiritual eyes of faith. Thus, there is both an objective and subjective aspect of beauty. The objective form of revelation is inherently beautiful in its splendor and has a counterpart in the subjective apprehension and experience of that beauty. It is here that Balthasar's concept of perception becomes all important in understanding his theological aesthetics. This perception includes both a vision or spiritual sight of God's revelation as well as a rapture or transport into the revelation.[123]

For Balthasar, the experience of faith is not merely an intellectual exercise but God's meeting with the whole person, soul and body, in all its created sensory fullness. God created the senses in order to be a means

118. Schindler, *Hans Urs von Balthasar and the Dramatic Structure of Truth*, 169.
119. Schindler, *Hans Urs von Balthasar and the Dramatic Structure of Truth*, 25.
120. Nichols, *The Word Has Been Abroad*, 29.
121. Balthasar, GL 1, 28.
122. Balthasar, *Herrlichkeit* 1, 26.
123. Balthasar, *Herrlichkeit* 1, 120.

of encountering him. The meeting with God in his beauty and glory usually begins with one or more of the senses and proceeds to engulf all the senses. The "whole man" becomes "a space that responds to the divine content."[124] In this beautiful passage, a person who has been prepared or "attuned" by faith is compared to a violin that is ready and prepared for the touch of the bow, material in the hands of the builder for a house, and the rhyme for the poet. Faith makes man a work of art in the hands of the Creator, but it also makes him an artist.[125] The beauty of obedience of the believer unfolds and becomes an apologetic for the onlooking world. The believer is called to situate himself before the "form of revelation" so that he can live in light of, and even within this revelation. The process of receiving and being brought up into the revelation happens when the whole person is attuned to the revelation. Balthasar explains, "Before the beautiful—no, not really *before* but within the *beautiful*—the whole person quivers. He not only 'finds' the beautiful moving: rather, he experiences himself as being moved and possessed by it."[126] Rather than thinking of this merely as a spiritual reality, Balthasar takes pains to emphasize that this is both a corporeal and physical experience as well as a spiritual experience.

Thus, for Balthasar, both subjectivity and objectivity are important elements for theological aesthetics. Nichols explains, "To his mind, the subject only comes to itself through the object, while the object only possesses its full significance on its entering the sphere of the subject."[127] The meeting place of the subject and object is in the act of perception. When the object is God's revelation, the beautiful form of Jesus Christ, the act of perception is faith that brings about rapture and transformation and creates dramatic action. This meeting of the subject with the beautiful object in such a way that creates a beautiful life is the heart of Balthasar's theological aesthetic.

## THE THEORY OF RAPTURE

In the last section, I explored the programmatic volume, *Seeing the Form*, that develops the main concepts of Balthasar's theological aesthetics.

---

124. Balthasar, *GL* 1, 221.
125. Balthasar, *GL* 1, 221.
126. Balthasar, *GL* 1, 247.
127. Nichols, *The Word Has Been Abroad*, 29.

Volumes 2–6 of *The Glory of the Lord: A Theological Aesthetics* build on the theological aesthetic framework presented in Volume 1 through studies of representatives from the history of the church, philosophy, and biblical theology. *The Glory of the Lord: A Theological Aesthetics* comes to a climax in the seventh volume, *The New Covenant*. The study of this volume in scholarship on Balthasar is underrepresented. As Balthasar looked back on his life and the reception of his works, he noted the tendency that people read the first volume, *Seeing the Form*, and think they have understood his theological aesthetics.[128] This tendency is true in scholarship on Balthasar as well. However, one cannot understand Balthasar's theological aesthetics without paying proper attention to the concluding volume.

In Volume 7, Balthasar builds the synthesis of the "theory of vision" with the "theory of rapture" through an exposition of the New Covenant in three parts, namely: Part 1: *Verbum Caro Factum* (the Word made flesh), he explores the significance of the Word taking on flesh; Part 2: *Vidimus Gloriam Eius* (we have seen his glory), wrestles with tension of glory of God that was displayed as well as hidden in the work of Christ; Part 3: *In Laudem Gloriae* (in praise of glory) where Balthasar explains the process of the Spirit's work in the heart of the perceiver to bring about transformation and glorification. In this section, I begin with showing how Balthasar completes his synthesis of the theory of vision and the theory of rapture in *The New Covenant*. The next two sections provide an overview of the main contributions of this volume to Balthasar's theological aesthetics. In the first of these I demonstrate that the incarnation is the epiphany of love and beauty that constitutes the primary form of theological aesthetics. The form of Christ as presented in his incarnation, death, and resurrection must be the object of perception for a person to perceive God and respond appropriately. I then conclude this section with where Balthasar concludes his work, focusing on the perceiving subject's glorification. I demonstrate that Balthasar's aesthetics concludes in the transformation of the person who truly perceives the form of Christ.

## Synthesis of the Theory of Vision and the Theory of Rapture

In Volume 7, Balthasar's goal was not necessarily to give a theology of the New Covenant, but to present Jesus Christ and his form to evoke

---

128. Balthasar, *My Work in Retrospect*, 96.

an aesthetic sense of wonder.[129] Jesus Christ and his action in history is the greatest art ever created. *The New Covenant* can be seen as a book-length exposition of the inference made in *Seeing the Form,* that the *ars divina* (divine art) is God's action "that begins with the creation, unfolds throughout the salvation-history of the Old and New Covenants and is consummated in the Resurrection." Balthasar goes on to ask, "Should we not rather consider this 'art' of God's to be the transcendent archetype of all worldly and human beauty?"[130] For Balthasar, the greatest art is God's divine action in Jesus Christ. This art gives meaning to all worldly beauty. Volume 7, *The Glory of the Lord: The New Covenant* examines this divine art.

In keeping with this, Jesus Christ is presented as the climax of all philosophical and theological reflections concerning beauty and glory. He is also the climax of history because all history builds up to him with great momentum. Balthasar argues that the New Testament presents the "absolute contradiction" of the glory of God in the person and work of Jesus Christ. The presentation of Jesus Christ in his humility and glory is the form that contains the splendor that unites God and the world in the New Covenant.[131] The form of Jesus Christ must be grasped by eyes of faith and true perception so that the believer stands before God in adoration and then moves to the action of the disciple.[132] Jesus Christ is the beauty of God because he is the specific self-disclosure of God. Therefore, theological aesthetics must be oriented around the beauty, glory, and majesty of God displayed in Jesus Christ who "transcends, criticizes, and brings to fulfillment general aesthetic concepts."[133] Jesus transcends the general beauty of creation and the arts because he is Lord over all beauty. For Balthasar, the form of Christ stands above general aesthetic concepts because he is the norm and standard of true beauty. Yet, Jesus also brings general creational beauty to fulfillment because every aesthetic truth is based on him and his beauty and finds its meaning ultimately in him.

*The New Covenant* focuses on Jesus Christ as the central figure of theological aesthetics, with a focus on how the perceiver is drawn into

---

129. Balthasar, *GL* 7, 10.

130. Balthasar, *GL* 1, 70. "Oder hat nicht gerald diese Kunst Gottes als das überschwängliche Urbild aller Welt-und Menschenschönheit zu gelten" Balthasar, *Herrlichkeit* 1, 65.

131. Balthasar, *GL* 7, 14.

132. Balthasar, *GL* 7, 15.

133. Balthasar, *GL* 7, 22.

rapture by beholding his form in the incarnation. Balthasar presents the form of Jesus Christ that includes his person and work in a way that further explains the discussion of the form of Jesus Christ presented in *Seeing the Form*.[134] In *Seeing the Form*, Balthasar explained that theological aesthetics develops in two phases. First is *the theory of vision*. This theory of vision emphasizes aspects of foundational theology and includes the nature of form and splendor which was discussed above and how the subject perceives God's revelation in Christ. Second is the *theory of rapture*. The theory of rapture is a treatment of dogmatic theology and "the incarnation of God's glory and the consequent elevation of man to participate in that glory."[135] Although Balthasar says this happens in two "phases," he is clear that vision and rapture are simultaneously experienced in the subject as the individual perceives the form of Jesus Christ. These two theories are developed throughout the Balthasar's theological aesthetic project. The themes in the rest of his seven-volume project revolve around the understanding of theological aesthetics as the vision of the form of God's revelation in Christ and the rapture of the person into the splendor of God's glory in that revelation. In *The New Covenant*, Balthasar brings to completion his discussion of the two phases of theological aesthetics. He explains, "Theological aesthetics began as a 'coming to see' the form in which God's Word comes to us, gives itself to us and loves us. In this act of seeing, there already lies the 'rapture': a breaking out from ourselves in the power of our being called and affected, in the power of the divine love which draws near to us and enables us to receive itself."[136]

As in *Seeing the Form*, Balthasar emphasized that even in this rapture, the subject-object distinction remains and is not blurred. However, there is a sort of coming together of subject and object in the beholding of Jesus Christ as the Holy Spirit works within the perceiving subject and causes a "rapture" that transforms the life of that person. Thus, the subject—object distinction is maintained, but the subject is transformed as

---

134. Nichols, *The Word Has Been Abroad*, 226.

135. Balthasar, *GL* 1, 125. The whole context is as follows, and may be the most important section for understanding Balthasar's theological aesthetics: "Die vorausgesetzt, muss eine theologische Ästhetik sachgerecht in zwei Zeiten entwickelt werden. Sie umfasst: 1. Die Erblickungslehre—oder Fundamentaltheologie; Ästhetik (im kantian Sinn) als Lehre von der Wahrnehmung der Gestalt des sich offenbarenden Gottes. 2. Die Entruckungslehre—oder dogmatische Theologie; Ästhetik als Lehre von der Menschwerdung der Herrlichkeit Gottes und von der Erhebung des Menschen zur Teilnahme daran." Balthasar, *Herrlichkeit* 1, 118.

136. Balthasar, *GL* 7, 389.

he or she encounters the beauty of the object. Balthasar maintains that it is not simply a beholding of the glory of God external from the perceiver, but a participatory transformation of rapture within that person who sees the glory of Christ. The synthesis of the subject and object in the act of perception was developed in the previous section, where I showed that Balthasar does not argue for a mystical mingling of subject and object. Instead, this synthesis is created as the subject perceives the beautiful form of Christ in contemplation and faith. Balthasar's treatment of *The New Covenant* is a cataphatic declaration of the revelation of God's beautiful form in Jesus Christ and the Incarnation, with a special emphasis on the cross, but in a way that maintains the mystery of the rapture of the perceiver and apophatic nature of "speechless" wonder at this event.[137] Balthasar's articulation of the meeting of the subject and object in the act of perception is carefully nuanced in a way that establishes and maintains the Creator-creature distinction, but at the same time argues for a deep and real transformation of the perceiver through the contemplation of faith. The strength of Balthasar's synthesis is maintaining the distinction between God and humanity, while at the same time establishing the mystery, wonder, and transformative effects of the meeting of God and man.

## The Revealed and Hidden Glory of the Incarnation

In Part I of *The New Covenant*, "Verbum Caro Factum," Balthasar builds up to the climax of the cross and the descent into hell. He begins by building a bridge with his exposition of the Old Covenant in Volume 6 of *The Glory of the Lord: A Theological Aesthetics* and then moves to the turn of the ages in the events surrounding the birth of Jesus and the ministry of John the Baptist. God worked to establish the New Covenant in a decisive shift from the Old, but John stands as the bridge between the Old and the New as he gathers all the Old Covenant into himself in a symbolic way and hands it over to Jesus Christ, the Word of God made flesh.[138]

Jesus Christ both builds upon the Old Covenant, but also establishes something fundamentally new in a way that both takes up and transcends the Old Covenant. The Old Covenant's relation to the New Covenant has an analogy in the relationship between nature and grace. Howsare explains Balthasar's position, "just as the natural order was made for the

---

137. Nichols, *The Word Has Been Abroad*, 211. Balthasar, *GL* 7, 10.
138. Balthasar, *GL* 7, 40.

supernatural—and therefore is not destroyed when it is taken up into it—the old covenant was designed to be fulfilled in the new, and, again is not destroyed when taken up into it."[139] Balthasar argues that the New Covenant is like an arch that is held up by two pillars that the Old Covenant established. The first pillar is the word of God that seeks to establish righteousness. The second pillar is the atoning-mediator who is prophesied in the Old Testament to establish the covenant by his own atoning sacrifice.[140] Jesus Christ is the word of the Lord and the atoning-mediator. He unites these two pillars of the covenant and recapitulates the history of Israel within himself.

As Balthasar orients his reader to the heart of the New Covenant, he does not proceed in linear fashion. He uses a metaphor from art and treats the New Covenant like a painting which has the climactic scene of the New Covenant standing at the foreground. He examines this climactic scene first and then looks at the corners of the painting to see what is around that scene. This is done in Section 1.2, "Orientation," which brings the climactic event of the cross to the front and then steps back to make statements about the receiving subject, the nature of theology, the incarnation, discipleship, and a theology of time. He then looks in more depth at the central event or climax of the cross and the descent into hell.[141]

In this "Orientation," Balthasar shows the center of God's glory in the death of Christ. Jesus transcends and takes into himself the law of Moses, the glory cloud of the Old Covenant, and all its images or types. He then brings all these things to their completion as their embodying synthesis and goal. It is particularly in Jesus's death that he does all this. In his death, Jesus overcomes the "inner impossibility" of the Old Covenant, which is the impossibility of a covenant between mortals with the Immortal God. He also conquers the persistent problem of death. Jesus takes on the problem of death and becomes the atoning mediator between God and man. In the death of Jesus Christ all the impossibilities of covenant between God and man are resolved. The irony is that the Word of God had to become *silence* and not a word, by entering death, for this to be made possible. Balthasar explains, "the death of Christ is no longer a word; it is silence, the silence and death of God as the fulfillment

---

139. Howsare, *Balthasar: A Guide for the Perplexed*, 86.
140. Balthasar, *GL* 7, 34.
141. Balthasar, *GL* 7, 77–114.

of the speaking, promising, living God."¹⁴² The cross, then, is the center of revelation or "midpoint of theology" when the Word of God became silence and not a word.¹⁴³ This explains the hiddenness of God's glory in the cross that Balthasar comes to in later sections. The cross, in the silence of death, becomes the concealed revealing of God's glory. The cross is the climax of history and the momentum of God's love toward the Church. Yet, the cross is a hidden glory and since the mission of the cross is a hidden glory, the rest of Jesus's mission is revealed concealment.¹⁴⁴

It is tempting to see a parallel between Balthasar and Luther's theology of the cross. However, Howsare notes a crucial difference.¹⁴⁵ The difference is, for Luther, the God revealed in the cross is not how God is in himself, but rather the God who is revealed to sinful human beings. For Balthasar the cross reveals the very essence of God. The cross reveals the essence of God's self-giving love and the measure of all earthly beauty. Howsare explains, the cross "is an act of beauty even as it confronts everything which is beautiful and ugly."¹⁴⁶ Therefore, Balthasar attempts a synthesis of a theology of the cross and a theology of glory. He appreciates and uses Luther's theology of the cross as a critique of the overreach of natural theology, but believes that a theology of the cross is congruent with a theology of glory.¹⁴⁷ For Luther, the cross was ugly and the contradiction of beauty and God's glory was revealed even in this ugliness. For Balthasar, on the other hand, the cross was inherently beautiful. God's glory was hidden, but in the hiddenness the beauty was also revealed and the hiddenness itself became an aspect of Christ's beauty. The difference between these two theologians fundamentally has to do with their approach to sin. Luther viewed the cross as a display of sin and curse in such a way that it appears evil.¹⁴⁸ Balthasar's theology of the cross is that it is an act of beauty that confronts evil.¹⁴⁹

Balthasar, having oriented the study around the momentum of God's love displayed in the cross, then moves on to describe his Christology. Jesus is presented as a paradox. He is at once the absolute judge

---

142. Balthasar, *GL* 7, 81.
143. Balthasar, *GL* 7, 113.
144. Nichols, *The Word Has Been Abroad*, 231.
145. Howsare, *Balthasar: A Guide For the Perplexed*, 89.
146. Howsare, *Balthasar: A Guide For the Perplexed*, 89.
147. Howsare, *Balthasar: A Guide For the Perplexed*, 92.
148. Kolb, "Luther on the Theology of the Cross," 49.
149. This difference will be addressed further in chapter 6.

with all authority, and at the same time the one who took on absolute poverty.¹⁵⁰ Jesus is the synthesis of authority and poverty. This synthesis is another expression of hiddenness of the glory of God. In his flesh, his glory was hidden, though secretly building a momentum toward cross and resurrection and the brilliant display of his glory. The momentum leads to a radical collision of the infinite love of God with the abyss of sin and hatred in the radical self-abandonment of kenosis, cross, and the descent into Hell.¹⁵¹ Jesus was the one who was abandoned on all sides to the judgment of the cross. The hidden glory of the cross is the deep irony of the crucifixion and "the raising up upon the cross and the raising up into glory are one single event."¹⁵²

In Part II of *The New Covenant*, Balthasar focuses on the hidden glory of Christ in the incarnation. He begins with explaining the movement from Christology to trinitarian glory. Jesus Christ reveals the glory of the Trinity. Jesus Christ has the threefold glorification by the Father, Spirit, and Church.¹⁵³ In this glorification of Jesus Christ, the meaning of glory is revealed. Father, Son, and Spirit reveal that glory is "the trinitarian love that has come into the world" and "is drawing the Church and the redeemed world into the light."¹⁵⁴ This is done by the presentation of the obedience and love of the Son, and the Father, Spirit, and Church's glorification of the Son. Balthasar states, "The central concern of a theological aesthetics must correspond between obedience and love, between self-emptying into hiddenness and being raised up into manifestness."¹⁵⁵ In Christ Jesus, the obedience and love of self-emptying moves into hiddenness and manifestation so that the trinitarian glory may be seen and experienced by the receiving subject. Nichols notes about this section, "Balthasar has reached the true climax of *Herrlichkeit* which does not wish to be a theological aesthetics save in that Christocentric—but not Christomonistic—fashion Balthasar learned from Barth."¹⁵⁶

Balthasar goes on to explore the dialectic that Jesus is the appearing of God's glory in the world that is a hidden appearing.¹⁵⁷ It is through

150. Balthasar, *GL* 7, 115–139.
151. Balthasar, *GL* 7, 210.
152. Balthasar, *GL* 7, 228.
153. Balthasar, *GL* 7, 239–261.
154. Balthasar, *GL* 7, 260.
155. Balthasar, *GL* 7, 262.
156. Nichols, *The Word Has Been Abroad*, 232.
157. Balthasar, *GL* 7, 264–286; 318–385.

Jesus Christ that the image of God appears in the world. Jesus's boundless obedience manifests the Father's boundless self-giving love.[158] Because Jesus is the appearing or epiphany of the glory of God, a new emphasis emerges on seeing this form presented in the incarnation. However, the emphasis on sight does not undermine the need to hear the word. This seeing is more than simply physical sight. It is indeed a spiritual *knowing* rather that understands both sight and listening in a spiritual way.[159]

This section of *The New Covenant* demonstrates Balthasar's Christocentrism. In my opinion, this is where Balthasar makes his most important contribution to theological aesthetics. His metaphysics, theory of perception, and concept of form and splendor are all important aspects of his work. However, his deliberate and careful focus on Christ as the form of God's beauty truly allows his theological aesthetics to be grounded on Jesus Christ and the incarnation. Balthasar's Christ-centered theological aesthetics provides a solid theological grounding for this field and also provides a corrective to those who follow Rahner by merely looking for the revelation of God in the beauty of art. Art and beauty may indeed reveal God, but Balthasar provides the necessary theological backdrop to make sure that this does not become idolatry. Furthermore, Balthasar's focus on the event of the incarnation reminds us that the beauty of Christ is not static, but dynamic. It is inherently connected with moral goodness that leads to not mere contemplation on his beauty, but to action as well.

## The Perceiving Subject's Glorification

In Part III, "*In Laudem Gloriae*," Balthasar focuses on the glorification of the person who has seen the glory of God in the form of Jesus Christ and experienced the rapture of participation in him. In the previous two parts, Balthasar focused on the objective beauty of God displayed in the form of Christ. In this part, he focuses on the perceiving subject's rapture and glorification. He begins with a restatement of his whole theological project. Theological aesthetics allows us to see the form of God. When the subject sees and believes, he is enraptured and drawn into the trinitarian glory through Christ.[160]

---

158. Balthasar, *GL* 7, 283.
159. Balthasar, *GL* 7, 277.
160. Balthasar, *GL* 7, 389.

Balthasar, therefore, brings to completion his explanation of perception that has been developing throughout his project. This perception, as we have seen, is the relation between the theory of vision and the theory of rapture. Balthasar explains that there are three stages to true spiritual sight.[161] Again, these three "stages" may be simultaneous rather than necessarily a temporal succession of stages. They are stages in the sense of logical succession. The first stage is the vision or catching sight of the form of Christ. This happens at the base level of God's presentation of his self-giving love in Jesus Christ. This is tied intrinsically to the historical seeing of the eyewitness of Jesus Christ in the flesh and their subsequent testimony. The Apostles' testimony of what they heard, saw, and touched becomes the basis for our "seeing" the obedience and love of the person of Jesus in his work.[162] Because of the dialectic of hiddenness and appearing, the witness of the Apostles and the eyes of faith are necessary. The eyewitnesses account then becomes an "epiphany of absolute love" that must be seen by faith rather than by physical sight.[163] This is the first stage of vision. Second, is the beginning stage of rapture, where the perceiving subject not only engages in a seeing of the external facts, but begins to see the things signified, the self-giving love of God, in the signs. The third stage is the completion of rapture when the perceiving subject is seized by the object of revelation. God himself grasps the perceiving subject and empowers him or her to truly see and be enraptured by the beauty of the absolute love of the Son. With this final stage the perceiving subject is drawn into infinite love and God imprints His own image on the perceiving subject in an act of transformation.

Once this seeing and rapture has occurred, the subject is freed and empowered by the Spirit to live a life of glorification that glorifies the glory we have seen.[164] The action of God on the perceiver as he beholds the beauty of the form of Christ establishes the perceiving subject's glorification and is the link between theological aesthetics and theo-drama. The theo-drama of God shows that the theological aesthetics happens within the context of God's dramatic action of salvation. The perceiving subject is not glorified in a vacuum, but on the stage of God's action where that perceiving subject is then given a part to play.

---

161. Balthasar, *GL* 7, 287.
162. Balthasar, *GL* 7, 290.
163. Balthasar, *GL* 7, 291, 391.
164. Balthasar, *GL* 7, 293.

The believer who has perceived the form of Christ then follows his pattern or image. The perceiving believer then becomes a reflection of that image.[165] Glorification and imaging God in this world is a work of "appropriation and expropriation."[166] God has given himself over to us in the form of Jesus Christ and the believer appropriates God's handing over through the event of vision and rapture and then an expropriation or living response of that appropriation.[167] Thus, God himself gives us himself and we appropriate this gift to our lives and live out this appropriation in our own lives. Living out this appropriation of the form of Christ in our lives is the heart of glorification and produces fruit in our lives for the glory of God. Nichols highlights that the conclusion of the theological aesthetics focuses on the glorification of God in the life of the believer and the life of the Church where the form of Christ is seen in the world in a reflected glory.[168] Thus, the conclusion of Balthasar's theological aesthetics is very concrete, but also dynamic as it moves to the life of the believer in the here and now. Concluding with an emphasis on the life of the believer in response to the form of Jesus Christ sets the stage for the theo-drama.

## THE RELATION OF THEOLOGICAL AESTHETICS TO THEO-DRAMA AND THEO-LOGIC

Balthasar's trilogy is based on his unique exposition of the transcendentals. The transcendentals exist because of the self-showing (beauty), self-giving (goodness), and self-expression (truth) of the triune God.[169] Balthasar's theological aesthetics, theo-drama, and theo-logic correspond to beauty, goodness, and truth. These transcendentals are objective as God's gift of Being and are existentially appropriated by the human subject as he or she receives this gift and responds in aesthetic wonder, dramatic goodness, and speaks and lives the truth. As the previous section showed, theological aesthetics refers to the experience of the glory of the form of Christ in vision and rapture that leads to a life of glorification where Christ is imaged in the life of the believer and in the Church. These transcendentals

---

165. Balthasar, *GL* 7, 398.
166. Balthasar, *GL* 7, 399.
167. Balthasar, *GL* 7, 400–401.
168. Nichols, *The Word Has Been Abroad*, 253.
169. Schindler, *Hans Urs von Balthasar and the Dramatic Structure of Truth*, 367.

are objective and outside of the subject, but they are to be received, or in Balthasar's language "appropriated," by the receiving subject.[170]

From an existential standpoint, theological aesthetics and the appropriation of the glory of God leads to living out of the theo-drama and speaking the truth of the theo-logic. Metaphysically, these transcendentals co-inhere within one another and cannot be divided.[171] However, when they are existentially appropriated, there is a sense in which they can be seen separately or in relation to one another in how each of them complements the other two. Balthasar begins with theological aesthetics because experiencing the glory of Christ generates a life of goodness and truth. Thus, Balthasar begins *Theo-Drama: Theological Dramatic Theory* with the explanation, "At the heart of the *Aesthetics*, the 'theological drama' has already begun."[172] The good of theological dramatics is action on the world stage (*Welttheater*), which is a response to seeing the form of God in the dramatic event of the incarnation.

The combination of theological aesthetics and the theo-dramatic was especially developed in Balthasar's treatment of Dante. Balthasar portrayed Dante as the creator of a new way to do theology that captured this combination of aesthetics and ethics and rejected the essentialist worldview of scholasticism. Balthasar, like Dante, argued for the "primacy of ethics," even in aesthetics, that finds expression in "concrete personal existence."[173] As beauty and goodness coinhere, so also the theological aesthetics establishes the dramatic response of the person who has seen the form and is caught up in God's cosmic drama of redemption. The person aesthetically delights in God and is invited to play a part in the cosmic theater.[174] Therefore, Balthasar emphasized the saints and the believer as the primary form where beauty is seen on this earth. The life of the saints is the primary place where the beauty of Christ is now seen by a watching world.[175] Saints make the form of Christ public as the Spirit glorifies that person in God's theater of the world.[176] Balthasar's aesthetic approach to ethics and his dramatic ethical approach to aesthetics provides a corrective to the tendency of a hard separation between aesthetics and ethics.

170. Schindler, *Hans Urs von Balthasar and the Dramatic Structure of Truth*, 367.
171. Schindler, *Hans Urs von Balthasar and the Dramatic Structure of Truth*, 402.
172. Balthasar, *TD* 1, 15.
173. Balthasar, *GL* 3, 34.
174. Balthasar, *TD* 1, 15.
175. Balthasar, *GL* 1, 494.
176. Moss, "The Saints," 81.

The life of the saints in the world is the culmination of Balthasar's *Theo-Logic*.[177] *Theo-Logic* is concerned with the truth and speaking correctly about God and his divine agency. Balthasar argued that truth as a transcendental immediately presents itself to everyone who has experienced consciousness.[178] Truth is apparent and unconcealed in everyday life. Truth has three stages. The first stage of truth is the revelation of the truth of Being. This stage is merely the fact that things and Being in general exist as a revelation of the truth. The second stage includes a knowing subject who has consciousness and an implicit awareness of the revelation of truth in everyday life. Truth by nature is unconcealed and open for all to see, though the knowledge of this truth may merely be implicit in the consciousness of the knowing subject. The third stage is the knowing contemplation of the subject on the object of truth. At this stage, the subject must consciously place himself in front of God's truth.

In *Theo-Logic*, the transcendentals, beauty, goodness, and truth, again find their basis and culminative expression in Jesus Christ and the incarnation. Truth is the self-expression of God in Jesus Christ. This truth of God is designed to be received by the subject and lived out in concrete existence. When it comes to truth, the life of the believer is a "living exegesis of the truth."[179] God's self-expression and revelation of truth inspire awe and a truthful life. The theologian's task then is to speak the truth concerning God's revelation in such a way that assists the believer to grasp the form of God's revelation in aesthetic wonder and help them become a reflection of that form and live a life of truth.[180] This life of truth is inherently beautiful and good. In this way, the transcendentals can be seen within one another, both in God's activity of revelation in Jesus Christ as well as in the perception and response of the subject.

## BALTHASAR ON CREATED BEAUTY

Although Balthasar wanted to emphasize that his work was not a theology of the arts, but a theology of the revelation of Jesus Christ, his work has profound implications for created beauty and the arts.[181] Viladesau

---

177. Mose, *Love Itself is Understanding*, 225.
178. Balthasar, *TL* 1, 35.
179. Mose, *Love Itself is Understanding*, 225.
180. Moss, "The Saints," 80.
181. Balthasar, *My Work in Retrospect*, 96.

notes that Balthasar's approach to theological aesthetics is Barthian.[182] It is an aesthetics focused on the glory of God revealed in Christ. However, at the same time his theological aesthetics is a response to Barth's rejection of the analogy of being. Balthasar gives a theology of beauty that is Christ-centered, but at the same time appreciates and utilizes the analogy of being in light of Jesus Christ. For Balthasar, the mystery of Being and every particular entity within Being is related to Jesus Christ. Jesus Christ, as the second person of the Trinity, gives the transcendentals meaning. Jesus Christ and his drama is the meaning of all existence. Balthasar explains, "God's incarnation perfects the whole ontology and aesthetics of created Being."[183] Thus, for Balthasar, it is meaningless to have theology of beauty that does not have its foundation in Jesus Christ. Theological aesthetics for Balthasar is "a theology that does not primarily work with the extra-theological categories of a worldly philosophical aesthetics (above all poetry), but which develops its theory of beauty from the data of revelation itself with genuinely theological methods."[184]

This means that Balthasar's theology of the inner-worldly beauty of creation and art is a derivative concern of his theological aesthetics rather than a central concern.[185] However, Balthasar's theological aesthetics does have implications for inner-worldly beauty. His theological aesthetics, though focused on the spiritual beauty of the glory of God in Jesus Christ, demonstrates the corollary that it is possible for this glory to be expressed by means of worldly beauty. Jesus Christ revealed the essence of being as glory, particularly as a self-giving act of love of the triune God.[186] Balthasar's insistence on the Creator-creature distinction and the theophanic nature of creation allows the creature to enjoy the glory and mystery of Being without fear of idolatry.[187] The enchanting wonder of Being and its variety of expressions in inner-worldly beauty is a reception of God's gift and brings people into deeper relationship with Christ.

Balthasar's clearest treatment of how inner-worldly beauty relates to his theological aesthetics occurs in the first volume of the *Theo-Logic: Truth of the World*. Balthasar seeks to explain the relationship the perceiving subject has with the phenomenal images in the world. Balthasar notes

182. Viladesau, *Theological Aesthetics*, 30.
183. Balthasar, *GL* 1, 29.
184. Viladesau, *Theological Aesthetics*, 32.
185. Viladesau, *Theological Aesthetics*, 32.
186. Balthasar *GL* 7, 391.
187. Levering, *The Achievement of Hans Urs von Balthasar*, 194.

that the temptation is for the subject to project meaning onto all things, including the beautiful things, that he experiences in creation. He notes this is especially the case in rationalism and mysticism.[188] Significance and meaning do not lie in the subject's conceptions, but rather within the object itself. Yet the object, whatever it may be, a work of art or beauty in creation, is at once revealed to sense experience and is at the same time mysterious. It has significance, but its significance is in a sense a wordless and mysterious display of the splendor of Being. Balthasar notes, "The whole world of images that surrounds us is a single field of significations. Every flower we see is an expression, every landscape has its significance, every human or animal face speaks its wordless language."[189] This significance paradoxically defies the conceptual or interpretive analysis but also invites it. Balthasar says that the reason art and created beauty defies interpretive analysis is because mystery is an abiding property of truth and Being. The splendor of Being shines from the form of this beautiful entity and it is inherently mysterious.

Balthasar comes the closest to defining created beauty when he says, "Beauty is the aspect of truth that cannot be fit into any definition but can be apprehended only in direct intercourse with it."[190] He goes on to describe created beauty, "It is the inexplicable active irradiation of the center of being into the expressive surface of the image, an irradiation that reflects itself in the image and confers upon it a unity, fullness, and depth surpassing what the image as such contains." Beauty is primarily the event of the encounter of the sense (*Sinn*) of the subject and the image (*Bild*) of the beautiful object. In this event of encounter, the mysterious splendor of Being as God's gift of love radiates to and is received by the subject. Therefore, all created reality is inherently enchanted with the grandeur of God and every entity has an eternal and mysterious "more" that it reveals. Balthasar says this is the remedy for boredom. Once a beautiful entity is conceptually analyzed and categorized and is stripped of its mysterious splendor, it becomes inherently boring. However, if the essence of Being remains in the background of everything we encounter, every entity, even those that surround us daily, becomes a "perennially inexhaustible wonder."[191]

---

188. Balthasar, *TL* 1, 136.
189. Balthasar, *TL* 1, 140.
190. Balthasar, *TL* 1, 136.
191. Balthasar, *TL* 1, 143.

This does not mean that we merely live the life of the aesthete on the surface of things.[192] We live in "perennial inexhaustible wonder," but at the same time seek to understand the truth of the world considering the Word of God who reveals its ultimate meaning. Balthasar is arguing against a cheap interpretation of the mystery of Being that leads to boredom, rather than seeking to understand all of beauty in light of the self-giving mystery of the love of God in Christ. Because beauty is the gift of God, co-extensive with Being, beauty is "on every street corner."[193] It encompasses all entities, even the beholder, "Beauty's radiance overspreads all who behold it, just as the sun overspreads a landscape."[194] Beauty gives joy and is fundamentally communication between God and the human person. Because of this, beauty in creation can have either a material dimension or a dramatic dimension. Balthasar explains, "beauty can seem, from one point of view to consist entirely in measure, in proportion, in delimited form, as if the image, understood as the appearance of the essence, were its true home. But in the twinkling of an eye, beauty can also appear to consist essentially in movement, in the rhythm of communication itself." Beauty is the self-communicative gift of God. It is received as a gift.[195] This is another strength of Balthasar's theological aesthetics. His aesthetics has the movement of life within it, and he approaches all life as part of God's gift of Being and revelation. Theological aesthetics moves toward dramatic action in life.

## BALTHASAR'S CRITIQUE OF PROTESTANTISM IN CONTEXT

In light of Balthasar's metaphysics and theological aesthetics, it is now possible to understand his critique of Protestantism in context. Balthasar both appreciated and gave a resounding critique of Luther and Protestant Christianity. In chapter 6, I will evaluate Balthasar's understanding of Luther and Protestantism. Here I simply present Balthasar's interpretation of Luther and Protestant approaches to beauty.

---

192. Balthasar, *TL* 1, 144.
193. Balthasar, *TL* 1, 224.
194. Balthasar, *TL* 1, 224.
195. Balthasar, *TL* 1, 224.

Balthasar notes that Luther's approach to theology was fundamentally actualist, anti-contemplative, and anti-Catholic.[196] Luther's actualism and focus on the event of the cross would not allow for a systemizing or synthetic approach of the neo-Scholastics. Balthasar states that, for Luther, the Neo-Platonic scholastics aesthetically presented their intellectual schemas and thus emptied the cross of its folly and power.[197] Luther, therefore, would not allow harmonization or intellectual synthesis of revelation with the "whore Reason" and established a sharp dialectic between God and creation. This stance of Luther, Balthasar said, was a "cold methodological protest" that gave birth to schism after schism within Protestantism.[198] This stance also began the crusade of eliminating the aesthetic from theology and isolating the aesthetic dimension from logic (truth) and ethics (goodness). Kierkegaard furthered this insulation of beauty from truth and goodness by emphasizing interiority at the expense of the aesthetic. With Kierkegaard, the beautiful became opposed to the religious.[199] After Kierkegaard, 20th Century Protestantism continued this emphasis in the writings of Scheler, Brunner, Buber, and Bultmann. This was the case until Barth had to return to a pre-Reformation theology to develop a theological approach to beauty because it had no root in Protestant theology.

Balthasar's summary of the history of Protestant theology brings him to the point of his critique. Balthasar writes, "Contemporary Protestant theology nowhere deals with the beautiful as a theological category ... The only question posed by Protestants is that concerning the relationship between revelation and this worldly beauty—certainly a justified question, but not a sufficient one."[200] It is instructive to note that he does not criticize Protestants for their iconoclasm or their rejection of the arts. Balthasar's critique is not that art has been eradicated from Protestantism. His critique is that Protestantism does not have the theological foundations to understand beauty in any sense. He notes that when Protestants talk of beauty, they speak of "the relationship between revelation and this worldly beauty."[201] In other words, Balthasar saw that

196. Balthasar, *GL* 1, 45.
197. Balthasar, *GL* 1, 45.
198. Balthasar, *GL* 1, 49.
199. Balthasar, *GL* 1, 51.
200. Balthasar *GL* 1, 56–57.
201. "Dort wird das Schöne als eine theologische Kategorie nicht gesichtet, und es bleibt einstweilen bei der gewiss nicht unberechtigen, nur ungenügenden Fragstellung

Protestants do discuss the relationship of theology and the arts, but his criticism goes deeper. Protestants, he says, have no theology of beauty and have eliminated beauty from theology as superfluous and even dangerous. This has implications for theology itself as well as the relationship between theology and the arts. Balthasar notes, "Such elimination has meant, broadly, the expulsion of contemplation from the act of faith, the exclusion of 'seeing' from 'hearing', the removal of the *inchoatio visionis* from the *fides,* and the relegation of the Christian to the old age that is passing away."[202]

Protestants must evaluate whether Balthasar's criticism is justified. In chapter 2, I demonstrated that evangelical Protestants do have some aspects of a theology of beauty. However, it is underdeveloped when compared to the history of theology and Balthasar's theology of beauty. Considering chapter 2 and chapter 3, I agree with Barrett's assessment that, in spite of some bright spots such as Edwards and Wolterstorff, "theological reflection on the significance of aesthetic phenomena has usually been sporadic and often peripheral within the Protestant heritage."[203] This is especially the case when comparing it to Balthasar's robust theology of beauty. Barrett goes on to note, "The logic of Balthasar's work illustrates how theological aesthetics must inform and flow from the most basic dynamics of Christianity, rather than being a mere doctrinal appendage."[204] Developing the beginnings of an evangelical Protestant theological aesthetic through a synthesis of chapters 2–5 is the aim of chapters 6 and 7. At one level, Balthasar's critique of Protestantism is legitimate. However, Balthasar's theological aesthetics may assist in the development of evangelical Protestant aesthetics. This is due to what Barrett notes as some "family resemblances" between Balthasar and Protestantism that make his theology of beauty "amenable to Protestant appropriation," such as a high regard for Scripture, an epistemological priority of the *analogia fidei* to the *analogia entis,* a distinction between justification and sanctification, and the centrality of Christ's work on the cross.[205]

---

zwichen der Offenbarung und dem innerweltlichen Schönen, einer Fragestellung, zu der eine gewichtige protestantirche Stimme sich mit eigenartiger Antwort meldet" Balthasar, *Herrlichkeit* 1, 65..

202. Balthasar, *GL* 1, 70.
203. Barrett, "Von Balthasar and Protestant Aesthetics," 97.
204. Barrett, "Von Balthasar and Protestant Aesthetics," 97.
205. Barrett, "Von Balthasar and Protestant Aesthetics," 98.

## CONCLUSION

In this chapter, I presented an overview of Balthasar's theological aesthetics and answered the subsidiary question, "How does Balthasar's development of theological aesthetics explain his critique of the Protestant approach to beauty?" Beauty, for Balthasar, is a complex theological category intrinsically connected to his metaphysics of Being. I analyzed various aspects of Balthasar's theology of beauty as it relates to God and his action, transcendentals, Being, form and splendor, the form of Christ, and inner-worldly beauty. Balthasar's project is truly polyphonic in nature. He synthesizes and incorporates many systems of thought into his project, while at the same time critiquing the elements that contradict the revelation of Jesus Christ. This is seen in his synthesis of systems of thought such as existentialism, Neo-Platonism, transcendental idealism, realism, phenomenalism, and personalism. In order to appreciate Balthasar's synthesis, it is important to understand his appropriation and critique of these different systems of thought.

The most fundamental synthesis that Balthasar builds is his synthesis of foundational and dogmatic theology. Balthasar built this synthesis through his metaphysics, which he articulated through the fourfold distinction and the categories of Being and the transcendentals. However, his approach to theology is also existential as he desired to present theology as the human person experiences it. Balthasar's theology of form and splendor is the meeting place between his metaphysical categories of Being and the transcendentals and the subject's aesthetic existential perception of the form in vision and rapture. For Balthasar, the form of Jesus Christ is the primary form of theological aesthetics and is the place where God's self-giving, self-showing, and self-speaking are most clearly seen. When the perceiving subject sees this revelation, the subject-object distinction is maintained, but the perceiver experiences a rapture and transformation by this perception. This leads to a life of faith and glorification. I argued that this transformation leads into the theo-drama and theo-logic. For Balthasar, the life of the saint who is truly perceiving the form of Christ is itself a form of beauty.

Balthasar's project is refreshing in its emphasis on the essential elements of beauty and goodness in theology. Too often theology is only concerned with truth, while beauty and goodness are neglected. Theologians must take Balthasar's project seriously by allowing beauty and goodness to be restored to theology. While Balthasar's project is insightful and refreshing, his method of constructing a theology as the human subject experiences it makes his project complex and cryptic. One cannot fully grasp his project or method until the *Epilogue*, which was published at the end of his life in 1987. He was a theologian who approached the transcendentals and Being in an original way, but his vast output and synthesizing methodology conceal rather than reveal his most original contributions. I noted in this chapter that in addition to his methodology, one of the major weaknesses of Balthasar's project is an underdeveloped theology of sin and its effects on both creation and the individual person.

In the *Epilogue*, Balthasar says something that could be said of his whole theological project.[206] His work is like a bottle thrown into the sea and for someone to find it, it would be a miracle. Unfortunately, his main contributions often get lost in the sea of his work. However, what I have presented in this chapter is my attempt to situate his approach to beauty in the context of his understanding of God's revelation in Christ and the gift of Being and the transcendentals. The field of theological aesthetics would benefit from a deeper and more robust interaction with Balthasar's project. The strengths of his work are clearly seen in his developed metaphysics of Being and the transcendentals, the Creator-creature distinction, his detailed articulation of the nature of perception, and his Christ-centered foundation of beauty. Those engaged in the field of theological aesthetics cannot overlook his contribution.

Nichols argues that Balthasar's New Covenant theology is essentially a "Johannine Christology of glory."[207] The Apostle John's writings provide a summary of the Biblical approach to theological aesthetics. Therefore, the following chapter explores the John the Evangelist's theology of beauty, specifically as it relates to Jesus Christ, before moving to a synthesis and construction in chapter 6 and 7.

---

206. Balthasar, *Epilogue*, 11.
207. Nichols, *The Word Has Been Abroad*, 238.

# 5

# Beauty and Perception in John

In Balthasar's understanding, theological aesthetics is the study of the objective glory and beauty of God as well as the subjective perception of that glory and beauty. The Apostle John presents a theology of the objective glory of God as well as the subject's perception of glory. This chapter begins the construction of a biblical foundation for evangelical theological aesthetics.[1] In this chapter, I examine what the writings of John the Evangelist teach about the revelation of God's glory and true perception. Although this construction of the biblical teaching is preliminary in that it focuses on the theology of the John the Evangelist, John provides some of the clearest texts that deal with the motifs of theological aesthetics. Not only this, but John also takes up themes related to theological aesthetics developed in the Old Testament and interprets them considering the incarnation of Christ. While a further study may examine theological aesthetics from other passages of Scripture, we may be confident that studying the writings of John provides a solid foundation for the construction and synthesis in the two following chapters.

This chapter begins with the prologue of the Gospel of John (John 1:1–18), where John presents Jesus as related to all created reality. The incarnate Word is *the* revelation of God's glory, as well as the need for human perception of that glory. Indeed, the heart of theological aesthetics finds its expression in the pronouncement: "And the word became flesh and dwelt among us and we beheld His glory, glory as of the only begotten from the Father, full of grace and truth" (John 1:14).

---

1. For a broader overview, see Parkison, *To Gaze Upon God*, 22–60

Next, I examine the relationship of spiritual regeneration and perception of glory, especially as John develops it in John 3:1–15 and John 12:27–36. This is followed by a discussion of the nature of the glory of God from Jesus's High Priestly Prayer, with special emphasis on John 17:1–5. I then explore John's theology of witness and the relation of perception and belief from John 20:24–21. The conclusion of this chapter moves to John's eschatological conclusion in the book of Revelation. This section demonstrates the eschatological importance of the glory and beauty of the nations and created beauty as the nations bring their glory into the heavenly kingdom. This climactic text reveals the eschatological significance of theological aesthetics as well as general aesthetics for the glory of God. In the eternal state, the glory of God will be perceived and experienced in eschatological fullness and the materially beautiful will be redeemed and restored to its intended purpose. As a result, this chapter provides the groundwork for constructing evangelical theological aesthetics on the foundation of Scripture considering the current and historical context. John presents God's glory as most clearly revealed and demonstrated in the incarnation and the cross of Christ. However, aesthetic categories are essential in understanding this revelation of God's glory because it is a revelation in the flesh. Material creation is the context of this revelation and provides rich metaphors for understanding what happened in the incarnation. The theology of the incarnation can thus be approached and understood aesthetically. Furthermore, I argue that John the Evangelist has a theology of perception of the glory that indicates sensory perception is not sufficient in and of itself. Regeneration and the eyewitness accounts in Scripture are needed for true faith. Sensory perception of the incarnation and death of Christ by eyewitnesses was the necessary precondition for the spiritual perception of faith.

## THEOLOGICAL AESTHETICS AND JOHN'S PROLOGUE

### The Structure of the Prologue

D.A. Carson calls the prologue of John the "foyer" to the rest of the Gospel as it draws the reader in and introduces the main themes of the book.[2] The prologue functions as a hermeneutical key for the gospel, and many

---

2. Carson, *The Gospel of John*, 111.

themes and motifs that John introduces in the prologue are developed later in the Gospel.³ For the purposes here, I highlight the motifs that have a bearing on theological aesthetics that are found within the structure of the prologue itself.

Since Jerome, the traditional structure of the prologue is considered John 1:1–18.⁴ This is reinforced by the *inclusio* of verses 1 and 18 that focuses on the Logos and his divinity and relationship with the Father. The prologue relates to the themes of theological aesthetics in the following ways: (1) the creation of the world and how it relates to Jesus Christ, (2) the incarnation of Jesus as the manifestation of the glory of God, (3) the beholding of Christ and becoming children of God, and (4) the witness and signs pointing to Jesus Christ. These four themes will be presented thematically from John 1:1–18 rather than verse by verse.

## The Word and Creation

John opens the prologue to his Gospel with an allusion to the opening chapters of Genesis. John's reference to the creation of the world is unique among the Gospels. With this reference to creation, John reminds his reader of the creation event with the purpose of revealing more about this event. Creation is now looked at through the lens of further revelation and given new meaning, a meaning that was there all along but had been hidden until now. This new revelation would have been surprising to John's first readers who would have been expecting "In the beginning *God*," but instead says, "In the beginning was the *Word*." John 1:1 clearly echoes Genesis 1:1.⁵ The Gospel of John develops the trinitarian doctrine that is introduced in this passage. John introduces us to the personified Word who is both identified with God and was with God.⁶

Much has been written about why John uses λόγος ("Word") to designate the one who was "with God and was God." Miller lists nine different potential sources for John's choice of this word.⁷ However, Carson is most likely right to emphasize that the primary source was the Hebrew Old Testament Bible because of the Old Testament echoes and

---

3. Romanowski, "When the Son of Man is Lifted Up," 101.
4. Carson, *The Gospel of John*, 113.
5. Culpepper, *Designs for the Church in the Gospel of John*, 303.
6. Holmes, *The Quest for the Trinity*, 53.
7. Millar, "The Johannine Origins of the Johannine Logos," 448–49.

allusions in this section.⁸ Craig Keener follows this line of thinking and specifically builds on the verbal association of λόγος to the Old Testament Torah, God's Word, and the wisdom tradition.⁹ He argues that John's presentation of Jesus as the λόγος establishes Jesus as the embodiment of Torah and Wisdom. Although the Old Testament is most likely the primary source for the use of this word, it seems possible that John may have had the Stoic idea and the wisdom tradition in mind as well.¹⁰ In the Stoic understanding, the λόγος is the "universal reason at work in the world as well as the rational order that bound the cosmos together."¹¹ This is congruent with a wisdom Christology that sees a connection with the Word and his creative activity and the activity of Lady Wisdom in Proverbs 8. Even though this cannot be proven, especially considering the lack of Wisdom terminology in John, there are recognizable parallels between the Stoic λόγος and the Wisdom tradition and the activity of the Word.¹²

The activity of the personified and divine λόγος is described in John 1:3–5. John 1:3 is very emphatic, captured by the NASB: "All things came into being through Him, and apart from Him not even one thing came into being that has come into being." Thomas notes that this is Greco-Roman Jewish monotheistic language that establishes the status of the Son as the one God who is the sovereign creator over all things.¹³ John first states the positive assertion that everything was generated through him and then reaffirms with the parallel negative statement that nothing was made without him.¹⁴ Keener notes that everything was not only created by the Word, who was God's Wisdom and the source of Torah, but also sustained by this personified Word, Wisdom, and Torah.¹⁵ Just as

8. Keener, *The Gospel of John*, 115.
9. Keener, *The Gospel of John*, 360–63.
10. Thomas, *John*, 28.
11. Kling, "Wisdom Became Flesh," 186.
12. Carson, *The Gospel of John*, 115.
13. Thomas, *John*, 29.
14. The use of πάντα is anarthrous, emphasizing each individual thing as opposed to the usages in Colossians 1:20 and Ephesians 1:10 where the article is used and the whole of creation is in view. McHugh 2009, 11. The aorist ἐγένετο emphasizes the decisive act of creation while the perfect ὃ γέγονεν, "has been made," highlights the abiding effect of this creation. The use of the perfect infers that ὁ λόγος created things with an abiding structure and may allude to the fact that the Logos also upholds all things (Heb 1:3).
15. Keener, *The Gospel of John*, 380.

God created the world and brought life and light, so now the Logos will enter the world and bring light and life to the spiritual darkness.[16]

For theological aesthetics, the implication is that all of creation must be understood considering this Logos, through whom the world was created. General aesthetics and an understanding of this world are simply not enough. Theology is needed to establish a theological aesthetics that perceives the world in reference to Jesus Christ. John is presenting a new way of perceiving the world theologically and aesthetically through Jesus Christ. The Logos, therefore, is the key to true perception. In this text, John is not simply explaining how the world was created. This text has teleological and epistemological implications. The thrust of this text is that creation can only find its true meaning in reference to the Logos. God created everything through the Logos and designed that all things relate to him.[17] Structurally and objectively, everything within creation and creation depends on him for its existence and purpose.

This is emphasized in verse 4 and 5, which bring in the metaphors of life and light to explain the continued relationship that the Logos has with his creation. John uses these metaphors to emphasize the Logos is the source of light and life for creation and in a way that anticipates salvation. What Carson says of verse 5 is true of both these verses, "it is a masterpiece of planned ambiguity."[18] Those who would read this text without knowledge of the Gospel would think that this refers exclusively to creation. John intentionally alludes to the creation of light and life in Genesis 1 to explain the activity of the Word in his incarnation and the event of New Creation.[19] This is the genius of the prologue: all of creation is gathered up and find its meaning in the salvation of Jesus Christ. The Logos was the source of life (ἐν αὐτῷ ζωὴ ἦν) in creation, in a way that would be revealed more clearly in salvation. The pre-incarnate Christ, the Logos, is the life giver and the one who sustains the life of humanity, and this anticipates the fact that the spiritual life of humanity after the fall will only be found again in him. Therefore, the Logos is the source of physical, eternal, and physical life. "This life," John says in 1:4b, is the life and light of all humanity.[20] The Logos is the source of light for creation, and this anticipates the light that will shine in the spiritual darkness. John

16. Thomas, *John*, 29.
17. Morris, *The Gospel According to John*, 71.
18. Carson, *The Gospel of John*, 115.
19. Keener, *The Gospel of John*, 385–386.
20.. Τῶν ἀνθρώπων is generic. Harris, *John*, 23.

masterfully brings both creation and redemption together in this text and emphasizes that they can only be understood Christologically.

This reinforces the implications for theological aesthetics. All of creation finds its meaning and purpose in Jesus Christ. In a limited way, nature or creation enables people to understand aspects of God's character and activity. Creation is created and upheld by the Logos and provides metaphors for understanding spiritual realities. John's use of life and light emphasize that the source of these created things was the pre-incarnate Christ, but also that these were created with the capacity to be metaphors or signs that point to deeper realities. Thus, John sets the stage for his Gospel in the midst of creation and explains the existence and meaning of creation through the Word and uses creation metaphors to explain truths about that Word. In other words, the Word explains creation, and creation can be used as a metaphor to explain and reveal truths about him. The world finds its source and purpose in the Logos and aspects of the world become symbols and signs that point to him. The planned ambiguity or anticipation of these verses,[21] is also a planned ambiguity and anticipation inherent in the creation act. The purpose of creation was a mystery that waited and anticipated the day when the Word would reveal it. In his prologue, John captures the planned ambiguity and anticipation inherent in all of creation before the New Covenant. Yet, even in the intentional ambiguity of these first few verses, he hints that the resolution is found within the Word. As the text progresses, the planned ambiguity and anticipation continues until the clarity of verses 9–14 and 16–18.

## The Aesthetics of God's Glory and the Incarnation of the Word

John continues his use of the metaphor of light in verses 9–14 and 16–18. These verses summarize what will be revealed fully in the Gospel of John. In John 1:5, this light continually and presently shines in the darkness. The Logos not only has life, which is light for men (John 1:5), but he is the "genuine," "authentic," or "true" light that was coming into the world. Again, for first time readers, the nature of this light is shrouded in ambiguity. In verse 10, the clarity begins that will resound in verse 14. The Light is personified and was in the world, even though the world was made through him. The phrase δι' αὐτοῦ ἐγένετο, rendered as, "was

---

21. Carson, *The Gospel of John*, 115.

made through him," echoes back to verse 3 and hints that the identity of this light is the same as the Logos.

John 1:10–11 expands on the theme developed in 1:5.[22] Even though he is the creator of the world and the One who "gives light to everyone," the world did not know him, and his own people did not receive him. Herman Ridderbos notes that in the Gospel of John the "world" has a dual meaning. The first meaning is that the Logos has entered his creation, the human world, "that belongs to God and alongside God, the object of God's love (cf. 3:16)."[23] The second meaning of "world" is estranged humanity apart from God. The Logos/Light was shining in this world, and yet humanity, and even his own people (John 1:11), did not know or receive this light. In verse 11, the second use of καί is adversative, emphasizing that despite the Logos's creation of the world, giving of light, and coming to his own, they still did not receive him. The Light's incarnation and spiritual shining in the darkness creates the irony that the light is shining yet people are still in spiritual darkness.[24] Although this Logos/Light is the source of creation and physical light and people only have life in him, the world cannot see or receive his spiritual light. Thus, even though creation finds its true meaning in the Logos, those in spiritual darkness only stay on the surface of things.

However, these verses reveal creation is the context for the New Creation. Creation is a sign and symbol of New Creation realities. Humanity's rejection of the Word is ironic because they want to receive from him light and life and the blessings of creation, but, for the most part, do not want to press through to deeper New Creation realities. Light is a metaphor for God's glory (John 1:14; Revelation 18:1; 21:23).[25] People gladly receive physical light from God but will not receive the spiritual light of God's glory, which the physical light points to. This

---

22. The darkness, humanity's blindness or willful evil, does not κατέλαβεν the light. This aorist active form of καταλαμβάνω either means "overcome" or "overpower" (ESV, RSV, CSB), or "understood" or "comprehend" (NASB, NIV, NKJV). The darkness, words, does not overtake this light. Barrett catches these meanings with his translation, "The darkness neither understood nor quenched the light." Barrett, *The Gospel According to St. John*, 158.

23. Ridderbos, *The Gospel According to John*, 44.

24. Verse 10 emphasizes that the world did not "know" the light with the use of the aorist form of γινώσκω. This is possibly an ingressive "did not begin to recognize," but more likely constative "did not know" emphasizing either a failure or refusal to know the light. Harris, *John*, 30.

25. Keener, *The Gospel of John*, 385.

dynamic is seen at other instances in the book of John. It is Jesus's point in John 6:26, when he says, "You are not seeking me because you saw the signs, but because you ate your fill of the loaves." Jesus is the bread of life (John 6:35), but the world only wants the physical bread to fill their physical bodies. All of creation is meant to point to the Logos who is the light (John 8:12–30), the life (John 11:17–27), the bread of life (John 3:26–35), the door (John 10:1–18), the true vine (John 15:1–6). Humanity enjoys creation and rejects the one who created it and to whom it refers (John 3:19–20).

The tendency to stay on the merely physical demonstrates the usefulness of theological aesthetics to complement general aesthetic theory to move toward the source and true meaning of creation and its beauty. If one merely stays at the level of general aesthetics and art, the meaning and purposes of beauty and creation allude the grasp. Theological aesthetics provides a framework to understand the purpose and nature of beauty and art revealed in creation in a Christ-centered way. The Gospel of John provides exegetical warrant and even a moral imperative for going deeper into the nature of created beauty than general aesthetics does to reveal the Logos as the source, meaning, and purpose of all created beauty. Creation and created beauty simply cannot be understood or truly enjoyed apart from the Logos. The Gospel of John also gives warrant for seeing created reality as revelatory in that it provides metaphors for understanding Christ.

In John 1:14, the ambiguity and anticipation of the previous verses breaks forth into a clear statement, "And the Word became flesh and dwelt among us, and we have seen his glory, glory as of the only Son from the Father, full of grace and truth." In this verse, there are three stages. The first is the event of the Word becoming flesh and dwelling with humanity. Secondly, the result of this action of the Word is the beholding of glory (δόξα). I examine this in a following section, along with verses 12–13. Thirdly, John explains the nature of this glory was δόξαν ὡς μονογενοῦς παρὰ πατρός, πλήρης χάριτος καὶ ἀληθείας, meaning, "glory as of the unique Son from the Father, full of grace and truth."[26]

Up to this point, the focus is on the divine nature of the Word, his activity in creation and the Word's identity as the light of the world. In verse 14, John turns to identify this Word with Jesus of Nazareth.[27] The

---

26. Translation mine.
27. Ridderbos, *The Gospel According to John*, 49.

Word became flesh.[28] In other words, Jesus was truly flesh, just as the rest of humanity. "Flesh" is the material side of creaturely existence. It is shocking that John uses the word σὰρξ (flesh), rather than ἄνθρωπος (man) or σῶμα (body).[29] The use of "flesh" emphasizes the materiality of the Word in the face of the heresy of Docetism, which argued that it only seemed like Christ was truly man. In response to this heresy, John is clear that the Word became flesh and truly human. John would later emphasize this in 1 John 4:2, "By this you know the Spirit of God: every spirit that confesses that Jesus Christ has come in the flesh is from God." John emphasizes the materiality, the *flesh*, of the Word.

The fact that the Word, who was God, and the life and light of men, became flesh is an eternal wonder. The incarnation has profound implications for theological and general aesthetics that cannot be overstated. It is in this flesh, this material side of creaturely existence, that the glory of God was put on display. Ridderbos explains, "The flesh is the medium of the glory and makes it visible to all people... the entire Gospel of John is proof of it: proof of that abundant glory, a glory manifested before the eyes of all."[30] In other words, the flesh was the medium that revealed the glory.[31] Because of God's creation of the material and because the Word was God enfleshed, we should note that the material creation is the place where humanity should expect to encounter the glory of God. The creation of the world and the incarnation enchants all of reality with wonder and glory. Because John made creation the context for the incarnation, it is right to speak of the world as the theater of God's glory that is itself glorious. Not only that, but the stage of creation also has its own glory because it was made to reveal and be the stage upon which the drama of the incarnation was revealed. The theater context itself as well as the drama on the stage, especially in the climax of the incarnation, reveals the glory of God.

The Word became flesh and answered the longing of the human heart to see the glory of God. The drama of the Old Testament was bursting with anticipation of the climactic revelation of the glory of God. John

---

28. In this passage, σὰρξ (flesh) is an anarthrous qualitative predicate nominative and indicates that Jesus did not become "*the* flesh" or "*a* flesh," but highlights the qualitative nature of Jesus's flesh. Wallace, *Greek Grammar*, 264.

29. MacLeod, "The Incarnation of the Word, 74.

30. Ridderbos, *The Gospel According to John*, 49.

31. Bultmann, *The Gospel of John*, 63.

1:14 has conceptual echoes from Exodus 33–34.[32] Moses's request to see God's glory (Exodus 33:18), has now been decisively answered in Jesus Christ. Therefore "grace and truth" and "grace upon grace" have been seen in Jesus Christ. The revelation of the glory of God is full of grace and truth and is now clearly on display. Ardel Caneday explains, "the grace of the law mediated through Moses (διὰ Μωϋσέως ἐδόθη) found its fulfillment and replacement in the grace (χάριν ἀντὶ χάριτος, 1:16) that came through Jesus Christ."[33] Just as the glory of God has been revealed in the flesh of the Word, so also grace and truth have become incarnate. Because of the conceptual echoes of Exodus 33–34, it is no surprise that John uses the phrase, ἐσκήνωσεν ἐν ἡμῖν ("dwelt among us").[34] The link with the tabernacle is significant. The Logos became flesh and "pitched his tent among us" or "tabernacled among us."[35] The tabernacle, and later the temple that replaced it, has profound implications for aesthetics and becomes a point of intersection between aesthetics and theological aesthetics.

In a study on the aesthetics of the tabernacle, Maurice Schmidt notes that in the Israelite mindset, the aesthetic adorns what is truly precious. He explains, "The beauty of things is an antechamber, a vestibule, a veil or covering, a garment covering something still more precious."[36] Yet, the tabernacle was a majestic display of beauty. It was a work of visual art that symbolized through the relationships of form, space, and color.[37] Like the holy garments designed for the High Priest, the tabernacle was constructed for the purpose of displaying "glory and beauty" (Exodus 28:2; cf., Exodus 25:2–8). The tabernacle was a work of art that symbolized the heavenly sanctuary.[38] The tabernacle was to be mobile so that God's glorious presence would go with Israel. When John says the Word "pitched his tent among us," he was recalling the glory of God that dwelt among Israel in the tabernacle and later the temple. After the completion of the

---

32. Caneday, "Glory Veiled in the Tabernacle of Flesh," 58.

33. Caneday, "Glory Veiled in the Tabernacle of Flesh," 60.

34. The aorist active verb ἐσκήνωσεν comes from the form σκηνόω, which means "to live in a tent [σκηνή]." Harris, *John*, 35. Therefore, the word ἐσκήνωσεν is related to the word for tent (σκηνή) which recalls one of the names for the Tabernacle (Exodus 25:9). Janzen, "The Scope of the High Priestly Prayer in John 17," 2.

35. Beale and Kim, *God Dwells Among Us*, 82.

36. Schmidt, *The Tabernacle as a Work of Art*, 11.

37. Schmidt, *The Tabernacle as a Work of Art*, 35.

38. Beale, *The Temple and the Church's Mission*, 373.

Tabernacle, God's glory visibly filled the tabernacle (Exodus 40:34–35). Here, John's allusion to the tabernacle shows that the incarnate Word is now the place where God dwells among us and the place, we should expect to see God's glory. In the Old Testament, the Holy of Holies was filled with the presence of God, but now God's presence is mediated through Jesus and the glory of God breaks into the world through him.[39] That Jesus is the fulfillment of the tabernacle and temple and the place where God's presence and glory dwell is a motif in the Gospel of John.[40] Jesus's fulfillment of the tabernacle and temple would have been well understood by a Jewish audience.

John emphasizes that the glory revealed in the becoming flesh of the Word is the glory of the Son from the Father. It is here where the Trinitarian implications of verse 2 are more fully developed. In the Farewell Discourse, John will include the Holy Spirit in his trinitarian discussion, but in the prologue, he focusses on the relationship of the Father and Son. The Word is the Son who was God himself and was with God, the Father. The nature of the glory revealed in the Word becoming flesh is a trinitarian glory. The phrase ὡς μονογενοῦς παρὰ πατρός (as the unique Son from the Father) introduces this Father and Son relationship. Etymologically, "Μονογενής" (unique) is from μόνος + γενής and has a familial meaning indicating the only child in a family.[41] It indicates the special relationship between the Father and his "one and only" or "unique" Son.[42] This uniqueness in this context highlights the uniqueness of Jesus's manifestation of glory as the μονογενής. Like the relationship between the Father and the Son, the glory in the incarnation of the Word is a μονογενής manifestation, meaning a one and only type of glory. This manifestation of glory is unique, in a category of its own set apart from all general creation displays of God's glory, but it is also preeminent in the clarity of its manifestation. No other revelation of glory is this clear. Therefore, the allusion to the tabernacle indicates that the glory of God dwelling on the tabernacle was in a sense a lesser glory that pointed forward to the glory of the incarnate Word.

---

39. Beale and Kim, *God Dwells Among Us*, 82.
40. Attridge, "Temple, Tabernacle, Time, and Space," 261–69.
41. Harris, *John*, 35.
42. Carson, *The Gospel of John*, 128. This does not contradict, but rather establishes the doctrine of eternal generation. The eternal generation is the basis of the Son's uniqueness.

The clarity of the glory of God preeminently revealed in the μονογενής is important to remember in discussing the relationship of theological aesthetics and the beauty of created reality. The beauty of creation and the arts indeed may reveal the glory of God, but only in a secondary way. The only one who perfectly reveals the glory of God is the unique and only Son of the Father. Any beauty that supplants the glory of Jesus Christ in the affections of the beholder is inherently idolatry. All earthly beauty that reveals the glory of God reveals the glory of God only as it relates to Jesus Christ. This is because of the metaphysical reality that Jesus is the μονογενής. Therefore, experiences of transcendent beauty are ultimately Christological rather than simply referring to a nebulous and undefined transcendent experience. The truth that Jesus is the only one from the Father provides the basis for the truth that beauty reveals transcendent and sublime truths that ultimately find content and meaning in Jesus Christ as the revealer of the triune God.

The greater glory of the incarnate Word is also the point of verses 15–17. The incarnate Word is greater than John the Baptist, Moses, and the law. In the Word, in Jesus Christ, the fullness (πλήρωμα) of the glory of God is manifested and received. This use of πλήρωμα has both a passive and active meaning. It is passive in that Jesus's fullness is a fullness from the Father. This fullness is such that it is a perfect representation and image of the Father's own fullness. Yet, at the same time the fullness is actively pouring out and filling creation and people with grace. It is not a simple replacement, but a renewing and distribution of a greater grace than the grace that was found in Moses and the Law.[43] Schmidt describes the aesthetics of the tabernacle as an "antechamber, a vestibule, a veil or covering, a garment covering something still more precious."[44] The Apostle John is clear that Jesus Christ, the incarnate Word is the "still more precious" beauty that the tabernacle and the Old Testament pointed to. The symbol of the Old Covenant, though beauty and grace, is now superseded by the fullness.

John then moves to show the uniqueness of the trinitarian glory revealed in Jesus Christ: "No one has ever seen God; the only God, who is at the Father's side, he has made him known" (1:18). This verse further explains the nature of the glory that was made manifest. It emphasizes the fact that no one has seen God with the perfect form of ὁράω and

---

43. Keener, *The Gospel of John*, 420.
44. Schmidt, *The Tabernacle as a Work of Art*, 11.

the emphatic adverb πώποτε, meaning, "at any time." John is ironic in this statement because the context has spoken of both Moses and the tabernacle. Moses was one who saw a glimpse of God's glory and the tabernacle was the place where God's glory was seen. Yet, there was a provisional and limited nature of the Old Covenant manifestations. This verse stresses both the divinity of the Son as well as his relation to the Father. The unique Son who is only God, has a unique intimacy with the Father. Later in the Gospel, this eternal relationship of intimacy is described as "glory" (δόξα; John 17:5). Sinclair Ferguson describes the glory of this relations, "Only the Son (always in and with the Spirit) is able to love in return with an intensity that preserves him from being consumed by the holiness of the Father."[45] The one who lived in this eternal triune relation with the Father became flesh. He revealed God and his glory in an unprecedented way. Verse 18 reinforces and intensifies John's claim, "we have seen his glory, glory as of the only Son from the Father" (1:14).

For theological aesthetics, the previous section noted the implications of Christology for all of creation. Creation finds its source and meaning in the Logos, who became Jesus Christ of Nazareth. While the previous section has implications for creation in general, this section highlights that the glory of God is manifested most clearly in Jesus of Nazareth. The Logos became material flesh and in this flesh the glory of God was manifested. This is ironic because while the tabernacle manifested the beauty and glory of God aesthetically, Jesus Christ manifested the glory of God in a hidden way. The dialectic of the glory of God manifest, yet hidden in the humility of flesh, is developed through the Gospel of John. Jesus has made the glory of God known as the unique and only Son in whom the fullness of God dwells. Theological aesthetics must see the world in light of Christ and see the pinnacle of the glory of God in Christ himself. Theological aesthetics and its relation to general aesthetics must take into consideration that the Son is the μονογενής and thus reveals the glory and beauty of God in a unique and unprecedented way. The last word of the prologue opens the way for us to read the rest of the Gospel of John and look at the life of Christ as the manifestation of the one who has made God the Father and his glory known.

---

45. Ferguson, *Some Pastors and Teachers*, 456. It is here that we must be extremely cautious not to fall into any sort of social trinitarianism. Yet, at the same time, even Augustine (*On the Trinity* XV.7) and Aquinas (*ST* 1.37.2) were comfortable speaking of a sense in which the persons of the Trinity share a mutual love in some sense.

## True Perception and Beholding the Glory

The previous two sections expounded on the objective aspects of God's glory. The glory of God is seen most clearly in Jesus Christ, the Word become flesh. This glory also reveals a trinitarian glory and is revealed in the context of material creation. Creation itself was the work of God and it anticipated the clear revelation of the glory of God in our midst. The clarity of the manifestation of the objective revelation of God among humanity invites people to perceive and respond to this glory. In John 1:12–14, perception and faith are introduced as a key motif developed in the Gospel of John.

The phrase "No one has ever seen God" (John 1:18) poses a problem for theological aesthetics. God's invisibility would make *seeing* God impossible. However, the Son alone sees God the Father and it is because of the Son's relation with God that he can manifest the Father.[46] Thomas points this out and says that Jesus is the unique "eyewitness" of the Father. Because of the Son's direct, eternal, and unmediated vision of the Father, not to mention possessing the same essence, the Son is in the unique place of displaying the Father perfectly in the flesh.[47] Therefore, Jesus manifested God from within creation to the senses. He who saw the Father eternally, now allows others to look on him in the flesh and see the invisible God manifested (John 14:8–9). The Gospel of John emphasizes sight and eyewitnesses because the invisible God has now become perceptible. The incarnation made speaking of theological aesthetics a theological possibility. John 1:14 indicates this by the pronouncement that the result of the incarnation of the Word is that we have *seen* God's glory (ἐθεασάμεθα τὴν δόξαν αὐτοῦ). Thomson notes that this first reference to sight in the Gospel of John is significant because it theologically identifies the Word with Jesus Christ.[48] The Word and glory of God is *perceived* in the flesh in Jesus of Nazareth. It is not simply that the glory of God was objectively manifested and displayed, John also wants to emphasize the subject's perception of that glory.

John the Evangelist makes a similar statement to John 1:14 in 1 John 1:1, "That which was from the beginning, which we have heard, which we have seen with our eyes, which we looked upon and have touched

---

46. Holmes, *The Quest for the Trinity*, 52.
47. Thomas, *John*, 35.
48. Thomas, *John*, 33.

with our hands, concerning the word of life."⁴⁹ John's polemic against Docetism and Gnosticism on the flesh of Jesus emphasizes the physicality of the incarnation and uses the senses to prove his point. Dorothy Lee explains John's use of the five senses in his Gospel.⁵⁰ She argues that the Gospel of John emphasizes the use of the senses to demonstrate the physical fact of the incarnation. This is seen in the materiality of the incarnation as well as the various metaphors and images John uses to describe Jesus. However, the most significant sense utilized by the Gospel of John is sight.⁵¹ The usages of words indicating sight or perception throughout the Gospel. Likewise, the commands to "behold" Jesus in the Gospel is the call to perceive him (John 1:29, 36, 12:15). These commands allude to John 1:14 and remind the reader that in Jesus the invisible God has been made visible (John 1:18; 5:37; 6:46; 14:7–9).

The prologue not only deals with the objective manifestation of the glory of God in Christ, but verses 10–13 also explains two different types of perception of the glory of God in the flesh of Jesus Christ. Verse 9 and 14 describe the fact of the incarnation and declare that "we have seen his glory." John uses the first-person plural, "we," to indicate that the believing community are the ones who have truly seen the glory of God in Christ.⁵² Those outside of the community refused to receive him and did not see his glory, even though it was in the world.

Verses 10–13 describe these two types of sight, one of believers and one of unbelievers. Verses 10–11 demonstrate that even though the Logos/Light was in the world, the world did not know or receive him. The fact that the Light was in the world (ἐν τῷ κόσμῳ ἦν), emphasized by the participle ἦν, is explained by verse 14 and the statement that the "Word became flesh." Yet, the irony is that even though the Logos/Light was in the world and created the world, the world did not know him. Here, the knowledge implies a true knowing. The world perceived him and saw him, but they did not know him. This indicates that mere physical perception is not enough. The mere sight of the Logos/Light in the flesh is not sufficient. A true knowledge that brings about belief is what is needed.

---

49. John uses the same word in the aorist first person plural (ἐθεασάμεθα, "we have seen").
50. Lee, "The Gospel of John and the Five Senses," 115.
51. Lee, "The Gospel of John and the Five Senses," 117.
52. Lee, "The Gospel of John and the Five Senses," 117.

Verse 11 goes on to intensify the statement that the world did not know the Logos/Light. It was not only the general world that did not know him, but his own people did not receive him.[53] This intensification highlights the hiddenness and the concealment of the manifest glory, but also fallen nature of the world (and particularly the Israelite nation of John's day). This dynamic is developed further in John 3:16–21. John 3:19 echoes 1:11 with the statement that the light has come into the world but gives a further explanation why his own people did not come to the light. John explains, "The light has come into the world, and the people loved the darkness rather than the light because their works were evil. For everyone who does wicked things hate the light and does not come to the light, lest his works should be exposed" (John 3:18–20). The refusal to know and receive is an affectional refusal. The glory was manifested and seen but it was not known or received because of the hatred of the light.

On the other hand, verse 12–13 describes the opposite response of those who received him. The ones who do receive the Christ are those who have been given the authority to become the children of God. The word ἐξουσίαν can be translated "right," "freedom," or "authority."[54] This emphasizes a granted authority or freedom that no human effort can produce. God is the only one who can grant this. Those who receive Christ and become his children are described as those who believe in the name of Jesus. The change to the present tense in the verb "believe" (πιστεύουσιν) emphasizes that this is a present reality for any person who responds to Jesus by believing. The reception of Jesus happens at belief.[55]

For the purposes of this study, it is crucial to note that there is a parallel between those who receive Christ, believe in his name, and are born of God. This is contrasted with those who did not know him, did not receive him, and merely operate at the level of natural human existence. Natural human existence is indicated by being born of "blood," "the will of flesh," and the "will of man." The use of σαρκὸς (flesh) in this passage is instructive because, as I noted in the discussion in the previous section, Word became flesh. "Flesh" in this verse indicates that simply being in the flesh and the desiring of the flesh is not sufficient for producing the

---

53. The aorist active indicative παρέλαβον is a constative aorist that sums up the reception, or lack of reception, that Jesus experienced in his lifetime. Harris, *John*, 30.

54. Keener, *The Gospel of John*, 403.

55. Cornelia van Deventer demonstrates John's complex use of the concept of belief throughout this Gospel, which invites the reader to participate in the mosaic of belief in Christ. van Deventer, "The Mosaic of Belief in the Fourth Gospel," 165.

kind of belief and spiritual perception that is needed to be children of God. The flesh is not sufficient in itself for spiritual insight. Regeneration, being born of God, is needed to believe and receive Christ. In theological aesthetics terminology, true perception of Christ and his glory has the prerequisite of being born of God. This is crucial because it shows that materiality and creation are a prerequisite, but not sufficient for God's purpose for humanity. Being born of God thus enables one to perceive Christ rightly, not merely with physical eyes, but with the eyes of faith. These are the ones who can truly see and perceive the manifested glory of God in Christ.

## The Function of Witness and Created Signs and Symbols

John 1:6–8, 15 introduce the concept of the witness of John that is further explained in 1:19–34. John the Baptizer is presented as the paradigmatic witness to Jesus. He testifies with the purpose that all might believe through him (1:7). John testifies in order that spiritual perception of Christ through faith might happen by means of his witness. It is ironic that John is testifying about the Light (1:7). The Apostle's irony here is that the Light should be self-evident and have no need of witness and testimony. However, the darkness's hatred of the light and the spiritual blindness necessitated a testimony.

For theological aesthetics and the intersection with created beauty and the arts, this passage shows that created beauty itself is not enough to cause true spiritual perception. Created beauty and the arts may refer to God and even testify about God, but they must include verbal testimony for true spiritual perception of the Christ to begin. In other words, encountering beauty, even if its source is God, is not salvific. It must include positive content about the message of Jesus Christ. Mere apophatic experiences are not enough to produce children of God. The cataphatic must be included as it is the content of the witness of the Gospel that allows people to spiritually perceive Jesus Christ.

In verse 15, John the Baptist is portrayed as continuing his testimony about Jesus.[56] John's testimony of Jesus continues into the present day through the Gospel account of the Apostle John. John's voice testifies and cries out into the present-day calling people to behold the Lamb (1:36)

---

56. The hendiadys "testifies" and "cries out," are, respectively, a historic present (μαρτυρεῖ) and stative perfect (κέκραγεν) that dramatically portrays John the Baptist's continued testimony into the present day. Carson, *The Gospel of John*, 130. Ridderbos, *The Gospel According to John*, 55.

and believe in him. This is a crucial concept for theological aesthetics because Christ is both presented and testified to by the Scriptures. Through the act of hearing or reading John's testimony about Jesus, it is as if the voice of the prophet is still crying out. The same is true of the perception of Christ. Through the eyewitness accounts of the Apostle John and the other gospels, indeed all the Scriptures, Jesus Christ is presented vividly and dramatically. The testimony of Scripture gives a type of perception of Christ by faith. In the testimony of John the Baptist and John the Apostle, we not only hear their active and continued witness about the Christ, but Christ is spiritually presented to the eyes of the heart calling for the belief of reception of Christ. The biblical witness allows a spiritual perception of Christ.

In interpreting and demonstrating the text, an untapped resource in the history of interpretation is an exploration into how artists have portrayed the text through visual exegesis.[57] While there are limits and even dangers to visual exegesis, artists can present a powerful interpretation of the text of Scripture that commentaries may miss. Like commentaries, works of art can misinterpret the subject or limit the meaning of the text by the individual painter's particularity.[58] However, when it comes to considering the witness of John the Baptist, the work of Mattias Grünewald in portraying John in the *Isenheim Altarpiece* is a brilliant work of visual exegesis of John 1:6–8 that enriches the interpretation of the text.[59] Grünewald's portrayal of John is a prime example of visual exegesis that "can broaden the viewer's knowledge and transform or intensify his or her vision of the subject."[60] John is enraptured in unrelenting and focused witness. In the scene, John is portrayed in a way that is detached from the action of the rest of the scene. While Jesus Christ dies, those to the left of the cross are caught up in the agony of grief over the crucified Messiah. However, John simply stands and witnesses in a timeless way. Grünewald thus captured John the Apostle's vision of John as witness who testified about the Christ. John is surrounded with other symbols that he takes up and explains. Most notably, the lamb next to John symbolizes the sacrificial system and reminds of John's witness, "Behold, the Lamb of God who takes away the sin of the world" (John 1:29). John also holds a book that symbolizes the Old Testament Scriptures. Grünewald thus identifies John

---

57. O'Kane "The Artist as Reader of the Bible, 338.
58. O'Kane "The Artist as Reader of the Bible, 373.
59. See the image in the previous chapter.
60. O'Kane "The Artist as Reader of the Bible, 372.

with the Scriptures in their pointing to Christ. In the prologue of John, the Old Testament is also symbolized in John. John is put in a parallel explanatory relationship with Moses in verses 15–17. In this way, John is both a bridge from the Old Covenant to the New, but in such a way that he carries into himself all of grace of the Old Covenant, the Law, and Moses and points to and testifies of the "higher" grace of Christ who existed before. Grünewald's hermeneutical aesthetics demonstrate John's action of timeless, unrelenting witness and his relation to the sacrificial system and the Old Testament Scriptures.

The prologue has profound implications for the theology of perception and its relation to Christology. It clear that the Logos became flesh and was presented to the senses. Yet, it is also clear that mere sight or perception is not enough. Accompanying the perception of Jesus must also be a corresponding knowledge and reception of Jesus. This has implications for theological aesthetics and its relation to general aesthetics. The physical world is endowed with dignity, value, and beauty, but it is not sufficient. There must be a deeper and spiritual sight that allows the perceiver to enjoy the wonder of creation and material beauty but presses through to glory. Theological aesthetics in accordance with the prologue of John is that all of creation must be truly seen in relation to the enfleshed Logos. The prologue also teaches us that in order for us to understand the deepest realities of existence, the person does not go beyond the material creation but looks to the truth of the glory of God that walked among us in the flesh. The reader is called to behold Jesus Christ and see the glory of God in his flesh yet calls for something deeper than mere sight perception. Sight perception is not sufficient because even those who saw the incarnate Word with their physical eyes "did not receive him." The glory was manifest and perceived, but true perception calls for believe and reception. This type of true spiritual perception of faith and belief is based on the testimony of witnesses.

## SPIRITUAL REGENERATION AND THE PERCEPTION OF THE GLORY OF THE CHRIST

### Spiritual Regeneration and Perception in John 3:1–15

In the discussion on John 1:13, I mentioned that the prologue demonstrates the need of regeneration for true perception of the Word, the Light that came into the world. In John 1:12–13 there is a parallelism between those who receive Christ, believe in his name, and are regenerated or born of God. This was contrasted with those who did not know him, did not receive him, and merely operate at the level of natural human existence. Jesus's conversation with Nicodemus in John 3:1–15 is a narrative demonstration of the need of regeneration, or being born of God, to understand the Christ and his mission.

John sets up this pericope by introducing Nicodemus as a "man of the Pharisees . . . a ruler of the Jews" (John 3:1). It is ironic that Nicodemus came to Jesus when it is night (John 3:2).[61] The coming to Jesus at night is a reminder to the reader of the incarnation of the Word into the darkness (σκοτία). This was emphasized in John 1:3 and is alluded to again in John 3:19. "Night" (νυκτός) in the book of John often has a double meaning. John uses the physical phenomenon of night to be a symbol of blindness, evil, and spiritual darkness. In John 11:10, Jesus says "If anyone walks in the night, he stumbles because the light is not in him." Thus, for Nicodemus to come to Jesus in the night is a symbol of his lost state.[62] "Night" is also used in John 9:4, John 13:30, and possibly John 21:3 as a physical phenomenon that symbolizes and emphasizes spiritual darkness. The question concerning Nicodemus is this: is he irrevocably in the darkness and stuck in spiritual night and darkness? Nicodemus's conversation with Jesus in the verses following communicates what must happen for Nicodemus, and every person, to be led out of the darkness of night. Although John hints literarily in 3:1 that Nicodemus was lost in the darkness that engulfed humanity, he is beginning a character arc that he intentionally develops and returns to near the end of the Gospel.

Although it was night, John emphasizes that Nicodemus *came* to Jesus. John's commentary in 3:19–20 on Jesus's interaction with Nicodemus infers that this was a positive thing. The fact that Nicodemus came to Jesus (John 3:1; οὗτος ἦλθεν πρὸς αὐτὸν), who himself is the Light, is viewed favorably, because it is contrasted with the wicked who do not

---

61. By putting the word night in the genitive case, the author using what has been called the genitive of time. John says, οὗτος ἦλθεν πρὸς αὐτὸν νυκτός (he came to him by night). He uses a genitive of "night" to highlight the time Nicodemus came to him. Daniel Wallace emphasizes that if John had used the dative case, the point would have emphasized that Nicodemus came at a particular time of night. However, the genitive of time focuses on the *kind* of time, meaning that it is a time filled with symbolic or spiritual significance. John chose the genitive case to place an emphasis on the kind of time it was and make a spiritual point. This is a literary device used by John to remind the reader of the prologue. Wallace, *Greek Grammar*, 123–124.

62. Barrett, *The Gospel According to St. John*, 204. Morris, *The Gospel According to John*, 211.

come to the light. This is demonstrated by the similarity of the language of John 3:1 (οὐκ ἔρχεται πρὸς τὸ φῶς; John 3:20). The text in John 3:20 is clear that the wicked do not come to the light at all. On the contrary, Nicodemus came to Jesus, the Light, with sincere questions. Keener likewise notices the narrative is bracketed with Nicodemus's visit by night (3:2) and the statement in John 3:21 that believers come to the light.[63] Therefore, the text leaves the reader with the question of whether Nicodemus will truly come to the Light or refuse to come and remain in the darkness of night. Grochowski also notices this inherent tension that marked Nicodemus, "a contrast between coming to Jesus (the act of a beginner in faith) and doing it "at night" (i.e., in a counterpoise to Jesus who is 'the Light'—cf. 8:12, 9:5, 12:46), rendering the situation ambiguous and ultimately improper."[64]

The content of the conversation between Nicodemus and Jesus reveals what the unbelieving world, including Nicodemus needed. In 3:2, Nicodemus makes a statement about his belief that Jesus came from God because of his ability to perform signs. This section of John is part of the "Book of Signs" which goes from John 1:19—12:50.[65] Brandon Crowe argues convincingly that the Book of Signs in the Gospel of John is made up of six signs that Jesus performed, and the book that follows, the Book of Glory (John 13–20), then recounts the death and resurrection of Jesus as the climactic seventh sign.[66] The purpose of the signs are symbolic and prophetic acts that witness to the identity of Christ.[67] However, the response to these signs is ambivalent. This is the case for Nicodemus as well, because his "belief" in the signs is to be read in light of John 2:23–25, where many "believed" in Jesus, but he did not entrust himself to them. This introduces the theological concept of a category of belief that is not saving or true belief.[68] John develops this in his recounting of Jesus's conversation with Nicodemus in order to demonstrate the nature of true belief. Those who "believed" in Jesus in 2:23–25 and Nicodemus were focused on the "signs" Jesus was performing. In the Gospel of John, the "signs" are both revelatory and condemning. The signs function as a witness to the identity of the Word. These signs are important in this

63. Keener, *The Gospel of John*, 536.
64. Grochowski, "Nicodemus," 643.
65. Kruger, "John," 121.
66. Crowe, "The Chiastic Structure of the Seven Signs," 65–81.
67. Kruger, "John," 121.
68. van Deventer, "The Mosaic of Belief in the Fourth Gospel," 160.

work on theological aesthetics because they emphasize the aesthetic and sensory and present how the Bible approaches symbolic signs experienced through the senses. The physical and material signs were designed to evoke an aesthetic response of wonder and transformative belief.

The signs also have an ironic effect. At one level, they displayed the glory and majesty of Jesus to the physical senses. This is seen especially after the miracle at Cana. The glory of Jesus was revealed in the aesthetic sensation of feasting and taste at the wedding at Cana where Jesus turned the water into wine.[69] This reveals the wonderment of God's use of creation as a vehicle to reveal his glory. John 2:11 is thematically similar to John 1:14 in that it speaks of the sign as a manifestation of God's glory. John says that this manifestation of his glory was the first of Jesus's signs (σημεῖον). This sign manifested his glory and pointed toward Jesus's identity as Lord and Messiah.[70]

When Nicodemus states his belief that Jesus is from God because of the sign, Jesus moves deeper to show that mere belief in the physical phenomenon of the sign is not enough. Belief must go deeper than the sensory and physical to grasp that which the sign signifies. Therefore, John's theology of signs is both positive and negative. Signs are designed to create belief, and are, therefore, good. However, when a sign meets an unbelieving heart in spiritual darkness that has not experienced the new birth or regeneration, it can only lead to a false belief in the physical sign itself or lead to unbelief. No sign automatically leads to true belief even though many initially respond to the phenomena of the sign with a type of belief.[71]

This is the irony of the signs in the Gospel of John. They lead to an initial belief in Jesus (John 6:2, 14, 26, 30; 7:31; 9:16; 11:47; 12:18), but often lead to unbelief because the crowd seeks the signs themselves rather than let them be witnesses to Jesus Christ. This is seen especially in John 6, which has been identified as a pivotal sign in the Gospel, where Jesus and the crowd both use the word "sign," but in very different ways.[72] In John 6:26, Jesus said, "You are not seeking me because you saw the signs, but because you ate your fill of the loaves." The irony is that the miraculous feeding recounted in 6:1–15 was a sign like the making of wine in Cana. Falconer has demonstrated a sacramental theology in John

---

69. Falconer, "Johannine Magical Realism," 335.
70. Falconer, "Johannine Magical Realism," 333.
71. Crowe, "The Chiastic Structure of the Seven Signs," 65–81.
72. Crowe, "The Chiastic Structure of the Seven Signs," 76–77.

6:26–58 in light of turning water into wine (John 2:1–11) and the feeding of the five thousand (John 6:1–15).[73] However, the crowd misses the substance by seeking the sign. They ask Jesus for a sign and hints that a sign like manna in the wilderness would be sufficient (John 6:30–31). Jesus points out that they were seeking him not because they saw the sign, but merely because they ate the bread.

The meaning of the signs was not self-evident but relied on the explanation of their meaning.[74] Jesus, therefore, explains the meaning of the sign. Jesus pointed to the need to believe and abide in the Son and participate in him, symbolized through eating and drinking (John 6:56) Therefore, Jesus was calling them to truly perceive the sign in such a way that they understood its spiritual meaning. In other words, he was calling them to a theological aesthetic perception that understood the sign and the physical vehicle of the sign considering the deeper meaning that Jesus gave to it. Crowe convincingly argues that this sign of the bread has a pivotal role in the Gospel that informs the other signs. Based on this central sign, the purpose of the signs was to point people to faith in Jesus and thus invite to participation in Christ. Tragically, the people only responded with a general aesthetic delight in the bread rather than in the one the bread pointed to (John 6:35). As the Israelites grumbled before the mana came, the Jews of Jesus's day grumbled even when they had the bread of life right in front of them.[75]

This ironic dynamic of the signs not creating true belief should make sense to the reader if the content of Jesus's teaching in the Nicodemus dialogue is understood. John intentionally relates this conversation to the signs by recounting that the signs are what brought Nicodemus to Jesus in the first place. However, in response to Nicodemus's initial statement of belief, Jesus immediately jolts the conversation in a surprising direction and describes the necessity of the new birth. In doing this, Jesus implies that Nicodemus's belief is not sufficient.[76] Jesus was teaching Nicodemus that belief in the mere external physical signs is not sufficient, even though they objectively manifest the glory of God (John 2:11). Regeneration, the new birth, is necessary for true perception and belief.

Jesus then teaches on the nature of true belief and the duality of the flesh and the spirit. This duality is introduced in verse 6 where Jesus clearly

73. Falconer, "Johannine Magical Realism, 337.
74. Crowe, "The Chiastic Structure of the Seven Signs," 76.
75. Falconer, "Johannine Magical Realism, 338.
76. van Deventer, "The Mosaic of Belief in the Fourth Gospel," 160.

says, "That which is born of flesh is flesh, and that which is born of the Spirit is spirit." However, this contrast between flesh (σάρξ) and spirit (πνεῦμά), is not a hard contrast against one another as though one was good and the other bad. This is seen in the context of the rest of the prologue, which I explored in the previous section, that Jesus Christ became flesh (1:14). Rather, the flesh becomes a necessary precondition, though was not sufficient in and of itself, for entering the Kingdom of God.[77] Therefore, Jesus does not denounce the first birth, but simply states that a person must be born from above (John 3:3) in order to see the kingdom of God. From the perspective of theological aesthetics, it is all important that Jesus here uses a word that describes the sight or perception of the kingdom of God (3:3; οὐ δύναται ἰδεῖν τὴν βασιλείαν τοῦ θεοῦ). The ability to see the kingdom is dependent on whether someone has been born from above. It is true that this ability to see may have eschatological import, indicating an entry into the kingdom. However, in the context of Nicodemus's mention of the signs and the discussion of true belief, Jesus seems to also imply that the new birth is the prerequisite for the sight of the kingdom even while being on the earth and perhaps through these signs.

This could be the reason that Jesus says in verse 12, "If I told you earthly things and you did not believe, how will you believe if I tell you heavenly things?" The earthly things (τὰ ἐπίγεια) refer to the fact that humans who are in the flesh must also be born from above. Nicodemus was having a hard time believing the simple fact that on earth people must be born from above in order to see the kingdom. Since Nicodemus had a hard time understanding this rudimentary "earthly" side of things, it was certain that he would not understand the heavenly things.[78] In verses 13–15, Jesus then goes on to explain the heavenly things (τὰ ἐπουράνια) that Nicodemus will certainly not understand, at least for the time being. In a way that alludes to the prologue, Jesus presents himself as the key to the mystery of the new birth because he is the one who descended from heaven. The mystery of the Spirit that Jesus described in verse 8 finds its meaning and explanation in these verses. Verses 5–12 anticipate the content and explanation of verses 13–15. Ole Filtvedt rightly notes, "Only a correct understanding of who Jesus is and what his mission entails can explain what makes birth from above possible."[79] Yet, these verses are themselves anticipatory for the meaning to be explained and fulfilled in

77. Filtvedt, "Revisiting Nicodemus's Question," 138.
78. Filtvedt, "Revisiting Nicodemus's Question," 139.
79. Filtvedt, "Revisiting Nicodemus's Question," 139.

the rest of the Gospel. Jesus refers to the greatest sign, the lifting up on the cross, which displays the glory of God and calls for belief. The cross will effectively reveal true belief and the new birth in the hearts of people. Those who have been born of the Spirit will be able to see the kingdom of God even in this lifting up. More than that, regeneration and spiritual sight is only made possible by the objective and spiritual healing of the flesh provided in this lifting up.

At the end of the character arc, Nicodemus shows that he has been transformed by Jesus Christ. John 19:39 says, "Nicodemus also, who earlier had come by night, bringing a mixture of myrrh and aloes, about seventy-five pounds in weight." John reminds the reader that Nicodemus at one time had come to Jesus by night but now shows that Nicodemus again comes to the crucified Lord. The text begins somewhat ambivalent toward Nicodemus because it groups him with Joseph of Arimathea who was a disciple of Jesus, but "secretly for fear of the Jews" (John 19:38). Nicodemus, along with Joseph, is here presented as one of the leaders who secretly believed in Jesus but did not openly acknowledge Jesus for fear of the Pharisees (John 12:42). However, the action of Joseph and Nicodemus brings them out of the shadows of secrecy to a bold identification with the crucified Christ. Grochowski argues that this text is the culminating moment of "the process of Nicodemus's ascending from the darkness of fear and disbelief."[80] He argues from the intertextual development of Nicodemus between 3:1–2, 7:50, and 19:39. Nicodemus has now identified with Jesus in the day, because the "the funeral of the Master had to be carried out during daytime, before the sunset according to the Jewish custom, defined in the Law."[81] In narrative form, Nicodemus demonstrates his identification with Jesus and a true coming to the Light. Considering his conversation with Jesus in John 3, Nicodemus demonstrates that he has experienced the new birth that was initially so confusing to him.

A powerful visual exegesis that captures this climactic moment for Nicodemus is *Descent from the Cross* (1650–1652) from Rembrandt's workshop. This painting puts Nicodemus in focus and offers a powerful exegesis of the significance of this moment. In this painting, Nicodemus is put in closest proximity to Jesus, recalling that Nicodemus *came* to Jesus. Nicodemus is basked in light and completely illuminated, signifying that he is no longer in the night. Nicodemus's face is transfixed in love,

---

80. Grochowski, "Nicodemus," 639.
81. Grochowski, "Nicodemus," 654.

grief, and wonder on the crucified Christ. The sheet that covers one eye conveys the unveiling of Nicodemus's face so that he is now enabled to see the Christ. However, one eye is still veiled to convey that his vision is still not complete. This could point toward the coming resurrection as the moment when the vision will be complete. This depiction of the descent allows the viewer to get a glimpse of Nicodemus's spiritual perception of Christ that John seems to highlight in the character development of Nicodemus. This painting also highlights the proximity of Nicodemus to the dead body of Jesus Christ. Michael Chung notes that Nicodemus's association with and touching of the corpse of Jesus is the clearest demonstration of his new birth and saving faith.[82] Joseph and Nicodemus's action would have rendered them unclean and lead to shame and disgrace because of the inability to celebrate the Passover. Nicodemus was essentially choosing Christ, the substance, over the shadow of the Passover.

The Nicodemus dialogue and character arc has many implications for theological aesthetics. Jesus's discussion with Nicodemus reinforces the teaching of John 1:12–13, that true perception of the glory and kingdom of Christ are only possible after the new birth has happened. The earthly manifestation of this is a mystery from the human perspective as the Spirit is like the wind and goes where he wills (John 3:8). The new birth is necessary because no one in the flesh has ascended into heaven (John 3:13), but John also notes a few verses later that it is also because men love the darkness rather than the light (John 3:19). True perception and belief presses through the mere appearance of things by the enabling power of the Spirit, who allows people to see Jesus and believe in him in even his crucified glory (John 3:14–15). It is this true perception caused by the new birth that enables people to rightly believe in the signs that manifest his glory. Thus, the signs may only be truly perceived if they are seen by the power of the new birth and in reference to the foundational sign of the lifting up, which I examine in the next section. These signs demonstrate John's theology of things of creation as signs that point to greater spiritual realities. Like light and life in the prologue, the physical is used to explain spiritual realities.

---

82. Chung, "Nicodemus," 34.

*The Descent from the Cross* (1650) by Rembrandt van Rijn. Public Domain / Wikimedia Commons

Theological aesthetics, therefore, relies heavily on the use of metaphors from the created order so that the spiritual realities may be understood. Metaphors are essential to theology. Theology itself is dependent on the use of metaphors and enriched by these metaphors.[83] A metaphor builds a bridge from the known, the metaphor, to the unknown thing the metaphor is pointing to. The utilization of metaphors invites comprehension of a new perspective.[84] In the Gospel of John, the use of metaphors abounds. Here, Jesus uses the metaphor of physical birth to explain regeneration. In Jesus's use of the metaphor of birth, physical birth becomes an

83. Laniak, *Shepherds After My Own Heart*, 35–39.
84. Laniak, *Shepherds After My Own Heart*, 39.

analogy and helpful metaphor for describing what is spiritually needed. Likewise, wind becomes a metaphor for the activity of the Spirit. Thus, the good things of creation, the earthly things, become symbols and metaphors that point to a greater and more necessary spiritual reality of heavenly things. Yet, in Christ the things of heaven have descended to the realm of the flesh so that the glory of heaven may be perceived in the flesh.

## The Perception of the Glory in the Lifting Up in John 12:27–36

John 12:27–36 is in the context of Jesus's prediction of his death. The narrative is moving toward a culmination in the cross and the resolution of the resurrection. In this passage John brings to completion his development of the light/darkness contrast that began in the prologue (John 1:4–9; 3:19–21; 8:12; 9:4–5; 11:9–10).[85] The event of the incarnation is again metaphorically symbolized by the light (John 1:35–36). Here, however, the light is brought to a culmination in its revelation in being lifted up. Yet, Jesus implies that after this event the light will be taken away (John 1:35). However, the climactic display of the light is described as the glorification of Jesus and the very reason he came (John 12:27).

The song of the Suffering Servant (Isaiah 52:13—53:12) provides the background for this text.[86] John frames this section of his Gospel in light of Isaiah 53:1 and 6:10 in order to make sense of Jewish unbelief (John 12:37–43). John's use of ὑψόω ("lifted up"; 12:32, 34) and δοξάζω/δόξα ("glorified/glory"; 12:16, 23, 28) needs to be seen in relation to one another and mutually interpreting.[87] The uses of these words also allude to Isaiah 52:13 where Isaiah says the Suffering Servant will be lifted up and glorified.[88] I would add to this that Jesus intentionally uses the metaphor of light to interpret the lifting up of Christ and glorification in a way that alludes to Isaiah's theology of light (e.g., Isaiah 9:2; 42:16; 60:3). The options Jesus presents are similar to the thought in the Dead Sea Scrolls, either one walks in the light or in the darkness.[89] Jesus and the Dead Sea Scrolls build this theology of walking in the light from the Old Testament. However, the crucial difference is that Jesus commands the people

---

85. Estes, "Dualism or Paradox," 116.
86. See Lett's discussion in "The Divine Identity of Jesus."
87. Lett, "The Divine Identity of Jesus," 169.
88. Romanowski, "When the Son of Man is Lifted Up," 115.
89. Morris, *The Gospel According to John*, 533.

to "believe in the light" (John 12:36), while the Dead Sea Scrolls simply assume that the community are already walking in the light.[90] In this passage, Jesus is presented as the light of the world that will be lifted up for all people to see and responded to. Therefore, Jesus's statement in John 12:32 and John's commentary in 12:33 along with his further explanation in verses 35–36 must be understood as mutually interpreting texts concerning the glorification of the Father and Son, the metaphorical contrast of light and darkness, and the ironic unbelief of the Jews. I explore these themes further in what follows.

Jesus's statement, "And I, when I am lifted up from the earth, will draw all people to myself" (John 12:33), is a part of a series of statements in the Gospel of John that describe Jesus being lifted up. The first of these was in the dialogue with Nicodemus (John 3:14–15). In those verses, Jesus likened himself to the serpent that Moses lifted up in the wilderness. Just as the people in the wilderness viewed the serpent and were healed, so also those who believe in the Son when he is lifted up will have eternal life. The second "lifted-up" saying is John 8:28, where Jesus tells the Pharisees, "When you have lifted up the Son of Man, then you will know that I am he, and that I do nothing on my own authority, but speak just as the Father taught me." In this final saying in John 12:32–33, John makes explicit what was implicit in the previous two texts. The lifting up Jesus speaks of was the ironic lifting up on the cross in death as well as simultaneously being honored by the Father.[91]

The lifting up on the cross was designed by the Father as an act of glorification of the Son. He is lifted up and glorified (Isaiah 53:12), but this refers to his death (John 12:33). In these verses, complex trinitarian theology is introduced. "Lifted up" and the glorification language are to be mutually understood.[92] The language of "lifted up" is not merely symbolic.[93] It refers to a real historical event of the lifting up of Jesus Christ on the cross. However, the "lifted up" sayings reveal that the cross was not what it appeared. From all appearances, it was a moment of shame and death, but in reality, it was an exaltation. This as a Johannine paradox, because this lifting up in exaltation hardly fits the shame and horror of the cross.[94] In John 12:33, it explains that Jesus said he would be lifted

---

90. Morris, *The Gospel According to John*, 554.
91. Romanowski, "When the Son of Man is Lifted Up," 101.
92. Lett, "The Divine Identity of Jesus," 169.
93. Romanowski, "When the Son of Man is Lifted Up," 107.
94. Keener, *The Gospel of John*, 881.

up, in order to signify or show what kind of death he was going to die. The word translated as "show" in the ESV, is the present active participle of σημαίνω. This is significant because of its verbal association with the word "sign" and the theological significance of the signs in the book of John.[95] The lifting up becomes one of the signs that manifest his glory.

It is instructive to see who is lifted up and who is glorified in this passage. First, the Son is glorified. Jesus makes the statement that the hour has come for the Son to be glorified (John 12:23). This frames the discussion and emphasizes the connection between the Son's lifting up and glorification. Secondly, in this same event, the Father is glorified in the lifting up of the Son. This is seen in John 12:28 where Jesus prays that the Father will glorify his name. This prayer will be developed in the High Priestly prayer which also prays for God's glory.[96] The Father responds in a voice from heaven, "I have glorified it and will glorify it again" (Καὶ ἐδόξασα καὶ πάλιν δοξάσω).[97] Carson indicates that this glorification is, "apparently throughout Jesus' earthly ministry, in the incarnation (1:14) and especially in the powerful signs."[98] Therefore, the Son and the Father are simultaneously glorified in the incarnation and the cross. As Carson noted, this reminds the reader of the prologue, "We have seen his glory, the glory of the one and only Son, who came from the Father" (John 1:14). This is also further emphasized by Jesus in John 12:44–45. Believing in Jesus is equated with belief in the Father; looking at the Son is "seeing" the Father. Perception and belief are placed side by side and equated as are the Father and the Son. This is particularly instructive in light of the context of seeing the Son being lifted up. The implications of this text are, if you want to see the Father and his glory, look to the crucifixion of the Son. This dynamic of the shared and manifested glory of the Father and Son will be developed further in the discussion on the High Priestly Prayer in John 17.

In the lifting up/death of the Son, the Son and Father are both glorified.[99] This is further metaphorically described by Jesus by the shining of the light. In this passage, the light that shines in the darkness is Jesus in the work of his ministry and being lifted up and glorified. Yet, Jesus

---

95. Keener, *The Gospel of John*, 881.
96. Keener, *The Gospel of John*, 874.
97. The aorist ἐδόξασα most likely refers to the glorification of the Father through the incarnation and signs the Son manifested.
98. Carson, *The Gospel of John*, 441.
99. Romanowski, "When the Son of Man is Lifted Up," 115.

warns those who are in the darkness of unbelief, that night is coming, and his ministry is being drawn to a close. Jesus's words in John 12:35–36 seem to have a double meaning. The close of Jesus's ministry is coming, but so is the opportunity to respond rightly to the light. Jesus is the light of the world, and he appeals to them to no longer stay in the darkness (12:46) and become children of the light through belief (12:36). Ironically, the light was rejected because people love the darkness more than the light and their eyes were blinded (12:40).

John's comment that Jesus "left and hid himself from them" (12:36) is designed to be an enactment of Jesus's statement that they were going to have the light just a little while longer.[100] When Jesus hides himself, the result is, "Even after Jesus had performed so many signs in their presence, they still would not believe in him" (John 12:37). This is designed to be a warning about what would happen after the light was removed. Unbelief would persist even after the light of the incarnation. However, even though the reality of unbelief persists, the thrust of John's work is designed to confront his audience with the necessity of belief in Jesus. This section calls the reader to see the glorification of the Father and Son in the death of Christ and presses for belief. The text implies that the way to continue seeing Jesus, even after his death. Filtvedt notes the irony, "Readers of the gospel know that Jesus is only hidden from the eyes of the world. They permanently see him."[101]

This is important for theological aesthetics because it reveals the *claritas* of God's "light." The glory of God is most clearly displayed in the incarnation and death of Christ, and it is perceived through the means of true belief. This is ironic and counter-intuitive, because the glory of God is revealed in the very place it is hidden, in the death of Jesus through crucifixion. This reemphasizes the need for the birth from above and the need to be children of the light to be enabled to truly perceive the glory of the Father and Son in the scandal and shame of the cross. Therefore, the glory of God is most clearly manifested in the cross and the perception of that glory is belief in Jesus Christ. The incarnation, and specifically the cross, is the starting point of theological aesthetics according to the Gospel of John.

---

100. Harris, *John*, 235.
101. Filtvedt, "Revisiting Nicodemus's Question," 116.

# THE TRIUNE GLORY REVEALED IN CHRIST IN JOHN 17:1–5

The economic relation of the Father and Son is climactically developed in the High Priestly Prayer in John 17. This prayer is the climactic expression of the words, metaphors, and themes John introduced in the prologue.[102] In the prologue, John dramatically stated, "No one has ever seen God" (John 1:18). However, the invisible God was manifested by the incarnation of the Word who was God. John continued, "the only God, who is at the Father's side, he has made him known" (John 1:18). This special relation between Father and Son and the Son manifesting the Father continues throughout the Gospel (John 3:35; 4:34; 5:18–23; 7:16, 28–29; 8:16–19; 10:46; 12:45; 14:9–11; 15:23; 16:15). The High Priestly Prayer develops this theme and explains the simultaneous glorification of the Father and Son and the manifestation of that glory to the world. Not only this, but the prayer itself is an enactment of the actual relationship between the Father and Son and gives a glimpse into the glory, intimacy, and unity of that relation.[103] The traditional name, "The High Priestly Prayer," also notes that Jesus functions as a High Priest and bears the believing community into the presence of God through His intercession.

Jesus returns to the theme of the glorification of the Father and Son in John 17:1, "Father, the hour has come; glorify your Son that the Son may glorify you." The hour of the glorification of the Son was also referenced in John 12:23 and referred to the lifting up of crucifixion. In John 17:1, Jesus prays to the Father that he would glorify the Son. In the lifting up of the crucifixion, we learn that the Father is performing the action of glorifying the Son with the purpose clause, introduced by the ἵνα, "that the Son might glorify you." This is the outworking of the themes introduced in the prologue in John 1:14–18. Keener says, "Jesus's crucifixion and exaltation to the Father is the theophany that will reveal the divine name to the disciples."[104] The cross is simultaneously God's expression of love for the world as well as a manifestation of the love between the Father and Son. The Son loves the Father and the Father glorifies the Son.

---

102. Janzen, "The Scope of the High Priestly Prayer in John 17," 1.
103. Holmes, *The Quest for the Trinity*, 52.
104. Keener, *The Gospel of John*, 1053.

Jesus then says that he has glorified the Father on the earth and accomplished the work the Father gave him (17:4–5). This implies that Jesus's incarnation and the works he did revealed the glory of the Father on the earth. The incarnation was the manifesting of the glory of God. Charles Gieschen presents a compelling case that this glory that Jesus mentioned in these verses, which was revealed during his earthly ministry is the same glory that was revealed in the Old Testament glory theophanies, especially of Exodus, Isaiah, and Ezekiel.[105] Gieschen says, "There is significant interest within the Gospel of John in beholding Jesus as the visible image or form of God, the Glory of YHWH seen by Moses at Sinai, by Israel in the tabernacle and temple, then by the prophets Isaiah and Ezekiel in their call visions."[106] The disciples are shown the glory of God and are brought by Jesus into God's presence. Therefore, the glory of God is both seen and actively participated in through the purification that Jesus gives.[107] It is for this reason that as Jesus prays, he notes that the climactic hour of glory has come. As Jesus glorified the Father through his life and works, now the climax of glory will be revealed in the crucifixion. Gieschen summarizes, "The lifting up of Jesus on the cross becomes the holy place where one sees the ultimate vision of the enthroned Glory."[108]

In verse 5, Jesus prays that he would again be glorified in the Father's own presence, like he was before creation. Carson notes that this does not mean that Jesus is asking for a "de-incarnation."[109] The glory that Jesus is asking for from the Father is the same glory he had with the Father from before the beginning. However, Jesus now brings his incarnated, glorified flesh into this glorious relationship because the incarnation was not a temporary condition. The incarnation of the Son was the necessary condition for the world to be shown and brought into the glory of the Father and Son. What Jesus is asking for is to return, in his glorified flesh, to the Father's side in the intimate relation of love (John 1:18; 17:24). The relation between Father and Son has not changed, but in the economy the possibility has been opened for those who believe in Christ Jesus to behold this glory and be united with the Father and the Son.

---

105. Gieschen, "The YHWH Christology of the Gospel of John," 13.
106. Gieschen, "The YHWH Christology of the Gospel of John," 13.
107. Janzen, "The Scope of the High Priestly Prayer in John 17," 5.
108. Gieschen, "The YHWH Christology of the Gospel of John," 13.
109. Carson, *The Gospel of John*, 557.

The incarnation made an intimate relationship with God possible. This is shown in an artistic way in John 13:23. The beloved disciple was reclining at the "side" of Jesus (ἐν τῷ κόλπῳ τοῦ Ἰησοῦ; John 13:23) just as the Son was at the "side" of the Father before the incarnation (ὁ ὢν εἰς τὸν κόλπον τοῦ πατρός; John 1:18). The incarnation thus opened the way for humans to live in intimate relation with God. Because the Son alone had this close relationship with the Father, the Son took on flesh to invite people into close relationship with himself and the Father. Jesus made a way for people to enter the glory of the triune God. This is what Jesus means in John 17:22, "The glory that you have given me, I have given to them, that they may be one even as we are one." The believers in Christ participate in the glory, but only by beholding the glory of Jesus who manifests the glory of the Father (17:24).[110] It is this reason that Jesus prays for the glorification in 17:5. He desired the glory of close intimacy with the Father that he had for eternity, and he longs for the fruit of believers to enter this glory through seeing and believing at his glorification. This is what John 17:3 means when it speaks of eternal life as the knowledge of God. This knowledge of the one true God only comes through the mission of Jesus Christ who was sent. This knowledge is special and salvific, based on belief in Jesus Christ and his accomplished mission through the cross.

For theological aesthetics, this shows the categories of trinitarian *ad intra* glory. This glory is primary and objective from all eternity, based on the relations of the Trinity of knowledge and love. The glory of the Trinity that was possessed from all eternity went public and was manifested through the work of Jesus Christ (John 1:14; 17:4). Therefore, as much as theological aesthetics deals with an aesthetic perception of the glory of God, the incarnation and cross must be the starting point and center of theological aesthetics. The incarnation and the cross, then, is the *sine qua non* of theological aesthetics. The cross is where the objective glory of God was most perfectly revealed and true perception of God is only possible to those who see, believe, and know this glory (17:3, 24).

---

110. Ferguson, *Some Pastors and Teachers*, 458.

## WITNESS AND THE PERCEPTION OF BELIEF IN JOHN 20:24–31

After the Gospel of John recounts the climactic event of the crucifixion of Christ, John's narrative turns to the event of the resurrection. The resurrection of Christ Jesus is of central importance to theological aesthetics. The resurrection of Christ Jesus in the flesh, which John takes pains to note (John 20:17, 25; 21:12–13), was the definitive establishment of the eternal permanence and value of redeemed material creation. The Word who became flesh was raised bodily in the flesh. Therefore, there remains an eschatological day when all eyes will see the Christ in the flesh. Until that time, the believing community perceives him by faith through the testimony of the eyewitnesses. This is main theological point of John 20:24–31.

John 20:24–29 is in the literary convention of a recognition scene. These recognition scenes were common in ancient literature and utilized by John throughout the Gospel (John 1:29, 35, 40–42, 45–50; 4:7–29; 5:2–15; 18:3–8; 20:11–16; 21:2–8).[111] Thomas refused to believe the eyewitness testimony of the disciples that they saw the Christ. In keeping with the Gospel of John's emphasis on sight, the disciples testified to Thomas that they had seen the Lord (John 20:25). However, Thomas says he will only believe if two sensory demands are met. He demands visual and tactile confirmation. If this sensory condition is not met, Thomas emphatically says he will never believe.[112]

In dramatic fashion, the text then shows Jesus meeting these two conditions. Eight days have passed after Thomas's emphatic pronouncement of disbelief (John 21:26). Thomas's obstinacy is perhaps the reason that the disciples did not obey the command recounted Matthew 28:7 and Mark 16:7 to go to Galilee.[113] Yet, despite Thomas's unbelief and obstinacy, Jesus meets him where he is at. Jesus commands Thomas to touch him with his fingers and hands (John 20:27) and to see his resurrected, but scarred hands. Caravaggio's *The Incredulity of Saint Thomas* is a visual exegesis of this event. Caravaggio's depiction emphasizes the sensory nature of this event. Thomas's finger is literally in the side of Christ Jesus and the eyes of Thomas are transfixed in wonder and shock on the physical body and scars of Jesus. Thomas's whole body is oriented toward Christ and his left-hand grips himself as if to communicate that Jesus's

---

111. Harstine, "Thomas: Recognition Scenes in the Ancient World," 439.
112. Thomas uses the emphatic negative (οὐ μή).
113. Harris, *John*, 333.

body is as real as his own. It is a work that evokes wonder at the physical body of Christ and those perceiving it.

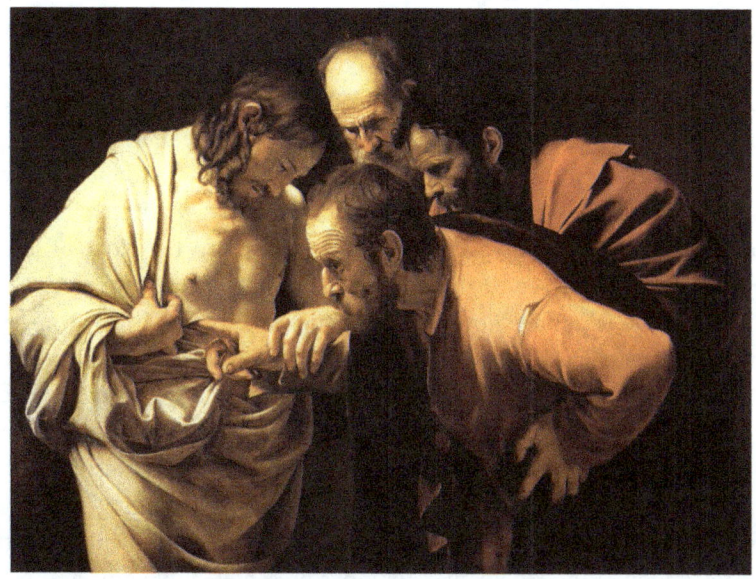

*The Incredulity of Saint Thomas* (1601–1602) by Caravaggio.
Public Domain / Wikimedia Commons

The necessary conditions for belief were met by this sight and touch and Thomas responds with a dramatic confession in the Lordship and divinity of Jesus Christ (Ὁ κύριός μου καὶ ὁ θεός μου). Jesus condescended to meet Thomas's conditions in order to pronounce a blessing on those who do not see and yet believed. Thomas's exclamation is the Gospel's climactic Christological statement. Murray Harris explains, "The apostle [John] found in Thomas's cry a convenient means by which he might bring into sharp focus at the end of his gospel, as at its beginning (1:1, 18), the ultimate implications of his portrait of Jesus."[114] Thomas's expression forms an *inclusio* with the prologue of John, emphasizing the divinity of Jesus Christ.[115]

From a theological aesthetics standpoint, the objective revelation of who Jesus is, Resurrected Lord and God, is presented. On the other side, the personal subject's perception of Jesus is also developed. For Thomas, this perception was a visual and tactile encounter. However, John used

114. Harris, *John*, 334.
115. Keener, *The Gospel of John*, 1211.

Thomas's encounter with the Resurrected Jesus to introduce a new and more blessed way of perception. Thomas, due to his skepticism, becomes a powerful witness to the Lordship of Jesus. Thomas becomes an eyewitness of the glory of Christ and invites others to believe and truly perceive through faith.

The new way of perception is introduced by Jesus in John 20:29. Jesus's response is, "Have you believed because you have seen me? Blessed are those who have not seen and believed." In Jesus's pronouncement of blessedness, belief is given as a blessed substitute for sight. In the incarnation, the glory of Jesus was seen, after the ascension the glory of Jesus will be "seen" or perceived through belief. The participle, ἰδόντες, referring to "those who have not seen" is a timeless aorist.[116] This is timeless in the sense that Jesus has now established belief as the central element of blessed perception for the indefinite future. In John 20:30–31, John moves to show what this belief is based on. The belief of those who do not see with their physical eyes is based on belief in the eyewitness testimony of those who saw Jesus in the flesh. After the resurrection, "seeing" Christ is through the eyewitness testimonies of those who did see him and through the testimony of the Holy Spirit. John has presented a dynamic and performative concept of belief. Those who believe are "immersed in the unfolding action of believing" that responds with dynamic and continuous faith in Jesus.[117] This belief must be based on the eyewitness testimony.

Faith is a spiritual sight that rests on the physical sight of the eyewitnesses. Filtvedt states, "Even if readers of the gospel also 'see' Jesus, they can only do so in a metaphorical sense through hearing the testimony (cf. 16,10; 20,29). However, this metaphorical seeing is rooted in events that were once physically seen and are made continuously present for the readers by the Spirit."[118] The age when Jesus is no longer seen in the flesh becomes a time of mission where the eyewitnesses beckon to all humanity, "Come and see" (1:39, 46; 4:29; 12:21; cf., 20:18). Scripture is the place where people can spiritually perceive Jesus. Therefore, theological aesthetics is concerned with the sight of God that is most fundamentally provided through the eyewitness testimony of the authors of Scripture. As all of creation and the Old Testament Scripture anticipated and moved toward Jesus Christ, now those who truly perceive Jesus Christ through belief can look through Jesus and the testimony concerning him and aesthetically

---

116. Harris, *John*, 334.
117. van Deventer, "The Mosaic of Belief in the Fourth Gospel," 167.
118. Filtvedt, "Revisiting Nicodemus's Question," 118.

apprehend the purpose and meaning of creation. Theological aesthetics provides a way to perceive the world in light of Christ, and the theological foundation necessary for learning about Christ through the things of the earth such as light, life, bread, weddings, water and wine, and so on.

## THE ESCHATOLOGICAL GLORY OF THE NATIONS AND THE GLORY OF GOD IN REVELATION 21:22—22:5

In the book of Revelation, John the Evangelist receives visions from the risen Christ about "what soon must take place after this" (Revelation 4:1).[119] The book of Revelation is apocalyptic literature that is an unveiling and unmasking of the world and its structures to allow it to be seen

---

119. It is contested that Revelation was written by the same John who wrote the Gospel and the epistles. However, I follow the traditional approach that argues that it was the same John, who was the apostle, that wrote these books. An exhaustive study of this issue exceeds the boundaries of this book. Some argue that the John of Revelation is not specifically identified with John and argues against apostolic argument, though this is an argument from silence. Beasley-Murray (*The Book of Revelation*, 33–34) argues that the well-established authority of John among the Asia Minor churches makes it likely that the author was John who was known as the apostle. Another objection, noted as early as the third century by a bishop of Alexandria named Dionysius, is that there is a marked difference in the style, tone, and grammar between Revelation and the Gospel of John (Beasley-Murray, *The Book of Revelation*, 32–36). However, this is not determinative because of the difference in genre makes many differences expected. There are also many similarities and points of contact in the grammar, syntax, tone, and phraseology as well (ibid; Poythress "Johannine Authorship," 329; Smalley, *Thunder and Love*; Beale, *The Book of Revelation*, 35). Beale (*The Book of Revelation*, 34) has given three potential options for the authorship of Revelation: 1) John the apostle/evangelist; 2) another John (such as "John the Elder"); or 3) someone who used "John" as a pseudonym. He argues the third option is highly unlikely because a pseudonym would have specifically identified himself as the apostle John. Cotro ("Could the Author of Revelation Step Forward, Please?," 89) has recently considered all the arguments for and against John the Evangelist's authorship of Revelation and concluded that it is still an open question. However, he argues that because the internal and external evidence at least suggest that the author was a Palestinian, Jewish rooted Christian, the Apostle John should be considered a viable option (ibid). Beasley–Murray (*The Book of Revelation*, 36) urged caution but was open to the authorship being John the Evangelist; he says, "Readers who have trodden the familiar paths of speculation regarding the authorship of the Fourth Gospel will be aware that conjecture follows conjecture in this area, and it is not a profitable exercise." Beale's conclusion (*The Book of Revelation*, 35–36) is similar. He contends that though it is possible that John the Evangelist wrote the book, it is not essential for the message of the book. For this study, I build on the argument that John the Evangelist was the author (Mounce, *The Book of Revelation*, 8–15) to provide a unified vision of his theological aesthetics.

for what it really is.[120] Richard Bauckham notes that the original audience in the province of Asia were confronted with images of the Roman Empire and its vision of the world.[121] He continues, "Civic and religious architecture, iconography, statutes, rituals and festivals, even the visual wonder of the cleverly engineered 'miracles' (cf. Rev. 13:13–14) in the temples—all provided powerful visual impressions of Roman imperial power and of the splendor of pagan religion."[122] It was in this context, Bauckham notes that the apocalyptic symbolism in Revelation provided Christian counter-images that cleanse the imagination through visual power. However, it is worth noting, that this visual power is only accessed through the Apostle John's recounting of what he saw. Like John's Gospel, Revelation relies on the written word given by the one who saw the vision. The perception of these counter-images is conditioned on the reader's belief in the testimony of the seer. Theological aesthetics again begins with the foundation of the perception of belief in the written word, which then allows the reader to see and perceive all of reality in a new and theologically aesthetic way.

There are many passages and themes in the book of Revelation that could be used to further develop a Biblical approach to theological aesthetics. This section will focus on three important themes developed in Revelation 21:22—22:5. John's vision of the new Jerusalem in particular invites his audience to "participate in a vision of cosmic wholeness" in such a way that provides an alternative to Babylon and Rome, the symbols of this world's systems and evil.[123] This passage brings to culmination three important biblical theological concepts that relate to aesthetics and theological aesthetics. Firstly, this passage shows the eschatological creation of the new heavens and new earth as a worldwide "paradisal City-Temple."[124] Secondly, inside the new heavens and earth, the nations will bring their glory and honor. The arts and aesthetics of the nations has a theological and eschatological teleology. The eschatological purpose of the nations' artistic beauty correlates general aesthetics with theological aesthetics. Thirdly, this passage describes the day when the goal of theological aesthetics will be realized, namely, seeing the face of God (Revelation 22:4).

120. Smith, *Desiring the Kingdom*, 92.
121. Bauckham, *Revelation*, 19.
122. Bauckham, *Revelation*, 19.
123. Schellenberg, Schellenberg "Seeing the World Whole," 467.
124. Beale and McDonough, "Revelation," 1155.

The context of this passage is John's final vision of the new creation. Revelation 21:9—22:5 is the seventh and climactic segment of the book.[125] John describes the vision of the new heaven and new earth (Revelation 21:1). This vision is rich with allusions to Isaiah, who prophesied a permanent new heaven and earth (Isaiah 66:22.)[126] The new Jerusalem is then showed to John, which is at once a bride prepared for her husband as well as the dwelling place of God with man (Revelation 21:2, 10). The bride, the city of Jerusalem, is presented in apocalyptic imagery as the alternative to Babylon, the harlot city.[127] Yet, the symbolism of being a bride does not make this new Jerusalem lose its character as a special dwelling place where God meets with his people. The old Jerusalem was understood to be the center of the earth, the place where the Lord reigned. Now, in this eschatological vision, the heavenly Jerusalem is the perfect antitype of the earthly Jerusalem where God will dwell with his people (Revelation 21:3).[128]

John is shown the city of the new Jerusalem in such a way that highlights its aesthetic quality. The city has the "glory of God" (Revelation 21:11) and is described as having the appearance of jasper, the same "rare jewel" that described the one seated on the throne in Revelation 4:3. Revelation 21:11–21 then describes the brilliance or splendor (φωστήρ; Revelation 21:11) of this city that shines with God's glory. Craig Koester notes that φωστήρ usually refers to a light-giving body.[129] Therefore, the city itself shares in the glory of God which it radiates. The glory of God and the splendor is described using material creation. The glory of God in this passage is directly linked with precious stones that are the materials which make up the new Jerusalem and its decorations. This emphasizes the dignity and value that God places on the material creation. He does not simply recreate using a different substance besides matter, but rather recreates the new heavens and earth with the most precious and beautiful matter. The new creation is more beautiful but is made from the same substance. It is also worth noting that the glory of God radiates through the precious materials that make up the new Jerusalem. In this eschatological vision, the new heavens and earth will radiate the glory of God in a similar way as our current world does. As Balthasar notes, "The

---

125. Beale, *The Book of Revelation*, 1040.
126. Beale and McDonough, "Revelation," 1150.
127. Tabb, *All Things New*, 174.
128. Schellenberg "Seeing the World Whole," 468.
129. Koester, *Revelation*, 814.

Bride of the Lamb does not go up from earth to heaven; together with Christ she comes 'down from God' (Rev 21:10)."[130] However, at that time the glory of God will shine in creation with eschatological fullness and clarity without the effects of sin in creation or in the perceiver.

After John's description of the bride, the new Jerusalem, he moves in verse 22 to describe what he did not see in this new creation. He did not see the temple because the Lord God Almighty and the Lamb are its temple. Beale noted, "God and the Lamb have filled the entire new creation with their glorious presence, a glorious presence formerly sequestered in the holy of holies and in the heavenly temple."[131] God then becomes the temple that radiates throughout the new heavens and earth. The division between the sacred and the common or mundane will be irrevocably erased as all is permeated with the holiness of God.[132] The presence of God and his omnipresent glory is emphasized in the following verse where it is said that God himself not only takes the place of the temple of worship, but also takes the place of the sun and moon as the source of light. In John 1:4–5, John stated that the Word was the light of all mankind and that in his incarnation he shined in the darkness. John now alludes to this and identifies the Messianic nature of this light, but the light is now apparent and visible in the new creation without being hidden.[133] The glory of God and the light of the Lamb will go public in such a way that it is as visible as the sun and moon (Revelation 21:23). The light of the glory of God will be seen clearly and no longer hidden.

The nations walk in the light of the glory of God, but they also bring their glory into the new heavens and earth. This is significant because the promises of the covenant people have now been extended perfectly to the nations.[134] This is the culmination and eschatological fulfillment of God's promise to Abraham that all the nations of the earth would be blessed in him (Genesis 12:1–3). The kings of the earth in Revelation 21:24–26 are symbolic of the international makeup of those who believe in Christ in the eschatological kingdom.[135] Revelation 21:26 explains verse 24 further and says, καὶ οἴσουσιν τὴν δόξαν καὶ τὴν τιμὴν τῶν ἐθνῶν εἰς αὐτήν, meaning that the nations will bring their glory and honor into the

---

130. Balthasar, *GL* 1, 662.
131. Beale and McDonough, "Revelation," 1153.
132. Schellenberg, "Seeing the World Whole," 473.
133. Koester, *Revelation*, 821.
134. Bauckham, *Revelation*, 137.
135. Beale, *The Book of Revelation*, 1101.

new Jerusalem. The question is, what exactly is this glory (δόξαν) and honor (τιμήν) the nations bring? Revelation 21:24–26 is an allusion to either Isaiah 60:1–7 or Zechariah 14:9–21.[136] While Isaiah 60 emphasizes the physical riches and wealth of the nations such as herds of rams and camels, gold and incense, and adornments for the temple, Zechariah 14 emphasizes the kingship of God, based on Psalm 2, and the worship of the nations. In the rest of the book of Revelation, glory and honor are on the lips of those who praise God (Revelation 1:6; 4:9, 11; 5:12–13; 7:12; 15:4; 19:1, 7).[137] Revelation 21:24–26 undoubtably means that the nations will verbally worship and ascribe praise to the Lord in this glory and honor, but the text does not demand that this simply be the worship of praise songs. The allusion to Isaiah 60 is clear, especially given the fact that Isaiah 60:1 speaks of the light of the glory of the Lord that is shining. Furthermore, Zechariah 14:14 speaks of the plunder of the nations that will be collected, so it is likely that Zechariah's vision of the nation's pilgrimage to Jerusalem includes the homage of material gifts rather than only verbal homage. Therefore, the glory and honor of the nations in Revelation 21:26 should include the material wealth and artistry that is alluded to in Isaiah 60. The glory and honor of the nations (τὴν δόξαν καὶ τὴν τιμὴν τῶν ἐθνῶν) includes the artistic and material beauty of the nations wielded in worship and service of the Lord God Almighty.

In this way, the gifts of the Magi to the Christ in Matthew 2:1–12 are thematically alluded to in Revelation 21:24–26. The intertextual link between Revelation 21:24–26 and Matthew 2:1–12 is that both passages allude to Isaiah 60.[138] Matthew's description of the Magi's worship of the Christ becomes a picture of the nations walking in the light of the glory of God and bringing their wealth and majesty to praise him. Matthew 2:11 describes the Magis' worship, "they fell down and worshiped him. Then, opening their treasures, they offered him gifts, gold and frankincense and myrrh." Likewise, in the new heavens and earth, the nations bring their glory and honor and offer it to the King. This is significant because it reaches back into the present and gives worth and value to the "glory and honor of the nations" in the present time. This includes not only the material wealth, but also the artistic beauty of the nations. Everything in cultures from all over the earth that is distinctively beautiful to those nations will be transformed into vessels of praise and honor of God. In

---

136. Baines, "The Identity and Fate of the Kings," 84.
137. Baines, "The Identity and Fate of the Kings," 84.
138. Blomberg, "Matthew," 5. Beale and McDonough, "Revelation," 1153.

this way, the nations will bring their own honor into the new Jerusalem and wield this honor in praise of God. This eschatological vision is the culmination of the creation mandate given in Genesis 1. The cultural artifacts and arts that were ironically first developed in Genesis 4:20–22 under the line of Cain will be eschatologically redeemed and purged of evil and turned into instruments of worship. This then shows an inherent correlation between general aesthetics and theological aesthetics. It is not only that the perception of beauty in creation, culture, and the arts gives a glimpse of the glory of God, but that the use and creation and generative aspects of artistry has a teleological and eschatological purpose of the glory of God. The arts, with international and variegated beauty and diversity, will be brought to God into the new heavens and earth. They will be for God's glory and will themselves radiate his glory.

Revelation 22:1–5 further describes the vision given in Revelation 21. This is seen especially in the repetition in Revelation 22:5 of the fact that God is the light in the new Jerusalem. This repetition emphasizes that this text is to be taken with the previous. However, the angel in this texted moved on to show John more details of the new Jerusalem. The symbolic imagery of the apocalyptic genre must be kept in mind rather than be taken as a literal description of the new heavens and new earth. It is possibly a literal description, but the symbolism of apocalyptic visions provides a check. Regardless, the symbolic imagery moved from the description of a city in Revelation 21:9–21, to the focus on God's omnipresence in contrast to the absence of temple, sun, and moon in 21:22–26, and now moves to the description of a garden in 22:1–5. John was shown that heaven will be a city-temple-garden permeated with the presence of God. Like Revelation 21:22 and John 1:9, the spiritual light that has its source in God will be seen visibly. Therefore, the new heavens and earth are not only the eschatological fulfillment of Jerusalem and the temple, but the Garden of Eden itself. Revelation 22:1–5 is rich with allusions to the Garden of Eden and provides an inclusio for the entire biblical story. Brian Tabb explains, "in this glorious vision of the new creation, the tree of life and river of life flowing from the divine throne provides eschatological food and drink for God's multi-ethnic people, who will perfectly carry our humanity's original calling to rule and serve as priest-kings."[139]

For theological aesthetics, this passage has two implications. The first is the emphasis on the eschatological eradication of evil, suffering,

---

139. Tabb, *All Things New*, 188.

and curse. The leaves of the tree of life provide healing for the nations (Revelation 22:2). Considering the discussion on Revelation 21:24–26 this verse demonstrates what is wrong with the current age and what hinders the glory and honor of the nations. In the present age, the wealth and arts of the nations are shot through with curse, evil, and sin. This is the reason that wealth and the institutions of culture can be so perverted and used for evil in this present age. The nations do not yet have eschatological healing and restoration. The present age still looks forward to the day that the curse will be removed (Revelation 22:3). Therefore, aesthetics, both general and theological, must not develop an over-realized eschatology in the present age. The nations have not yet experienced healing from any curse (πᾶν κατάθεμα). This could be translated as "any curse" (NIV) or "anything accursed" (ESV). The meaning of πᾶν κατάθεμα encompasses both translations. There will no longer be any accursed thing, all evil will be removed (cf., Revelation 21:8). Because all accursed things will be removed and the nations will experience healing, the curse of God that was over sinful humanity and over creation will also be removed. Humanity in the new Eden will be freed to live as servants before the throne of the holy God and reign with him (Revelation 22:4–5).

Instead of the curse or anything accursed, there *will be* the throne of God and the Lamb (22:4). This is the second implication this text has for theological aesthetics. Since the fall, creation has been cursed. Goodness, truth, and beauty are seen throughout creation, but so is the curse. In the eternal Kingdom, creation will no longer be cursed, and the presence of God will be the most fundamental reality. At that time, God's people will see his face and live in his light. The Old Testament longing to see the face of God and have his countenance shine on the community will be finally realized (Numbers 6:25–26; Psalm 4:5; 11:4–7; 31:16; 67:1).[140] In all theological aesthetic discussion, this eschatological fullness must be kept in view. The sight of God is an eschatological reality and cheap substitutes in this life should not be accepted. The transformative nature of seeing God (*visio Dei*) was emphasized by John in 1 John 3:2, "but we know that when he appears we shall be like him, because we shall see [ὀψόμεθα] him as he is." This transformative vision is the theological basis for being enabled to serve before him in holiness and even have the honor bestowed of ruling with him for eternity, which was promised to those who kept the faith earlier in the book (Revelation 22:5; 3:21; 5:10). Theological aesthetics

---

140. Beale and McDonough, "Revelation," 1154.

looks forward to the day of eschatological fullness when the perception of faith and belief established in the Gospel of John is transformed into the perception of sight in the new heavens and new earth.

## CONCLUSION

In this chapter, I explored the Christological theological aesthetics based on the Gospel of John and the final eschatological vision in the book of Revelation. In summary, God's glory is most clearly displayed in the incarnation of Christ and his exaltation on the cross. The glory of the incarnation explained and gave meaning to the glory of God revealed in creation. All true perception of God's glory must be seen through faith in Christ and the new birth.

The prologue of John's Gospel has implications for both general aesthetics and theological aesthetics. The prologue describes the objective glory of God seen in the incarnation of the Word and the perception of that glory. The incarnation is situated in the context of creation, reaffirming the goodness of material creation. It also takes pains to note that the Word who was God took on flesh or materiality and manifested the glory of God. Creation therefore is the stage of the incarnation and has inherent value. Creation anticipates the incarnation but also is used as a metaphor to explain the importance of the incarnation. Created realities such as light and life become metaphors for what was accomplished in the incarnation, and all of creation can be understood considering Jesus Christ and his incarnation. Because Jesus Christ manifested the glory of the invisible God in the flesh, it should not be surprising that we are expected to find the glory of God in material creation. Even in creation's beauty, the glory of God cannot be fully perceived apart from Jesus Christ. Therefore, theological aesthetics and the perception of God's glory is inherently Christological. However, the High Priestly Prayer of John 17 reveals that this Christological glory is only understood in light of trinitarian glory. The incarnation of Christ was the external display of an eternal inner-trinitarian glory.

The Gospel of John develops a theology of perception for theological aesthetics. The light of Christ was manifested, but the human condition under sin leads people to love the darkness and refuse to see the light. True perception is hindered from a moral inability and love for evil rather than the glory and beauty of God. The condition for true perception is to become a child of God. True perception allows the individual subject to perceive Christ and understand all created reality in light of him. Creation is an analogy for teaching about Christ and salvation, and Christ, in turn, explains the meaning of creation. This type of perception provides an all-encompassing vision of the world.

The discussion with Nicodemus in John 3 and demonstrates the need for the second birth for this type of perception. The perception of God's glory must press deeper than the surface level. The signs and miracles of Jesus were not enough because people needed to see the climactic sign of Jesus's death on the cross and believe in this sign. True perception, in the theological aesthetic sense, has regeneration as its prerequisite. The individual has this perception if he or she sees the glory of God manifested in the climactic event of the cross and believes in Jesus Christ. Theological aesthetics is not only Christ-centered but also cross-oriented. In the cross the glory of God was most perfectly shown and true perception made possible.

Jesus's interaction with Thomas (John 20:24–31) indicates that true perception of God's glory is based on the eyewitness testimony of the Scripture. Therefore, theological aesthetics is based on the eyewitness authority of the authors of Scripture and perception is faith rather than sight until the eschatological completion. Revelation 21:22—22:5 has profound implications for theological aesthetics because it develops the eschatological aspect of theological aesthetics. The eschatological hope of theological aesthetics is to see the face of God, which is promised in Revelation 22:4. However, this beholding of God is also transformative and participatory. The one who beholds God has been redeemed and saved from all evil and is eternally purified to behold, serve, and reign with God Almighty. This eschatological vision of God remains the teleological end of theological aesthetics. Theological aesthetics, therefore, must always be oriented eschatologically. The context of this vision of God is also important for theological aesthetics in the present age. The eschatological vision of God will take place in the new heavens and the new earth. This will be a created place similar to the old earth, but with the curse and sin forever removed (Revelation 21:1; 22:4). That the eternal dwelling place is similar to the current creation indicates the value and dignity of the current creation in spite of its present brokenness. The fact that God's glory is seen in the precious jewels in the new creation indicates that God is the creator of aesthetic beauty and his glory shines through created reality. Theological aesthetics, therefore, provides a theological foundation and teleological framework for understanding general aesthetics. Finally, the glory and honor of the nations, which is the culmination of the material and cultural wealth and the beauty of common grace, will be brought into the eternal kingdom and utilized for the glory of God. This eschatological perspective reaches back into the present to establish the legitimacy and purpose of wealth, art, and culture. Everything that the nations produce, which has truth, beauty, and goodness, will be eschatologically redeemed in the new heavens and new earth for the worship and honor of God Almighty.

# 6

# An Evangelical Protestant Theological Aesthetic

As we have seen, a theological account of beauty in evangelical Protestantism is present but underdeveloped.[1] Balthasar's critique against Protestantism in general applies to evangelical Protestants as well. Evangelicals continue the trend Balthasar noticed in Protestants by focusing on the relationship between theology and the arts rather than developing a theology of beauty. I respond to Balthasar's critique in this chapter by developing evangelical Protestant theological aesthetics. Balthasar's insights inform this chapter, but I seek to set them within the theological tradition of evangelical Protestantism. The possibility of theological aesthetics is based on metaphysical realities of how God structured Being and reality. God also designed human persons to fit within this structure of reality and experience the wonder of perception. I begin this chapter by discussing the objective aspects of theological aesthetics and the relation between glory and beauty. Then, I proceed to examine the subjective element of true perception.

---

1. With notable exceptions, such as the work of Jonathan King and Samuel Parkison. This work is complementary to King's and Parkison's work. The distinction is the emphasis on perception and the spiritual sense. Parkison develops the impact of regeneration on the spiritual sight from the perspective of classical theology and the doctrine of the beatific vision. My work here seeks to complement his work with some distinct emphases on the theological nature of beauty and perception in dialogue with modern philosophers and theologians.

## OBJECTIVE ASPECTS OF THEOLOGICAL AESTHETICS

### Immanent (Ad Intra) Glory, External (Ad Extra) Glory, and the Beauty of the Lord

In the previous chapters, I discussed the tension and ambiguity between spiritual and physical beauty. This tension was observed by philosophers such as Plato and Aristotle and continues to the present day.[2] Chapter 3 delved into the theological response to this tension in the history of doctrine. Theologians such as Athanasius, Augustine, Aquinas, and Luther grappled with this tension and ultimately developed a theology that sees Jesus Christ and his incarnation as the resolution. The second person of the Trinity took on flesh to reveal true beauty. Related to this, one of the issues in the field of theological aesthetics is the relationship between the glory of God and his beauty. As I noted in chapter 2, evangelicals often equate the glory of God with the beauty of the Lord without a clear distinction. King, who filled the lacuna with his work on theological aesthetics from an evangelical perspective, argues that the beauty of God in Scripture is "most basically associated" with his glory.[3] He nuances the relationship, "To be clear, beauty is not identical or does not equate to the glory or the objective forms that God's glory takes—beauty is *not* a synonym for glory, in other words. The distinction here is a subtle one but important to grasp."[4] King goes on to make the distinction between the glory of God and the beauty of God, "the beauty of God manifested economically (*pulchritudo Dei ad extra*) is expressed and perceivable *as a quality of the glory of God* inherent in his work of creation, redemption, and consummation. The display of God's glory is thus always beautiful, always fitting, always entails an aesthetic dimension to it."[5]

King's definition of the beauty of God comes from the classicist theory of beauty, which claims beauty has certain qualities such as "proportion, unity, variety, symmetry, harmony, intricacy, delicacy, simplicity, or suggestiveness," which evoke delight and pleasure when they are perceived.[6] This theory of beauty is represented in Aquinas's theology of

---

2. Sammon, *The God Who Is Beauty*, 15.
3. King, *The Beauty of the Lord*, 31.
4. King, *The Beauty of the Lord*, 51.
5. King, *The Beauty of the Lord*, 51.
6. King, *The Beauty of the Lord*, 51.

beauty. For Aquinas, most basically, the beautiful is known when it is seen and gives pleasure.[7] *Claritas* is the condition of the beautiful form that evokes pleasure and displays the proportion, unity, and other conditions of beauty. It is the light that causes aesthetic seeing and evokes delight.[8] When seen in conjunction with King's definition of God's beauty, Aquinas's theology of beauty underlines the fact that the beauty of God should evoke pleasure and delight. God's work and glory are by nature objectively beautiful and entail an aesthetic dimension. The necessary conclusion from a classic theology of beauty would seem to be that all people would respond to this beauty with aesthetic delight. However, the fact remains that many find the works of God and the gospel of Jesus Christ dull, questionable, or even morally repulsive. This demonstrates the need to further develop the theology of the subjective side of perception. Based on the findings from the Gospel of John, I argue that regeneration is the prerequisite for the true perception of the objective beauty of the glory of God. A theology of spiritual perception is the key area where more work needs to be done to construct evangelical Protestant theological aesthetics. Balthasar is an excellent dialogue partner because he approaches God's beauty from the vantage point of perception.

Regarding the objective side of God's beauty, King's definition is consistent with the context of historical theology explored in chapter 3. The history of theology adds nuance and depth to his excellent definition of the beauty of God. In King's definition of God's beauty, the primary focus is on the objective element of beauty. God and his work are objectively beautiful and presented in space and time history. Barth emphasized a covenantal aspect of beauty that sees beauty as inherently relational. For Barth and King, beauty is a subset of God's glory. Barth defined glory as his "self-revealing sum of all his divine perfections. It is the fullness of God's deity . . . fullness, the totality, the sufficiency, the sum of the perfection of God."[9] Likewise, King says that the immanent glory of God is the "altogether perfection of God" and utilizes the doctrine of divine simplicity to demonstrate the simple unity of the manifold perfections of God in the fullness of his glory.[10] King, however, develops the trinitarian aspect of God's beauty more than Barth ever did. Both these

---

7. Aquinas, *ST* I.5.4 *ad* 1.
8. Eco, *The Aesthetics of Thomas Aquinas*, 119.
9. Barth, *CD* II.1 § 31,643, 645.
10. King, *The Beauty of the Lord*, 48.

writers distinguish between the immanent glory of God and the glory of God displayed in his works.

Barth offers a definition of the immanent glory of God as the "fullness, the totality, the sufficiency, the sum of the perfection of God."[11] If we synthesize this with Edwards's and King's trinitarianism, we are reminded that the "fullness, the totality, the sufficiency, the sum of the perfection of God" is an eternal reality in the triune unity of the Father, Son, and Spirit. This was also seen in the previous chapter in the High Priestly Prayer in John 17. In his prayer, Jesus speaks of the glory shared with the Father before creation. The prologue of John already spoke of Jesus being at the Father's side (John 1:18). This introduced the theme of the special relation of Father and the Son (John 3:35; 4:34; 5:18–23; 7:16, 28–29; 8:16–19; 10:46; 12:45; 14:9–11; 15:23; 16:15). The Spirit is also introduced in the Gospel of John as the third person of the Trinity (14:15–21, 26; 15:26; 16:7–11, 12–15). From the Gospel of John, we understand that the immanent glory of God is the "fullness, the totality, the sufficiency, the sum of the perfection of God," experienced in the fullness and glory of the triune relations.[12] This is the immanent (*ad intra*) glory that the Father, Son, and Holy Spirit shared in eternity.

Glory and beauty are mutually interpreting concepts. The concept of God's *ad intra* "glory" emphasizes the objective excellence and incomparable perfection of God himself. Edwards claimed that God displayed his *ad intra* (immanent) glory *ad extra* (outside himself) to creatures through creation and redemption. There is a distinction, therefore, between the *ad intra* glory of God and the *ad extra* glory of God. The glory displayed in creation, humanity, the arts, redemption, and all the works of God flow from his eternal trinitarian glory. The concept of "beauty" is related to this. Beauty has both objective and subjective elements. The subjective aspect of beauty does not mean that beauty is relative, but beauty is inherently seen and delighted in by a perceiving subject. In other words, glory refers to the objective aspect, while the concept of beauty emphasizes the subjective aspect of perception and aesthetic delight.

Barth's development of the distinction between glory and beauty guards us from thinking of God's glory as a brute fact of cold and detached omnipotence.[13] Glory emphasizes the objective reality, but it comes and meets creatures who *perceive* that glory as beauty and respond

---

11. Barth, *CD* II.1 § 31, 643, 645.
12. Barth, *CD* II.1 § 31, 643, 645.
13. Kirkland, "Glory Over Sublimity," 1014.

in aesthetic delight. Therefore, God's beauty is an aspect or quality of his glory. Beauty approaches glory from the vantage point of the beholder.[14] Beauty is the attractive power of glory that draws people in and evokes aesthetic delight and wonder. The objectivity of glory is presupposed, but it is nuanced in that this glory meets the perceiver and pleases because it is beautiful in such a way that it evokes aesthetic "desire, joy, pleasure, yearning, and enjoyment."[15] In his emphasis on the freedom of God and God as the subject, Barth spends most of his time defining the objective glory of God. However, as I noted in Chapter 3, Barth's comment that he could rewrite *Church Dogmatics* from the perspective of beauty was an invitation to develop theological aesthetics from the perspective of the perceiving subject.[16] Balthasar's theological aesthetics are the response to this invitation.[17]

To summarize, the concept of "glory" has two aspects. The first is the glory of God of the Trinity (*ad intra*), which is the fullness of his perfection. The second aspect of glory is the display of God's glory outside himself (*ad extra*). It is this second aspect of glory that Barth argues is the subset of beauty. The beauty of God is the subject's perception of God's glory that evokes aesthetic delight. King is somewhat more precise to speak of beauty as a "quality" of God's glory. He explains, "The display of God's glory is thus always beautiful, always fitting, and always entails an aesthetic dimension to it."[18] In other words, the beauty of the Lord is the intrinsically aesthetic dimension of God's glory when it is perceived.

Is it proper, therefore, to speak of the *ad intra* beauty of God, or is beauty always an aspect of the external display of God's glory? For Barth, the answer is that the beauty of the Lord is a subset of his *ad extra* glory that emphasizes perception. This is perhaps the most precise way for theologians to discuss the beauty of the Lord. However, suppose one synthesizes Barth's contribution with Augustinian, Thomistic, and Edwardsian trinitarianism. In that case, there is also a sense in which one can speak of the *ad intra* beauty of the Lord. If the *ad intra* glory of the Lord is the sum of the perfections of God shared in the triune life, speaking of the *ad intra* beauty of the Lord emphasizes the "perception" and delight that the triune God has in the trinitarian fullness. The beauty of

14. Navone, *Toward a Theology of Beauty*, 29.
15. Barth, *CD* II.1 § 31, 654.
16. Barth, *CD* II.1 §31, 657.
17. Kerr, "Assessing this 'Giddy Synthesis,'" 9.
18. King, *The Beauty of the Lord*, 24.

the Lord within the Trinity is seen most clearly in Aquinas's development of an Augustinian theme: the Holy Spirit is the bond of love between the Son and the Father.[19]

As I demonstrated in chapter 3, Aquinas maintained that love is the proper response to beauty.[20] When applied within the triune relations, love for the beautiful perfections of God radiates within God because the Father eternally delights and loves the beauty of his image in the Son. To speak in this way again makes beauty a subset of glory that emphasizes the side of perception. In this case, it speaks of the perfect perception and delight in the glory of God manifested in the beauty of the eternal Son. The reason this *ad intra* beauty of the Lord is an important concept to add to the discussion will be seen later in this chapter when I develop the Christological aspects of glory and beauty. If we are consistent in our emphasis that glory and beauty are interrelated, with glory emphasizing the objectivity of perfections and beauty emphasizing the subjectivity of perception, the *ad intra* beauty of the Lord can only be understood in trinitarian categories. *Ad intra* beauty emphasizes the full and infinite delight and love that the triune God experiences in response to his own glory. The *ad intra* beauty is a subset or quality of God's *ad intra* glory that emphasizes the delight and love experienced within himself. Edwards described this as the "respect to himself, or an infinite propensity to, and delight in his own glory" experienced within the triune God.[21] For Edwards, this trinitarian *ad intra* beauty is the essence of holiness because it is God's infinite love for himself and his perfections.[22] King, similarly, speaks of the *ad intra* beauty of the Lord as understood from the doctrine of the Trinity as the basis of God's own blessedness and beatitude and the "eternal condition in himself of absolute felicity, delight, satisfaction, and repose."[23]

## The Beauty of the Lord and Created Beauty

The classic philosophical tension between spiritual beauty and material beauty is resolved in Christian theology by maintaining that the ultimate

---

19. Aquinas, *ST* I.37.1.
20. Aquinas, *ST* I.26.2.
21. *WJE* 8:439.
22. Sherry, *Spirit and Beauty*, 85.
23. King, *The Beauty of the Lord*, 53.

source of all material beauty is the spiritual beauty of the triune God. Material beauty is a display of God's *ad extra* glory designed to evoke a sense of aesthetic delight. Beauty exists because of God's pleasure of showing his glory to creatures. God, from all eternity, is "the superabundant source . . . of every beautiful thing."[24] For Pseudo-Dionysius, "all being derives from, exists in, and is returned toward the Beautiful and the Good."[25] God is the Source of all being because everything proceeds from him and returns to him. All of reality, therefore, is theophanic in that it reveals the glory and majesty of God. Balthasar developed his entire theological aesthetics around this concept and called it the "double and reciprocal *ecstasis*."[26] The double movement begins with God, who creates and moves toward the creatures whom he created. The secondary movement is the return of the creature who responds in pleasure and delight in encountering the beauty of the Lord and return to him. Louth explains, "The theophanic beauty reminds those beings who are struck by this beauty of their own derivation from the source and cause of all."[27] Therefore, for Pseudo-Dionysius, there is no tension between the spiritual beauty of the Lord and material beauty because material beauty refers to the spiritual as its source.[28]

The relationship of spiritual beauty to material beauty is also clear in Edwards's theology. However, Edwards made his argument more robustly trinitarian than Pseudo-Dionysius and Balthasar. He argued that the fullness of God's trinitarian glory and beauty led him to share it with creatures. For Edwards, God's eternal communication and perception of glory and beauty within himself "causes him to incline to its being abundantly diffused, and to delight in the emanation of it."[29] He is a God who communicates beauty because of his prior delight in that beauty. This communication of beauty included physical beauty, but most fundamentally, the divine beauty of redemption and Jesus Christ. Therefore, Edwards makes a distinction between primary beauty and secondary beauty. Primary beauty is the spiritual beauty of God himself, while secondary beauty is a physical pointer to that primary beauty.[30]

24. Pseudo-Dionysius, *Divine Names* 701C, 76.
25. Pseudo-Dionysius, *Divine Names* 705D, 79.
26. Balthasar, *GL* 1, 126.
27. Louth, "Apophatic Theology," 79.
28. Balthasar, *GL* 2, 179.
29. *WJE* 8:439.
30. *WJE* 8:565

In this way, Edwards would have described material beauty in creation and the arts as theophanic.

Edwards's distinction between primary (spiritual) beauty and secondary (created) beauty allows for easing the tension without advocating for equating the two. Without differentiating the two, one runs into the danger Rahner fell into when he equated the infinity and incomprehensibility of God with Dürer's "The Hare."[31] The designation of "secondary beauty" does not undermine the value of this beauty in any way. It establishes that this secondary beauty is not the primary beauty of God, who alone is worthy of worship. Secondary beauty is a pointer to primary beauty. Balthasar is close to Edwards in his emphasis on this fundamental difference between God and the theophanic reality that reveals him.

If this is the case, why is there such a perceived tension between spiritual and created beauty? Augustine's theology reveals where the real tension lies between God's beauty and the beauty of created things. He urged caution because sinful humanity misuses creation. The fall blinds the perceiver from seeing the beauty of God in creation and leads to the tendency toward misusing creation. The power of created beauty on the fallen heart inevitably produces idolatry. For Augustine, idolatry is delighting in the beauty of creation in a way reserved for God.[32] Theologians such as Pseudo-Dionysius, Edwards, and Balthasar demonstrate no real tension between the Lord's beauty and creation's beauty in Christian theology. Material beauty has its origin and telos in God himself. He is the Creator of material beauty, and it is designed to lead back to him and give a glimpse into his glory. However, Augustine helps to locate where the tension exists. The tension between spiritual and material beauty is not a metaphysical problem, but rather an existential problem in the heart of man. The problem has to do with worship. In his fallen state, man refuses to allow material beauty to reveal the beauty of the Lord as God designed it. When secondary beauty is confused with or equated with primary beauty, it leads to idolatry. Created beauty is elevated to the place only primary beauty should occupy. This is the very process Paul warned about when he described the human propensity for idolatry in Romans 1:25. However, although this is the case, the abuse of created beauty does not undermine the proper use and enjoyment of created beauty as a revealer and pointer to the glory of God.

---

31. Rahner, "Theology and the Arts," 29.
32. Smith, *On the Road with Saint Augustine*, 82.

The real tension is primarily anthropological rather than metaphysical. The tension comes from an inability to perceive primary beauty in secondary beauty. As I demonstrated in chapter 4, it is in this area that evangelical Protestants must develop different theological aesthetics than Balthasar. Balthasar did not give enough credence to the pervasive effects of the fall on perception and humanity. I address this more in the second half of this chapter on the subjective aspects of theological aesthetics.

## The Christological Aspects of Glory and Beauty

The field of theological aesthetics is inherently Christ-centered because in Jesus Christ the glory of God was made manifest, and the beauty of God is perceived. One of Balthasar's primary contributions to theological aesthetics is the focus on Jesus Christ as the pinnacle of God's beauty.[33] This emphasis on Jesus Christ is not an idiosyncratic theology of Balthasar. It is exegetically established in the writing of John the Evangelist. The central problem for theological aesthetics is the invisible nature of God. As John explains, "No one has ever seen God" (John 1:18). Because God is invisible, revelation to the senses is needed in theological aesthetics. This need was met in the person and work of Jesus Christ.

However, before speaking of the work of Christ, it is important to note that the pre-incarnate Christ, the second person of the Trinity, shared in and enjoyed the *ad intra* glory of the triune God. It is proper to speak of the beauty of each person of the Trinity because each one is fully divine and possesses the whole fullness of divine perfections. However, Aquinas notes that the divine beauty most properly refers to the Son, even from eternity past.[34] Beauty, in Aquinas's theology, most properly belongs to the Son because of the unique role of the Son as the perfect image of the Father. The Son, from all eternity, perfectly images the Father. By extension, one could argue that the Spirit is also perfectly imaged by the Son. Aquinas emphasized that the proportion and harmony of the Son in his representation of the Father is exact and perfect. In Aquinas's theology of the Spirit, the Spirit is the personified love of God for his own perfect image.[35] Therefore, the *ad intra* beauty of the Lord focuses on the Son as the perfect image of the Father, who evokes aesthetic delight.

---

33. Balthasar, *GL* 7, 276. Nichols, *The Word Has Been Abroad*, 232.
34. Aquinas, *ST* 1.39.8. Sevier, *Aquinas on Beauty*, 104.
35. Aquinas, *ST* I.37.1.

While Aquinas focused on the beauty of the pre-incarnate Son, most other theologians emphasized the beauty of Christ in creation and his redemptive work. For Athanasius, creation only makes sense in light of Jesus Christ. Athanasius built this theology in reference to the prologue of John's Gospel and emphasized that the Logos is impressed on all creation as he is its pattern and archetype. This is because the Father, as the "Maker and Artificer," created through the Logos, the eternal Son.[36] He created in such a way that the Logos was imprinted on all of creation and revealed his glory.[37] The perfect image of the Father was both the instrument and archetype of creation. Creation is theophanic and revelatory because the Word, the Image of God, is revealed in creation.[38] This is why Genesis 1 is replete with the phrase, "And God saw that it was good." God aesthetically delights in his creation because it is a display of the Word's glory. To emphasize the Christological aspects of beauty in creation in no way creates an "asymmetrical trinitarianism."[39] As Ortlund shows, Jesus Christ perfectly revealed the Trinity and is the exact imprint of the Father (Heb. 1:1–3), so that when one sees Christ they have seen the Father and the Spirit (John 12:45; 14:9). Even though Jesus Christ is emphasized as the revelation of God's glory, to glorify one member of the Trinity is to glorify the other members as well.

The revelation of God's glory in creation through Christ is also a key feature in Balthasar's work. In Athanasius's *On the Incarnation*, the Logos is imprinted on every aspect of creation. This is the same for Balthasar. Jesus Christ is the splendor of the form of creation. Balthasar explains, "The whole world of images that surrounds us is a single field of significations. Every flower we see is an expression, every landscape has its significance, every human or animal face speaks its wordless language."[40] Every entity has its significance because it is theophanic and revelatory of the splendor of Being, which reveals the form of Jesus. However, Balthasar's focus falls on the form of Christ in his incarnation and work as the place where the beauty of God is most perfectly revealed. For Balthasar, "God's incarnation perfects the whole ontology and aesthetics of created Being."[41] Therefore, in Athanasius and Balthasar's view, even though creation can

---

36. Athanasius, *On the Incarnation* §27.
37. Athanasius, *On the Incarnation* §11, 39.
38. Leithart, *Athanasius*, 92.
39. Ortlund, "Christocentrism," 315.
40. Balthasar, *TL* 1, 136.
41. Balthasar, *GL* 1, 29.

be said to reflect the beauty of Christ, the incarnation perfects the beauty of nature. This is consistent with John's use of creation in his Gospel's prologue. The world was made through the Logos and is upheld by the Logos. Creation anticipates its teleological purpose: the day when the Logos is manifested in the flesh. Beauty in creation points to Jesus Christ. The Word, the second person of the Trinity, provided the blueprint for the architecture of creation.

## The Theology of the Cross as the Gateway to Beauty

Even though created beauty is inherently theophanic and revelatory, the presence of sin impacts creation and created beauty at two levels. Sin twists created beauty both ontologically and subjectively. Athanasius argued that the fall ontologically impacted creation by marring it.[42] The theophanic revelation is still present, but sin impacts creation so it needs redemption. At the level of perception, humanity refused to see the beauty of God in the beauty of creation. They decided to worship created beauty rather than divine beauty. For Athanasius, the incarnation was the dramatic event of the Word becoming flesh so that all would see his form and look at him. In the climactic moment of the cross, Jesus paradoxically becomes formless, shamed, cursed, and judged, but simultaneously reveals the infinite beauty of God's love. This revelation, Athanasius argued, was the center of our faith and what was necessary to objectively restore creation and subjectively reveal the beauty of God to idolatrous humanity.[43]

Athanasius's theology of the cross was later developed by Luther. Luther's theology of the cross is the foundation for an aesthetic approach to beauty seen through the cross. An aesthetics of glory attempts to get around the cross and avoid it as the ugly or the obscene. However, in the aesthetics of the cross, God judges and purifies the beauty of the world through the cross and resurrection. This does not destroy earthy beauty, but rather establishes it and nuances it based on God's perspective and wisdom rather than man's. Evangelical theological aesthetics is an aesthetics of the cross. In the Heidelberg Disputation, Luther says, "That wisdom is not of itself evil. . . but without the theology of the cross a person misuses the best things in the worst way."[44] Like wisdom and phi-

---

42. Athanasius, *On the Incarnation* §14, 41.
43. Athanasius, *On the Incarnation* §19, 48.
44. Luther, *Annotated Luther* 1, 101.

losophy, aesthetics and created beauty are not evil in and of themselves. However, to approach beauty, in whatever form, apart from the cross, is misusing the best thing in the worst way. An aesthetic without the cross is a theological aesthetic of glory, which Luther critiques.[45] Theological aesthetics that has no reference to the cross makes the same mistake of Aristotle and the scholastics. These theologians of glory accept the good in creation but avoid the cross and thereby misuse the good of creation, which is redeemed by the cross. The cross then becomes the door through which humanity must enter if they are to enjoy worldly beauty as God has intended it to be used. Once one goes through the cross, God invites humanity again to enjoy creation. The resurrected Christ comes with all the good gifts of creation, purchased by the cross and enjoyed based on the cross and says, "Come and have breakfast" (John 21:12). While Viladesau's theology of the cross is closer to Balthasar's than Luther's, he represents both when he says, "The cross of Christ must always be seen in light of the resurrection."[46] For Viladesau, the cross is not a beautiful object but the beautiful *denouement* of the theo-drama. As the *denouement* of all of existence, nothing can be truly perceived or understood apart from it.

The cross solves the ontological and existential brokenness that impacts created beauty and its perception since the fall. As Stephen Fields argues, "however much the cross of Christ sets the standard for beauty, it cannot be understood to destroy the integrity of worldly aesthetics. It must somehow give this integrity its center."[47] This is true of Luther's theology of the cross, which is the crucial foundation for constructing an evangelical theological aesthetic. The cross is the standard of beauty because it reveals the love of God in the hiddenness of an ugly and humiliated form. The cross destroys all worldly and created beauty because it stands as a critique of all beauty apart from God. The cross tests all things, including created beauty. Therefore, at one level, I disagree with Viladesau, who says the cross is not a contradiction of "worldly beauty," but agree with him when he says that the cross elevates worldly beauty to its "fullest and most complete level."[48] The cross first contradicts humanity's idolatrous use of worldly beauty, but then establishes the proper use of beauty once the believer passes into resurrection life in Christ.

45. Rosebrock, "The Heidelberg Disputation and Aesthetics," 352.
46. Viladesau, *Theological Aesthetics*, 197.
47. Fields, "The Beauty of the Ugly," 174.
48. Viladesau, *Theological Aesthetics*, 198.

The cross gives integrity to all worldly beauty because it objectively restores beauty to its original intention. Specifically, the way the cross destroys created beauty is not that it destroys created beauty per se, but it destroys humanity's inclination to sin and idolatrous perceptions of that beauty. It allows the one who lives under the cross, who has encountered the beauty of God in the ugly event of the cross, to now look at beauty in light of the cross. Thus, the existential or subjective problem of truly seeing beauty rightly is solved because all of reality is seen from this reference point. Humanity's problem with beauty is fundamentally located in the perception, cognition, and desires.[49] This Augustinian teaching is consistent with Luther's theology of the cross. The bondage of the will creates in humanity the urge to seize and possess what we desire violently. This bondage of the will and proclivity of humanity is confronted and destroyed in the cross where God's suffering beauty reorients our cognitive and affective nature so that we can now see beauty, both spiritual and created, rightly. In the following section, I demonstrate how the theology of the cross establishes a spiritual sense in redeemed humanity that functions in a way somewhat similar to how Kant described transcendental apperception. Because of the cross, humanity can now enjoy created beauty without it becoming idolatrous. Therefore, created beauty, even though it is critiqued and seemingly destroyed by the cross, is established and finds its integrity and purpose in the cross.

In chapter 4, I noted the fundamental difference between Luther and Balthasar's theology of the cross. The difference is that Luther viewed the cross as the revelation of God to sinful beings, while Balthasar maintained that the cross was the revelation of God's essence of love.[50] Balthasar's theology of the cross reveals a deficiency in his doctrine of sin. For Balthasar, natural theology and a theology of glory do not contradict a theology of the cross.[51] Luther argued that the cross contradicts all theologies of glory and the natural man. For Balthasar, the cross was the culmination and fulfillment of natural beauty, but for Luther, natural beauty must die in Christ and rise again. For Balthasar, the cross reveals the beauty of the love of God. According to Luther, the cross is at once beautiful but also fundamentally ugly because it reveals the curse of sin. However, because of the cross, beauty and its proper use is established.

---

49. Garrett, "A Peculiar Beauty," 37.
50. Howsare, *Balthasar: A Guide for the Perplexed*, 89.
51. Howsare, *Balthasar: A Guide for the Perplexed*, 91–92.

One can understand why Balthasar critiqued Luther so harshly. Balthasar critiqued Luther because his dialectic of the cross confronted and contradicted worldly beauty and wisdom. For Balthasar, Luther's theology of the cross was excessively apophatic and led to the deconstructionism of protest and negation rather than upbuilding.[52] Balthasar argued that the proper way to speak of the dialectic revealed in the cross of the "exuberant outpouring of the Gospel's nuptial love" that demands a self-surrender on the part of man.[53] Luther understood that the cross is only beautiful to those who have been crucified with Christ and had their sin dealt with at the cross. Luther and Balthasar would have agreed with Augustine when he asked, "What is it we love in Christ — his crucified limbs, his pierced side, or his love? When we hear he suffered and died for us, what do we love? Love is loved. He loved us that we might in turn love Him."[54]

The theology of the cross is one of the most important elements of evangelical theological aesthetics. Balthasar's theology of the cross too quickly synthesized with a theology of glory because of his deficient understanding of a theology of sin. However, Balthasar cautions Protestant theologians who only emphasize the negation of the cross and apophatic rather than cataphatic theology. Balthasar's caution allows Protestants to recover Luther's full intention in the theology of the cross. The cross not only deconstructs worldly beauty but reestablishes it through redemption. As Rosebrock explains, "The theologian of the cross is the only one who can properly delight in the aesthetic because he or she has died and continues to die daily to the sinful allure that beauty can be captured by his or her efforts."[55] The cross of Christ is indeed the pinnacle of beauty, but it destroys humanity's attempts to possess beauty. The cross brings humanity into a new way of receiving God's good gifts. The cross of Christ unites spiritual beauty with created beauty and gives created beauty its transcendent nature. As it relates to Christ and the cross, created beauty truly is theophanic. In the next section I explore the subjective aspects of theological aesthetics.

---

52. Balthasar 1982, *GL* 1, 48.
53. Balthasar 1982, *GL* 1, 48.
54. Quoted by Garrett, "A Peculiar Beauty," 30.
55. Rosebrock, "The Heidelberg Disputation and Aesthetics," 354.

## SUBJECTIVE ASPECT OF THEOLOGICAL AESTHETICS

### Embodied Nature of the Perceiving Subject

The study of theological aesthetics is informed by theological anthropology. God created humans to perceive and enjoy beauty. Part of what it means to be human is to have a physical body. John of Damascus recognized, "body-ness is a *sine qua non* feature of the whole human existence: the body is not something man has, but the basis of his/her essence."[56] Before him, Augustine reflected on the nature of man as body and soul, but Augustine tended to minimize the body because of the temptations it offered. Because evangelical theological aesthetics appreciates the profound impact of sin on desires and perception, the goodness of material and created beauty must be emphasized.

John of Damascus provides a healthy corrective to the iconoclastic tendency of rejecting the material. He rejoiced in the material nature of man and the need for the senses, not only for perception but also for understanding spiritual truths. God's design in creating humans with both material and spiritual aspects established the possibility of theological aesthetics. Created persons are not only able to respond aesthetically to created beauty and art, but God has given them the capacity to respond with all the aesthetic varieties of wonder to the beauty of God revealed in created beauty. As John of Damascus and Pseudo-Dionysius emphasized, the beauty of God and the spiritual realm is not encountered in a disembodied spiritual state but through the materiality of sense experience as it encounters created or artistic beauty.[57] Because of the structure of anthropology and the truth of embodiment, it is easy to recognize with John the value and importance of the use of material and creative means for understanding and enjoying spiritual truths.

This approach provides a philosophical foundation and minor corrective for James K.A. Smith's theological anthropology presented in *Desiring the Kingdom: Worship, Worldview, and Cultural Foundation*. I here present a summary of his argument as a movement toward a theological anthropology that fits within the insights of theological aesthetics. However, I also offer an appreciative critique of his anthropology based on Balthasar's theology of the coinherence of the transcendentals. Smith

---

56. Adrahtas, "The Notion of Symbol," 16.
57. Dyrness, *Visual Faith*, 5.

developed a theological anthropology based on insights from Augustine and Heidegger.[58] Smith argues from the Augustinian insight that our hearts are oriented by desire and love: "To be human is to be just such a lover—a creature whose orientation and form of life is most primordially shaped by what one loves as ultimate, which constitutes an affective, gut-like orientation to the world that is prior to reflection and even eludes conceptual articulation."[59] This orienting desire of love is "prereflective, imaginative 'attunement' to the world that precedes the articulation of ideas and even belief."[60] For Smith, embodied nature means that the senses are portals to the heart that shape and mold our core affectional dispositions and identity.[61] Because of this, the senses are the training ground for the affections and loves. The senses should be guided by practices, habits, and liturgies that form the heart to love God as ultimate and at the same time guard the heart from disordered loves.[62]

Smith's work presents a model for forming the heart through liturgical practices, but it is also a polemic against an overly intellectual approach to pedagogy. He argues that the dominant model of pedagogy for Christian centers of learning is dominated by a Cartesian anthropology that views people as essentially "thinking things that are containers for ideas" because it reduces Christian formation to "a set of ideas, principles, claims and propositions that are known and believed."[63] He, therefore, rightly critiques the dominant model as reductionistic, focusing on one aspect of anthropology at the expense of a more holistic approach.

These insights are consistent with theological aesthetics. However, while he offers a philosophical framework for the importance of liturgies, he overcorrects the current emphasis by devaluing the propositional and rational aspects of theological anthropology. He does not believe his project undermines the intellectual, but propositional truth and doctrine are devalued in the commendable process of emphasizing the beauty of practice and liturgy. In the second volume of the series, *Imagining the Kingdom*, Smith responds to his critics that this was not his intention. However, he then reaffirms, "The driving center of human actions and behaviors is a nexus of loves, longings, and habits that hums under the

---

58. Smith, *Desiring the Kingdom*, 25, 28.
59. Smith, *Desiring the Kingdom*, 51.
60. Smith, *Desiring the Kingdom*, 28.
61. Smith, *Desiring the Kingdom*, 58.
62. Smith, *Desiring the Kingdom*, 28.
63. Smith, *Desiring the Kingdom*, 32.

AN EVANGELICAL PROTESTANT THEOLOGICAL AESTHETIC    219

hood, so to speak, *without needing to be thought about.*"[64] Thus, he is right to critique the intellectual overemphasis, but he does so in such a way that devalues the cognitive and propositional.

Smith's devaluing of the propositional is on display when he ridicules of those who emphasize the Creator-creature distinction. I have emphasized that the Creator-creature distinction is the starting point for any orthodox theological aesthetics. Smith, however, critiques this. He quotes a poem by Anne Sexton, "the hair I brush each morning, in the Canon towel newly washed, that I rub my body with each morning, in the chapel of eggs I cook each morning in the outcry from the kettle that heats my coffee . . ." She concludes, "All this is God."[65] Smith approves of this and says, "While the doctrine police get worried about blurring the Creator/creature distinction and thus position themselves at a distance from this enchanted space, they unwittingly evacuate the world of its charge and grandeur."[66] This is one example of the over-correction of Smith's approach. Sexton's poem aligns with Rahner's argument that the infinity of God looks at him through Dürer's "The Hare."[67]

Although there is a distinction, there is also a similarity between Smith's phenomenological anthropology and Rahner's spiritual existential. Smith does not go to Rahner's extreme, but Rahner demonstrates the extreme position phenomenology can reach. Rahner developed the possibility of an "anonymous Christian" who could experience God's grace in the midst of life even if this was a preconscious experience.[68] Rahner did this through adapting Kant's transcendental apperception to Heidegger's phenomenology. The overlap with Rahner and Smith is due to the influence of phenomenology and the emphasis on the category of preconscious knowledge of the embodied subject. Smith's argument is built on the phenomenology of Heidegger and Merleau-Ponty.[69] Smith follows these philosophers and says the human person experiences life as "being-in-the-world" and is interwoven with the context of the world. Phenomenology argues that there is a preconscious knowledge that all people have based on their experience. Smith explains, "The body carries a kind of acquired, habituated knowledge or know how that is irreducible

64. Smith, *Imagining the Kingdom*, 12.
65. Smith, *Desiring the Kingdom*, 147.
66. Smith, *Desiring the Kingdom*, 147.
67. Rahner, ". "Theology and the Arts," 29.
68. Little, "Anthropology and Art in the Theology of Karl Rahner," 941.
69. Smith, *Imagining the Kingdom*, 44.

and inarticulable, and yet fundamentally *orienting* for our being-in-the-world."[70] Therefore, the theological anthropology of Smith emphasizes the value of an "antepredicative" and "preconscious knowledge" that forms the practices and habits and forms the heart and loves.[71]

If Smith's approach is consistently applied, doctrine and theology will be undervalued, and the arts and social imaginary will reign without the foundation that doctrine supplies. Smith's approach demonstrates what often goes wrong in the theological aesthetic project. Proponents of theological aesthetics rightly note an overemphasis and lack of health in the dominant approach to theology. In theological discussion, truth is deemed as more important than beauty. As a result, theological aesthetic proponents are in danger of overcorrecting this and rejecting doctrinal clarity and precision. This overcorrection results in a blurring of the Creator-creature distinction and movement toward pantheistic articulations. When those who emphasize doctrine, or in Smith's language, "the doctrine police,"[72] caution about potential danger, the response is not heeded because it comes from someone who overemphasizes the propositional nature of theology. However, the danger of doctrinal heresy is a real and present danger.

While Smith notices an overemphasis in intellectualist approaches, his solution is also an overemphasis. Balthasar's theology of the transcendentals provides a healthy corrective not only to those who overemphasize the propositional and intellectual aspects of doctrine but also a corrective to the current field of theological aesthetics, which tends to follow Rahner and overemphasize beauty and the arts at the expense of doctrinal truth. Balthasar reminds that truth and beauty coinhere in one another, along with goodness. Truth complements and transforms beauty, and beauty complements and transforms truth. Truth without goodness and beauty is no longer truth; beauty without truth and goodness is no longer beauty.

Therefore, theological anthropology will recognize human's need for truth, beauty, and goodness. The affections and loves are shaped through practices, habits, liturgies, and the senses, but also through the intellect and the beauty of truth. For Edwards, love and affections can only be based on rational understanding.[73] Edwards was clear, love can only be

70. Smith, *Imagining the Kingdom*, 45.
71. Smith, *Imagining the Kingdom*, 53.
72. Smith, *Desiring the Kingdom*, 147.
73. McClymond, "Spiritual Perception in Jonathan Edwards," 208.

set on something that is an object of the understanding. In Smith's project, Edwards would be guilty of excessive intellectualism. For Edwards, Smith's concept of the preconscious relation to love would be nonsensical. However, Smith and Edwards complement each other wonderfully, even though their emphasis is radically different. While both are Augustinian in their argument of the importance of the affections and rightly ordered love, they move into different streams of emphasis. Smith emphasizes the tactile and sensory aspects of affections, desires, and love, while Edwards emphasizes the intellectual and cognitive aspects.

Balthasar's use of Aquinas shows us how to navigate between overemphasis on either the side of the body or the side of the mind. Balthasar's theological anthropology establishes the unity of body and mind.[74] Balthasar viewed the human person as a "corporeal-psychic totality."[75] The unity of the body and intellect in the human being establishes a theological anthropology that emphasizes both aspects. Similarly, Aquinas recognized the interplay of reason, emotion, and the physical body as the person encounters the beautiful.[76] However, Aquinas provides a needed warning that the unity of this interplay between the senses and intellect follows a process that is "defined, secured, and ordered."[77] In other words, while Smith overemphasizes the corporeal and Edwards overemphasized the intellectual, Balthasar's synthesis of the two leads to a conflation of physical and intellectual that weakens the distinctive contribution of both. Aquinas's ordered process of moving from sense perception to reason and the intellect presented in chapter 3 allows for an appreciation of both aspects.

Balthasar's doctrine of the transcendentals and how they are experienced by the personal subject presented in chapter 4 reminds us that the sensory and intellect are not at odds with one another, but mutually interpret and coinhere in one another. Balthasar reminds us of the need for balance in theological anthropology with the reminder that God has revealed himself as true, good, and beautiful to the whole man. Therefore, evangelical theological aesthetics will consider the unity of the body and intellect and their distinction.

---

74. McInroy, *Balthasar on the Spiritual Senses*, 155.
75. Balthasar, *GL* 1, 385.
76. O'Reilly, *Aesthetic Perception*, 17.
77. Eco, *The Aesthetics of Thomas Aquinas*, 63.

## Bondage, the Physical Senses, and the Spiritual Sense

Theological aesthetics in the Balthasarian tradition is the perception of the glory of the Lord and a type of existential "interiority" generated by that perception.[78] McInroy explains that Balthasar united perception of the physical senses with the perception of the spiritual splendor of God.[79] In other words, the physical senses have the ability to perceive supernaturally.[80] In chapter 3, I demonstrated that the doctrine of the spiritual sense is also a key theological concept for Edwards. Scholarship on Edwards's use of the spiritual sense enlightens the discussion here. There are three ways the spiritual sense may relate to the bodily senses: (1) The spiritual sense may have no connection to the bodily senses; (2) the spiritual sense supernaturally may be interwoven into the physical senses; or (3) the spiritual sense is a new sense in that it allows for the perception of the spiritual beauty of God. This debate within Edwards's scholarship demonstrates the different approaches to the spiritual sense and how it relates to the body's physical senses.

In the first view, there is a division between spiritual and corporeal. In this view, the spiritual sense has little to do with the senses of the body. The second and third views are similar, but slightly distinct. In the second view, the spiritual sense is united with the bodily senses. This describes Balthasar's approach. McInroy concludes his study on Balthasar's approach to the spiritual sense, "Balthasar thoroughly conjoins spiritual and corporeal perception such that the two occur in a single unified act. Spiritual perception does not occur without its corporeal counterpart."[81] This approach has much to offer it. In Balthasar's understanding, this unification is at once the synthesis of the bodily senses and the spiritual sense as well as the unification and synthesis of foundational and dogmatic theology. Balthasar's project synthesized the newness and objectively other of dogmatic theology with the immanence of Rahner's theological anthropology.[82] While Balthasar effectively did this, as mentioned above, the issue with his synthesis is that he did not fully appreciate a doctrine of sin. Therefore, for Balthasar, like Rahner, the revelation of God and the

---

78. Balthasar, *GL* 1, 298.
79. McInroy, *Balthasar on the Spiritual Senses*, 134.
80. Balthasar, *GL* 6, 35. McInroy, *Balthasar on the Spiritual Senses*, 158.
81. McInroy, *Balthasar on the Spiritual Senses*, 187.
82. McInroy, *Balthasar on the Spiritual Senses*, 176.

spiritual sense are inherent and intrinsic within man. However, this tacit knowledge must be drawn out by encountering God's revelation.

Balthasar's understanding of the spiritual sense does not take into consideration the impact of the bondage to sin. This is why, for Athanasius, Augustine, Aquinas, Luther, and Edwards, the doctrine of sin was a crucial aspect in their development of theological aesthetic concepts. The reception of a spiritual sense is an essential aspect of understanding the existential interiority of the subject. Without this spiritual sense, the person bound in sin will not be able to see the beauty of God or spiritual things. The heart is "dead in sin" (Ephesians 2:1), and without the new birth, there will be no way to perceive the beauty of God. Those outside of Christ may have experiences of the sublime or transcendent, but it will not be an experience leading to worship of the triune God. When the person who does not believe in Christ experiences the transcendent, he or she receives an inkling of God's grandeur. However, even though the experience has value in and of itself, it falls short of the teleological goal inherent in God's purpose for creating the world.

The beauty and splendor will remain hidden and obscure and often even appear ugly or evil. While Balthasar argues that the spiritual sense is united to the bodily senses, the biblical witness is clear that regeneration is necessary. The natural man does not have the spiritual sense. The necessity of regeneration was seen in the previous chapter in the discussion on John 1:13 and John 3:1–15. Natural humanity does not receive Christ's light and does not perceive him rightly (John 1:12–13). In John 3:1–15, Nicodemus is presented as the paradigmatic human who comes to Jesus in the dark of night without understanding even though he had a shallow faith in Jesus. Nicodemus needed Jesus to open his eyes to understand spiritual things. Jesus taught Nicodemus that true perception is only possible when the Holy Spirit enables people to see the glory of God, which would be displayed in Jesus's lifting up (John 3:14–15). John 3 clearly shows that only the regenerated or born again can see Jesus Christ and know the splendor of his beauty. They have "the eyes of their hearts enlightened" (Ephesians 1:18) to see the beauty of God. The blinding effects of the sin nature and the demonic forces are undone, and the glorious beauty of God is perceived. In the new birth, a new perception of Christ or new sense is given to the soul (2 Corinthians 4:4–6).

In the theology of the cross, this new birth can only happen because the sinful nature and the bondage to sin have been destroyed by Christ's work on the cross. The cross accomplished redemption objectively and is now able to be applied to the personal subject by the Spirit. In the event of regeneration, the ability to truly perceive spiritual beauty has been given. Before that event, natural man could use his senses to see beauty, but it always stayed on the physical level. Even though God's spiritual beauty is inherent within created beauty, the natural man is blinded from seeing that spiritual beauty. The fallen nature impacts every aspect of life. It is here especially that Smith's work on the preconscious practices that form our lives is perceptive and distinct from Balthasar's theological anthropology.[83] Smith critiques the intellectualist accounts of sin and temptation because these approaches make every sin a deliberate choice. Instead, Smith argues that our sinful nature manifests itself in our habitus, preconscious practices, and way of life. Not only that, but we unconsciously absorb the narratives and systems that project themselves on us with metaphorical power. This is what Paul spoke of when he said that humankind are the "sons of disobedience" who follow the "course of this world" (Ephesians 3:1–3).

However, when regeneration occurs a new spiritual sense is given, and true perception of God and his beauty are seen wherever the regenerated person looks. This event of regeneration and obtaining a new sense is what Edwards describes as "the divine and supernatural light" being imparted to the soul.[84] Edwards's language here is based on the Johannine language that was seen in the last chapter. For Edwards this "light" or spiritual sense is nothing less than God's own Spirit and delight within the human being. In Ryan Martin's study of Jonathan Edwards use of the affections, he shows the relation of the spiritual sense to the affections.[85] The Spirit gives a new, spiritual sense to the believer and the believer now has a new love and affection for spiritual beauty.[86] When Edwards says, "true religion, in great part consists in holy affections," he is building on an Augustinian theology of rightly ordered love, which is possible for the believer who now has the new spiritual sense. For evangelical theological aesthetics, the new birth and the receiving of the spiritual sense is where a true perception of God and love for his beauty begins. In Balthasar's theological anthropology, this spiritual perception begins at birth and needs to be more fully formed or uncovered, but from a biblical perspective the true perception of Christ only comes at the new birth.

83. Smith, *Imagining the Kingdom*, 140.
84. *WJE* 17:413.
85. Martin, *Understanding Affections in the Theology of Jonathan Edwards*.
86. Martin, *Understanding Affections in the Theology of Jonathan Edwards*, 234.

From the Protestant perspective, the solution to the difference between Balthasar and Protestants on the spiritual sense is to appropriate Balthasar's theology of the spiritual sense to the believer. While the Protestant cannot accept that the unbeliever has a spiritual sense, he can agree with Balthasar's insights on the spiritual sense for believers. Clarity in the distinction of who has this spiritual sense and how it operates is a crucial distinction for the future of the field of theological aesthetics. If one assumes a general spiritual sense for all mankind, theological aesthetics will lose its distinctively orthodox moorings. At the same time, I must note that there is apologetic value to the unbeliever's limited sense of experiencing God's beauty in creation. Indeed, this experience may lead to an experience of *Sehnsucht* explored in chapter 2 that brings a person to Christ.[87] God may work in that experience to lead the person to himself and impart that "divine and supernatural light."

However, the question arises: how does the spiritual sense operate in the believer? Another question is how the cross relates to the perception of created beauty. First, Luther's theology of the cross is essential to evangelical Protestant theological aesthetics to keep it from becoming a theological aesthetics of glory. As I mentioned above, Balthasar critiqued Luther's theology of the cross for its deconstructionism. It is best to summarize Luther's atonement theology and theology of the cross as a combat against sin, death, the law, and the devil.[88] Falconer demonstrates that Luther's theory of the atonement was multifaceted and nuanced.[89] Luther's theology of the cross is often misunderstood and overly simplified. It includes a theology of the resurrection. In this way, Luther's theology of the cross establishes a theology of aesthetics.[90] Theological aesthetics of the cross does not constantly gaze at the cross but presses through to resurrection life because of the cross. A theological aesthetic of the cross embraces resurrection life and sees all of reality in light of the cross.

Once the cross has been spiritually apprehended by faith, Luther says that the believer is now permitted, and even invited, to enjoy the good gifts of creation.[91] Luther viewed music as a mirror of God's beauty that reached the soul directly.[92] However, this is only true for the

87. Lewis, *Surprised by Joy*, 14–18.
88. Falconer, "Crux Sola Est Nostra Theologia," 292.
89. Falconer, "Crux Sola Est Nostra Theologia," 293.
90. Rosebrock, "The Heidelberg Disputation and Aesthetics," 354.
91. Heal, *A Magnificent Faith*, 17.
92. Viladesau, *Theological Aesthetics*, 149.

one who approaches music through the cross. As Owen Strachan puts it, "Now we have seen the God-man. We have found the one who brings light back into our eyes and hope back into our souls."[93] The spiritual sight of Christ in faith changes the way we view everything.

Once Luther's biblical theology of sin and the solution of the cross is properly appreciated, Balthasar's insights on the spiritual sense can be appropriated. The person who sees Christ and believes the gospel is the one who has received the spiritual sense and has the eyes of their heart enlightened (Ephesians 1:18). While Balthasar wants to equate the spiritual sense and the physical senses, the theology of the cross teaches us that the spiritual sense transforms the physical senses. In the life of the believer, the physical senses are experienced only in light of the truth of the cross and resurrection of Christ.

Though there are significant differences, Kant's discussion of perception in his development of transcendental apperception can help demonstrate how the spiritual sense operates in the life of a believer. With Balthasar, we note that Kant was misguided in his persistent focus on perception and thought rather than objectivity.[94] However, also like Balthasar, we note that Kant said some profound things about the nature of perception. For Kant, the "transcendental aesthetic" describes how the subject perceives the sensory impressions and unifies the experience by imposing "pure *a priori* intuitions" of space and time onto the experience.[95] From the perspective of theological aesthetics and the nature of the spiritual sense, the reception of these phenomena and appearances are *in themselves* objectively charged with the beauty of God or the ugliness of the curse or a simultaneous mixture. The spiritual sense, therefore, gives a new taste or new aesthetic to respond to these phenomena. In Edwards's language, the spiritual sense is a newfound ability to respond at the level of the affections to these impressions with either a love and delight or a repulsion. In Luther's language, it is a new ability to see things the way God sees them and through God's wisdom rather than the world's wisdom.

For this reason, a believer and an unbeliever can receive the same perception of phenomena by the physical senses. However, because of the spiritual sense, the believer can perceive more than what is on the

---

93. Strachan, *Reenchanting Humanity*, 282.
94. Levering, *The Achievement of Hans Urs von Balthasar*, 34.
95. Kant, *Critique of Pure Reason*, 114.

surface. Augustine demonstrated that the person with the spiritual sense can enjoy sensory beauty because it becomes an analogy for God's beauty.[96] Edwards sees a flower and says that he sees the love and purity of Christ.[97] John the Evangelist sees light, and he was reminded of the light that came into the world (John 1:9). The things of creation are enjoyed for their intrinsic beauty as an expression of God's glory. They also become metaphors that teach the believer about God. The believer, therefore, is invited to look at the things of creation and discover truths about God. Jesus invites people to "look at the birds of the air" (Matthew 6:26–34).

Taking Smith's warning about the over-emphasis on the intellectual, at another level, God's beauty in creation and the arts is not valuable only because of the metaphor or analogy it provides but because it simply *is* the beauty of God in a way meant to be enjoyed and delighted in for its own sake. Balthasar captures this, "Beauty is the aspect of truth that cannot be fit into any definition but can be apprehended only in direct intercourse with it."[98] The spiritual sense allows this experience and delight in God's beauty and allows this perception to be reflected upon in the intellect.

Therefore, the person with the spiritual sense may be looking at the same object as someone without the spiritual sense, and yet see something completely different. To see with the spiritual sense is to see truly. Alister McGrath shows that this is the point of Lewis's *The Pilgrim's Regress*. Lewis's early allegory describes two journeys.[99] The first journey is toward a mysterious island and the second is the return back home. In these two journeys, even though he is looking at the same landscape, his perception of that landscape has completely changed. After the allegorical conversion, the pilgrim's sight has completely changed, and he is now "seeing the land as it really is."[100] The spiritual sense operates in the same way. It transforms the perception of all reality. This happens for every believer at regeneration. However, the spiritual sense needs formation.

The new sense and the new affections need to be trained and developed. It is not as though those with the spiritual sense always respond in a way appropriate or in line with God's perspective. This is due to the nature of indwelling sin in the life of the believer. Even though the spiritual sense has been given, the wisdom of God must still form and transform

---

96. Augustine, *Confessions* X.6, 212.
97. *WJE* 13:279.
98. Balthasar, *TL* 1, 136.
99. McGrath, *Born to Wonder*, 66.
100. McGrath, *Born to Wonder*, 67.

our minds. Unlike Kant's transcendental unity of apperception, the impressions made on our senses through experience are not automatically and simultaneously placed into concepts and categories during our experience. These concepts and thoughts are not a synthetic *a priori* based on the constitution of being a new creation in Christ with a spiritual sense. These thought processes must be created in the understanding by the Scriptures. The Holy Spirit works alongside and within the believing individual so that in the operation of the spiritual sense the person begins to love the things that God loves. The believer's mind begins to think God's thoughts after him as the Scriptures shape it. Not only that, but the spiritual sense begins to form a bodily basis of holiness.[101] There is a unity of body and mind as Balthasar's and Smith's theological anthropology reminds us. Therefore, not only is the believer's mind formed, but the practices and habits of formation and way of being in the world are also transformed.[102]

This is what Balthasar means when he speaks of the theory of vision and the theory of rapture. The spiritual sense that is functioning properly will impact the body, affections, and intellect. The person with this spiritual sense that is being formed will respond rightly to the perception of God's beauty in Jesus Christ and be brought up into him in the rapture of love. For Balthasar, the spiritual sense and perception is nothing less than faith in Jesus Christ, and at the same time, seeing all of reality through the lens of faith and using the physical senses to perceive Christ and the beauty of God.[103]

## Theological Aesthetics and Wonder

Theological aesthetics and the nature of the spiritual sense has profound implications for the individual's everyday life. I explore many of these implications in the next chapter. However, one of the ways theological aesthetics and the spiritual sense impact the believer's daily life is that it provides a capacity to wonder at the beauty of God. Building on Charles Taylor's *A Secular Age*, Owen Strachan demonstrates that mankind in the modern age is fundamentally *disenchanted* and needs to be *reenchanted* by Christ to return to the state God intended. He claims God created a

---

101. Smith, *Imagining the Kingdom*, 113.
102. Smith, *Imagining the Kingdom*, 114.
103. Maeseneer, "Retrieving the Spiritual Senses," 277.

world that is enchanted, that is, full of wonder and transcendent majesty. In Balthasar's language, the world is theophanic. However, because of sin and the fall, mankind needs to be reenchanted, and their eyes reopened to the glory they live in.[104]

In Balthasar's metaphysics, beauty is inherent in all being and seen everywhere. Balthasar explains that all created reality is inherently charged with the grandeur of God and every entity has an eternal and transcendent "more."[105] Everything is enchanted with a "perennially inexhaustible wonder."[106] However, as Balthasar noted, even though created reality is enchanted in this way, the dullness of humanity and their disenchanted state keeps them from truly seeing reality. He explains:

> Works of art can die as a result of being looked at by too many dull eyes, and even the radiance of holiness can, in a way, become blunted when it encounters nothing but hollow indifference. But this remains an external offence to beauty which may be rectified by purifying the heart and by exhuming what has been buried under the ruins.[107]

The dull eyes described here are the result of a disenchanted state of existence that is characterized by a loss of wonder.[108]

The natural person can discern beauty in nature and the arts. However, as Kierkegaard demonstrated, this mode of life only stays on the surface of things. The aesthetic must go deeper than the mere surface, no matter how beautiful the surface is. However, those who remain on the surface of reality can achieve a measure of reenchanting themselves to see beauty. They awake themselves to see the beauty of creation or the arts. This, in fact, is often the function of the arts, to help "rehabilitate the lost wonder of the squandered ordinary."[109] However, general aesthetics ultimately attempts do what is only possible after they have been enlightened by the spiritual sense.

Theological aesthetics shows how Jesus Christ solved both the objective and subjective (perceptive) problem of beauty. Jesus Christ restored beauty through his work on the cross and resurrection and also

---

104. Strachan, *Reenchanting Humanity*, 53.
105. Balthasar, *TL* 1, 136.
106. Balthasar, *TL* 1, 143.
107. Balthasar, *GL* 1, 23.
108. McGrath, *Born to Wonder*, 143.
109. Viladesau, *Theological Aesthetics*, 181.

provided the spiritual sense in regeneration to solve the problem with perception. The theology of the cross offers the solution to the "offense to beauty... by purifying the heart and by exhuming what has been buried under the ruins."[110] Created beauty is perceived with regenerated eyes. As Kierkegaard's stages reveal, an encounter with God does not destroy the aesthetic, but rather transforms and redeems it.

The person with the spiritual sense can respond properly in wonder to the beauty of God, wherever it is seen. The Christian, therefore, is a person who has been reenchanted with the inexhaustible wonder of all of life.[111] Craig Baron describes this well, "For the person of faith, the re-enchanted sense of 'wonder' about nature draws the imagination upward to glimpse a divine source and eternal destiny."[112] The spiritual sense, if properly developed in the believer's life, allows the individual to awaken to the wonder of God's beauty in the world. This wonder is an affective joy that hungers for the divine and sees all created beauty as a sign that signifies God.

Wonder is not unique to the believer. It is an experience of common grace. However, for the believer, wonder does not end in puzzlement as to the meaning of wonder, but in worship. Sherry demonstrates from Plato, Aristotle, Kant, and Wittgenstein that wonder is the beginning of the philosophic endeavor.[113] McGrath, likewise, argues that wonder is the root of the scientific enterprise.[114] Sherry says that wonder is closely linked to "powerful human responses like admiration, fascination, delight, fear or horror, gratitude, and worship."[115] Wonder can be evoked at a sense perception or an intellectual reflection. Charles Taylor speaks of works of art, such as Chartres Cathedral or *The Divine Comedy*, that have an "epiphanic transcendent reference."[116] In other words, created beauty or art reveals a transcendent reality that evokes wonder. Taylor goes on, "Here the challenge is to the unbeliever, to find a non-theistic register in which to respond to them without impoverishment."[117] Therefore, Balthasar indicated that the Christian faith provides the only non-tragic

---

110. Balthasar, *GL* 1, 23.
111. Balthasar, *TL* 1, 143.
112. Baron, "Christian Theology and the Re-Enchantment of the World," 119.
113. Sherry, *Spirit and Beauty*, 341–343.
114. McGrath, *Born to Wonder*, 142.
115. Sherry, *Spirit and Beauty*, 341.
116. Taylor, *A Secular Age*, 607.
117. Taylor, *A Secular Age*, 607.

justification for worldly beauty. The experience of wonder leads to reflection about that experience and can give no satisfactory answers for it.[118] Even the epiphany of wonder for the unbeliever turns into an "existential black hole" because the source of transcendent beauty is unknown.[119] For the unbeliever, the referent of the transcendent is fundamentally unknown, but for the believer the transcendent is known and loved.

The spiritual sense opens the way for the aesthetic enjoyment of creation and the arts. It fuels wonder at epiphanic theophanies of the transcendent God in everyday life. This wonder is not cheapened by an immediate move toward the intellectual explanation of how this relates to Jesus Christ and the cross. Instead, the evoked wonder draws the person into worshiping the God who is there and revealed in that moment.

## SUMMARY

In this chapter, I explored the objective and subjective aspects of the beauty of the Lord. The objective aspect begins with distinguishing *ad intra* glory, the glory of God experienced within the Trinity, and *ad extra* glory, the glory of God displayed outside of himself in creation. Glory and beauty are different, but fundamentally related. God's glory emphasizes the objective nature of the worth and majesty of God, while the beauty of the Lord emphasizes the intrinsically aesthetical dimension of God's glory when it is perceived.

Theological aesthetics teaches us that there is no inherent tension between the beauty of God and created beauty. The beauty of creation is a revelation of God and is inherently theophanic. However, the perceived tension between the beauty of the Lord and the beauty of creation is primarily anthropological or existential. It arises from humanity's refusal to acknowledge God's beauty in creation, instead choosing to worship and possess created beauty without acknowledging the glory of God. I underscored that an evangelical Protestant theological aesthetic must grapple with a theology of sin. I then proceeded to demonstrate how Jesus Christ is the solution to the problem of sin through his redemptive work on the cross and resurrection. Thus, evangelical theological aesthetics is firmly rooted in a theology of the cross, where worldly beauty is restored and humanity's bondage to sin is addressed. Those who respond to Christ in

---

118. McGrath, *Born to Wonder*, 162.
119. McGrath, *Born to Wonder*, 162.

faith have the spiritual sense. The spiritual sense allows all of reality to be seen in light of Christ's work on the cross and resurrection. The spiritual sense also informs the use of the physical senses and allows the physical senses to perceive God's beauty revealed in creation. The spiritual sense, when it is properly developed, also opens humanity's eyes to the wonder of God in all reality. Those with the spiritual sense see all things in relation to God and creation, and worldly beauty may be enjoyed with wonder and delight because they reveal God's beauty. In the next chapter, I give examples of how evangelical theological aesthetics find expression in the individual and church life.

# 7

# The Aesthetics of the Theo-Drama

THE TRANSCENDENTALS—THE GOOD, THE true, and the beautiful—are metaphysically united. However, they also may be existential realities. Goodness, truth, and beauty coinhere and are displayed in the life of the individual believer and the community of the local church. This chapter explains how theological aesthetics leads into the theo-drama. This movement demonstrates how the moral agent is transformed by the perception of the beauty of God and sent out into the world to participate in and display that beauty publicly. James K.A. Smith speaks of this as the "transformative 'spiritual work' of *leitourgia* (Rom. 12:1) in order to be transformed, rather than being conformed to the world; and yet even this is for the sake of the world."[1]

In this chapter, I begin with a discussion of the movement from theological aesthetics to theo-drama. Theological aesthetics and the theo-drama have implications for the believer, whose life becomes a work of art that displays beauty. Lilias Trotter is given as an example of a believer whose life was a beautiful work of art. However, theological aesthetics also has implications for art creation and enjoyment. Theological aesthetics invites the pursuit of art that has an iconic effect and avoids the extremes of kitsch and apophatic art. This chapter concludes with some reflections on the implications theological aesthetics has for the artist and the theologian.

---

1. Smith, *Awaiting the King*, 58.

## LITURGY AND THE THEO-DRAMA

Balthasar's second series of work in his trilogy, *Theo-Drama: Theological Dramatic Theory* (4 volumes) focuses on the theo-drama. Wesley Vander Lugt provides an extensive bibliography of those who have expanded on the metaphor of drama and its implications for ethics and theology.[2] The theo-drama is God's action in the history of redemption that invites the audience to participate in this drama and play their own part.[3] However, it is a distinctive emphasis of Balthasar to insist that the theo-drama rests on a proper understanding of theological aesthetics.[4] The connection between theological aesthetics and the theo-drama rests on the inherent connection between beauty and goodness.[5] Most treatments of theological aesthetics fail to realize the inherent connection between aesthetics and ethics.[6] Goodness is a form of moral beauty. Kant argued that beauty in nature and the arts are a "symbol of the moral good."[7] Beauty in nature and art is indeed symbolic. Augustine, John of Damascus, and Jonathan Edwards especially saw that beauty in creation and the arts is a sign or symbol that refers to a deeper, more primary beauty. Beauty points to the transcendent beauty of God. This transcendent beauty is not static, as if the beauty remains "out there" for mere observation. This is even true of seeing the beauty of God in created beauty. The beauty of God in nature and art is dynamic and transformative.

Balthasar's use of Pseudo-Dionysius's theology of procession and return demonstrates that God's outpouring and revelation demands a response and return from the perceiving subject. Balthasar calls this the "double and reciprocal *ecstasis*."[8] In Balthasar's theology this procession and return are what unites theological aesthetics and the theo-drama. The first procession is the beauty that proceeds from God, the Source. The second procession is from the receiving human subject who responds to God's revelation of beauty by returning to him in love and delight. This return to God is the glorification of man as he responds in faith to God. Theological aesthetics in the Balthasarian tradition emphasizes that

---

2. Vander Lugt, "Church Beyond the Fourth Wall," 7.
3. Balthasar, *TD* 1, 151. See also: Vanhoozer, *The Drama of Doctrine*, 78.
4. Balthasar, *TD* 1, 15.
5. Garrett, "God's Beauty-in-Act," 413.
6. Jantzen, "Beauty for Ashes," 428.
7. Kant, *Critique of the Power of Judgment*, 225.
8. Balthasar, *GL* 1, 126.

God's procession and revelation finds its pinnacle in Jesus Christ. The Transcendent One was revealed in the realm of our senses. It is through the pinnacle of this revelation that the return to God begins. The cross and resurrection of Christ is where moral beauty or goodness is re-established in the middle of the broken stage in the cosmic drama. As people respond in faith to the splendor of the good news of what Jesus Christ accomplished in the cross and resurrection, they are united with Christ and set on the return to God culminating in glorification in the eschaton.

Those who respond in faith are united to Jesus and participate in him. Balthasar explains, "The object with which we are concerned is man's participation in God, which, from God's perspective, is actualized as revelation (culminating in Christ's Godmanhood) and which, from man's perspective, is actualized as 'faith' (culminating in participation in Christ's Godmanhood)."[9] This participation is at once beholding and becoming. The perceiving subject beholds the glory of Christ and becomes like him. The one who has faith in Christ is immersed in the "unfolding action" and "performative nature" of believing.[10] One of Balthasar's paradigmatic texts describing this is 2 Corinthians 3:18, "And we all with unveiled face, beholding the glory of the Lord, are being transformed into the same image from one degree of glory to another. For this comes from the Lord who is the Spirit." The beholding of Christ, through the eyes of faith, works a transformation in the beholder. This is the basis of imitation of Christ as the beholding perceiver becomes more and more like Christ, the One he is united to by the Holy Spirit. This participation and transformation based on the perception of faith is the beginning stages of glorification where that person is pulled in as an actor in the theo-drama.

The actor participates in God's drama as a result of communion with the triune God. This is the reason the public event of worship and liturgy is so important.[11] The liturgy is the space where our "loves are recalibrated" and where "God sanctifies our perception so that we can see reality more clearly."[12] The local church is the space where true perception and aesthetic delight in God is learned and received and then carried out into the world. Willis Saliers notes, "In corporate worship, Christians engage in activities which articulate and shape how they are to be disposed

9. Balthasar, *GL* 1, 125.
10. van Deventer, "The Mosaic of Belief in the Fourth Gospel," 168.
11. Smith, *Awaiting the King*, 61.
12. Smith, *Awaiting the King*, 224.

to the world."[13] Likewise, Vander Lugt develops the metaphor of drama by emphasizing that the theo-drama is an interactive theater.[14] One of the difficulties with the metaphor of theater is that it distinguishes between the performers and the audience. Interactive theater helps overcome this difficulty by allowing the audience a role in the theater. The metaphor of interactive theater can also help one understand the mission of the church in the world. The liturgy and lives of believers are extensions of the theo-drama that invites the onlooking world to participate.[15]

When Christians gather on Sunday, they rehearse and participate in God's covenant with his people.[16] This liturgy is a public event, a proclamation of the specifics of the story of the gospel and God's inbreaking into history. The worship forms a community and at the same time forms the individuals who make up that community. For Pseudo-Dionysius, the liturgy of a worship service reflects the rhythms of life and demonstrates the procession from God in creation and the return to him in redemption and restoration.[17] The liturgy is an art form that displays and proclaims the way God has created and designed all of life. The congregation participates in this liturgy and its impact extends to the rhythms of their daily lives. The liturgy is composed of the cataphatic theology presented in the Scriptures and the person of Jesus Christ, but also evokes apophatic humility before transcendence as we return to the God who will redeem and restore us.[18] Worship, then, is a reenactment and proclamation of the truths of how God is restoring all things. Thus, worship reminds us that we live and participate in God's story. Not only that, but the church's worship proclaims God's rule and reign over the public sphere.[19]

The reenactment of God's works in the past reminds the believer of God's covenant and continued action in the present. The liturgy is not simply a reminder of God's work in the past, but an encounter with Christ that forms the moral life.[20] The worship service is a call to remember and move into every area of life as an actor on God's grand stage. The stage metaphor was a favorite of Calvin's who points out that

13. Saliers, "Liturgy and Ethics," 176.
14. Vander Lugt, "Church Beyond the Fourth Wall."
15. Vander Lugt, "Church Beyond the Fourth Wall," 12.
16. Smith, *Awaiting the King*, 60.
17. *Ecclesiastical Hierarchy* 3.3.3. See Louth, "Apophatic Theology," 80.
18. Louth, "Apophatic Theology," 81.
19. Smith, *Awaiting the King*, 67.
20. Steck, "Graced Encounters," 256.

we live our daily lives in the theater of God. Vanhoozer reminds that church worship is not "dead theater" where the Bible is attempted to be mechanically reproduced, but rather an event where God's actions are remembered and pressed into the lives of the particular actors present at the worship service.[21] Those actors themselves leave the worship service ready to engage in the part that God has ordained them to play on his stage in front of the watching world.

Balthasar saw that there is a flawless movement from theological aesthetics into the theo-drama.[22] This is the reason Balthasar's theological aesthetics only indirectly speak of art and created beauty. Balthasar was most concerned with the movement of drama, and he understood that this movement begins as a person truly perceives the beauty of God in Jesus Christ. Christopher Steck explains, "The story of Christ reveals a divine drama at the same time as it invites us, directly and personally, to take up our role within it."[23] The person sees the activity of God in the history of redemption through the spiritual sense. The perception of faith reveals something that is not contradictory to the physical senses but transforms them and gives them meaning and purpose. What is *seen* is not a physical object, but God's revelation, his dramatic action on the stage he created. Balthasar explains, "God's revelation is not an object to be looked at: it is his action in and upon the world, and the world can only respond, and hence 'understand' through action on *its* part."[24] The act of perception creates a dramatic movement as the perceiving person is transformed and lives out a beautiful life on the stage of God's creation. The person perceives God and his drama in aesthetic delight and is given a part to play. The worship on Sunday, therefore, must be a theologically aesthetic event where the beauty of God is displayed, and each person is reminded of their part.

The accomplishment of redemption was the action of the Trinity. Now, the Holy Spirit is active in the application and formation of beauty in the space of the local church and the lives of her members. The Holy Spirit is the person of the Trinity who "breathes beauty into the world."[25] The Holy Spirit is active and breathes the breath of life on the congregation and the individuals of the community are conformed into the image of Christ.

21. Vanhoozer, *Faith Speaking Understanding*, 3.
22. Balthasar, *TD* 1, 15.
23. Steck, "Graced Encounters," 259.
24. Balthasar, *TD* 1, 15.
25. Sherry, *Spirit and Beauty*, 82.

Garrett explains, "We are attracted to and drawn into God's triune life of love, thereby entering into the dramatic movements of the risen Christ in the Spirit."[26] The work of the Spirit forms the believers into the image of Christ and presses the drama of Jesus's self-giving life into the lives of believers. In this way, the believer is enabled to walk in imitation of Christ and the "Spirit of glory" shines through that believer no matter what the circumstances, even suffering (1 Peter 4:14). It is a miracle of grace that one of the ways the Spirit breathes beauty into the world is by beautifying the lives of believers and sending them out into the world.

The life of a believer who has been transformed from the kingdom of darkness into the Kingdom of Christ, therefore, radiates the beauty of Christ in the corrupt world. The drama of redemption radiates the splendor of Jesus Christ and redeems worldly beauty. The Holy Spirit hovers over all creation applying the accomplished redemption to individuals by regenerating them and causing them to see the Son who was lifted up (John 3:1–21). The beauty of Christ's resurrection forms the believer in the present as they await their own resurrection. The believers are formed into a Kingdom of righteousness, a city on a hill that shines in splendor in the world and cannot be hidden (Matthew 5:14). In this way the eschatological reality that the believer will shine like the sun at the sight of Christ is a reality experienced already in this life (Matthew 13:43). The splendor of the treasure in the weak clay pot shines through with radiance (2 Corinthians 4:7–9). This is what Balthasar means when he says the true Christian is the highest created beauty.[27]

Therefore, the life of a believer is a work of art. God is the Master Artist who sculpts and crafts a beautiful life for the watching world to see and glorify him (Matthew 5:15). The moral life of a believer is the place where theological aesthetic beauty is lived out and put on display. Steck likewise argues, "The moral life continues the work of the liturgy: it itself becomes a liturgy for others."[28] In other words, the life of the individual Christian represents Christ. The world encounters an albeit imperfect image of Christ in the imitator of Christ. Steck continues, "The moral life is an occasion for grace in the life of the one witnessing its action because of its evocative power, which, in the Spirit, can be made to manifest

---

26. Garrett, "God's Beauty-in-Act," 447.

27. "*Die gelingende Gestalt des Christen ist das Schönste, was es im menschlichen Bereich geben kann.*" Balthasar, *Herrlichkeit* 1, 26.

28. Steck, "Graced Encounters," 267.

Christ and to lead the other to encounter him."[29] Balthasar used the metaphor of music to communicate this dynamic. The believer is like a violin that was ready to be played by God, the Great Musician.[30] Yet at the same time God is playing the instrument, the metaphor shifts and the believer himself becomes the musician who will produce something beautiful in his or her life for the glory of God.

## A LIVING WORK OF ART: THE EXAMPLE OF LILIAS TROTTER

Theological aesthetics' emphasis on the theo-dramatic and moral goodness does not devalue the beautiful in creation or the arts. However, the emphasis on moral beauty recognizes the centrifugal force of the beauty of the drama of redemption. The beauty of Christ draws the person into an encounter with him and that encounter transforms the individual and the watching world should be able to recognize that "they had been with Jesus" (Acts 4:13). As I demonstrated in the last chapter, the whole stage of the cosmos radiates beauty that finds its source and sustaining power and *telos* in the Son. The person who has perceived the beauty of Christ and been enlivened by the spiritual sense now sees created beauty in a new way. The next section develops the worldview implications for how the spiritual sense given at regeneration transforms the worldview and perception of created beauty. However, to spotlight how theological aesthetics leads into the theo-drama and the beauty of moral goodness, Lilias Trotter is given as an example.

In Kierkegaard's stages or spheres, there is a movement from the aesthetic stage, to the ethical, and finally to the religious. The aesthete must be transformed by the ethical. The moral goodness of the ethical stage confronts the aesthetic and creates an either/or dialectic. If the person rejects the ethical, that person stays in the aesthetic stage, which means for Kierkegaard that they only stay on the surface of things. If, however, the ethical is chosen, the aesthetic is taken up and deepened and creates a moral beauty. Finally, the ethical stage runs into the religious stage where the individual meets God and the aesthetic and the ethical are transformed in relationship to God. Kierkegaard's philosophy sounds obtuse and abstract, but it is in fact very concrete and personal.

---

29. Steck, "Graced Encounters," 267.
30. Balthasar, *GL* 1, 221.

Kierkegaard's existentialism demonstrates the necessary path for the true believer in Christ. The aesthetic stage should not remain simply on the surface of things but must go deeper to the persons relationship with God. Kierkegaard's purpose was not to develop a philosophical system, but to provide existential categories that can be seen in the concrete individual's life.

Kierkegaard viewed the lives of the saints in the biblical narrative as icons of the eternal.[31] In the lives of concrete individuals in history, Kierkegaard saw the eternal at work. Therefore, the observer can look back on the lives of faithful believers through history and see a living icon. Sittser has demonstrated something similar in evangelical biographies of Protestant missionaries. He explains, "In the pens of their biographers, therefore, Protestant missionaries become written icons of faith. They point beyond themselves to the Incarnation and show readers what it means to reflect the divine glory."[32] The life of the believer is the place where God's beauty is reflected.

Lilias Trotter provides an example of pressing through the aesthetic stage to the religious in true relation to God. Lilias Trotter lived a life that refused to stay on the surface of things, or, in Kierkegaard's language, in the aesthetic stage. She pressed deeper to a moral goodness and a religious beauty in the sight of God. Trotter had a natural appreciation for created beauty. As a child when she saw the Alps, she wept.[33] Not only that, but she also was naturally gifted at painting. By a chance meeting, she met John Ruskin who was immediately impressed with her natural talent displayed in her watercolor paintings. He attempted to convince her to work with him as his pupil. Ruskin used her work as examples in his classes at Oxford and told her that if she devoted herself to art, "she would be the greatest living painter in Europe and do things that would be immortal."[34] Trotter's definition of immortal was much different than Ruskin's. Rather than being his pupil, she decided to work among the poor women and prostitutes of London and later as a missionary in Algeria. Through refusing to stay on the surface of things and to pour her life out for the sake of others, Trotter played her part in the theo-drama well. Not only that, but she made beautiful art that has existential and narrative depth because of her story. The art itself may not have been

31. Barnett, *The Dynamics of Faith*, 183.
32. Sittser, "Protestant Missionary Biography as Written Icon," 304.
33. Ramsey, *Rembrandt is in the Wind*, 193.
34. Ramsey, *Rembrandt is in the Wind*, 199.

as beautiful as it would have been had she studied under Ruskin, but because of the life she chose her art is given a theo-dramatic depth. The content of her life is poured into her artwork. In her rejection of becoming a painter, she herself became something even more beautiful, a work of art in the hands of the Great Artist. She pursued the beauty of Christ, and his life of self-sacrifice was reflected in her life. She found the beauty she looked for. At the end of her life, one of the last things she said was, "I see many, many beautiful things."[35]

"Travel Journal" (1893) by Lilias Trotter. Used with Permission from Lilias Trotter Legacy and Arab World Missions

Trotter's life is a life full of beauty that demonstrates the connection between theological aesthetics and the theo-drama. Does this mean that art and created beauty must always be given up for the sake of something else? Not at all. In Trotter's life, created beauty and art fueled her theo-dramatic response and informed and adorned her as she generated a beautiful work of art with her life. She was on a quest to see and create beauty. When she arrived in Algeria she said, "Oh how good it is that I have been sent here to such beauty."[36] She celebrated the beauty of Algeria and the people through drawings in her journal. Generating art in her

35. Ramsey, *Rembrandt is in the Wind*, 204.
36. Ramsey, *Rembrandt is in the Wind*, 201.

journals helped her to keep seeing the beauty of the world around her. She even kept in correspondence with Ruskin and continued to send him some of her paintings.

In addition to her watercolors and paintings, she often saw the beauty around her as a metaphor for her life and work. She viewed her work among the Muslims of Algeria as the morning star and she longed for the dawn of the Gospel. She was inspired by the beauty of flowers, and they taught her lessons about her work. She took Jesus's call to consider the flowers literally and their beauty became spiritual symbols for her (Matthew 6:28). She wrote, "The autumn-crocus is the snowdrop as it were of these lands, breaking out of the hard ground and laughing at the barrenness of everything around in its faith that the rains are coming . . . Wonderful things may be waiting in the ages to come as the fruit of Christ's sacrifice, but nothing can come up to the joy of being part of His 'autumn-crocus.'"[37] She viewed her work as a firsthand enjoyment of the "autumn-crocus" of the gospel in Algeria. Her use of natural beauty is also on display when God teaches her about her mission work through a bee. Trotter says:

> A bee comforted me very much this morning concerning the desultoriness that troubles me in our work. There seems so infinitely much to be done, that nothing gets done thoroughly . . . We seem only to touch souls and leave them. And that was what the bee was doing, figuratively speaking. He was hovering among some blackberry sprays, just touching the flowers here and there in a very tentative way, yet all unconsciously, life-life-life was left behind at every touch, as the miracle-working pollen grains were transferred to the place where they could set the unseen spring working. We have only to see to it that we are surcharged, like the bees, with potential life. It is God and His eternity that will do the work. Yet He needs His wandering desultory bees.[38]

Trotter's life was a work of art. Even though she renounced the opportunity of being an artist, she delighted in the beauty of creation and cultivated her love and delight in beauty as she sacrificed herself for others. In this way, her life itself became a living and dramatic work of art. For her, this meant giving up the potential of becoming a great artist to meet God in suffering. In Kierkegaardian terms, she pressed through the aesthetic

---

37. Quoted by Sinclair, "The Legacy of Isabella Lilias Trotter," 34.
38. Quoted by Tait, "Lilias Trotter."

stage of existence to the religious. She became a living work of art on the stage of the theo-drama. Her life has an iconic effect because it points beyond herself to the glory of God.

Theological aesthetics places primary importance on the individual and the life that is generated from a result of perceiving Christ. In a sense, the person who has perceived Christ in the Gospel and lives in light of that perception becomes an icon by reflecting the eternal. The emphasis on the lives of individuals is primary in theological aesthetics in the Balthasar tradition because theological aesthetics is intrinsically tied to the theo-drama. Balthasar explained, "At the heart of the *Aesthetics*, the 'theological drama' has already begun."[39]

Those who know the beauty of Christ will have his life pressed into their lives. The part that each individual plays will be different. Theological aesthetics teaches that each believer will be enraptured by the beauty of Christ and his work and live a life that reflects him. This will look differently for every individual person depending on context, personality, and situation. However, theological aesthetics invites the enjoyment of the beauty of Christ and allows the beauty of the arts and creation to inspire discipleship and imitation of Christ. As theological aesthetics leads into the theo-drama, the life that is produced is at once mimesis and poiesis. Mimesis emphasizes conformity and representation while poiesis "sees the world as so much raw material out of which meaning and purpose can be created by the individual."[40] The theo-dramatic life incorporates both. It is mimesis because the life of Christ is perceived aesthetically as inherently beautiful and inspires replication and imitation. It is also poiesis in the sense that each individual creates something new and beautiful given their own particular circumstances and part in the theo-drama. That person creates something new and beautiful with the life given to him or her and imitates Christ in his own context. As Garrett explains, "Authentic expressions of Christ have nothing to do with the popular notion of being 'authentic to oneself', for such expressions are unfitting. Rather, our performances are beautiful when our lives are attuned to the life of Christ in the Spirit."[41]

---

39. Balthasar, *TD* 1, 15.
40. Trueman, *The Rise and Triumph of the Modern Self*, 39.
41. Garrett, "God's Beauty-in-Act," 478.

# THEOLOGICAL AESTHETICS, THEO-DRAMA, AND ART

## Material Beauty as Communicative

The life of the believer is the primary work of art as he or she lives in aesthetic delight, captured in the vision and rapture of the perception of God's revelation. This is the person who is truly beautiful. Balthasar is often quoted appreciatively by those who write on theology and the arts. However, robust interaction with Balthasar is usually quite limited in works on theology and the arts because it falls outside his emphasis. Balthasar's concern was not the arts *per se* but rather the perception of God as he has revealed himself. Balthasar approvingly spoke of Dante as "the great lover of every embodiment of form, of all radiant beauty" who ironically "has no interest in the visible beauty of the Church on earth."[42] This is because for Balthasar and Dante before him, the beauty of the Church and the individuals within the Church is lived out in lives of humility, love, and obscurity.[43] In fact, Balthasar believes opulent beauty is a sign of moral evil.[44] However, Balthasar's theological aesthetics has profound implications for a theology of the arts. His emphasis on the co-inherence of goodness, truth, and beauty reminds that we are not merely after beautiful art, but a beautiful life.

Theological aesthetics in Balthasar's tradition emphasizes the theo-dramatic and action that happens as a result of seeing the beauty of God. This emphasis distinguishes it from the study of general aesthetic theory and the study of theology and the arts. However, theological aesthetics has implications for art and its creation. Art is most potent if beauty, truth, and goodness are displayed not only in the work of art itself but in the life, affections, and creative process of the artist. This does not mean that general aesthetics and the discussion of art and theology are unimportant. Rather, theological aesthetics provides a metaphysical and theological grounding for beauty and gives a broader context that helps understand art and beauty more fully. As in the life of Lilias Trotter, the perception of beauty became instrumental not only in the creation of art but also in generating a beautiful life of faith. Theological aesthetics, therefore, impacts the believer's perception or worldview of beauty

---

42. Balthasar, *GL* 3, 21.
43. Balthasar, *GL* 3, 21.
44. Balthasar, *GL* 3, 22.

and art as well as how they generate art. Balthasar's theological aesthetics relationship to theo-dramatics fits well with Wolterstorff's aesthetics. For Balthasar and Wolterstorff, art appreciation as well as creation are action within the world.[45]

Wolterstorff reminds us that art is embedded in a large diversity of actions by human agents who are using art in such a way that it plays its own role in human action.[46] Art can be viewed and analyzed as an artifact with the principles provided by general aesthetics, but for art to be more fully understood the analysis must go beyond this. Art ultimately can only be understood considering its broader embeddedness and the part that the artist and the art itself plays in the theo-drama. In chapter 2, I showed that many evangelicals examine art to determine the worldview behind it. An artwork's theo-dramatic embeddedness is (but not less) than the worldview of the author who created that work of art. Wolterstorff argues that the institution of high art prefers not to look at the worldview or embeddedness of a work of art: "The institution much prefers simply to stay on the surface of things and look at the resultant work, or to offer purely psychological accountings."[47] However, in order to understand a work of art, one must see the art as it is an artifact in the broader context of the theo-drama and created and perceived by actors who play their own role in the theo-drama.

Every form of beauty, whether it is art or the beauty of creation, is a gift from God and a self-communication of his nature and beauty. Different forms of beauty reveal different aspects of who God is or tell a part of the story of his theo-drama. Even though art invites an interpretation that seeks to understand the artwork itself as well as its embeddedness, ultimately all forms of beauty are to be received and surrendered to as a gift of God.[48] Balthasar, even in the attempt to give a theological account of beauty, shied away from a definition of beauty. He said, "beauty is the aspect of truth that cannot be fit into any definition but can be apprehended only in direct intercourse with it."[49] Something that is beautiful by nature is a communicative event between the perceiver and God himself. This is why Balthasar was quick to move from a beautiful object to the communicative and dramatic purpose for that object. He explained

45. Wolterstorff, *Art in Action*, 5.
46. Wolterstorff, *Art in Action*, 5.
47. Wolterstorff, *Art in Action*, 221.
48. Balthasar, *TL* 1, 224. Levering, *The Achievement of Hans Urs von Balthasar*, 200.
49. Balthasar, *TL* 1, 136.

this movement from object to communication and drama, "beauty can seem, from one point of view to consist entirely in measure, in proportion, in delimited form, as if the image, understood as the appearance of the essence, were its true home. But in the twinkling of an eye, beauty can also appear to consist essentially in movement, in the rhythm of communication itself."[50]

Beauty, in creation or art, is an invitation to the perceiver to live a life awake and in a "perennial inexhaustible wonder" at the mystery of beauty and the God who created and communicated it.[51] There is a tension between the need to understand the worldview and embeddedness of art and the need to not reduce the wonder of beauty by interpretive analysis. It is here that a distinction between beauty and art can be understood. Beauty is the splendor that communicates an aspect of the goodness and truth of God and evokes pleasure and awe in the perceiver. Beauty can be perceived clearly in creation. Art may or may not be a medium of the beautiful. However, art is a communicative event. The artist himself communicates something through his art. Furthermore, if the work of art is a medium of the beautiful, God is communicating something through that art as well that cannot be fully analyzed. A work of art, then, is inherently communicative. The primary focus of theological aesthetics is on the beautiful as a theological category that is understood in relation to Jesus Christ and the drama of redemption and the recognition that all created beauty relates to him. When it comes to created beauty, theological aesthetics reminds that God is communicating with the perceiver through the medium of material creation and the arts. The work of Jesus Christ provides the foundation for that communication because it upheld and redeemed the beauty, as well as redeemed the perceiver through the Gospel and has given him or her the spiritual sense.

Biblical hermeneutics provides an analogy of how theological aesthetics helps in interpreting a work of art. In the grammatical-historical method, the interpreter seeks to understand the original intent of the human author of Scripture. It helps to understand the language, culture, and *Sitz im Leben* (situation) of the original author. However, because the Scripture is inspired by God, the meaning of the divine author in the unfolding story of the canon must also be taken into consideration. God's intention may transcend the full understanding of the original author,

---

50. Balthasar, *TL* 1, 224.
51. Balthasar, *TL* 1, 144.

though is never contrary to that author's intent. General aesthetics in this analogy is like linguistic, textual, and literary criticism in biblical interpretation. It studies the form, shape, and structure of the passage and is valuable in its own right. Worldview analysis of the work of art is like seeking to understand the authorial intent of the human author. Theological aesthetics is concerned with both of these, but goes beyond art criticism and worldview analysis to seek to experience and perceive the *sensus plenior* of the work of art as an aspect of God's communication and invitation to live in his drama in light of redemption in Christ. This is where the analogy of Biblical hermeneutics breaks down. In Biblical hermeneutics, the text is the medium of communication and the divine author is never at odds with what the human author was communicating. In the general revelation of art, God always transcends and at times contradicts the message of a human artist. But even this contradiction is an act of communication. The human artist and the art may be a foil to the truth God communicates through that very work of art. God's communication may work in an opposite direction.

It is at this point that the theology of the spiritual sense developed in the previous chapter helps us understand how a person can perceive what God is communicating. The spiritual sense enlightens the physical senses and teaches the believer what God wants to communicate to him through his physical senses. In this way, the communication between God and the believer in that moment is intensely personal. What God communicates through a beautiful object to one believer may be different than what is communicated to another believer. This does not turn into mere romanticism or projection of meaning onto the beautiful object because the Holy Spirit is leading the spiritual sense to perceive true communication from God through a beautiful material object. To return to Lilias Trotter as an example, the bees hovering over flowers communicated to her something different than it would have communicated to another person. This is not subjectivism because it recognizes, as Begbie explains, "There is a fullness or plentitude of meaning in the world that is inexhaustible, that outperforms our perception."[52] Begbie also explains that the arts also have "a capacity to draw on and generate potentially inexhaustible dimensions of meaning."[53] God's communication through created, natural, and artistic beauty is variegated and personal. For the believer, beauty is

---

52. Begbie, *Redeeming Transcendence in the Arts*, 161.
53. Begbie, *Abundantly More*, 94.

always perceived through the cross and is tested by the truths of Scripture. Theological aesthetics does not demand a development of its own theological aesthetic art criticism. Theological aesthetics is content with allowing and utilizing the contributions of aesthetic theory, art criticism, and worldview analysis. However, it goes beyond these to insist on the need to recognize God's communication through the beautiful to the individual who lives in the theater of God.

## The Iconic Effect of Art and Extremes of Kitsch and Apophatic Art

Theological aesthetics views material beauty as inherently communicative. When it comes to the beauty of creation, God's wordless sermon is always speaking and communicating (Psalm 19:1–6). However, when it comes to art, the exact content of what God is communicating is ambivalent. Nevertheless, theological aesthetics teaches that there is a distinctively Christian way to enjoy and create art as communion with God in the context of the theo-drama. This guides the Christians appreciation and creation of art. The spiritual sense informed by the Scripture shapes the taste and judgement of art for the believer. Not only this, but the artist who has been enlivened by the spiritual sense to perceive God's communication in the beauty of the world has the task of creating art that helps others see that beauty. The artist is therefore given a part to play in displaying the beauty, truth, and goodness of God. Artists who take the contribution of theological aesthetics into consideration will be informed by the Creator-creature distinction, the mystery and transcendence of beauty, the goodness of material creation, the communicative nature of beauty, and the theo-dramatic action of art. An exhaustive examination of the implications of theological aesthetics for art creation goes beyond the parameters of the current work. However, I will limit myself to examining apophatic and kitsch art as two extremes to avoid and demonstrate that the goal of art creation should have an iconic effect.

Theological aesthetics helps shape good taste in artistic beauty. It provides categories for how to understand beauty and helps one in discerning when the beautiful is seen or experienced in a work of art. When beauty is present in art there is both form and content. Part of the content of a beautiful work of art is God's transcendent communication of goodness, truth, and beauty through that work. The splendor of God's beauty shines through the form and is perceived. This is why truly beautiful art is not simply concerned with form, but with the content as well. The message of the work of art should resonate with the truth of God and his moral goodness in such a way that the beauty evokes a wonder and pleasure in the perceiver. The reason truly beautiful art evokes *Sehnsucht* or longing within humanity is because the content of the art communicates the mystery of the beauty humans were created for. Wolterstorff explains, "Aesthetic delight is a component within and a species of that joy which belongs to the shalom God has ordained as the goal of human existence, and which here already, in this broken and fallen world of ours is to be sought and experienced."[54] We were designed for aesthetic delight in the beautiful. Wolterstorff goes on to describe the responsibility the artist has, "Since it belongs to the shalom that God intends for each of us, it becomes a matter of responsible action to help make available, to ourselves and others, the experience of aesthetic delight."[55]

Since it is part of our responsible action to pursue and make available aesthetic delight, it is important to know what kind of aesthetic delight is part of the shalom God intended. Theological aesthetics does not give insight into what particular style of art or art form is better than the rest, but it does require that art at once draws the perceiver to the form of the art and also signifies something greater than the work of art itself. When it comes to appreciating and creating beautiful art, apophatic art and kitsch art are different extremes that need to be avoided.[56] Apophatic art denies form in an attempt to open up space for transcendence, while kitsch art denies transcendence by refusing to refer to something beyond itself. In this way, kitsch art functions similarly to an idol while apophatic art rejects the transcendent in the immanent. Kitsch art overemphasizes immanence while apophatic seeks sheer transcendence. Theological aesthetics invites the creation of art that functions similarly to how John of Damascus envisioned the icon functioning: manifesting transcendence through immanence.

To begin with one extreme, kitsch art functions like an idol because it does not refer to anything beyond itself. In chapter 2, I argued that kitsch art is popular in evangelicalism. Theological aesthetics reveals the reason kitsch art is so detrimental. Art is meant to be communicative and has the potential of communicating God's beauty. Kitsch trades the

54. Wolterstorff, *Art in Action*, 169.
55. Wolterstorff, *Art in Action*, 169.
56. Schindler, "Beauty in the Tradition."

revelation of transcendent beauty for a substitute, namely, that particular work of art itself.[57] Kitsch art does not properly engage the viewing subject because it does not allow for the communication of true beauty and does not signify anything beyond itself. At the same time, we must hear Wolterstorff's plea to guard against elitism in art.[58] Christopher Watkin gives a similar warning: "One can imagine a particularly serious and conscientious Christian affirming with pride, 'I detest Kinkade. I only ever read Dostoyevsky, and I watch *The Handmaid's Tale* on a loop to make sure that I avoid Christian kitsch.'"[59] What is often called "kitsch" is simply popular art. Popular art has its place within evangelicalism and coincides with the desire to reach and influence as many people as possible. Popular art is not necessarily kitsch art if it refers to a beauty beyond itself.

Kitsch art, when it does not signify anything beyond itself, functions in the same way an idol functions. Like the idol, it "reduces the invisible to the visible."[60] Jean Luc Marion in *God Without Being* explains the difference between an idol and an icon. With the idol, the focus of attention terminates in the perceived object itself. The gaze rests upon the object and stays there.[61] The teleological end of the idol is itself and invites the observer to grasp the divine and come to rest in it. Marion alludes to the Augustinian teaching of the restlessness of our hearts. The perceiver seeks to satisfy his or her restlessness by seeking to rest in the idol and "reveals a sort of essential fatigue."[62] Rather than creating *Sehnsucht* or communicating the splendor of transcendent beauty, the idol or kitsch work of art invites the perceiver to find his rest in this form here and now.

Good art on the other hand has a different impact on the perceiver: it points beyond itself to transcendent beauty and becomes the place where God communicates with the perceiver. Marion gives an example of this type of art in his discussion of an icon. The icon "summons the gaze to surpass itself" and moves back "up the infinite stream of the invisible."[63] Pseudo-Dionysius emphasized this as well in his distinction of the icon and the idol. Louth explained Pseudo-Dionysius's theology of

---

57. Scruton, *Beauty*, 188.
58. Wolterstorff, *Art in Action*, 30–32.
59. Watkin, *Biblical Critical Theory*, 174.
60. Begbie, *Redeeming Transcendence in the Arts*, 57.
61. Marion, *God Without Being*, 12.
62. Marion, *God Without Being*, 13.
63. Marion, *God Without Being*, 18.

the icon, "What distinguishes icon from idol is that apophatic moment: the creation of a distance across which the icon points, across which the icon carries our veneration."[64] Thus, an element of the apophatic is essential in the enjoyment of art or beauty in order for it not to become idolatry. However, the extreme of apophatic art is also avoided in the icon because there is a clear form. In fact, art that functions in an iconic fashion engages the perceiver and even examines him. Marion explains, "The icon regards us—it *concerns* us."[65] In some instances, "The icon lays out the material of wood and paint in such a way that there appears in them the intention of a transpiercing gaze emanating from the icon."[66]

From an evangelical Protestant perspective, the depths of the depravity of the human heart makes icons and their veneration dangerous. Not only that, but iconography has developed into an inherently idolatrous institution. The theology of the icon is problematic and heterodox. While John of Damascus and Marion's theology of the icon may *technically* guard from idolatry, the Protestant is aware of the heart's tendency to make an icon into an idol. Any object can be turned into an idol by the perceiver even if this was by no means the intention of the creator. In the Old Testament, this is demonstrated in the case of the bronze serpent. The bronze serpent was a work of art that symbolically represented God's healing and ultimately was a type of Christ (John 3:14). However, rather than a work of art that pointed beyond itself as was intended, it became an idol and object of worship (2 Kings 18:3–4). This instance demonstrates the necessity of the creation of art that has the iconic effect of regarding the viewer as well as pointing beyond itself, but also the need for the perceiving subject to see and use art rightly. Every type of art, especially art that truly communicates beauty, can be twisted into idolatrous use. Balthasar noted that the iconoclast argument through church history acted as a needed reminder of the Creator-creature distinction. Balthasar speaks of the need for a "constant vigilance required to keep the transcendental beauty of revelation from slipping back into equality with an inner-worldly natural beauty."[67] The vigilance required here does not discourage the enjoyment and creation of art, but rather is a reminder of the tendency of the human heart to make beauty into an idol and worshipping creation rather than the Creator (Romans 1:25). From

64. Louth, "Apophatic Theology," 82.
65. Marion, *God Without Being*, 19.
66. Marion, *God Without Being*, 19.
67. Balthasar, GL 1, 40.

a Protestant perspective, the icon itself poses too much of a temptation for the heart and invites idolatry. However, Pseudo-Dionysius, John of Damascus, and Marion's theology of the icon demonstrate the need for art that "regards us" and communicates transcendence.[68] This art "allows the invisible to saturate the visible."[69] This is the kind of art that invites the perceiver into aesthetic wonder and invites an appropriate response in the theo-drama.

A painting that is not an icon but conveys this iconic and theo-dramatic sense is Rembrandt's *The Storm on the Sea of Galilee*. The work is full of theo-dramatic movement and force representing the events of Mark 4:35–41. The waves on the sea threaten the disciples as they battle the storm and Christ appears asleep. There is potential subtle reference to the cross by the mast which features prominently in the center of the painting. In Rembrandt's style, he also brings in the iconic gaze by painting himself in the boat looking out at the viewer. Russ Ramsey explains, "By peering through the storm and out of the frame to us, he asks if we are not on the same boat."[70] Rembrandt regards us through the painting and brings us into the theo-dramatic action. The painting seems to ask us, how will you respond and play your part when Christ appears to sleep and not hear your prayers when the chaos of life strikes? The iconic effect of *The Storm on the Sea of Galilee* communicates the transcendent, examines the viewer, and moves the viewer to a response.[71]

Art with this iconic effect provides a strong contrast to the extremes of kitsch and apophatic art. Kitsch and idols are one extreme that "reduces the invisible to the visible."[72] The other extreme is apophatic art that removes the visible for the sake of the invisible. Apophatic art does not allow the perceiver to grasp the beauty of the form. The emptiness of form seeks to convey splendor or transcendence but at the end of the day falls short in conveying true beauty. A classic example of a work of art that is apophatic in nature is Rothko's chapel that was completed in 1971 in Houston, Texas. Rothko said that his work was an attempt to

---

68. Marion, *God Without Being*, 18.
69. Begbie, *Redeeming Transcendence in the Arts*, 57.
70. Ramsey, *Rembrandt is in the Wind*, 74.
71. See another example of the iconic effect of art in Begbie's discussion of Kollwitz's *The Downtrodden* in *Abundantly More*, 107–108. This is a more distressing work of art, but it is iconic because it concerns us. "We discover something of that it means to be in the midst of the gray, numbing prison of poverty. Indeed, we are granted a particular understanding of poverty that would be hard if not possible to achieve by any other means."
72. Begbie, *Redeeming Transcendence in the Arts*, 57.

express the "infinite eternity of death."⁷³ Stoker describes Rothko's chapel as "radical transcendence" and uses Millbank's words to describe it, "absolutely unknowable void, upon whose brink we finite beings must dizzily hover."⁷⁴ This type of apophatic art contrasts with the transcendence displayed in the incarnation.

*The Storm on the Sea of Galilee* (1633) by Rembrandt van Rijn. Public Domain / Wikimedia Commons

However, the apophatic has its place. Pseudo-Dionysius emphasized that the apophatic is primarily a response and can only be properly utilized if the cataphatic guides the apophatic response.⁷⁵ Paul Rorem,

73. Quoted by Gottschaller, *Art and Activism*, 144.
74. Stoker, *Where Heaven and Earth Meet*, 121.
75. Louth, "Apophatic Theology," 73.

likewise, has demonstrated that the apophatic can only be appreciated in relation to the cataphatic.[76] There is a distinction to be made then between an apophatic response of silence before transcendent beauty and apophatic art that conveys emptiness and a sheer transcendence like Rothko's chapel.

Davies describes the aspect of apophasis as a response, "Apophasis in this sense articulates human response to a divine communicative presence, and it is burdened as much by an excess of presence as it is by an endemic sense of absence."[77] The apophatic in this sense is an aesthetic response to transcendence, as opposed to the apophatic being an art form. This is also seen in Athanasius's theology of the incarnation. Athanasius maintained that "apophatic reverence" is the only fitting response to the Incarnation.[78] Theological aesthetics is in line with Athanasius's apophatic theology and invites for the creation of art that conveys more than emptiness and space but a fullness of transcendence within immanence. Beauty and art signify a splendor and transcendence beyond the form. However, form is just as important because it becomes the medium through which the splendor shines through.

Apophatic approaches to art are pessimistic about the ability of the form to signify transcendence. This approach recognizes the brokenness of creation and the need for beauty that transcends this world. However, John of Damascus demonstrated how the incarnation and Jesus's work of redemption restored the ability of signs and art forms to signify deeper spiritual realities. John of Damascus argued that Jesus restored "the meaning and relatedness of the created order and human life within it by entering into the 'order of signs'. . . to heal brokenness and restore meaning and relatedness."[79] John maintained that created beauty and art can be the vehicle for God's communication of transcendent beauty because Jesus Christ has established this as a possibility. Not only that, but as I demonstrated in the last chapter, the redemption of Christ has restored the possibility for fallen creatures to see transcendent beauty through the spiritual sense's operation in the physical senses. Therefore, theological aesthetics establishes that created beauty and art is inherently Christological because Jesus Christ has made God's communication in that beauty an objective reality and a possibility for the perceiver. All created

---

76. Rorem, "Negative Theologies and the Cross," 314.
77. Quoted by Begbie, *Redeeming Transcendence in the Arts*, 117.
78. Anatolios, *Athanasius*, 98.
79. Louth, "Beauty Will Save the World," 75.

beauty is created and redeemed by Jesus Christ and refers to the Source of Beauty, evokes *Sehnsucht*, and is an analogy for the beauty of God. When it comes to art, the extremes of apophatic and kitsch art are unable to produce the iconic effect of engaging the perceiver with transcendence through immanence.

## THEOLOGICAL AESTHETICS IMPLICATIONS FOR ARTISTS AND THEOLOGIANS

### Christian Artists as Theologians of the Cross

While general aesthetics is most concerned with the work of art itself, theological aesthetics is more concerned with the individual and his or her perception of God's beauty and the life that is inspired from that perception. Theological aesthetics assists with the evangelical tension between the arts and ministry mentioned in chapter 2. William Dyrness notes that evangelicals' neglect of beauty and art comes from an emphasis on spiritual beauty rather than the physical.[80] However, the development of an evangelical theological aesthetics will help evangelicals get beyond the tension they feel between creation and the arts and discipleship and ministry. Theological aesthetics demonstrates that the beauty of Christ establishes every form of beauty and ultimately refers to him. Material and physical beauty do not compete with spiritual beauty, but rather manifest it and become a place where the individual can perceive truth about God.

As we have seen, theological aesthetics leads into the theo-drama, and maintains that the life of the individual becomes a work of art. It is not just the missionary or pastor who ought to become a living work of art, but every believer. This is also true of the Christian artist as well. In the creation of art, God cares not only for the form and content of the art being created, but also the form and content of the artist himself. There are artists who can create great works of art that are objectively beautiful but lack the moral beauty of goodness if they are done for the wrong ends. In the mercy of God, after a work of art is produced it takes on a life of its own that may be somewhat detached from its artist. For this reason, beautiful cathedrals that were funded through usury or indulgences are not disqualified from communicating the beautiful and inspiring worship.

80. Dyrness, *Visual Faith*, 149.

Although the creation of that art was made possible through moral evil, the irony is that God allows the evil choices of moral agents to ultimately accomplish good in this fallen world (see Genesis 50:20). This, though, in no way allows for the ends to justify the means in the creation of art.

The content of the artist's life, that is, the motivations, heart posture, and affections ultimately are more important to God than the art form produced. In this way, God puts to shame the standards of the fine arts. The creative act that generates art that is considered crude, dull, or even "kitsch" by the world's standards, but made in a heart posture of worship with right affections, is glorifying to God. Objective beauty is not the only important element in the creation of art. This means that at the affectional level the individual who is creating will be loving the things that Christ loves and hating the things that Christ hates or at least striving in this direction. Garrett explains, if participation in the theo-drama is the goal, the training and formation of the affections provided in the liturgy of the local church is necessary.[81] He goes on, "If fitting participation is the goal, then the forming and shaping of our imaginations will lead us into strict training (1 Cor. 9:24–27) as we seek to break old habits and ways of thinking (Col. 1:21)."[82] The artist will allow this strict training of the cross to test all artistic endeavors. The cross, or rather, God himself through the cross, tests the affections of the artist as to whether they are operating as a theologian of glory or a theologian of the cross in their artistic creation. If the cross is the door through which humanity must enter in order to enjoy worldly beauty, the artist himself must enter the artistic endeavor through the cross. If the cross shapes the artist existentially, the resurrected life of Christ mediated by the Spirit will enable the artist to see and create and use the good aesthetic gifts of God properly. The artist marked by a theology of the cross does not first and foremost have to do with the art created, but who the artist is existentially.

However, this does not encourage poor craftmanship. The objective beauty of the art is important. Theological aesthetics also places a high value on the role of physical beauty and calls for artists who can create the type of art that transposes the transcendent into the art form and uncovers the beauty that God formed into creation.[83] The artist first must perceive the beauty of the risen Christ and allow the Spirit to shape a fitting response in the artist's action and the work of art created. Garrett

81. Garrett, "God's Beauty-in-Act," 478.
82. Garrett, "God's Beauty-in-Act," 478.
83. Begbie, *Redeeming Transcendence in the Arts*, 131.

explains that the "fitting movements of the risen Christ in the Spirit serve as the patterns that educate and form the imaginations of properly perceiving subjects, enabling them to envision their role and perform their parts in God's drama of redemption."[84] The spiritual sense works to shape and form the imagination of Christian artists to help them perceive the beauty of God and then communicate it in an art form. The artist assists others with perceiving beauty and this assistance helps them to worship God, communicate with him, and inspires their theo-dramatic action. In other words, the artist seeks to transform his own imagination by the perception of the beauty of Christ through the Holy Spirit. He then artistically represents what has been seen and imagined in faith. The goal of this is to display to others what has been perceived in faith. The art created in turn shapes the imagination of those who view it. This is why, as Peterson says, the creative task is "profoundly spiritual, and therefore profoundly mysterious."[85]

Theological aesthetics, therefore, establishes the importance of both the life of the artist as well as the art they generate. For the Christian artist, theological aesthetics demonstrates that this beauty begins with the spiritual perception of the beauty of Christ and seeing all beauty in relation to him. Therefore, the artist must live awake in aesthetic wonder at the beauty around him that refers to the transcendent beauty of God, and then seek to bring that awe to others in the art form.[86] Artists then play the crucial role of awaking the one who perceives their art to the transcendent beauty that is all around them and remind them of the part they play. As Andrew Peterson explains, "God allowed. . . stories to lift the veil on the imaginary world to show me the real world behind it—which ended up being, in the end, the one I was already in."[87] God speaks through different art forms and reveals truth, beauty, and goodness through them in such a way that transforms the perceiver. Vanhoozer has demonstrated that the resurrection gives the metaphysical grounding for the hope, consolation, and joy that art gives.[88] Beautiful art conveys a world that can only be true if the cross and resurrection are true. Therefore, Vanhoozer says, the type of art that Christians should strive to produce is art that communicates

---

84. Garrett, "God's Beauty-in-Act," 479.
85. Peterson, *Adorning the Dark*, 85.
86. Wolterstorff, *Art in Action*, 169.
87. Peterson, *Adorning the Dark*, 71.
88. Vanhoozer, "What Has Vienna to Do with Jerusalem," 146.

"the consolation of a fallen and redeemed creation."[89] This type of art is art that truly displays a theology of the cross and manifests the power of the resurrected Christ making all things new by his Spirit. This art reveals beauty and the God who stands behind that beauty and inspires theo-dramatic action.

## Theologians Awake to Beauty

It is not only the artist whose craft is influenced by theological aesthetics. Theological aesthetics is primarily a field in theology and calls for theologians to come awake to the beauty of its Subject. Balthasar calls the theologian to write under the aesthetic wonder of the splendor of the beauty of Christ. Balthasar's decision to make beauty the point of departure for his theology was a self-conscious attack on the loss of beauty in theology. He argues that theology is the only science that can truly have beauty as its object.[90] He not only calls the theologian to consider beauty, but also lets beauty form the theological task as well. He explains, "A theology of beauty may be elaborated only in a beautiful manner. The particular nature of one's subject matter must be reflected first of all in the particular nature of one's method."[91]

However, Luther's caution of being a theologian of glory rather than a theologian of the cross is especially pertinent here. The theologian of glory will sound rhetorically beautiful and yet will use this rhetoric and beautiful theology to subvert the truth rather than celebrate it. This was one of Luther's primary critiques of Erasmus in *The Bondage of the Will*. According to Luther, Erasmus used his rhetorical skill and beautiful articulation in a way that twisted the truth and made no real assertions about God's revelation. Luther argued that the beauty of his theology was illegitimate because it was used as a weapon against the truth rather than a beautiful articulation of the truth. Beauty in theology rests on the clarity of Scripture, recognizing the alluring nature of revealed truth.

Balthasar also recognized the danger of beauty in theology and the temptation to make theology serve only what is beautiful by worldly standards.[92] Theological aesthetics, however, reminds of the axiom *fi-*

---

89. Vanhoozer, "What Has Vienna to Do with Jerusalem," 149.
90. Balthasar, *GL* 1, 19–20.
91. Balthasar, *GL* 1, 39.
92. Rosebrock, "The Heidelberg Disputation and Aesthetics," 350.

*nitum non capax infiniti* (the finite cannot contain the infinite), while at the same time maintaining that the finite reveals the infinite. Balthasar warned against this use of beauty in theology and called it "aesthetic theology" in distinction from theological aesthetics.[93] Barth also warned against an aestheticism that would undermine the freedom of God by equating it with an inner worldly beauty.[94] The Creator-creature distinction and the transcendent sovereignty of God does not allow the theology of revelation to be collapsed into a worldly beauty. This, however, explains the reason why Balthasar maintained that theology is the science that can help us properly understand beauty.[95] General aesthetics has its place but can only be rightly understood considering the theological account of beauty offered by theological aesthetics.

We have noted Balthasar's criticism: "Contemporary Protestant theology nowhere deals with the beautiful as a theological category. . . . The only question posed by Protestants is that concerning the relationship between revelation and this worldly beauty—certainly a justified question, but not a sufficient one."[96] I have shown that evangelical Protestants do indeed have a theology of beauty. I have sought to bring more clarity to this theology of beauty in my synthesis of this theology with Balthasar and historical theology, with Scripture as its foundation. As I demonstrated in chapter 2, apart from a couple notable exceptions, this theology of beauty in evangelical Protestantism remains mostly tacit and hidden in the background. Evangelical Protestantism for the most part has yet to discover a theological account of beauty that will help it through some of the impasses it faces between spiritual and material beauty and the intersection of art and theology. The purpose of this work has been to examine theological aesthetics in order to assist the evangelical community in getting its bearings on a theology of beauty.

However, a clear theological account of beauty only provides the theological framework for bringing beauty back into theology. Theologians also must awaken themselves to the aesthetic wonder of the beauty of God in Christ and seek his beauty all around in the world he created. In classic philosophy, wonder was the starting point of the philosophical venture.[97] Likewise, wonder at the beauty of God's revelation is the start-

93. Balthasar, *GL* 1, 90.
94. Barth, *CD* II.1 § 31, 653.
95. Balthasar, *GL* 1, 19–20.
96. Balthasar, *GL* 1, 56–57.
97. Sherry, *Spirit and Beauty*, 340.

ing point of theology and carries the theologian throughout the theological task. Like the artist, then, the theologian will seek to transpose the perception of beauty into his theology to awaken this perception in his or her readers. To assist with this, the theologian may recognize the place of art in assisting the theological task and method. As Garrett writes, "Art, in a broad sense, exercises our imaginations in ways that we would otherwise not, opening theology to new and creative ways of envisaging God's divine reality."[98] Art assists theology by waking it up from its tendency to move away from beauty; theology assists the arts by waking it up from its tendency to move away from truth. When the beauty of art and the truth of theology ring out together the coinherence of the transcendentals will be clearly manifested in the good life of the receiving subject.

To bring beauty into theology will also require the development of a theology that says things beautifully. Truth and precision do not need to be supplanted in order for theology to be articulated beautifully. This is where Balthasar's doctrine of the co-inherence of the transcendentals is vital. Beauty does not compete with truth. Rather truth in and of itself is beautiful and the beauty of truth calls the theologian to articulate with precision but in such a way that captures the beauty of doctrine. Theology itself should ring out beautifully. Theology gains its inspiration from the great theologians of the past who developed their theology in awe and wonder at the beauty of revelation.

This also means that theology makes space for the arts in the life of the church. The theologian does theology as a part of the body of Christ and creates theology that inspires and celebrates the arts and the artistic endeavors in the body of Christ.[99] The theologian speaks beautifully in such a way that the poet is given content and the preacher courage to proclaim the beauty of revelation to the church. Theologians will need to bridge the gap between art and theology, not merely by providing a theology of the arts, but by giving a theological account of beauty that inspires the arts.

---

98. Garrett, "God's Beauty-in-Act," 475.

99. Pearcey, *Saving Leonardo*, 275.

## CONCLUSION

The theologian has been given the sacred task of "seeing beauty" and then "saying beautifully."[100] The theologian has a crucial part in the body of Christ. However, the theologian is only one part of the church. The whole church together becomes the space where the beauty of God's revelation is remembered, celebrated, and proclaimed. The local church is the space where true aesthetic existence in relation to God becomes a reality. As Bonhoeffer said, "I wonder whether it is possible (it almost seems so today) to regain the idea of the church as providing an understanding of the area of freedom (art, education, friendship, play), so that Kierkegaard's 'aesthetic existence' would not be banished from the church's sphere, but would be re-established within it? I really think that is so."[101] This is especially the case if we think of the church as the local gathering of believers rather than a building. The aesthetic existence of these believers is recalibrated when they come together and remember and proclaim what God has done in Christ by the Spirit. Imagine what could happen if these members of the local church were awakened to the beauty of God and lived a life in wonder at his beauty. The local church and its liturgy would become the space where the believers are allured by the beauty of God and reminded of the part they play in the theo-drama. The church's proclamation then goes public in the lives of those who create moral beauty in the context of their own life.[102]

The purpose of this chapter was to answer the question, "How do theological aesthetics impact the individual's and the church's approach to beauty?" In this chapter, I followed Balthasar's connection between theological aesthetics and the theo-drama and demonstrated that the life of the believer is itself designed to be a work of art that displays God's beauty. The perception of God's beauty in the redemption of Christ transforms the individual and invites them to play their part in the theo-drama. Christian worship, or the liturgy, functions as the place where Christians perceive the glory of Christ and are sent out into the world to play their parts and image Christ. The church and the believer, therefore, not only approach and perceive beauty, but radiate that beauty in their own lives.

The theo-dramatic emphasis, however, does not undermine the value of physical beauty. Material beauty is part of the stage and provides

---

100. Piper, *Seeing Beauty and Saying Beautifully*, 1.
101. Bonhoeffer, *Letters and Papers from Prison*, 193.
102. Smith, *Awaiting the King*, 59.

inspiration for the actors of the theo-drama. I demonstrated that beauty in creation and the arts also has dramatic movement and plays an important role. Beauty is inherently communicative. God communicates through the beauty of creation and art in a way that inspires and motivates the believer in their theo-dramatic action. I argued that art that has an iconic effect in the type of art that is most fitting with theological aesthetics account of beauty. This is better than art that tends toward sheer immanence (kitsch) or sheer transcendence (apophatic). Art that has an iconic effect communicates the transcendent through immanence in such a way that "regards" the perceiver.[103] This type of art brings about transformation and inspires action. The artist himself is playing an important part in the theo-drama. Theological aesthetics places a high priority on the life of the artist. The Christian artist is one who is the theologian of the cross and has passed through the cross and into resurrection life. This artist seeks to perceive the beauty of Christ and shape the imagination in such a way that helps transpose the beautiful into his or her craft by the help of the Spirit. When this happens, the artist is being used by God to communicate the beauty of truth to others.

Likewise, the theologian attempts to do the same in theology. Theology begins in wonder at the beauty of God seen in the person and work of Christ. This wonder should permeate the work of theology and influence the method and articulation of theology. Theology will bring the beauty of God's revelation as a gift to the church. When those in the church are helped by the artist and the theologian to see the beauty of God, the fitting response is to receive this beauty and let it shape them. The church that receives the beauty of God in this way will inspire beauty in the lives of the members who are sent out into the world. In this way, the splendor of Christ will shine in the world.

---

103. Marion, *God Without Being*, 19.

# 8

# Conclusion

My aim in this book is to contribute to the field of theological aesthetics from an evangelical Protestant perspective through an engagement with the theological aesthetics of Hans Urs von Balthasar.[1] Theological aesthetics often bypasses thorough engagement with Balthasar. Evangelicals, like the Protestants Balthasar critiqued, have often neglected the development of a theology of beauty, especially a theology of the perception of beauty. While Balthasar's theological aesthetic is helpful, an evangelical Protestant theological aesthetic must take into consideration how a Biblical theology of sin impacts perception and theological aesthetics. A distinctively Protestant theology of beauty and perception must be developed through an emphasis on the theology of the cross and the spiritual sense received at the new birth. Sin and the fall impact the perception of beauty and the cross and the spiritual sense are necessary for the true perception of beauty.

This study also brings together the divergent streams of theological aesthetics. In chapter 1, I noted that theological aesthetics is defined in three different ways: (1) The theology of true perception of the beautiful splendor of God's revelation in Jesus Christ and all reality in him; (2) An approach to theology that is fundamentally shaped by the reality of the true perception of the glory and beauty of God's revelation; (3) A theology of beauty as it is perceived through the senses in creation and the arts

---

1. This work follows Garrett's advice for evangelicals "to consider one of the most prominent Catholic theologians of the twentieth century who can help evangelicals sharpen their theological discourse." Garrett, "The Dazzling Darkness of God's Triune Love," 428.

as revelatory of divine beauty. Works on theological aesthetics usually focus on one of these three definitions without reference to the other two. A robust theological aesthetics encompasses all three of these definitions. Theological aesthetics is a theology of the true perception of the beauty of Jesus Christ and how his beauty relates to the beauty perceived through the physical senses. The perception of God's beauty and created beauty shapes a distinctive approach to theology.

Balthasar's theology also reminds us of the connection between theological aesthetics and the theo-drama. It has been popular to explore the theo-dramatic nature of theology in recent years. However, the connection between theological aesthetics and the theo-drama, which Balthasar forged, is often overlooked. The practical aspect of this work recovers this connection and emphasizes that theological aesthetics generate a beautiful life. Those who perceive the beauty of God in Christ and all of life are reminded of the part they were designed to play in the theo-drama.

My greatest hope for this work is that the writer and the reader will be drawn to the beauty of God in Jesus Christ. The beauty of creation points to him. In praise of his beauty, it is fitting to conclude this work with the reflections of Jonathan Edwards:

> When we behold the fragrant rose and lily, we see his love and purity. So, the green trees and fields, and singing of birds, are the emanations of his infinite joy and benignity; the easiness and naturalness of trees and vines [are] shadows of his infinite beauty and loveliness; the crystal rivers and murmuring streams have the footsteps of his sweet grace and bounty. When we behold the light and brightness of the sun, the golden edges of an evening cloud, or the beauteous bow, we behold the adumbrations of his glory and goodness; and the blue skies, of his mildness and gentleness. There are also many things wherein we may behold his awful majesty: in the sun in his strength, in comets, in thunder, in the towering thunder clouds, in ragged rocks and the brows of mountains. That beauteous light with which the world is filled in a clear day is a lively shadow of his spotless holiness and happiness, and delight in communicating himself.[2]

He truly is, as Augustine said, the "beauty at once so ancient and so new."[3] He is the beauty that will save the world.

---

2. *WJE* 13:279.
3. Augustine, *Confessions* X.27, 231.

# Bibliography

Adrahtas, Vassilis. "The Notion of Symbol as a Logical/Aesthetic Category According to the Theology of St John of Damascus." *Phronema* 17 (2002) 15–34.

Anatolios, Khaled. *Athanasius: The Coherence of His Thought.* New York: Routledge, 2005.

Anderson, Hannah. *All That's Good: Recovering the Lost Art of Discernment.* Chicago: Moody, 2018.

Anderson, Cameron J. *The Faithful Artist: A Vision for Evangelicalism and the Arts.* Downers Grove: IVP Academic, 2016.

Anderson, Neil, Julianne Zuelke, and Terry Zuehlke. *Christ-Centered Therapy: The Practical Integration of Theology and Psycology.* Grand Rapids: Zondervan, 2000.

Anttilla, Miikka E.."Beauty Redeem""'s the World: An Introduction to Christian Aesthetics." *Word & World* 39 (2019) 35–41.

Aquinas, Thomas. *The Summa Theologiae of St. Thomas Aquinas.* Translated by The Fathers of the English Dominican Province. 1920. https://www.newadvent.org/summa/.

Arand, Charles P. "God's World of Daily Wonders." *Concordia* 46 (2002) 53–71.

Ashton, John. *Understanding the Fourth Gospel.* 2nd ed. Oxford: Oxford University Press, 2007.

Athanasius. *On the Incarnation.* Translated by A. Religious. Crestwood, New York: St Vladimir's Seminary, 1996.

Attridge, Harold W. "Temple, Tabernacle, Time, and Space in John and Hebrews." *Early Christianity* 1 (2010) 261–274.

———. "How Priestly is the 'High Priestly Prayer' of John 17." *The Catholic Biblical Quarterly* 75 (2013) 1–14.

Augustine. *Expositions on the Book of Psalms.* Translated by John Henry Parker. Oxford: Oxford, 1847.

———. *Confessions.* Translated by R.S. Pine-Coffin. New York: Penguin, 1961.

Austin, Michael A. *Explorations in Art, Theology, and Imagination.* New York: Routledge, 2005.

Avrahami, Yael. *The Senses of Scripture: Sensory Perception in the Hebrew Bible.* New York: T&T Clark, 2012.

Baines, Matthew C. "The Identity and Fate of the Kings of the Earth in the Book of Revelation." *The Reformed Theological Review* 75 (2016) 73–88.

Balmer, Randal H. "The Kinkade Crusade." *Christianity Today* 44 (2000) 48–55.

Balthasar, Hans Urs von. *Herrlichkeit. Eine Theologische Ästhetik.* Verlag: Johannes, 1989.

———. *The Glory of the Lord: A Theological Aesthetics*. 7 vols. Translated by Erasmo Leiva-Merkakis, Andrew Louth. Brian McNeil, Oliver Davies. Francis McDonagh, John Saward, Martin Simon, and Rowan Williams. San Francisco: Ignatius, 1982–1991.

———. *Theo-Drama: Theological Dramatic Theory*. 5 vols. Translated by Graham Harrison. San Francisco: Ignatius, 1988–1998.

———. *Theo-Logic*. 3 vols. Translated by Adrian Walker. San Francisco: Ignatius, 2000–2005.

———. *Truth is Symphonic: Aspects of Christian Pluralism*. Translated by Graham Garrison. San Francisco: Ignatius, 1987.

———. *Epilogue*. Translated by Edward T. Oaks. San Francisco: Ignatius, 2004.

———. *My Work in Retrospect*. San Francisco: Ignatius, 1993.

Barker, H. Gaylon. *The Cross of Reality: Luther's Theologia Crucis and Bonhoeffer's Christology*. Minneapolis: Fortress, 2015.

Barnett, Christopher B. *The Dynamics of Faith: The Spirituality of Søren Kierkegaard*. Minneapolis: Fortress, 2014.

———. "Painting with Words: Kierkegaard and the Aesthetics of the Icon." In *Kierkegaard, Literature, and the Arts*, edited by Eric Ziolkowski, 177–192. Evanston: Northwestern University, 2018.

Baron, Craig A. "Christian Theology and the Re-Enchantment of the World." *Cross Currents* 56 (2007) 112–123.

Barone, Marco. *Luther's Augustinian Theology of the Cross*. Eugene: Resource, 2017.

Barrett, C.K. *The Gospel According to St. John: An Introduction with Commentary and Notes on the Greek Text*. 2nd ed. Philadelphia: Westminster, 1978.

Barrett, Lee. "Von Balthasar and Protestant Aesthetics: A Mutually Corrective Conversation." In *Theological Aesthetics after von Balthasar*, edited by Oleg Bychkov and James Fodor, 97–106. New York: Routledge, 2008.

Barrs, Jerram. *Echoes of Eden: Reflections on Christianity, Literature, and the Arts*. Wheaton: Crossway, 2013.

Barth, Karl. *The Humanity of God*. London: Collins, 1967.

———. *Wolfgang Amadeus Mozart*. Translated by C.K. Pott. Grand Rapids: Eerdmans, 1986.

———. *Church Dogmatics*. Volumes 1–14. Translated by A.T. Mackay and T.H.L. Parker. New York: T&T Clark, 2004.

Bauckham, Richard. *The Theology of the Book of Revelation*. Cambridge: Cambridge University Press, 1993.

———. *The Climax of Prophesy: Studies on the Book of Revelation*. London: Continuum International, 1998.

Bauer, Katerina. "Iconic Light as Incarnate Grace." *Communio Viatorum* 52 (2010) 83–95.

Bautch, Richard, and Jean-François Racine, eds. *Beauty and the Bible: Toward a Hermeneutics of Biblical Aesthetics*. Atlanta: Society of Biblical Literature, 2013.

Beale, Gregory K. *The Book of Revelation*. NIGTC. Grand Rapids: Eerdmans, 1999.

———. *We Become What We Worship: A Biblical Theology of Idolatry*. Downers Grove: IVP Academic, 2009.

———. *A New Testament Biblical Theology: The Unfolding of the Old Testament in the New*. Grand Rapids: Baker Academic, 2011.

———. *The Temple and the Church's Mission: A Biblical Theology of the Dwelling Place of God*. Downers Grove: IVP Academic, 2014.

Beale, G.K. and Donald Carson., eds. *Commentary on the New Testament Use of the Old Testament*. Grand Rapids: Baker Academic, 2007.

Beale, G.K., and Sean M. McDonough. "Revelation." In *Commentary on the New Testament Use of the Old Testament*, edited by G.K. Beale and D.A. Carson, 1081–1160. Grand Rapids: Baker Academic, 2007.

Beale, G.K., and Mitchell Kim. *God Dwells Among Us*. Downers Grove: IVP, 2015.

Beasley-Murray, George R. *The Book of Revelation*. NCBC. Grand Rapids: Eerdmans, 1974.

———. *The Book of Revelation*. Eugene: Wipf and Stock, 2010.

Beek, Abraham van de. "The Relevance of Athanasius in Dogmatics." *Church History and Religious Culture* 90 (2010) 287–309.

Begbie, Jeremy S. *Voicing Creation's Praise*. Edinburgh: T&T Clark, 1991.

———. *Beholding the Glory: Incarnation through the Arts*. Grand Rapids: Baker Academic, 2000.

———. *A Peculiar Orthodoxy: Reflections on Theology and the Arts*. Grand Rapids. Michigan: Baker Academic, 2018.

———. *Redeeming Transcendence in the Arts: Bearing Witness to the Triune God*. Grand Rapids: Eerdmans, 2018.

———. *Abundantly More: The Theological Promise of the Arts in a Reductionistic World*. Grand Rapids: Baker Academic, 2023.

Behr, John. *Nicene Faith Vol 1*. Crestwood, New York: St. Vladimir's Seminary, 2004.

Belcher, Richard. *The Messiah and the Psalms: Preaching Christ from all the Psalms*. Fearne: Mentor, 2006.

Belden, Lane C. "Jonathan Edwards on Beauty, Desire, and the Sensory World." *Theological Studies* 65 (2004) 44–72.

Bielfeldt, Dennis. "Heidelberg Disputation." In *The Annotated Luther: The Roots of the Reformation*, edited by Timothy Wengert. Minneapolis: Fortress, 2015.

Biehl, Craig. *The Infinite Merit of Christ: The Glory of Christ's Obedience in the Theology of Jonathan Edwards*. Horsham: Pilgrim's Rock Press, 2014.

Bird, Michael F. *Evangelical Theology*. Second Edition. Grand Rapids: Zondervan Academic, 2020.

Blomberg, Craig L. "Matthew." In *Commentary on the New Testament Use of the Old Testament*, edited by G.K. Beale and D.A. Carson, 1–109. Grand Rapids: Baker Academic, 2007.

Bomer, Grace Carol. *The Mystery of Babel*. 2015. https://gracecarolbomer.com/section/297654-Global-City-Babel.html.

Bonhoeffer, Dietrich. *Letters and Papers from Prison*. New York: Touchstone, 1997.

Boyle, Marjorie O. "Christ the Eikon in the Apologies for Holy Images of John of Damascus." *The Greek Orthodox Theological Review* 15 (1970) 175–186.

Bradbury, Rosalene. *Cross Theology: The Classical Theologica Crucis and Karl Barth's Modern Theology of the Cross*. Cambridge: James Clark & Co, 2011.

Bray, Gerald. *The Attributes of God: An Introduction*. Wheaton: Crossway, 2021.

Brown, Christopher Boyd. "Art and the Artist in the Luther Reformation: Johannes Mathesius and Joachismsthal." *Church History* 86 (2017) 1081–1120.

Brown, Frank B. *Good Taste, Bad Taste, & Christian Taste: Aesthetics in Religious Life*. New York: Oxford University, 2000.

Bultmann, Rudolf. *The Gospel of John*. Translated by George R. Beasley-Murray. Philadelphia: Westminster, 1971.

Bychkov, Oleg V. "'Metaphysics as Aesthetics' Metaphysics in Present-Day Theological Aesthtics." *Modern Theology* 31 (2015) 147–178.
Bychkov, Oleg, and James Fodor, eds. *Theological Aesthetics after von Balthasar*. New York: Routledge, 2008.
Bychkov Oleg, and Anne Sheppard. *Greek and Roman Aesthetics*. Cambridge: Cambridge University, 2010.
Caneday, Ardel B. "Glory Veiled in the Tabernacle of Flesh: Exodus 22–34 in the Gospel of John." *Southern Baptist Journal of Theology* 20 (2016) 55–72.
Caponi, Francis J. "Beauty, Justice, and Damnation in Thomas Aquinas." *Pro Ecclesia* 19 (2010) 389–404.
Carson, D.A. *The Gospel of John*. Pillar. Grand Rapids: Baker, 1991.
———. *The Cross and Christian Ministry*. Grand Rapids: Baker, 2004.
———. *Christ and Culture Revisited*. Grand Rapids: Eerdmans, 2008.
Carter, Grayson. "C.S. Lewis and the Church." *Sehnsucht: The C.S. Lewis Journal* 5/6 (2011) 165–204.
Chapell, Bryan. *Christ-Centered Preaching: Redeeming the Expository Sermon*. 2nd ed. Grand Rapids: Baker, 2005.
———. *Christ Centered Worship: Letting the Gospel Shape our Practice*. Grand Rapids: Baker, 2009.
Chatraw, Joshua D. and Karen Swallow Prior, eds. *Cultural Engagement: A Crash Course in Contemporary Issues*. Grand Rapids: Zondervan, 2019.
Chesterton, G.K. *Thomas Aquinas*. New York: Doubleday, 1956.
Chung, Michael. "Nicodemus: From Darkness to the Light." *Theoforum* 49 (2019) 27–37.
Cirelli, Anthony. "Facing the Abyss: Hans Urs von Balthasar Reading of Anxiety." *New Blackfriars* 92 (2011) 705–723.
Clowney, Edmund. *Preaching and Biblical Theology*. Grand Rapids: Eerdmans. 1961.
———. *Preaching Christ in All of Scripture*. Wheaton: Crossway, 2003.
Cole, Graham A. *He Who Gives Life: The Doctrine of the Holy Spirit*. Wheaton: Crossway, 2007.
Cotro, Hugo A. "Could the Author of Revelation Step Forward, Please?" *DavarLogos* 14 (2015) 71–89.
Covington, Sarah, and Kathryn Reklis, eds. *Protestant Aesthetics and the Arts*. New York: Routledge, 2020.
Crain, Chris. "Turning the Beast into a Beauty: Towards an Evangelical Theological Aesthetics." *Presbyterion* 29 (2003) 27–41.
Crisp, Oliver. "Divine Beauty and Excellency: Some Lessons from Jonathan Edwards." *Crux* 44 (2008) 2–11.
Crawford, Matthew David. "C.S. Lewis's Concept of Sehnsucht: Philosophical Foundations, Aesthetic Analysis, and Implications for Evangelism and Apologetics." PhD diss., Southern Baptist Theological Seminary, 2015.
Crouch, Andy. *Culture Making: Recovering our Creative Calling*. Downers Grove: InterVarsity, 2013.
Crowe, Brandon D. "The Chiastic Structure of the Seven Signs in the Gospel of John: Revisiting a Neglected Proposal." *Bulletin for Biblical Research* 28 (2018) 65–81.
Culpepper, R. Alan. "The Pivot of John's Prologue." *New Testament Studies* 27 (1980) 1–31.
———. *Designs for the Church in the Gospel of John: Collected Essays 1980–2020*. Tübingen, Germany: Mohr Siebeck, 2021.

Dadosky, John D. "Recovering Beauty in the Subject: Balthasar and Lonergan Confront Kierkegaard." *American Catholic Philosophical Quarterly* 83 (2009) 509–532.

———. *The Eclipse and Recovery of Beauty: A Lonergan Approach.* Toronto: University of Toronto, 2014.

Davidson, Edward H. "From Locke to Edwards." *Journal in the History of Ideas* 24 (1963) 355–372.

Davies, Oliver. "Von Balthasar and the Problem of Being." *New Blackfriars* 79 (1998) 11–17.

———. "Soundings: Towards a Theological Poetics of Silence." In *Silence and the Word: Negative Theology and the Incarnation*, edited by Oliver Davies and Denys Turner, 201–222. Cambridge: Cambridge University, 2002.

DeCou, Jessica. "Relocating Barth's Theology of Culture: Beyond the 'True Words' Approach of *Church Dogmatics* IV/3." *IJST* 15 (2013) 154–171.

Delattre, Roland A. *Beauty and Sensibility in the Thought of Jonathan Edwards: an Essay in Aesthetics and Theological Ethics.* Pasadena: Wipf and Stock, 2006.

DeMoss, Nancy Lee. *Choosing Gratitude: Your Journey to Joy.* Chicago: Moody, 2009.

Deventer, Cornelia van. "The Mosaic of Belief in the Fourth Gospel." *Neotestamentica* 55 (2021) 155–170.

Dickens, William T. *Hans Urs von Balthasar's Theological Aesthetics.* Notre Dame: University of Notre Dame, 2009.

Djuth, Marianne. "Veiled and Unveiled Beauty: The Role of the Imagination in Augustine's Esthetics." *Theological Studies* 689 (2007) 77–91.

Dupre, Louis K. "Hans Urs von Balthasar's Theology of Aesthetic Form. *Theological Studies* 49 (1988) 299–318.

Dutton, K. "Von Balthasar as Transmodernist: Recent Works on Theological Aesthetics." *Religion and the Arts* 14 (2010) 332–340.

Dostoevsky, Fyodor. *The Idiot.* Translated by Alan Myers. New York, Oxford University. Kindle Edition.

Dyer, Justin B. "Lewis, Barth, and the Natural Law." *Journal of Church and State* 57 (2015) 1–17.

Dyrness, William A. "Aesthetics in the Old Testament: Beauty in Context." *JETS* 28 (1985) 421–432.

———. *Visual Faith: Art, Theology and Worship in Dialogue.* Grand Rapids: Baker Academic, 2001.

———. *The Earth is God's: A Theology of American Culture.* Eugene: Wipf and Stock, 2004.

———. *Poetic Theology: God and the Poetics of Everyday Life.* Grand Rapids: Eerdmans, 2010.

———. "Review of *Redeeming Transcendence in the Arts: Bearing Witness to the Triune God.*" *Interpretation* 74 (2020) 84–86.

Eco, Umberto. *The Aesthetics of Thomas Aquinas.* Translated by H. Bredin. Cambridge: Harvard University, 1998.

Edwards, Jonathan. *Works of Jonathan Edwards.* 26 vols. New Haven: Yale University Press, 1957–2008.

Emlet, Michael. *CrossTalk: Where Scripture and Life Meet.* Greensboro: New Growth, 2009.

Endean, Philip. "Von Balthasar, Rahner, and the Commissar." *New Blackfriars* 79 (1998) 33–38.

Ensor, Peter W. "The Glorification of the Son of Man: An Analysis of John 13:31–32." *Tyndale Bulletin* 58 (2007) 229–252.
Erickson, Millard J. *Christian Theology*. 3rd ed. Grand Rapids: Baker Academic, 2013.
Eswine, Zack. *Preaching to a Post-Everything World: Crafting Biblical Sermons that Connect with our Culture*. Grand Rapids: Baker, 2008.
Estes, Douglas. "Dualism or Paradox?: A New 'Light' on the Gospel of John." *The Journal of Theological Studies* 71 (2020) 90–118.
Evans, C. Stephen. *Kierkegaard: An Introduction*. Cambridge: Cambridge University, 2009.
Falconer, Robert. "The Lion, the Witch and the Cosmic Drama: An African Socio-Hermeneutic." *Conspectus* 22 (2016) 126–140.
———. "Crux Sola Est Nostra Theologia: Luther's Theology of Atonement and Its Development in Recent Theology on the Cross of Christ." *Conspectus* 24 (2017) 277–306.
———. "Architectonic Theology." *Pharos Journal of Theology* 100 (2019) 1–10.
———. "Johannine Magical Realism: A Trigger for Sacramental Realism in John 6:26–58." *Neotestamentica* 55 (2021) 323–345.
Farley, Edward. *Faith and Beauty: A Theological Aesthetic*. New York: Routledge, 2016.
Farlow, Matthew S. *The Dramatization of Theology: Humanity's Participation in God's Drama*. Eugene: Wipf and Stock, 2017.
Feijoo, Mary Lopez de and Myriam Protasio. "The Aesthetic Character of Existence in Kierkegaard Philosophy." *Journal of Health and Religion* 54 (2015) 1470–1480.
Ferguson, Sinclair B. *In Christ Alone: Living the Gospel-Centered Life*. Lake Mary: Reformation Trust, 2007.
———. *Some Pastors and Teachers: Reflecting a Biblical Vision of What Every Minister is Called to Be*. Edinburgh: Banner of Truth, 2018.
Fields, Stephen. "The Beauty of the Ugly: Balthasar, the Crucifixion, Analogy and God" *International Journal of Systematic Theology* 9 (2007) 172–183.
Fletcher, Daniel H. *Signs in the Wilderness: Intertextuality and the Testing of Nicodemus*. Eugene: Wipf and Stock, 2014.
Filtvedt, Ole J. "Revisiting Nicodemus's Question in John 3:9." *The Journal of Theological Studies* 70 (2019) 110–140.
Frame, John M. *The Doctrine of the Knowledge of God*. Phillipsburg: P&R, 1987.
———. *The Doctrine of the Christian Life*. Philipsburg: P&R, 2008.
———. *A History of Western Philosophy and Theology*. Phillipsburg: P&R, 2015.
Fritz, Peter Joseph. *Karl Rahner's Theological Aesthetics*. Washington DC: Catholic University, 2014.
———. *Freedom Made Manifest: Rahner's Fundamental Option and Theological Aesthetics*. Washington DC: Catholic University, 2019.
Forde, Gerhard O. *On Being a Theologian of the Cross: Reflections on Luther's Heidelberg Disputation, 1518*. Grand Rapids: Eerdmans, 1997.
Fortna, R.T. *The Gospel of Signs*. Cambridge: Cambridge University, 1970.
Foster, Charles. "The Veneration of Icons." *Contemporary Review* 278 (2001) 291–293.
Froehlich, Karlfried. "Pseudo-Dionysius and the Reformation of the Sixteenth Century." In *Pseudo-Dionysius: The Complete Works*, edited by Paul Rorem, 33–46. New York: Paulist, 1987.
Fujimura, Mukato. *The Splendor of the Medium*. Medellin: Poiema, 2004.

———. *Refractions: A Journey of Faith, Art, and Culture*. Colorado Springs: NavPress, 2009.

———. *Silence and Beauty: Hidden Faith Born of Suffering*. Downers Grove: InterVarsity, 2016.

———. *Culture Care: Reconnecting with Beauty for our Common Life*. Downers Grove: InterVarsity, 2017.

Garcia-Rivera, Alejandro. *The Community of the Beautiful: A Theological Aesthetics*. Collegeville: The Liturgical Press, 1999.

Garrett, Stephen M. "The Dazzling Darkness of God's Triune Love: Introducing Evangelicals to the Theology of Hans Urs von Balthasar." *Themelios* 35 (2010) 413–30.

———. "Beauty as the Point of Connection between Theology and Ethics." *European Journal of Theology* 20 (2011) 413–430.

———. "God's Beauty-in-Act: An Artful Renewal of Human Imagining." *International Journal of Systematic Theology* 14 (2012) 459–479.

———. "A Peculiar Beauty: The Theological Aesthetics of the Suffering Christ." In *New Perspectives on the Relationship between Pain, Suffering and Metaphor*, edited by N. Hinerman, 27–39. Leiden: Brill, 2019.

Garff, Joakim. *Søren Kierkegaard: A Biography*. Translated by Bruce H. Kirmmse. New Jersey: Princeton University, 2005.

Gibson, Michael D. "The Beauty of the Redemption of the World: The Theological Aesthetics of Maximus the Confessor and Jonathan Edwards." *The Harvard Theological Review* 101 (2008) 45–76.

Gieschen, Charles A. "The YHWH Christology of the Gospel of John." *Concordia Theological Quarterly* 85 (2021) 3–22.

Girard, Marc. "La Composition Structurelle des sept 'Signes' dans le Quatrieme Evangile." *Sciences Religieuses* 9 (1980) 315–324.

Goldsworthy, Graeme. *Preaching the Whole Bible as Christian Scripture: The Application of Biblical Theology to Expository Preaching*. Grand Rapids: Eerdmans, 2000.

———. *According to Plan: The Unfolding Revelation of God in the Bible*. Downers Grove: IVP, 2002.

———. *Gospel-Centered Hermeneutics: Foundations and Principles of Evangelical Biblical Interpretation*. Downers Grove: IVP, 2007.

Gottschaller, Pia. *Art and Activism: Projects of John and Dominique de Menil*. New Haven: Yale University, 2010.

Gouwens, David J. "Mozart Among the Theologians." *Modern Theology* 16 (2000) 461–474.

Greidanus, Sidney. *The Modern Preacher and the Ancient Text: Interpreting Preaching and Biblical Literature*. Grand Rapids: Eerdmans, 1988.

———. *Preaching Christ from the Old Testament: A Contemporary Hermeneutical Method*. Grand Rapids: Eerdmans, 1999.

Grube, Drik-Martin. "God or the Subject?: Karl Barth's Critique of the 'Turn to the Subject.'" *Neue Zeitschrift für Systematische Theologie und Religionsphilosophie* 49 (2007) 308–324.

Grudem, Wayne. *Systematic Theology*. 3rd ed. Grand Rapids: Zondervan, 2009.

Grochowski, Zbigniew. "Nicodemus: A Disciple Liberated by the Cross of the Christ from the Darkness of Fear and Disbelief." *The Biblical Annals* 10 (2020) 637–676.

Hanson, Jeffrey A. *Kierkegaard and the Life of Faith: The Aesthetic, the Ethical, and the Religious in Fear and Trembling.* Bloomington: Indiana University, 2017.

Harrison, Carol. *Beauty and Revelation in the Thought of Saint Augustine.* Oxford: Clarendon, 1992.

———. *Augustine: Christian Truth and Fractured Humanity,* Oxford: Oxford University, 2000.

———. *Rethinking Augustine's Early Theology: An Argument for Continuity.* Oxford: Oxford University, 2006.

Harris, Murray J. *Jesus as God: The New Testament Use of Theos in Reference to Jesus.* Grand Rapids: Baker, 2008.

Harris, Murray J. *John.* Exegetical Guide to the Greek New Testament. Edited by Andreas J. Köstenberger and Robert W. Yarbrough. Nashville: B&H Academic, 2015.

Harstine, Stan. "Thomas: Recognition Scenes in the Ancient World." *Perspectives in Religious Studies* 33 (2006) 435–447.

Hart, David B. *The Beauty of the Infinite: The Aesthetics of Christian Truth.* Grand Rapids: Eerdmans, 2003.

Heal, Bridget. *A Magnificent Faith: Art and Identity in Lutheran Germany.* Oxford: Oxford University, 2017.

———. "Luther, Cranach, and the Reformation Image." *Lutherjahrbuch* 85 (2018) 356–358.

Helm, Paul. "John Lock and Jonathan Edwards: A Reconsideration." *Journal of the History of Philosophy* 7 (1969) 51–61.

Henrici, Peter. "La Structure de la Trilogie." *Transversalités: Revue de l'Institut Catholiqeu de Paris* 66 (1997) 15–22.

Hofer, Andrew. "Proclamation in the Theological Aesthetics of Hans Urs von Balthasar." *Worship* 79 (2005) 20–38.

Holmes, Stephen R. *The Quest for the Trinity: The Doctrine of God in Scripture, History, and Modernity.* Downers Grove: IVP Academic, 2012.

Horton, Michael S. *Covenant and Eschatology: The Divine Drama.* Louisville: Westminster John Knox, 2002.

———. *Lord and Servant: A Covenant Christology.* Louisville: Westminster John Knox, 2005.

———. *Covenant and Salvation: Union with Christ.* Louisville: Westminster John Knox, 2007.

———. *Pilgrim Theology.* Zondervan: Grand Rapids, 2011.

Howsare, Rodney. *Hans Urs Von Balthasar and Protestantism.* New York: T&T Clark, 2005.

———. *Balthasar: A Guide for the Perplexed.* New York: T&T Clark, 2009.

———. "On True and False Humility: A Reading of Karen Kilby's Balthasar: A Very Critical Introduction." *Pro Ecclesia* 24 (2015) 439–451.

Iacovetti, Christopher. "God in His Processions: Aquinas, Palamas, and Dionysius on God's Relation to Creation." *Pro Ecclesia* 26 (2017) 297–310.

Jantzen, Grace M. "Beauty for Ashes: Notes on the Displacement of Beauty." *Literature and Theology* 16 (2002) 427–449.

Janzen, Gerald J. "The Scope of the High Priestly Prayer in John 17." *Encounter* 67 (2006) 1–26.

Jeffreys, David L. "Augustine on Beauty." In *The Edinburgh Companion to the Bible and the Arts*, edited by Stephen Prickett, 56–58. Edinburgh: Edinburgh University Press, 2014.
John of Damascus. *Saint John of Damascus Collection*. Translated by G.R. Woodward. New York: Aeterna, 2016.
Johnson, Marcus Peter. *One with Christ: An Evangelical Theology of Salvation*. Wheaton: Crossway, 2013.
Johnson, Dennis. *Him We Proclaim: Preaching Christ from All the Scriptures*. Phillipsburg: Presbyterian & Reformed, 2007.
———. *Heralds of the King: Christ-Centered Sermons in the Tradition of Edmund P. Clowney*. Wheaton: Crossway, 2009.
Jonge, Marinus de. "Signs and Works in the Fourth Gospel." In *Miscellanea Neotestamentica*, Volume 2, edited by T. Baarda, A.F. Klijn, and W.C. van Unnik. Leiden: Brill, 1978.
Kaai, Anneke. *The Psalms: An Artist's Impression*. Downers Grove: IVP, 1999.
Kallay, Katalin G. "Alternative Viewpoint: Edwards and Beauty." In *Understanding Jonathan Edwards*, edited by Gerald McDermott, 127–132. New York: Oxford University, 2009.
Kant, Immanuel. *Critique of the Power of Judgment*. Cambridge: Cambridge University, 2000.
———. *Critique of Pure Reason*. Translated by J.M.D. Meiklejohn. Waiheke Island: The Floating Press, 2009a.
———. *Religion Within the Bounds of Bare Reason*. Translated by Werner S. Pluhar. Indianapolis, Indiana: Hackett, 2009b.
Kearney, Dutton. "Von Balthasar as Transmodernist: Recent Works on Theological Aesthetics." *Religion and the Arts* 14 (2010) 332–340.
Keener, Craig S. *The Gospel of John*. 2 vols. Grand Rapids: Baker Academic, 2012.
Keller, Timothy, and John Inazu, eds. *Uncommon Ground: Living Faithfully in a World of Difference*. Nashville: Thomas Nelson, 2020.
Keller, Timothy. *Center-Church: Doing Balanced, Gospel-Centered Ministry in Your City*. Grand Rapids: Zondervan, 2012.
———. *Encounters with Jesus: Unexpected Answered to Life's Biggest Questions*. New York: Penguin, 2012.
———. *Jesus the King: Understanding the Life and Death of the Son of God*. New York: Penguin, 2016.
———. *Preaching: Communicating Faith in an Age of Skepticism*. New York: Viking, 2015.
Kelly, J.N.D. *Early Christian Doctrines*. 5th ed. New York: Bloomsbury, 1985.
Kerr, Fergus. "Assessing this 'Giddy Synthesis.'" In *Balthasar at the End of Modernity*, edited by Lucy Gardner, David Moss, Ben Quash, and Graham Ward, 1–15. Edinburgh: T&T Clark, 1999.
Kierkegaard, Søren. *A Kierkegaard Anthology*. Edited by Robert Bretali. New Jersey: Princeton University, 1951.
———. *Kierkegaard's Writings*. 26 vols. Princeton: 1990–2000.
Kilby, Clyde S. *The Arts and the Christian Imagination: Essays on Art, Literature, and Aesthetics*. Edited by William Dyrness and Keith Call. Wheaton: Mount Tabor, 2016.
Kilby, Karen. 2004. *Karl Rahner Theology and Philosophy*. New York: Routledge.

———. 2006. "Balthasar and Karl Rahner." In *The Cambridge Companion to Hans Urs von Balthasar*, edited by Edward Oakes and David Moss, 256-268. New York: Cambridge University.

———. 2012. *Balthasar: A (Very) Critical Introduction*. Grand Rapids: Eerdmans.

King, Jonathan. *The Beauty of the Lord: Theology as Aesthetics*. Bellingham: Lexham, 2018.

Kirkland, Scott A. "Glory Over Sublimity: Karl Barth's Theological Aesthetics." *The Heythrop Journal* 57 (2016) 1010-1018.

Kling, Sheri D. "Wisdom Became Flesh: An Analysis of the Prologue to the Gospel of John." *Currents in Theology and Mission* 40 (2013) 179-187.

Koester, Craig R. *Revelation: A New Translation with Introduction and Commentary*. The Anchor Yale Bible 38A. New Haven, Yale: Yale University, 2014.

Kolb, Robert. "Luther on the Theology of the Cross." *Lutheran Quarterly* 16 (2002) 443-466.

———. "Luther on the Theology of the Cross." In *The Pastoral Luther: Essays on Martin Luther's Practical Theology*, edited by Timothy J. Wengert, 33-58. Minneapolis: Fortress, 2017.

Kolbet, Paul R. "Athanasius, the Psalms, and the Reformation of Self." *The Harvard Theological Review* 99 (2006) 85-101.

Kooi, Cornelis van der. "Herman Bavinck and Karl Barth on Christian Faith and Culture." *Calvin Theological Journal* 45 (2010) 72-78.

Köstenberger, Andreas J. *John*. BECNT. Grand Rapids: Baker Academic, 2004.

———. *A Theology of John's Gospel and Letters*. Grand Rapids: Zondervan, 2009.

Kruger, Michael J. "John." In *A Biblical-Theological Introduction to the New Testament*, edited by Michael J. Kruger, 115-135. Wheaton: Crossway, 2016.

L'Engle, Madeleine. *Walking on Water: Reflections on Faith and Art*. Colorado Springs: WaterBrook, 2001.

Laniak, Timothy S. *Shepherds After My Own Heart: Pastoral Traditions and Leadership in the Bible*. NSBT. Downers Grove: InterVarsity, 2006.

Leclercq, Jean. "Influence and Non Influence of Dionysius in the Western Middle AgesIn *Pseudo-Dionysius: The Complete Works*, edited by Paul Rorem, 25-32. New York: Paulist, 1987.

Leithart, Peter J. *Athanasius*. Grand Rapids: Baker Academic, 2011.

Lee, Dorothy. "In the Spirit of Truth: Worship and Prayer in the Gospel of John and the Early Fathers." *Vigilae Christianae* 58 (2004) 277-297.

———. "The Gospel of John and the Five Senses." *Society of Biblical Literature* 129 (2010) 115-127.

Lee, Sang Hyun. "Edwards and Beauty." In *Understanding Jonathan Edwards*, edited by Gerald McDermott, 113-126. New York: Oxford University, 2009.

Lett, Jonathan. "The Divine Identity of Jesus as the Reason for Israel's Unbelief in John 12:36-43." *Journal of Biblical Literature* 135 (2016) 159-173.

Lewis, C.S. *Surprised by Joy: The Shape of My Early Life*. Orlando: Harcourt, 1955.

———. *The Four Loves*. San Diego: Harcourt, 1988.

———. *The Pilgrim's Regress: An Allegorical Apology for Christianity, Reason and Romanticism*. 3rd Ed. Grand Rapids: Eerdmans, 1992.

———. *Mere Christianity*. San Francisco: Harper, 2001a.

———. *The Problem of Pain*. New York: Harper, 2001b.

———. *The Weight of Glory*. San Francisco: HarperCollins, 2009. Kindle Edition.

———. *Till We Have Faces: A Myth Retold*. New York: Mariner, 2012.
———. *God in the Dock*. Grand Rapids: Eerdmans, 2014.
Lewis, Gordon and Bruce A Demarest. *Integrative Theology. Three Volumes in One*. Grand Rapids: Zondervan, 1996.
Levering, Mathew. *The Achievement of Hans Urs von Balthasar*. Washington DC: Catholic University of America, 2019.
Linnet, Ragni. "Kierkegaard's Approach to Pictorial Art, and to Specimens of Contemporary Visual Culture." In *Kierkegaard, Literature, and the Arts*, edited by Eric Ziolkowski, 193-222. Evanston: Northwestern University, 2018.
Lister, Rob. *God as Impassible and Impassioned: Toward a Theology of Divine Emotion*. Wheaton: Crossway, 2012.
Little, Brent. "Anthropology and Art in the Theology of Karl Rahner." *Heythrop* 70 (2011) 939-951.
Little, Marcus. "The Paradoxical Beauty of the Cross: Theological Aesthetics and the Doctrine of the Atonement in Athanasius' Contra Gentes-De Incarnatio." *Eleutheria* 1 (2011) 72-86.
Losinger, Anton. *The Anthropological Turn: The Human Orientation of the Theology of Karl Rahner*. Translated by Daniel O. Dahlstrom. New York: Fordham University Press.
Louie, Kin Yip. *The Beauty of the Triune God: The Theological Aesthetics of Jonathan Edwards*. Eugene: Pickwick, 2013.
Louth, Andrew. "Apophatic Theology: Pseudo-Dionysius the Areopagite." *Hermathena* 165 (1998) 71-84.
———. *Denys the Areopagite*. New York: Continuum, 2001.
———. "Beauty Will Save the World: The Formation of Byzantine Spirituality." *Theology Today* 61 (2004) 67-77.
Löwenich, Walter von. 1976. *Luthers Theology of the Cross*. Translated by Herbert J. A. Bouman. Minneapolis: Augsburg, 2000.
Luther, Martin. *The Roots of Reformation*. The Annotated Luther Volume 1, edited by Timothy Wengert. Minneapolis: Fortress, 2015a.
———. *Word and Faith*. The Annotated Luther Volume 2, edited by Kirsi Stjerna. Minneapolis: Fortress, 2015b.
Lyttle, David. "The Supernatural Light." In *Studies in Religion in Early American Literature*, 1-20. Lanham, MY: University Press of America, 1983.
MacLeod, David J. "The Incarnation of the Word: John 1:14." *Bibliotheca Sacra* 161 (2004) 72-88.
Maeseneer, Yves de. "Retrieving the Spiritual Senses in the Wake of Hans Urs von Balthasar." *Communio Viatorum*, 55 (2013) 276-290.
Marion, Jean Luc. *God Without Being*. Translated by Thomas A. Carlson. Chicago: University of Chicago, 1991.
Markos, Loius. *Restoring Beauty: The Good, the True, and the Beautiful in the Writings of C.S. Lewis*. Downers Grove: InterVarsity, 2010.
Marmion, Declan. "Review of *Karl Rahner: Theology and Philosophy*, by Karen Kilby." *The Way* 44 (2005) 120-121.
Martin, Jennifer N. *Hans Urs Von Balthasar and the Critical Appropriation of Russian Religious Thought*. Notre Dame: University of Notre Dame Press, 2015.
Martin, Ryan J. *Understanding Affections in the Theology of Jonathan Edwards: "The High Exercises of Divine Love."* New York: T&T Clark, 2019.

Masson, Robert. "Review of *Karl Rahner: Theology and Philosophy*, by Karen Kilby." *Modern Theology* 23 (2007) 157–160.
Mattes, Mark. *Luther's Theology of Beauty: A Reappraisal*. Grand Rapids: Baker Academic, 2017.
———. "Luther and Beauty." *Word and World* 39 (2019) 11–24.
———. "Luther's Theology of Beauty." *Lutheran Quarterly* 34 (2020) 42–60.
McClymond, Michael J. "Spiritual Perception in Jonathan Edwards." *The Journal of Religion* 77 (1997) 195–216.
McCosker, Philip. "Blessed Tension: Barth and von Balthasar on the Music of Mozart." *The Way* 44 (2005) 81–95.
McDermott, Gerald R. "How to Understand the American Theologian." In *Understanding Jonathan Edwards: An Introduction to America's Theologian*, edited by Gerald McDermott, 3–14. New York: Oxford University, 2009.
McGrath, Alister E. *Luther's Theology of the Cross*. Cambridge: Blackwell Publishing, 1990.
———. *Evangelicalism and the Future of Christianity*. Leicester: Inter-Varsity, 1995.
———. *The Open Secret: A New Vision for Natural Theology*. Oxford: Blackwell, 2008.
———. *C.S. Lewis A Life: Eccentric Genius, Reluctant Prophet*. Carol Stream: Tyndale, 2013.
———. *Born to Wonder*. Carol Stream: Tyndale, 2020.
McHugh, John F. *John 1–4: A Critical and Exegetical Commentary*. New York: T&T Clark, 2009.
McInroy, Mark. *Balthasar on the 'Spiritual Senses': Perceiving the Splendor*. Oxford: Oxford University, 2014.
McKnight, Scott. *The King Jesus Gospel*. Grand Rapids: Zondervan, 2016.
Meijering, Eginhard. "Athanasius on God as Creator and Recreator." *Church History and Religious Culture* 90 (2010) 175–197.
Michaels, J. Ramsey. *The Gospel of John*. NICNT. Grand Rapids: Eerdmans, 2010.
Miller, E.L. "The Johannine Origins of the Johannine Logos." *Journal of Biblical Literature* 112 (1993) 445–57.
———. "Jonathan Edwards on the Sense of the Heart." *Harvard Theological Review* 41 (1948) 123–145.
Miller, Paul. "Jonathan Edwards and the Beauty of God." *Touchstone* 36 (2018) 6–13.
Miner, Robert C. *Thomas Aquinas on the Passions*. Cambridge: Cambridge University, 2009.
Mitchell, Louis J. "The Theological Aesthetics of Jonathan Edwards." *Theology Today* 64 (2007) 36–46.
Morgan, Christopher, and Robert Peterson, eds. *The Glory of God*. Wheaton: Crossway, 2010.
Morgan, Jonathan. "A Radiant Theology: The Concept of Light in Psuedo-Dionysius." *St. Vladimir's Theological Quarterly* 21 (2010) 127–147.
Morris, Leon. *The Gospel According to John*. NICNT. Grand Rapids: Eerdmans, 1995.
Mose, Matthew A.R. *Love Itself is Understanding: Hans Urs von Balthasar's Theology of the Saints*. Minneapolis: Fortress, 2016.
Moss, David. "The Saints." In *The Cambridge Companion to Hans Urs von Balthasar*, edited by Edward T. Oaks and David Moss, 79–92. Cambridge: Cambridge University, 2004.

Mouw, Richard J. *He Shines in All That's Fair: Culture and Common Grace*. Grand Rapids: Eerdmans, 2002.
Mounce, Robert H. *The Book of Revelation*. NICNT. Rev. ed. Grand Rapids: Eerdmans, 1997.
Myers, Stephen G. "The Sufferings Are Better: Martin Luther and the Theology of the Cross." *Puritan Reformed Journal* 9 (2017) 84–100.
Narinskaya, Elena. "On the Divine Images: Theology Behind the Icons and Their Veneration in the Church." *Transformation* 29 (2012) 139–148.
National Association of Evangelicals. "What is and Evangelical?" https://www.nae.org/what-is-an-evangelical.
Navone, John. *Toward a Theology of Beauty*. Minnesota: Liturgical, 1996.
Ngien, Dennis. *Luther's Theology of the Cross: Christ in Luther's Sermons on John*. Eugene: Wipf and Stock, 2018.
Nichols, Aidan. *The Word Has Been Abroad: A Guide Through Balthasar's Aesthetics*. Washington DC: T&T Clark, 1998.
———. "An Introduction to Balthasar." *New Blackfriars* 79 (1998) 2–10.
———. *Redeeming Beauty: Soundings in Sacral Aesthetics*. Burlington: Routledge, 2007.
Niebuhr, H. Richard. "Toward the Independence of the Church." In *The Church Against the World*, edited by Richard Niebuhr and William Pauck and Francis Miller. Chicago: Willett, 1935.
———. *Christ and Culture*. New York: Harper and Brothers, 1956.
Noble, Bonnie. *Lucas Cranach the Elder: Art and the Devotion of the German Reformation*. New York: University Press of America, 2009.
Noll, Mark A. 1994. *The Scandal of the Evangelical Mind*. Grand Rapids: Eerdmans.
O'Connell, Robert J. *Art and the Christian Intelligence in St. Augustine*. Cambridge: Harvard University, 1978.
O'Connor, John D. "Theological Aesthetics and Revelatory Tension." *New Blackfriars* 89 (2008) 399–417.
O'Collins, Gerald. 2020. *The Beauty of Jesus Christ: Filling out a Scheme of St. Augustine*. Oxford: Oxford University, 2020.
O'Kane, Martin. "The Artist as Reader of the Bible: Visual Exegesis and the Adoration of the Magi." *Biblical Interpretation* 13 (2005) 337–373.
———. "Wirkungsgeschichte and Visual Exegesis: The Contribution of Hans-Georg Gadamer." *Journal for the Study of the New Testament*. 33 (2010) 147–159.
O'Meara, T.F. "Paul Tillich and Karl Rahner: Similarities and Contrasts." *Gregorianum* 91 (2010) 443–459.
O'Reilly, Kevin. *Aesthetic Perception: A Thomistic Perspective*. Dublin: Four Courts, 2007.
Ortlund, Duane C. "Christocentrism: An Asymmetrical Trinitarianism?" *Themelios* 34 (2009) 309–321.
Ortlund, Raymond. *Isaiah: God Saves Sinners*. Preaching the Word. Wheaton: Crossway, 2005.
———. *The Gospel: How the Church Portrays the Beauty of Christ*. Wheaton: Crossway, 2014.
Osborne, Grant R. *The Hermeneutical Spiral*. Second Edition. Downers Grove: InterVarsity, 2006.
Parkison, Samuel G. *Irresistible Beauty: Beholding Triune Glory in the Face of Jesus Christ*. Ross-shire: Mentor, 2022.

———. *To Gaze Upon God: The Beatific Vision in Doctrine, Tradition, and Practice.* Downers Grove: IVP Academic, 2024.

Pattison, George. "The Bonfire of the Genres: Kierkegaard's Literary Kaleidoscope." In *Kierkegaard, Literature, and the Arts,* edited by Eric Ziolkowski, 39–54. Evanston: Northwestern University, 2018.

Payton, James R. "John of Damascus on Human Cognition: An Element in His Apologetic on Icons." *Church History* 65 (1996) 173–183.

Pearcey, Nancy R. *Total Truth: Liberating Christianity from its Cultural Captivity.* Wheaton: Crossway, 2004.

———. *Saving Leonardo: A Call to Resist the Secular Assault on Mind, Morals, & Meaning.* Nashville: B&H, 2010.

———. *Finding Truth.* Colorado Springs, Colorado: David Cook, 2015.

———. *Love Thy Body: Answering Questions about Life and Sexuality.* Grand Rapids: Baker, 2018.

Pelikan, Jarislov. "The Odyssey of Dionysian Spirituality." In *Pseudo-Dionysius: The Complete Works,* edited by Paul Rorem, 11–24. New York: Paulist, 1987.

Perl, Eric. *Theophany: The Neoplatonic Philosophy of Dionysius the Areopagite.* Albany, New York: Suny, 2007.

Peterson, Andrew. *Adorning the Dark: Thoughts on Community, Calling and the Mystery of Making.* Nashville: B&H, 2019.

Peterson, Eugene H. *Eat this Book: A Conversation in the Art of Spiritual Reading.* Grand Rapids: Eerdmans, 2006.

———. *Christ Plays in Ten Thousand Places: a Conversation in Spiritual Theology.* Grand Rapids: Eerdmans, 2008.

Piggin, Stuart and Dianne Cook. "Keeping Alive the Heart in the Head: The Significance of 'Eternal Language in the Aesthetics of Jonathan Edwards and S.T. Coleridge.'" *Literature and Theology* 18 (2004) 383–414.

Piper, John. *God's Passion for His Glory.* Wheaton: Crossway, 1998.

———. *The Pleasures of God.* 2nd ed. Portland: Multnomah, 2000.

———. *Don't Waste Your Life.* Wheaton: Crossway, 2003.

———. *When I Don't Desire God: How to Fight for Joy.* Wheaton: Crossway, 2004.

———. *God is the Gospel.* Wheaton: Crossway, 2005.

———. *Seeing Beauty and Saying Beautifully. The Power of Poetic Effort in the Works of George Herbert, George Whitfield, and C.S. Lewis.* Wheaton: Crossway, 2014.

———. *Expository Exultation: Christian Preaching as Worship.* Wheaton: Crossway, 2018.

Platt, David. *Radical: Taking Back Your Faith from the American Dream.* Colorado Springs: Multnomah, 2010.

Potter, Brett D. "Living in the Moment: Mission as Improvisation in Samuel Wells, Kevin Vanhoozer, and Hans Urs von Balthasar." *McMaster Journal of Theology and Ministry* 15 (2013) 136–164.

Poythress, Vern. "Johannine Authorship and the Use of Intersentence Conjunctions in the Book of Revelation." *Westminster Theological Journal* 47 (1985) 329–336.

———. *The Shadow of Christ in the Law of Moses.* Phillipsburg: Presbyterian & Reformed, 1991.

———. *Redeeming Philosophy: A God-Centered Approach to the Big Questions.* Wheaton: Crossway, 2014.

Preus, Andrew, J. "The Theology of the Cross and the Lutheran Confessions." *Concordia Theological Quarterly* 82 (2018) 83–104.

Price, George. *The Narrow Pass: A Study of Kierkegaard's Concept of Man.* London: Hutchinson, 1963.
Priebbenow, Clarence. "A Study of 'Only' and 'Only Begotten.'" *Logia* 28 (2019) 35-39.
Pior, Karen Swallow. *The Evangelical Imagination.* Grand Rapids: Brazos, 2023.
Prosperi, Paolo. "Believing and Seeing." *Theological Studies* 78 (2017) 905-929.
Pseudo-Dionysius. *The Complete Works.* Translated by Colm Luibheid and Paul Rorem. New York: Paulist, 1987.
Quash, Ben. "Drama and the Ends of Modernity." In *Balthasar at the End of Modernity*, edited by Lucy Gardner, David Moss, Ben Quash, and Graham Ward, 139-141. Edinburgh: T&T Clark, 1999.
———. *Found Theology: History, Imagination and the Holy Spirit.* New York: Bloomsbury, 2013.
Rahner, Karl. "Thomas Aquinas on the Incomprehensibility of God." *The Journal of Religion* 58 (1978) 107-125.
Rahner, Karl. "Theology and the Arts." *Thought* 57 (1982) 17-29.
Ramsey, Russ. *Rembrandt is in the Wind: Learning to Love Art through the Eyes of Faith.* Grand Rapids: Zondervan, 2022.
Reeves, Michael. *Gospel People: A Call for Evangelical Integrity.* Wheaton: Crossway, 2022.
Rhodes, Michael Craig. "Handmade: A Critical Analysis of John of Damascus' Reasoning for Making Icons." *Heythrop* 52 (2011) 14-26.
———. "Handmade: A Critical Analysis of John of Damascus' Justification for Venerating Icons." *Heythrop* 54 (2013) 347-359.
———. *Pseudo-Dionysius: A Commentary on the Texts and an Introduction to their Influence.* New York: Oxford University, 1993.
Ridderbos, Herman N. *The Gospel According to John: A Theological Commentary.* Translated by John Vriend. Grand Rapids: Eerdmans, 1997.
Riga, Peter. "Signs of Glory: The Use of 'Semeion' in St. John's Gospel. *Interpretation* 17 (1963) 402-424.
Rigney, Joseph. *The Things of the Earth.* Wheaton: Crossway, 2015.
Rosebrock, Matthew. "The Heidelberg Disputation and Aesthetics." *Concordia* 38 (2012) 347-360.
Romanowski, John W. "'When the Son of Man is Lifted Up': The Redemptive Power of the Crucifixion in the Gospel of John." *Horizons* 32 (2005) 100-116.
Rorem, Paul. "Negative Theologies and the Cross." *Lutheran Quarterly* 23 (2009) 314-349.
Roselen, Grahame. "The Incarnational Christology of Athanasius." *Phronema* 35 (2020) 85-95.
Ryken, Leland, ed. *The Christian Imagination.* Colorado Springs: Waterbrook, 2002.
Saliers, Don E. "Liturgy and Ethics: Some New Beginnings." *Journal of Religious Ethics* 7 (1979) 179-189.
Salier, Willis Hedley. *The Rhetorical Impact of the* Semeia *in the Gospel of John.* Tubingen: Mohr Siebeck, 2004.
Sammon, Brendan T. *The God who is Beauty: Beauty as a Divine Name in Thomas Aquinas and Dionysius the Areopagite.* Eugene: Pickwick, 2013.
Sanders, Fred. *The Deep Things of God: How the Trinity Changes Everything.* Wheaton: Crossway, 2017.
Sayers, Dorothy L. *The Mind of the Maker.* New York: HarperCollins, 1987.
Schaeffer, Francis A. *Art and the Bible.* Downers Grove: InterVarsity, 1973.

Schellenberg, Ryan S. "Seeing the World Whole: Intertextuality and the New Jerusalem (Revelation 21–22)." *Perspectives in Religious Studies* 33 (2006) 467–476.

Schindler, David C. *Hans Urs von Balthasar and the Dramatic Structure of Truth: A Philosophical Investigation.* New York: Fordham University, 2004.

———. "Beauty in the Tradition: Hans Urs von Balthasar." Lecture. 2017. https://www.youtube.com/watch?v=b26vvB3-97g&t=1584s

Schmidt, Maurice. *The Tabernacle as a Work of Art: An Aesthetic of Monotheism.* Lewiston: Edwin Mellen, 2009.

Scruton, Roger. *Kant: A Very Short Introduction.* New York: Oxford, 2001.

———. *Culture Counts: Faith and Feeling in a World Besieged.* New York: Encounter, 2007.

———. *Beauty: A Very Short Introduction.* New York: Oxford, 2011.

Sevier, Christopher S. *Aquinas on Beauty.* Lanham, MY: Lexington Books, 2015.

Shaw, Lucy. *Breath for the Bones: Art, Imagination, and Spirit.* Nashville: Thomas Nelson, 2007.

———. *Thumbprint in the Clay: Divine Marks of Beauty, Order, and Grace.* Downers Grove: InterVarsity, 2016.

Sherry, Patrick. *Spirit and Beauty: An Introduction to Theological Aesthetics.* London: Oxford University, 2002.

———. "The Varieties of Wonder." *Philosophical Investigations* 36 (2013) 340–354.

Shultz, Walter. "Jonathan Edwards's 'End of Creation' an Exposition and Defense." *Journal of Evangelical Theological Society* 49 (2006) 247–71.

———. "Jonathan Edwards's Concept of an Original End." *Journal of Evangelical Theological Society* 56 (2013) 107–22.

Siedell, Daniel A. "Modern Art and the (Evangelical) Church." *Perspectives in Religious Studies* 32 (2005) 183–191.

———. "Between Art and Religion: Reflections on the Strange Place of God in the Gallery." *Cultural Encounters* 6 (2010) 67–71.

Sinclair, Lisa M. "The Legacy of Isabella Lilias Trotter." *International Bulletin of Mission Research* (2002) 32–35.

Sittser, Gerald L. "Protestant Missionary Biography as Written Icon." *Christian Scholar's Review* 36 (2007) 303–321.

Smalley, Stephen S. *Thunder and Love: John's Revelation and John's Community.* Eugene: Wipf and Stock, 1994.

Smith, James K.A. "Staging the Incarnation: Revisioning Augustine's Critique of Theatre." *Literature and Theology* 15 (2001) 123–139.

———. *Desiring the Kingdom: Worship, Worldview, and Cultural Formation.* Grand Rapids: Baker Academic, 2009.

———. *Imagining the Kingdom: Worship, Worldview, and Cultural Formation.* Grand Rapids: Baker Academic, 2013.

———. *You Are What You Love: The Spiritual Power of Habit.* Grand Rapids: Brazos, 2016.

———. *Awaiting the King: Reforming Public Theology.* Grand Rapids: Baker Academic, 2017.

———. *On the Road with Saint Augustine: A Real-World Spirituality for Restless Hearts.* Grand Rapids: Brazos, 2019.

Smith, Richard L. *Such a Mind as This.* Eugene: Wipf and Stock, 2021.

Sproul, R.C. *The Holiness of God.* Carol Stream: Tyndale, 1985.

———. *The Truth of the Cross*. Sanford: Reformation Trust, 2007.
Stan, Leo. "From Singularity to Universality and Back." *Rivista di Filosophia Neo-Scolastica* 105 (2013) 611–632.
Steck, Christopher. "Graced Encounters: Liturgy and Ethics from a Balthasarian Perspective." *Horizons* 30 (2003) 255–279.
Stoker, Wessel. *Where Heaven and Earth Meet: The Spiritual in the Art of Kandinsky, Rothko, Warhol, and Kiefer*. Amsterdam: Brill, 2012.
Stott, John. *The Cross of Christ*. 2nd ed. Downers Grove: InterVarsity, 2012.
Strachan, Owen. *Reenchanting Humanity: A Theology of Mankind*. London: Christian Focus, 2019.
Tabb, Brian. *All Things New: Revelation as a Canonical Capstone*. Downers Grove: InterVarsity, 2019.
Tait, Jenifer Woodruff. "Editors Note: Lilias Trotter." *Christian History Institute*. https://christianhistoryinstitute.org/magazine/article/editor-note-lilias-trotter-ch-148.
Taylor, Charles. *A Secular Age*. Cambridge: Belknap, 2007.
Terry, Thomas and J. Ryan Lister. *Images and Idols: Creativity for the Christian Life*. Chicago: Moody, 2018.
Thomas, Heath A. *Habakkuk, Two Horizons Old Testament Commentary* Series. Grand Rapids: Eerdmans, 2018.
Thomas, Marianne M. *John: A New Testament Commentary, New Testament Library* Series. Louisville: Westminster John Knox, 2015.
Thiessen Gesa, ed. *Theological Aesthetics: A Reader*. Grand Rapids: Eerdmans, 2005.
Treier, Daniel, Mark Husbands, and Roger Lundin, eds. *The Beauty of God: Theology and the Arts*. Downers Grove: IVP, 2007.
Tripp Paul, D. *Awe*. Wheaton: Crossway, 2015.
Trueman, Carl. *The Rise and Triumph of the Modern Self: Cultural Amnesia, Expressive Individualism, and the Road to the Sexual Revolution*. Wheaton: Crossway, 2021.
Tseng, Shoa Kai. "Paradox? Bringing Mozart's *Don Giovanni* to Terms with Kierkegaard's Religious-Life View." *Literature & Theology* 28 (2014) 411–424.
Turley, Stephen R. "Practicing the Kingdom: A Critical Appraisal of James J.K. Smith's *Desiring the Kingdom*." Calvin Theological Journal 48 (2013) 131–142.
Turner, S. *Imagine: A Vision for the Christians in the Arts*. Downers Grove: InterVarsity, 2001.
Wahlde, Urban von. *The Earliest Version of John's Gospel: Recovering the Gospel of Signs*. Wilmington: Michael Glazier, 1989.
Wallace, Daniel B. *Greek Grammar Beyond the Basics: An Exegetical Syntax of the New Testament*. Grand Rapids: Zondervan, 1997.
Watkin, Christopher. *Biblical Critical Theory: How the Bible's Unfolding Story Makes Sense of Modern Life and Culture*. Grand Rapids: Zondervan Academic, 2022.
Wellum, Stephen. *Christ Alone: The Uniqueness of Jesus as Savior*. Grand Rapids: Zondervan, 2017.
Wengert, Timothy J. "'Peace, Peace. . .Cross, Cross' Reflections on How Martin Luther Relates the Theology of the Cross to Suffering." *Lutheran Quarterly* 33 (2019) 304–323.
Wesche, Kenneth P. "Christological Doctrine and Liturgical Interpretation in Pseudo-Dionysius." *St Vladimir's Theological Quarterly* 33 (1989) 53–73.
Wheeler, Geraldine. "Three Theologians and Their Favorite Paintings." *ARTS* 18 (2006) 6–13.

White, Graham. *Luther as Nominalist*. Helsinki: Luther-Agricola-Society, 1994.
Wilson, James M. "Review of *Aesthetic Perception: A Thomistic Perspective*, by Kevin E. O'Reilly." *Christianity & Literature* 59 (2010) 727–732.
Wilson, N.D. *Notes from the Tilt-a-Whirl*. Nashville: Thomas Nelson, 2013.
Wittmer, Michael E. *Becoming Worldly Saints: Can You Serve Jesus and Still Enjoy Your Life?* Grand Rapids: Zondervan, 2015.
Wolterstorff, Nicholas P. *Art in Action: Toward a Christian Aesthetic*. Grand Rapids: Eerdmans, 1980.
———. *Art Rethought: The Social Practices of Art*. Oxford: Oxford University, 2015.
Woodell, Joseph D. "Jonathan Edwards, Beauty, and Apologetics." *Criswell Theological Review* 5 (2007) 81–95.
Wright, Christopher. *Knowing Jesus through the Old Testament*. 2nd ed. Downers Grove: IVP, 2014.
Wright, Nicholas T. *Jesus and the Victory of God: Christian Origins and the Question of God*. Minneapolis: Fortress, 1996.
———. *Simply Jesus: A New Vision of Who He Was, What He did, and Why He Matters*. New York: Harper Collins, 2018.
Wright, Stephen J. *Dogmatic Aesthetics: A Theology of Beauty in Dialogue With Robert Jenson*. Minneapolis: Fortress, 2014.
Vainio, Olli-Pekka. "Martin Luther on Perception and Theological Knowledge." *Neue Zeitschrift für systematische Theologie und Religionsphilosophie* 57 (2015) 87–109.
Vander Lugt, Wesley. "Church Beyond the Fourth Wall: Incorporating the Audience as Guest in Interactive Ecclesial Theater." *Cultural Encounters* 8 (2012) 7–22.
Vanhoozer, Kevin J. "What Has Vienna to Do with Jerusalem? Barth, Brahms, and Bernstein's Unanswered Question." *Westminster Theological Journal* 63 (2001) 123–150.
———. *The Drama of Doctrine: A Canonical-Linguistic Approach to Christian Theology*. Louisville: Westminster John Knox, 2005.
———. *Is There a Meaning in This Text?* Grand Rapids: Zondervan, 2009.
———. *Faith Speaking Understanding: Performing the Drama of Doctrine*. Louisville: Westminster John Knox, 2014.
———. *Pictures at a Theological Exhibition*. Downers Grove: InterVarsity, 2016.
———. *Biblical Authority After Babel*. Grand Rapids: Baker, 2016.
———. *Mere Christian Hermeneutics: Transfiguring What It Means to Read the Bible Theologically*. Grand Rapids: Zondervan Academic, 2024.
Vető, Étienne. "Kilby Verses Balthasar: A Cultural Divide?" *Pro Ecclesia* 24 (2015) 425–431.
Viladesau, Richard. *Theological Aesthetics: God in Imagination, Beauty, and Art*. New York: Oxford University, 1999.
———. "Review of *Karl Rahner's Theological Aesthetics*." *Modern Theology* 32 (2016) 125–127.
Yeager, D.M. "A Quality of Wonder: Five Thoughts on a Poetics of the Will." *Journal of the Society of Christian Ethics* 39 (2019) 213–235.
Zahnd, Brian. *Beauty will Save the World*. Lake Mary: Charisma House, 2012.
Ziolkowski, Eric J. "Kierkegaard's Concept of the Aesthetic: A Semantic Leap from Baumgarten." *Literature and Theology* 6 (1992) 33–46.
———. "Introduction." In *Kierkegaard, Literature, and the Arts*, edited by Eric Ziolkowski, 3–36. Evanston: Northwestern University, 2018.

www.ingramcontent.com/pod-product-compliance
Lightning Source LLC
Chambersburg PA
CBHW061432300426
44114CB00014B/1653